LIGHTHOUSE

Jerald and Sandra Tanner

LIGHTHOUSE

JERALD & SANDRA TANNER
DESPISED AND BELOVED CRITICS OF MORMONISM

RONALD V. HUGGINS

SIGNATURE BOOKS | 2022 | SALT LAKE CITY

To
Marlene Reeves
Wendell Crothers
Mark Reeves
Tony Higgins

Design by Jason Francis

FIRST EDITION | 2022

LIBRARY OF CONGRESS CONTROL NUMBER: 2022938540

Hardback ISBN: 978-1-56085-450-0
Paperback ISBN: 978-1-56085-454-8
Ebook ISBN: 978-1-56085-425-8

CONTENTS

INTRODUCTION

When I was approached about writing a biography of Jerald and Sandra Tanner, my first response was a sinking feeling. There were two interrelated reasons for this. The first was how daunting a task it would obviously be, from a number of angles. There was, to begin with, the enormous body of material I would need to come to terms with to do justice to the story. It is now sixty years since the Tanners produced their first reprint of an early Mormon document—the first of their many firsts of various kinds: the first-ever photo-mechanical reproduction of the 1833 Book of Commandments.

The first tract Jerald Tanner ever wrote was in 1959 on the Book of Mormon and race. But it was not until May 20, 1960, that the Tanners began distributing their writings on a larger scale after purchasing a mimeograph machine from a Sears store in California. What began as a tiny stream eventually became a mighty flood of controversy and publishing activity that, even though curtailed somewhat by Jerald Tanner's Alzheimer's diagnosis and subsequent death in 2006, has continued. Sandra continues with writing, speaking engagements, and interviews, including an appearance in the recent 2021 Netflix documentary series, *Murder among the Mormons*. The Tanners' activities also generated a substantial body of other materials, documents, letters, newspaper clippings, and photographs I would need to review carefully. These materials are cited throughout this book as "Tanner and Tanner, Papers." It is Sandra's intention to eventually donate them to the University of Utah's Marriott Library.

Given that the Tanners attracted controversy, I also knew that it would not suffice for me to simply familiarize myself with their material. I would also need to delve into the evidence and arguments of those the Tanners were in controversy with, who, taken together, represented dozens of people over many years. I also knew that, given the uncorrelated nature of the Tanners' work, a lot more people, including believing Mormon scholars, were reading and being influenced by the Tanners over the last sixty years than were probably willing to openly admit it. The Tanners, in other words, represented an important, but often unacknowledged, force contributing to the direction of Mormon historical studies throughout the second half of the twentieth century and into the present one. Indeed, given the large number of historical disputes the Tanners' research contributed to, it would be impossible to trace the course of Mormon history and historiography over the past sixty years without an understanding of their involvement.

The second reason for my sinking feeling was that I actually felt strongly that a biography of the Tanners should indeed be done but only if done right. And alongside this conviction I also had the uncomfortable suspicion that if that were going to happen, it could be that, whether I liked it or not, I might be the obvious person to take it on. There may have been other scholars at the time who could have done it, but they would have surely approached the task much differently than I, and my fear was that the result might echo a remark once attributed to Alexander Solzhenitsyn after reading a biography someone had written about him: It was like looking at my reflection in a puddle, on a windy day.[1]

We are often given the impression in textbooks that the writing of history is a wholly dispassionate exercise that follows firmly established and universally accepted canons and procedures. That is partly true, but there is another force playing in the background, summed up by Ralph Waldo Emerson when he said, "All biography is autobiography."[2] Speaking of authors writing biographies of Jesus, Albert Schweizer once insisted that "no vital force comes into the figure [the subject of a biography] unless a man breathes into it all the hate or all the love of which he is capable," and further that "the greatest of them are written with hate."[3] The reason

1. Paraphrase based on distant recollection.
2. Ralph Waldo Emerson, "Theodore Parker, An Address at the Memorial Meeting at the Music Hall, Boston, June 15, 1860."
3. Albert Schweizer, *Quest for the Historical Jesus*, 4.

this was so, said Schweizer, was that the authors' "hate sharpened their historical insight."[4] Granting that Jesus is a special case, I can hardly imagine anything that is further from the truth when it comes to writing biographies of ordinary human beings. Breathing all the love we are capable into a biography turns it into hagiography, a kind of extended edifying discourse that papers over faults with excuses and ignores complexities. The image of the subject of such a biography fails to ring true because it is informed, not by the inner dynamics of the person's own life, but by the biographer's own notions of what such an ideal person should look like. Such biographies parallel religious pictures that prettify their subjects, smoothing out wrinkles and removing blemishes as a way of making them seem more noble or otherworldly, but in reality only make them look artificial and untrustworthy.[5]

Schweizer's other claim, that the best biographies are the result of our breathing the most hate into them, is even more conspicuously off the mark and contradicts the common experience expressed so well by the seventeenth-century Protestant divine William Gouge: "Disturbed passions cast a mist before the understanding, so as a man cannot discern what is enough, what too much."[6] In the light of hostility, even the most innocent words and actions can seem to represent external expressions of underlying sinister motives. It is the Jungian problem of projection. When someone says or does something that makes us angry or hostile or arouses feelings of hatred in us toward them, it is easy for us to project those feelings onto the person who inspired them. We imagine that the problem is not that we feel angry, hateful, or hostile, but that the person who inspired those feelings in us actually personifies those things. Once projection occurs it is very difficult to walk it back and get a better view of things because, as Jung noted, "In a projection; you simply know it to be true, and you are inclined to resent any suggestion of error connected with it."[7] And unfortunately, as Jung says elsewhere, "most

---

4. Schweizer, 3.

5. As is done for example with the Catholic Saints, Martin Luther, or even Joseph Smith or early Mormon leaders.

6. William Gouge, *Of Domesticall Dvties*, 564 (6.47).

7. Jung, *Introduction to Jungian Psychology*, 83.

people are content to be self-righteous and prefer mutual vilification (if nothing worse!) to the recognition of their projections."[8]

I once asked Mormon and Western historian Will Bagley if he had ever considered writing a biography of Brigham Young. He responded with an emphatic, "NO!" When I asked him why not, he said with his usual unvarnished candor, "Because I don't like him!" And I agree with Bagley on this point. If he does not like Brigham Young then he probably shouldn't write a biography of him. And yet there are many Mormons and some non-Mormons (including scholars) who do not like the Tanners, even though they know a good deal less about them than Bagley knows about Brigham Young. I would not have counted it a positive development if one of these had elected to undertake a biography of the Tanners for the reasons just described.

In my view a credible biography of the Tanners would not involve breathing our love or hate into it at all. What it would involve rather is a determined process of removing ourselves from the story to the point that what ultimately emerges is a depiction of what the world looks like from the perspective of the subjects themselves and how that vision moved them to think and act as they did. To be sure, empathy is a necessary doorway into the story the historian and biographer tries to tell, with the questions always playing in the background: "What would I do and how would I feel if I were in the person's position in the particular situation I am describing?" Would I be happy? Sad? Angry? Elated? Bold? Intimidated? Would I be experiencing a sense of outrage? Personal triumph? What?

A biography produced without empathy is likely to remain on the level of bland, lifeless description. But empathy alone is not an adequate guide for imaginative biographical reconstruction. People differ in perspective, background, experience, personality, intelligence, and so on, so there is a great deal we could potentially get wrong if we rely on our own assumed responses as a template for interpreting the feelings and actions of others. I am grateful to Sandra Tanner for the many times she reviewed things I had written and pointed out places where I hadn't got the facts, the feel, the atmosphere, of particular incidents quite right, from her perspective.

---

8. Jung, *Aion*, 17.

Another challenge I faced was the fact that, although I knew Jerald Tanner fairly well and saw him quite often during his last six years, much of what I present in this book necessarily represents Jerald "insofar as he has been translated correctly" by Sandra. This was counterbalanced by all that Jerald wrote, so that in many cases I was able to compare the spoken Sandra with the written Jerald. Still, one cannot interrogate texts in the same way as they can a living person. And there were many times in the course of writing this book that I would have liked to have asked Jerald's perspective on things. I was also helped by others who knew him over a long period.

Jerald was in many ways a remarkable person. For example, many people have supported needy children through help organizations like World Vision. But few would have actually traveled to World Vision headquarters first to check them out, as Jerald did, and then eventually sign on to support as many as one hundred children at one time. Similarly, when he felt God was calling him to help out at the Salt Lake Rescue Mission, Jerald didn't do so half-heartedly. He jumped in and continued to volunteer every morning six days a week, year in and year out, for the rest of his life (see chapt. 13). Jerald was a man of regular habits, fastidious even about little things like following safety precautions, not jaywalking, returning to the store if the cashier had given him too much change, and driving under the speed limit in town.[9] But where this fastidiousness comes into play most decisively in this book is in Jerald's carefulness about getting at the truth, and his strong sense of the need to refute falsehood *wherever he found it*. Although Jerald was generally mild mannered, he could become firm and confrontational when he felt a point of truth and accuracy was at stake. This brought him into conflict not only with fellow Mormons, but also with fellow evangelicals and ex-Mormon Christians (see chapt. 18). Jerald made enemies in both groups, but at the same time earned the respect of others who came to understand that he would not hesitate to debunk non-truth wherever he found it, even when doing so seemed to knock the props out from under his own position. He is best known in this regard for

---

9. Out on the freeway he might open it up a little and drive as much as five miles over the speed limit, especially when everyone else was racing past him at twenty or thirty miles an hour over it.

coming out against the authenticity of Mark Hofmann's Salamander letter forgery eight months before the experts and the LDS Church declared it to be genuine. In recalling this particular incident, Will Bagley commented that "the honesty and integrity that was reflected when he [Jerald] rejected a piece of evidence that could have been easily used as a cudgel or a support for many of the Tanners' basic arguments reflects a commitment to the truth that all of us as historians no matter what our faith or religious commitments must honor" (see chapt. 19).

I frequently heard about Jerald's skepticism of Hofmann's forgeries, and it misled me for a time to assume that the story was better known that it apparently is. This was dramatically illustrated for me when a well-known Mormon writer Paul Toscano came out in a Mormon history Facebook group after the 2021 documentary on Hofmann, *Murder Among the Mormons*, bitterly complaining that the producers had no business including Sandra because the Tanners played no part in the Hofmann case at all. For me as the author of this biography, this represented an encouraging sign because I had previously assumed that Mormons, especially Mormon scholars and writers, knew more about the overall story told in this book than many do. In any case, Jerald's approach to the Salamander letter was typical of everything he and Sandra did, and it was what set them apart from many others who opposed the LDS Church.

Both scholars and lay people alike have given many reasons over the years for not liking the Tanners or crediting their work. Some have found the amateur appearance of their publications, their overuse of long quotations, using all-caps or underlining of words, and their limited educations reason enough to dismiss them out of hand. Some have even interpreted the capitals and underlining as reflective of their more general "anger, even rage."[10] But this is a mistake. The Tanners' usage followed the pattern of Jerald's mentors Pauline Hancock and James Wardle (chapt. 3). The old manual typewriters didn't have italics, so Hancock, Wardle, and the Tanners used caps and underlining for emphasis instead.[11] And just as no one who

---

10. Foster, "Career Apostates," 41.

11. The use of capitals and underlining was replaced by italics and bold type in 1979, though the older parts of *Mormonism: Shadow or Reality* continued to contain them.

knew Hancock and Wardle would ever describe them as angry people, the same is true of the Tanners.

But somehow for me these very same unpolished features contributed to what intrigued me about the Tanners in the first place. I first became aware of what might be called the Tanner difference in the early 1980s when Ed Decker's film *The God Makers* was creating a sensation on college campuses near where I lived. I found the contrast between Decker and certain other evangelical writers and what the Tanners were doing striking. Decker was sensationalistic and had evangelicals as his primary audience. He, along with other writers at the time, seemed to me at least to be more interested in entertaining evangelicals by scandalizing them than in communicating with Mormons. Decker's work was broad brush and emotional. The Tanners, on the other hand, were more of an enigma. Certainly the Tanners were critical and confrontational, but their work read more like in-depth investigative journalism and generally dealt with issues meaningful to Mormons—but of little interest to most evangelicals. But the thing that was most notable for me was that, despite their lack of formal education and the amateur look of their books and newsletters, they were remarkably good at what they did. It was an example of what Augustine of Hippo had been talking about when he said, "A thing is not necessarily true for being expressed eloquently, nor necessarily false if the sounds made by the lips are imperfectly pronounced . . . with wisdom and folly the same thing holds good as with wholesome and unwholesome food. You can have silver or earthenware dishes on the table, just as you can have a decorated or undecorated use of language; either kind of food can be served in either kind of dish."[12]

Because I am an academic with a doctorate myself and have spent most of my career in academia, I have little patience for academic colleagues who dismiss the Tanners on the basis of their limited educations. If my years of teaching graduate and postgraduate students and reading and engaging with the work of other academics has taught me anything, it is that getting a PhD is no sure sign of having a competent critical intellect. And this is especially relevant in relation

---

12. Augustine, *Confessions*, 5.6.10 (English trans., Rex Warner).

to Mormon studies, where without question some of the best published historical work over the last century has been done by people without doctorates. In addition to this I believe that anyone who has spent time with Sandra Tanner cannot help but find her to be unpretentious, thoughtful, articulate, and reasoned in her responses. She is a clearer communicator both verbally and in writing than Jerald and a good many academics I have known. Jerald, on the other hand, had an extraordinary ability to get to the bottom of things, and a unique genius for detecting literary forgeries (chapt. 15). This is granted even by the noted expert on nineteenth-century new religious movements Lawrence Foster, who may be the Tanners most vigorous academic critic, but who nevertheless described Jerald as "a brilliant analyst of detail, with an almost uncanny ability to spot textual inconsistencies that demand explanation" (chapt. 19).[13] Looking across the academic landscape in my own field, one of the few parallels I have encountered to Jerald's unique ability is the late Polish scholar Józef Tadeusz Milik who left me flabbergasted on one occasion by his seemingly miraculous ability to plausibly reconstruct even the tiniest fragments of the Dead Sea Scrolls.[14] While working through Jerald's material for this book I was often reminded of what noted biblical scholar F. F. Bruce once said about his father's being "a natural scholar and student [with a] finely balanced judgement. Although his period of formal schooling was brief, I never had to unlearn anything I learned from him."[15] The same can be said of Jerald.

The contrast I observed between the Tanners and others in the early 1980s revealed at once the inadequateness of reductionistic descriptions like "anti-Mormon" as a one-size-fits-all way of labeling and dismissing Mormons, ex-Mormons, and non-Mormons who challenged the veracity of the teachings and historical claims of the LDS Church. Yet "anti-Mormon" is only one of the terminological hotspots that called for careful negotiation throughout this book. Another problematic term is the word "Christian," as in the

---

13. Foster is perhaps best known for his *Religion and Sexuality: The Shakers, the Mormons, and the Oneida Community,* first published by Oxford University Press in 1981, and *Women, Family, and Utopia: Communal Experiments of the Shakers, the Oneida Community, and the Mormons,* by Syracuse University Press in 1992.

14. See my "A Canonical 'Book of Periods' at Qumran?"

15. J. D. Douglas, "A Man of Unchanging Faith," 16.

question: "Are Mormons Christians?"[16] A Mormon might feel that all one need do to prove they are Christian is to point to the name of their institution: The Church of Jesus Christ of Latter-day Saints. Indeed in 1995 the name "Jesus Christ" was made larger and given its own line in the church's logo, presumably to make just this point. This convention was continued in the new church "symbol" introduced in 2020, which now places the church's name in a rectangular shape beneath an image of Thorvaldsen's *Christus* statue as a way of reminding viewers that "Jesus Christ is the chief cornerstone."[17] Traditional Christians on the other hand might insist that affirmation of the teaching of the ancient creeds is an essential element of what it means to be a Christian. And since Mormons have as a foundational claim of their religion that God told Joseph Smith Jr. that "all their [i.e., the traditional Christians'] creeds were an abomination in his sight" (JS-H 1:19), it is scarcely surprising that traditional, creed-affirming Christians might have difficulty with that. The situation is further exacerbated by the fact that Joseph Smith's testimony, which contains this condemnation of the creeds, is highlighted in Mormon missionary presentations across the globe. The church distribution center up the street from where I live, for example, offers the "Joseph Smith Testimony" pamphlet on site for purchase in some thirty languages. Mormons may not like traditional Christians' unwillingness to call them Christians just as traditional Christians may feel the same about having their cherished creeds, the most important of which are affirmed in common by Eastern Orthodox, Roman Catholic, and the majority of Protestant Churches, damned as "an abomination." In both cases the usage is rooted in significant theological differences that cannot be marked down to a simple lack of courtesy on either side. Beyond this it is also cumbersome in a book like this one to always feel the need to preface retronyms like *traditional* or *non-Mormon* to the word "Christian" when describing adherents of traditional Christian teaching. So, although I sometimes do resort to retronyms, I have generally tried to fit the usage

---

16. See, for example, Robinson, *Are Mormons Christians?*
17. Russell M. Nelson, "Opening the Heavens for Help," *Ensign*, May 2020, 73; image and explanation on p. 129.

of terminology to the perspective of the particular individuals I am describing in a particular context.

Before getting far in the present work I became aware of another scholar who, I'm convinced, would have done a fine job had he taken on the task: David Conley Nelson, author of the book *Moroni and the Swastika: Mormons in Nazi Germany*, published by the University of Oklahoma Press (2015). At one point I asked David if he would be willing to take over and finish the project if anything happened to me. He graciously agreed. I am very grateful to David for this and his many encouraging words along the way. I am indebted to others who helped me in significant ways including especially Sandra Tanner, who read and reread the various drafts of the present work, to her staff, Marlene and Mark Reeves and Tony Higgins (see dedication), and to Dennis Tanner and H. Michael Marquardt. I am also indebted to many others who shared their memories and/or expertise with me in a more incidental manner, including Grant Palmer, Chris Vlachos, Sam Burton, Gary Bergera, Brent Metcalfe, Charles Larson, Curt Bench, Anne Wilde, D. Michael Quinn, Shannon Flynn, and Steve Mayfield. Special thanks finally to John Hatch of Signature Books, who edited the present work with great patience, skill and sensitivity. Finally, this book, its conclusions, and any errors, are mine, and mine alone.

1

MARRIAGE

Jerald Tanner and Sandra McGee married on June 14, 1959, in Mission Hills, California, north of Los Angeles, in Sandra's parents' spacious colonial-style home. Sandra wore the wedding dress her mother, Georgia, had originally made for her older sister. The dress was let out and lengthened, and Sandra helped with the lace and beadwork. Jerald looked dapper in a rented white tuxedo with black tie and matching cummerbund, the ensemble finished out with a pair of argyle socks, much to the consternation of the mother of the bride.

Although both were born into the Church of Jesus Christ of Latter-day Saints, they were no longer believers. They contemplated simply bringing in a justice of the peace, but Sandra's mother had secured James H. Kepler of the Granada Hills Congregational Church of Our Savior, whose Bible studies Georgia had attended, to perform the ceremony. The Reverend Kepler's claim to fame was that he was a spiritual advisor to Charlton Heston, who'd played Moses in Cecil B. DeMille's 1956 film classic, *The Ten Commandments*.[1] The ceremony went well, and was followed by a reception for the eighteen-year-old bride and twenty-one-year-old groom. It was a whirlwind romance for a couple who had been engaged for less than two months, and it was the start of a nearly half-century union centered on researching Mormonism and promoting mainstream Christianity.

The couple had met during Sandra's freshman year at Los Angeles Valley Junior College. Her grandmother Sylvia Young Rogerson came to California to stay the winter, and Sandra accompanied her back to Salt Lake City during spring break. Rogerson asked her granddaughter to drive her to a meeting she described as "sort of

---

1. Kepler, "Dare I, A Sinner, Play Christ?" *Modern Screen*, Jan. 1961, 1. Heston contributed a foreword to Kepler's novel, *The Jordan Beachhead: A Novel of Biblical Times*.

like a fireside."[2] The words "sort of" did not escape Sandra, but she decided to tag along to get her mind off the recent visit from her soon-to-be ex-boyfriend informing her of his intention to break off the relationship. She did not expect the meeting to be exciting; it was a distraction. She recalls, "I assumed it was a bunch of old Mormon people, and she didn't want to tell me that in case I wouldn't go. When this tall good-looking guy came to the door, I immediately got more interested."[3]

The LDS "fireside" wasn't LDS at all. It was a presentation by a small Restorationist sect called the Church of Christ (Bible and the Book of Mormon Teaching), headquartered in Independence, Missouri.[4] The group was pastored by Pauline Hancock, perhaps the first woman to lead a Mormon splinter group. The group accepted the Bible and the Book of Mormon but rejected other LDS scriptures, believing Joseph Smith was only called to bring forth the Book of Mormon. Jerald Tanner hosted the meeting and had asked James Wardle, an RLDS[5] barber, for a list of names of people in Salt Lake City who might be interested to hear about Pauline's teaching. Sandra's grandmother Sylvia was apparently on the list and she was interested.

Jerald and Sandra remembered their first impressions of each other the way most first impressions are made: by physical appearance. "I thought that she was a beautiful young woman," remarked Jerald, though he feared that Sandra was too wealthy and

---

2. Firesides are presentations or musical events held for LDS congregations, typically on Sunday evenings.

3. Tanner, Recollections.

4. Sometimes the group was referred to by outsiders as "Lukites," because it met in the home of Ervin Luke. Others referred to it as "The Basement Church," because its building never finished its upper level. The Church of Jesus Christ of Latter-day Saints in which the Tanners were raised is the largest of many groups descended from Joseph Smith's restoration movement. Many of these splinter groups claimed to be the only true and legitimate successors of Joseph Smith. The Church of Christ (Bible and the Book of Mormon Teaching) never did. Indeed, Pauline Hancock firmly rejected the idea: "The group became converted to THE LORD, before we had been converted to a church, there is a big difference, church is people, there are many churches. It is to the Lord that we must be converted, we are then willing to do His will." (Pauline Hancock to James Wardle, Jan. 31, 1950, 5. In Marquardt, Papers, box 9 fd. 1).

5. The Reorganized Church of Jesus Christ of Latter Day Saints (RLDS) changed its name to the Community of Christ in 2001, and is the second-largest Mormon denomination. I refer to it as the RLDS Church because all references to it in this book came before the name change.

sophisticated to have any interest in him.[6] Sandra's initial interest in Jerald was helped by his fastidious personal appearance, with special attention to his hair and his clothes. He was lucky: When Sandra received her first letter from him, she found Jerald's sloppy handwriting off-putting. Had she seen his handwriting before meeting him, she is certain they would not have ended up together.

Jerald's prominent Mormon ancestry belied his upbringing as a typical kid from Salt Lake City's west side. He was rebellious as a teen, not academically motivated, nor particularly ambitious. He wasn't interested in reading or education, despite coming from a family that placed a high value on it. He once scandalized his father, who had attended Massachusetts Institute of Technology, by proclaiming that "pumping gas in a filling station" was his most ambitious career choice. Meanwhile, he worked at Ray's Music Company, which dealt in vending machines and candy.

Jerald's one passion in high school was developing and performing magic shows. He spent hundreds of dollars, not an inconsiderable sum in the 1950s, purchasing trick equipment and trade secrets. After leaving Mormonism and converting to Christianity, however, Jerald demonstrated the depths of his new commitment to Jesus Christ. He burned all of his props in imitation of the Ephesian sorcerers who turned from magic to Christ and publicly burned their scrolls (Acts 19:19). He saved only two items, a trick sword that seemed to go right through you and come out the back and an endless handkerchief that just keeps coming as you pull it out of your clenched fist. The conflagration represented for Jerald a repudiation of deceptions, even those others might deem harmless.

Jerald's mother, Helen, was an active Mormon who tried to make sure he and his sisters attended LDS worship services while they were growing up. Jerald's father, George, was inactive and increasingly hostile towards religion, eventually becoming an outspoken atheist. Jerald had a few friends who, like him, drank and smoked and had little interest in school. These boys would settle into solid blue-collar jobs, as the ascendancy of the American middle class reached its apex. Jerald would have likely followed the same path

---

6. Tanner, *Jerald Tanner's Testimony*, 9.

after he graduated from West High School. He completed a year at the University of Utah, where he took remedial English,[7] but left the university to attend Salt Lake Trade Technical Institute to become a machinist, finishing the program not long before he married Sandra. But instead of a life of blue-collar work with a nuclear family raised by a stay-at-home wife, the future (or to Jerald's thinking, God) had other plans.

Sandra was a good student. Not top of her class but solid and involved socially. She had run for ninth-grade class president and won with the slogan, "Don't scratch your head like you had a flee, pick up your pen and vote for McGee." In high school and junior college, she studied speech, art, voice, drama, and business. Like most women at the time, she had no expectation that she would go to college and pursue her own career. She would be "treading water until marriage," acquiring such skills as she needed to tide herself over financially while single and then, once married, to make herself useful as a wife and mother.[8]

Sandra was very active in the LDS Church. On school days she would rise early to attend Mormon seminary held before her usual classes at San Fernando High.[9] When she was sixteen, her father bought her a car because, as Sandra recalls, "he hated getting up at 5 [a.m.] to take me to seminary, which was across town." She contributed a column called *The Eye Opener* to a small Mormon newsletter printed for Mormons living in the San Fernando Valley. Articles included news on current and past seminarians, such as Dianne Campbell who had gone to BYU on a scholarship and recently married Don Harris in the Los Angeles Temple; Bishop Floyd Weston, who had an operation and needed someone to fill in for him; Hollywood film director Cecil B. De Mille's sponsoring members of the Sherman Oaks seminary to attend the premier of *The Ten Commandments*; and a special Christmas breakfast event,

---

7. Tanner, Recollections.

8. Tanner.

9. LDS seminaries are part of the Church Education System and offer religious instruction before, and sometimes during, high school classes. These seminary classes are separate from public education. After high school, college-age students can attend LDS institutes of religion.

Marriage of Sandra McGee to Jerald Tanner, June 14, 1959.

which had as its closing number, "Oh, Come, All Ye Faithful," sung by Sandra Jacobson and Sandra McGee.[10]

After she finished seminary, Sandra attended the LDS institute for college-aged youth. In 1957 she was initiated into the Delta Gamma chapter of the LDS Lambda Delta Sigma fraternity/sorority where she became pledge master;[11] her initiation certificate was signed by LDS education luminary T. Edgar Lyon. After she graduated from

---

10. Tanner and Tanner, Papers, clipping of *The Eye Opener* column, 1956.

11. Laura Lee Smith, "The LDS 'Greeks' Lambda Delta Sigma and Sigma Gamma Chi," *Ensign*, Sep. 1986, 27–31.

high school, Sandra attended Los Angeles Valley Junior College, but she soon dropped out after meeting Jerald at that "sort of a fireside."

It was Sandra who took the initiative that night. She approached Jerald to talk about the meeting. Naturally he was eager to share both his discoveries about Mormonism and his own beliefs. By the end of the evening, Jerald had an invitation to come to dinner with Sandra and her grandmother. At their second dinner, on April 1, 1959, Sandra played an April Fool's joke on Jerald. She set the dinner table with cake pans and measuring cups—anything besides normal tableware. When Jerald arrived, he was so desperate to make a good impression he refused to act as though anything were abnormal. Sandra maintained her deadpan expression for as long as she could, waiting in vain for some glimmer of recognition of the joke on Jerald's face until she could stand it no longer and burst out laughing, "April Fools!" After that fiasco Sandra feared Jerald might lose interest, but he was not so easily put off. On April 6, Jerald sat next to Sandra for the first time at her grandmother's house under the pretext of showing her a photograph. On April 24, while sitting in the Tanner family's front room, their petting of a fat tabby cat sitting between them resolved, with a nudge of encouragement from Sandra, into their holding hands.

Three days later, Jerald and Sandra met to listen to a Pauline Hancock tape on Jerald's reel-to-reel player. The machine always worked before, but for some reason Jerald couldn't get it to play. Instead, they spent their time talking, and as the minutes ticked away the discussion veered from Mormonism to their relationship. Sandra's grandmother was in the front parlor watching television, while Jerald and Sandra sat side by side, holding hands in another room at the back of the house. Jerald told Sandra how much he loved being with her and then, gazing at their hands, said that he wanted to hold her hand forever. Sandra detected a proposal fluttering in the air and noticed that Jerald kept looking at her hand rather than her face. She asked him outright what he was trying to say, and Jerald stammered out his love and that he hoped they might marry, to which Sandra responded, "Wow! Me Too!" They kissed and started making plans. As soon as Sandra's mother and Aunt Lucille heard the news, they hurried from California to Salt Lake City.

A little over a month after they had met, Jerald and Sandra came close to eloping. While her grandmother, mother, and aunt were out visiting relatives, Sandra left a note. They fetched Jerald's mother to serve as witness and drove west from Salt Lake City for Wendover, Nevada. They got to the Great Salt Lake before Sandra felt guilty about how disappointed her mother would be, so they turned back. Sandra's mother had returned home before they arrived but hadn't yet seen the note. She might never have known anything had Sandra not asked, "Did you see the note?"

Sandra got along well with Jerald's mother, who was pleased to have her as a future daughter-in-law. But somewhere during the plan to elope to Wendover, she asked Sandra if she was certain she wanted to go through with it, since Jerald "didn't even have a job." After the wedding, what would the newly married couple do? But for the present, such questions would have to wait.

After the wedding, Jerald and Sandra spent their first night in a twin bed in a house her mother was remodeling to sell. Sandra recalled, "I changed into my nightgown in the bathroom, came out and jumped in bed. Jerald finished in the bathroom and came out and knelt to pray. I felt like a heathen. It hadn't occurred to me, and he hadn't said anything about praying together ... a failure to communicate."[12]

They added up the money they had been given in wedding gifts: two hundred dollars—half from Jerald's grandfather Caleb, and half from a mutual friend. The newlyweds headed north for a brief honeymoon in Yosemite National Park. On their return trip, they visited San Francisco and the infamous Winchester Mansion. Back in Mission Hills, they moved into small apartment behind the garage of Sandra's parents' home and Jerald got a job as a machinist. In October 1959 they got their own apartment in North Hollywood.

How was it that Jerald, the rebellious, unambitious teen, came to hold meetings to explain the teachings of a Mormon splinter group? Why would Sandra's LDS grandmother feel comfortable bringing her active LDS granddaughter to such a meeting? How was it that Sandra, who had so recently been an active LDS girl, came to reject

---

12. Tanner, Recollections.

the teachings of the LDS Church between spring break and her marriage just two months later? Why, given that Sandra was marrying a member of a Mormon splinter group, should she feel more comfortable with having a Protestant pastor perform their wedding than a Mormon Bishop?

How these two young people came to be "the Tanners" stretches back to old Mormon families whose spiritual and intellectual journeys went before and shaped them. Jerald's family was a well-known Mormon clan whose name appears on buildings around Salt Lake City to this day. Sandra's family, the Angells, descend from Mary Ann Angell, Brigham Young's first Mormon wife.

2

THOSE WHO CAME BEFORE

Jerald's Ancestry

Veritas is the single word emblazoned across the official shield of Harvard University. The earliest example of the familiar image is a crudely drawn doodle settled between briskly scribbled notes of the meeting of the governors of Harvard when the shield design was originally adopted.[1] It has been suggested that both the symbol and handwriting belonged to Harvard's first president, Henry Dunster.[2] Within ten years of making the doodle, however, Dunster would be driven out of both his position in the university and the city for seeking *Veritas* in a place not approved by Harvard University, in a place, in fact, that wasn't even legal. He had fallen, to quote Cotton Mather's magisterial *Magnalia Christiani Americana*, "into the errors of *Antipaedobaptism*,"[3] that is to say, he had become a Baptist, although the more common term in those days used by their detractors was *Anabaptist* (someone who baptizes again).

At the time Baptists were still something novel in the English-speaking world. It had only been a few years before when Thomas Helwys returned from religious exile in Amsterdam to found the first Baptist Church on English soil in 1612 at Spitalfields in London's East End. That same year Helwys was arrested and consigned to Newgate Prison where he died by 1616.[4] In America, Baptists were centered in Rhode Island, founded by Roger Williams, who was expelled from Massachusetts in 1636, not for becoming a Baptist,

---

1. College Book 1, 1639–1795, UAI 5.5, box 1, Harvard University Archives, http://lib.harvard.edu.

2. Dunster, *Henry Dunster*, 8; Davis, *Bibliographical Contributions*, 4, 10.

3. Mather, *Magnalia Christiani Americana*, 3:12.

4. See Early, ed. *Life and Writings of Thomas Helwys*, 44, and Burgess, *John Smyth the Se-Baptist*, 289.

but for insisting on "dyvers newe & dangerous opinions against the aucthoritie of magistrates." Williams said that the state has no jurisdiction over what people believe, only over how they behave, and that the Indians owned the land so if the English wanted some of it they needed to pay for it, rather than simply declaring it their own.[5] As a result of the former conviction, Rhode Island became a haven for people persecuted for their beliefs. Williams did become a Baptist for a time, founding the first Baptist Church in America in 1638 in Providence, Rhode Island. But he departed from it, apparently after only a few months, to become instead what some have called a "Seeker."[6]

In July 1651, John Clarke and Obadiah Holmes—both ministers in the second Baptist Church in America founded by Clarke at Newport in 1644—along with a layman named John Crandall, who was also Jerald Tanner's seven-times great-grandfather, crossed over from Rhode Island to Massachusetts to visit a blind fellow believer named William Witter who lived two miles outside of Lynn. Holmes had previously been a pastor in Massachusetts, but had gone to Rhode Island after getting in trouble for becoming a Baptist and having unauthorized religious services in private homes. On Sunday, July 20, while they were engaging in a private worship service at Witter's, two constables arrested them. The court fined Holmes £30—a sum equal to fines meted out for crimes like adultery, rape, and counterfeiting[7]—Clarke, £20, and Crandall, £5, to be paid *before* they could be released from prison, failing which "they are all of them to be well whipped."[8] Clarke's and Crandall's fines were paid by well-wishers, but Holmes refused to allow anyone to pay his. As a result, he was led out on September 5, 1651, and brutally given thirty lashes.[9] Clarke wrote about the incident in a book published in England and dedicated to the English Parliament, entitled *Ill Newes from New-England* (1652).

As J. T. McNeill pointed out, "Obadiah Holmes was publicly whipped (1651). But the embarrassing result was the conversion of

---

5. The specific charges are given in Williams, *Mr. Cottons Letter Lately Printed*, 4–5.

6. Fox and Burnyeat, *A New-England Fire-Brand Quenched*, 247; Winthrop, *Winthrop's Journal*, 309 (Jul. 5, 1639).

7. King, *Summer Visit of Three Rhode Islanders*, 57.

8. Clark[e], *Ill Newes*, 26–27.

9. Clark[e], 22.

Jerald Tanner's 7x great-grandfather John Crandall was arrested in Massachusetts in 1651 for leading an illegal worship service with John Clarke and Obadiah Holmes. *Artist: A. Frederick, Engraver: A. Bobbett, 1878.*

many to their [Baptists] views, of whom Henry Dunster, the president of Harvard, was the most distinguished."[10] In 1653 President Henry Dunster violated the laws of Massachusetts by refusing to bring his infant child—probably his fourth—to the baptismal font, and by repudiating infant baptism and defending believers' baptism from the pulpit.[11]

The dignity of Dunster's office as the president of the institution that identified itself with *Veritas*, and the fear of losing it, might have become a snare for him. But Dunster followed his conscience and was removed. And it was good for his relationship to *Veritas*, and to

10. McNeill, *History and Character of Calvinism*, 341.
11. Chaplin, *Life of Henry Dunster*, 101–18, esp. 108–10.

justice, that he did, because what began with the magistracy of Massachusetts whipping one Baptist in 1651 progressed to the hanging of three Quakers in 1659–60[12] and of numerous women during the witch craze of the 1680s and 1690s. The last mentioned of these actions was endorsed by no less distinguished a pen than that of the later Harvard president, Increase Mather.[13]

In 1665, as John Clarke's Newport Church became more dispersed geographically, it was decided they needed to found a daughter church at Westerly (now Hopkinton) Rhode Island, with Jerald Tanner's ancestor John Crandall serving as its first pastor. In time the church became Seventh-Day Baptists (Sabbatarians) when members began following the ancient practice of the Jews by keeping Saturday as their Sabbath.[14]

In 1708 the Westerly Sabbatarians moved to become two distinct churches, and it is in this connection that we encounter William Tanner, who was "prominent in founding the old Seventh-Day Baptist church in Westerly, now Hopkinton, and held an influential position therein. He was living as late as 1735 ... The date of his birth is unknown, but was probably about 1660–63. It is not known from what part of England he came, nor to what branch of the Tanners he belonged ... It is probable that William Tanner, and a brother or two brothers crossed the ocean to escape the rigorous measures against the Baptists in the time of Charles II."[15] Hence William Tanner, who married John Crandall's granddaughter Mary, was Jerald Tanner's earliest known Tanner ancestor in the New World. It is from William's great-grandson, John Tanner, that the vast majority of LDS Tanners trace their ancestry.

As Don A. Sanford writes in his recent history of the Seventh-Day Baptist movement, "Members of the First Hopkinton Church in Rhode Island provided the nucleus for new churches across the state of New York."[16] This was certainly the case of the descendants of William Tanner. By 1800 we find John Tanner and

---

12. Rogers, *Mary Dyer*, 46, 57–62.
13. Mather, *Further Account*.
14. Callender, *Historical Discourse*, 65.
15. *Encyclopedia of Genealogy*, 2:944.
16. Sanford, *A Choosing People: The History of the Seventh Day Baptists*, digital edition.

his father Joshua living in Argyle, Washington County, New York.[17] While there John married two successive wives in two years. In early 1800 he married Tabitha Bentley, who died in 1801 shortly after giving birth to John's firstborn son, Elisha. Before that year was out, he married Lydia Stewart.[18]

John Tanner had some sort of connection with the Bottskill Baptist Church. We know that his first wife, Tabitha Bentley, was the daughter of Elisha Bentley, the first appointed clerk of the church, who was also the first school master in the area,[19] and that a son of John Tanner and Lydia Stewart Tanner, who died in infancy in 1807, is buried in the Bottskill Baptist Church's Graveyard.[20] But John's name is not listed in the membership records of the church.[21] Yet some of his progeny did attend, as is seen by the sudden influx of six Tanners into membership of the Bottskill Church in 1816.[22] This was likely due to a religious revival that occurred throughout the region in 1816 and 1817.[23]

Yet there may be another explanation as to why John Tanner was not attending Bottskill Baptist Church, which we might find a hint of in a story that is sometimes told in relation to John Tanner's naming one of his sons Nathan, after an Elder Nathan Tanner (a distant relative), who might be the same person as the first pastor of the Bottskill Church. According to an early version of the story:

> Nathan Tanner, son of John and Lydia Stuart Tanner, was born in the town of Greenwich, Washington County, New York, May 14, 1815.

---

17. See the 1800 *New York State Tax Assessment Book* for Argyle, New York.

18. New York State Comptroller's Office Tax Assessment Rolls of Real and Personal Estates, 1799–1804, Series B0950, box 54, fd. 17, New York State Archives, Albany.

19. Thurston, *History of the Town of Greenwich*, 25. Tabitha had been received into membership in the Bottskill Church in 1794, see Foley, "Early Church Records: 'Names Belonging to Elder Nathan Tanner's Church at Bottenkill,' now Greenwich, N.Y., prior to 1815," *Early Settlers of New York State*, 35.

20. Wade, *Bottskill Baptist Church*, 31. *The New York Genealogical and Biographical Record* 48, Jan. 1917, 5, lists the name of the child, less plausibly, as "Willard."

21. Wright, *History of Shaftsbury Baptist Association*, 298; Foley, *Early Settlers of New York*, 38.

22. At least two of the new members appear to be John's children: Elisha Bentley Tanner (b. 1801) and William Stewart Tanner (b. 1802), neither of whom became Mormons.

23. "Revival of Religion in Greenwich, State of New-York," *Massachusetts Baptist Missionary Magazine*, Sep. 1816, 356–57; Edward Barber, "Letter to the Editor," *American Baptist Magazine and Missionary Intelligencer*, Jul., 1817, 152–53.

Three years before his birth, a Baptist preacher of the same name, and a distant relative, visited his parents, and sought and obtained their promise that if they ever had another son, they would call him by the said Baptist Elder's name. The Baptist Elder was a righteous man, who preached not for a salary, but for the pure love of the Gospel, and being full of the Holy Ghost prophesied many things concerning Nathan Tanner which have come to pass.[24]

The Nathan Tanner who was the first pastor of the Bottskill Church was defrocked and excommunicated when it was discovered that he was involved in money digging with a mineral rod and the aid of a "congurist,"[25] the latter probably helping Tanner cope with the spirits that were thought to serve as guardians of buried treasure.

The incident with Elder Tanner offers a clear picture of the attitude of a significant number of Baptist Church leaders toward the practice of using a mineral rod and a conjuror to dig for buried treasure along similar lines to what Joseph Smith Jr. was doing some decades later, giving credence to the report of a strong reaction to Smith's attempting to join the Methodist class in 1828 without first repenting of his role as a necromancer.[26]

It may be that John and his father, Joshua Tanner, did not agree with the church's censure, and continued to follow Elder Tanner after the Bottskill Baptist Church withdrew fellowship from him and those who followed him in 1794.[27] According to Asa Fitch, Elder Tanner was "restored afterward to the church but not to the ministry."[28]

Did John and Joshua start to meet privately for services in Elder Tanner's home after his fellowship had been withdrawn? Was he the Elder in the Tanner family's story who "preached not for a salary, but for the pure love of the Gospel, and being full of the Holy

---

24. George S. Tanner, Papers, box 33, fd. 8, 1. This is a fair copy of a document entitled "Life of Nathan Tanner: An Elder in the Church of Jesus Christ of Latter-Day Saints. Member of Zions Camp. Fronteersman. Missionary Etc," in the George S. Tanner, Papers, box 33, fd. 9. The version I use here includes a note identifying the paper as coming from "the papers of E. Pingree Tanner, of Magrath, Alberta. It is not dated and the author is not given. By G. S. Tanner."

25. Thurston, *History of Town of Greenwich*, 39.

26. According to Emma Smith's cousin Joseph Lewis, *The Amboy Journal*, Jun. 11, 1879, 1.

27. Thurston, *History of Town of Greenwich*, 43.

28. Fitch, *The Asa Fitch Papers*, 3, 20, sec. 436.

Ghost prophesied many things"? Though it seems probable, we ultimately can't be sure.

Jared Carter and his brother Simeon are responsible for bringing the Tanner family into Mormonism. Before his conversion to Joseph Smith's church, Jared had been a Freewill Baptist,[29] a denomination founded in 1780 by a New Hampshire sailmaker named Benjamin Randall, who had himself been converted to Christ under the preaching of George Whitefield. Jared's brother John Sims Carter had served as pastor of a Calvinistic Baptist Church in Benson, Vermont, prior to his excommunication "for denying eternal, personal, unconditional election."[30] Following his excommunication, John sought out the Freewill Baptists and became a presiding elder over a congregation of twenty-eight members in 1823, which included his brothers Gideon and Jared.[31] All three brothers would later convert to Mormonism.

By the time the Mormon Jared Carter wrote his 1832–33 diaries, his beliefs had little in common with those of the Freewill Baptists. Instead, his views mirrored an unrelated "restorationist" movement forming in Great Britain at the same time called the Irvingites, named for Edward Irving, whose principal idea was that all the offices—the gift of tongues, prophesy, and other miraculous manifestations of the early church—were beginning to be evidenced again. The Irvingite movement got off the ground in 1830 following the miraculous healing of two women in Scotland, Mary Campbell and Margaret Macdonald. The similarity between the early Latter-day Saints and the Irvingites did not go unnoticed. Emilius Guers's *Irvingism and Mormonism: Tested from Scripture* (1854) includes a section entitled "Parallel of Irvingism and Mormonism."[32] Joseph Smith is credited with saying, "The Irvingites are a people that have counterfeited the truth perhaps the nearest of any of our modern sectarians."[33]

---

29. Carter, Journal, typescript, 24.
30. Stewart, *History of the Freewill Baptists*, 380.
31. Johnson, *History of Washington Co.*, 452.
32. Guers, *Irvingism and Mormonism*, 85–90.
33. Smith, *Teachings of the Prophet Joseph Smith*, 210; "Try the Spirits," *Times and Seasons*, Apr. 1, 1842, 746. Also, Church Historian's Office, History of the Church, Apr. 1, 1842, 1309.

Left to Right: John Tanner (the first Mormon Tanner), Elizabeth Beswick Tanner (John's 3rd wife), Myron Tanner (Jerald's great-grandfather) and Louisa Maria Tanner Lyman (c. 1844). *Courtesy of the Church History Library, The Church of Jesus Christ of Latter-day Saints.*

Carter put a strong emphasis on the restoration of miracles, especially healing. In his journal he recounts expressing his view in a meeting of elders at Kirtland in the spring of 1832 that it was the privilege of Latter-day Saints "to rise above all afflicttions as disseases, feavers and curses."[34] Hyrum Smith, Carter reports, got up and "sanctioned or fellowshipped the doctrine and advanced additional proof of the propriety of the possibility that the members of this Church might come to the privilege of standing clear of all diseases an feavers or pane of sickness."[35] According to Carter, Reynolds Cahoon and Frederick G. Williams also endorsed the doctrine, while Thomas Marsh, who was "then un well" initially opposed it, but afterward accepted it, with the result that, Carter claims, Marsh

34. Jared Carter Journal, Manuscript, 55/Typescript, 9.
35. Carter, Ms., 55–56/Typescript, 9–10.

was healed.[36] Carter regularly commanded unwell people to "rise and walk" regardless of their particular affliction. Yet occasionally he did encounter people who really did have trouble walking. One such person was John Tanner, then living in Lake George, New York:

> on Sunday [September 16, 1832, at the earliest] held meeting to Brother Tanners and the and the preasanc of the Lord was powerfully manifested. after the meeting we baptized four. while we was here the Lord had mercy apon a lame man by the name of Taner who was so lame that he could not bear his weight on atol [at all] on one of his feet. he had been lame for months but we found he was a believer in the book of mormon. I asked him to indeavor to walk in the name of Christ. he agreed to undertake. I then took him by the hand and commanded him in the Name of christ to walk and by the Power of christ he was enabled to walk.[37]

Later reminiscent accounts more or less concur with Carter's journal, though as time passed, these depictions grew steadily more fantastic, complete with assurances that John was about to lose his leg or even die accompanied by increasingly horrifying descriptions of the sores that supposedly covered the leg.[38] The number and dignity of the physicians involved in the case also grew as the story passed along to the point that it was finally asserted that "seven of the most eminent physicians in the country" had tried and failed to help John Tanner.[39]

That same month John Tanner sent two of his sons, Nathan and John J., to Kirtland, Ohio, where they "got acquainted with the Prophet and the leading men of that day."[40] The following spring the brothers joined the Zion's Camp march to western Missouri, to aid Mormons driven from their homes. According to Nathan they contributed one animal shy of three teams of horses, and "put in very near half the money that paid the expenses of Zion's Camp."[41]

---

36. Carter, Ms., 56/Typescript, 10.

37. Carter, Journal, Ms., 117/Typescript,19.

38. Nathan Tanner, "Reminiscences," rpt. in Tanner, *John Tanner and His Family*, 380. Elizabeth Beswick Tanner, "Reminiscences," 1884, 1, and "Reminiscences" in Tanner, *John Tanner and His Family*, 375. Also "Sketch of an Elder's Life," in *Scraps of Biography*, 10.

39. "Sketch of an Elder's Life," in *Scraps of Biography*, 10.

40. Nathan Tanner, "Reminiscences," in Tanner, *John Tanner and His Family*, 382.

41. Tanner.

John's third wife, Elizabeth Beswick, said that her husband "had a comfortable home and was considered a wealthy man"[42] in New York. He "carried on farming extensively; stock raising and dairying on different farms; lumbering in all its branches, as he owned sawmills and planing mills, and owned some 2,200 acres of land with houses and barnes to accommodate a number of families; and orcharding in great abundance."[43]

The family arrived in Kirtland, Ohio, in March 1835 with "six teams and wagons, with merchandise and cash, altogether amounting to about $10,000—a very prosperous condition for those days."[44] When the family departed Kirtland three years later for Far West, Missouri, they were destitute.[45] They had to beg for food, and a young daughter died along the way. John's willingness to lend money to the church and its leaders, to co-sign loans and for goods they had taken out, and to extend them credit on goods in his store ruined him.

In fact, the Tanners were in Kirtland fewer than twenty-four hours when they were pressed for money. The mortgage payment on the farm on which the Kirtland Temple was to be built had to be made by the following morning. John loaned the church $2,000 on the spot. On top of his liberal donations for the temple construction, he also loaned the temple committee an additional $1,300.[46] In Missouri, the family continued to remain faithful and to defend their church.

By 1838, when Mormon–Missouri relations had again erupted into violence, Nathan, John J., and their brother Sydney appear to have participated in the notorious vigilante band known as the Danites. Nathan and Sydney added their signatures to the menacing June 1838 letter to Oliver Cowdery, William W. Phelps, David Whitmer, John Whitmer, and Lyman E. Johnson, warning them to leave Far West within three days or face "a more fatal calamity."[47]

---

42. Elizabeth Beswick Tanner, "Reminiscences," 1884, rpt. in Tanner, *John Tanner and His Family*, 375.

43. Nathan Tanner, "Reminiscences," (1884) in Tanner, *John Tanner and His Family*, 380.

44. Tanner, *Biography of Myron Tanner*, 4.

45. Elizabeth Beswick Tanner, "Reminiscences," 1884, 376.

46. "Sketch of an Elder's Life," in *Scraps of Biography*, 12, places the sum at $13,000, as does Elizabeth Beswick Tanner, "Reminiscences," 1884, 375–76. What Elizabeth had actually written in the original manuscript for the talk was not $13,000 but $1,300. "Elizabeth Beswick Tanner, "Reminiscences," (1884), 2 in George S. Tanner, Papers, box 22 fd. 10.

47. *Document Containing the Correspondence*, 103. Page 106 for the list of signatories.

Nathan and Sydney also participated in the Battle of Crooked River under Captain "Fear Not" Patton. John D. Lee reported that the participants in the battle "were nearly all, if not every one of them, Danites."[48] Sydney and John J. were also among those arrested and tried with Joseph Smith for high treason in relation with the 1838 Missouri War. However, Danite leader Sampson Avard named the two as being among the few men being tried who may not have taken the Danite oath.[49]

Another of John's sons, Myron, twelve at the time and later Jerald Tanner's great-grandfather, recalled one violent incident against his father. As John and Myron had taken their wagon out to a mill some twelve miles away, they saw a Missouri militia approaching. John ordered Myron to get out of the wagon, hide in the brush, then make his way back home and tell everyone what happened. A militiaman struck John on the head with the butt of a rifle and, according to Nathan, "cut a gash 7 inches long to the boan."[50]

John Tanner's wife, Elizabeth, describing the family's rapid descent into grinding poverty at Kirtland, poignantly writes:

> Our substance was divided from time to time for church purposes and to assist the needy even my own personal clothing. I divided until we were left in very destitute circumstances and lived as poor as it was possible to get along with our large family many times lacking such nourishment as I felt the need of to sustain myself through sickness and hard labor.[51]

Sydney's name appears immediately after Nathan's but his last name is mispelled as Turner, rather than Tanner.

48. Lee, *Mormonism Unveiled*, 73. Quinn, *Mormon Hierarchy: Origins of Power*, 487, credits Lee with saying that "all the participants in the Battle of Crooked River were Danites," but Lee wasn't perhaps quite as definitive in his statement.

49. *Document Containing the Correspondence*, 98. Sydney's last name is spelled correctly in the testimony, 153. Curiously, D. Michael Quinn cites Sampson Avard's testimony as proof that Sydney and John *were* Danites (Quinn, *Origins of Power*, 484). John J. was released for lack of evidence (*Document Containing the Correspondence*, 37), but Adam J. Job testified to having been taken captive by Sidney Tanner (143).

50. "Journal of Nathan Tanner," 6, rpt. in Smith, *John Tanner*, 395. See also Tanner, *Myron Tanner*, 6. Nathan Tanner, "Reminiscences," 395. The story also made it, for example, into Rigdon, *Appeal to the American People*, 78.

51. Elizabeth Beswick Tanner, "Reminiscences," (1884), 2, rpt. in Tanner, *John Tanner and His Family*, 376.

John's son Nathan once remarked on how it seemed to him "that Joseph [Smith] had the power to call money to his aide when He needed to a complish His ends at Will."[52] In so far as the money he called for from John Tanner, it does not seem that he, or the church, ever repaid the debts. As George S. Tanner wrote in 1974, "If he [John Tanner] ever collected any part of his considerable loans, there is no evidence of it."[53] Myron later recounted that by the time the family had passed through Kirtland and Far West to settle in Nauvoo, Illinois, his father "held notes against Joseph Smith" for over $3,300.[54] Poverty and hunger stalked the once prosperous family; some of the children did not have shoes.[55]

John, on at least one occasion, went to Hyrum Smith to ask that the $1,300 loan he had made to the temple committee be repaid. Hyrum however refused, suggesting that he try to sell the debt, which he managed to do, but for less than half the original value of the loan.[56] John also held "a note in the amount of thirty thousand dollars given for goods purchased in New York for the church that he and others signed in Kirtland."[57] "We were harassed," Myron recalls, "by the demands made upon my father for the payment of a note of $30,000 which he had endorsed for the Prophet Joseph. It took everything we could spare, except what we needed for the barest necessities of life, to relieve ourselves from the obligations of this note which was paid in the year 1845."[58]

John Tanner never wavered in his faith. A final incident comes shortly after the church's spring conference in 1844, not long before Joseph Smith's death. John went to Nauvoo and seeing Joseph on the street "he handed him his note for the $2,000.00 loaned in

52. Nathan Tanner, Journal, typescript, 1.

53. George S. Tanner, *John Tanner and His Family*, 104.

54. Myron Tanner to George A. Smith, Sep. 25, 1873, in Young, Office Files, box 35, fd. 1.

55. Tanner, *Biography of Myron Tanner*, 6–7.

56. Tanner to Smith, Sep. 25, 1873. He sold the debt to a certain Mr. Foster, who agreed to pay him $600 for it, of which only $500 was paid.

57. Tanner to Smith.

58. Tanner, *Biography of Myron Tanner*, 7. The claim, put forward by Andrew Jenson, that John was only ultimately held responsible for $100 of that $30,000 note (Jenson, *Latter-day Saint Biographical Encyclopedia*, 2:801), contradicts Myron's recollection of the incident. For further discussion, see Tanner, *John Tanner and His Family*, 102 and 107n12.

Kirtland, January 1835, to redeem the Temple farm. The Prophet asked what he wanted done with it, and father Tanner answered, 'Bro. Joseph you are welcome to it.' The Prophet laid his right hand heavily upon his left shoulder and said, 'God bless you Father Tanner, your children shall never beg bread.'"[59]

This blessing Joseph gave John Tanner for his help and generosity is legendary, and Myron's view of the matter was that so far as his father was concerned, "compared with the necessities of the Church and the financial relief of the Prophet in the hours of his distress, money to him was mere dross."[60]

After Smith was killed, thousands of Mormons chose to follow Brigham Young out of Nauvoo and across the plains to Utah. Myron Tanner enlisted in the Mormon Battalion during the Mexican–American War. He worked in various places across the country before eventually settling in Provo, Utah, to become a mill owner, member of the city council, and bishop of Provo's LDS Third Ward. As put by one of his two plural wives, Myron ended up "a nice fat old man" who was "just as good as he can be."[61]

One of the more persistent characteristics of the Tanner family has been their sense for business and ability to rebound from destitution. Most of Myron's children and grandchildren were educated, with a number continuing to prestigious universities. The Tanners came to be known as a family of educators. Joseph Marion Tanner, son of Myron and Jane Mount Tanner, attended Harvard Law School and became "perhaps the most distinguished educator of his place and time, at least one of the most distinguished."[62] Joseph Marion is better remembered today as the husband of Annie Clark Tanner, his second plural wife, who was the author of the moving memoir, *A Mormon Mother*.[63] He was also the father of Obert C. Tanner, a prolific writer, occasional instructor in religious studies at Stanford

59. Francis M. Lyman, "Reminiscences," in Tanner, *John Tanner and His Family*, 370.
60. Tanner, *Biography of Myron Tanner*, 7.
61. Tanner, *A Fragment*, 198–201.
62. Ward, *A Life Divided*, vi. For another presentation on the life of Joseph Marion Tanner, see N. Y. Schofield, "Delineation of Dr. J. M. Tanner," and John T. Miller, "Sketch of Joseph Marion Tanner," both in the *Character Builder*, May 1903, 13–18.
63. Tanner, *Mormon Mother*.

University, professor of philosophy at the University of Utah, author of numerous books, successful businessman, and philanthropist.

Jerald's grandfather Caleb, the son of Myron and his first plural wife Ann Crosby, studied geology at Harvard and afterward served as Utah State Engineer from 1905 to 1913 before going into private practice. Caleb's son George, Jerald's father, was a meteorologist. Beyond their professional lives, both Caleb and George ran the sizable Tanner farms and orchards in and around Provo.[64]

Sandra's Ancestry

Long before Joseph Smith introduced him to polygamy, Brigham Young married Mary Ann Angell. At the time of their union in 1834, Young was already a widower; his first wife, Miriam Works, died in 1832. Mary Ann, or "Mother Young" as she was sometimes called, was so respected in Utah that when she died on June 27, 1882, she was given what may be described as a state funeral, including an opening prayer by Daniel H. Wells, followed by adulatory speeches by such lights as Wilford Woodruff, John Taylor, and Joseph F. Smith, after which a large company of mourners processed to view Mary Ann's face one final time before she was carried out and buried beside her husband, Brigham Young.

Brigham seemed to have preferred maintaining some semblance of ordinary family life, as if he were a man with a wife and children, all living together in a single house. He had the Mansion House built for Mary Ann in 1854 at what would now be 119 East South Temple. It was also called the White House, because of its being the only whitewashed house in the territory, and the first in the state to have shingles on its roof.[65]

There he lived with her for a time along with their children until they all moved into the Beehive House. Mary Ann would move back to the Mansion House with her children after Brigham's plural wife, Lucy Ann Decker, replaced Mary Ann in Brigham's affections and moved into the Beehive House with him. Lucy Ann also held a special place as Brigham's first plural wife, whom he married on June 17, 1842. At the time Lucy was married to a certain William Seeley,

---

64. Tanner, *Biography of Myron Tanner*, 22.
65. Dykman and Whitley, "Settling in Salt Lake City," 96.

Jerald's grandfather Caleb Tanner (behind and to the right of the lone woman) in the group of Mormons studying at Harvard and other elite Boston area schools in 1893. Caleb's half-brother Joseph Marion Tanner is seated in the center with the mustache. *Courtesy of the Church History Library, The Church of Jesus Christ of Latter-day Saints.*

who was apparently not a Mormon.[66] Mary Ann's experience with Brigham had been unique in that she had him to herself in their early years. With the coming of polygamy, things changed. "God will be very cruel," Mary Ann once reportedly confided to a friend, "if he does not give us poor women adequate compensation for the trials we have endured in polygamy."[67] Sandra Tanner is the great-great granddaughter of Brigham Young through Mary Ann Angell.

Thomas Angell, Sandra's first Angell relative to arrive in America, was said to have traveled as a boy from England to America in 1631

---

66. Johnson, "Determining and Defining 'Wife,'" 5.
67. Quoted in "Mary Anne Angell Young," *Anti-Polygamy Standard*, Aug. 1882, 36.

Mary Ann Angell, Brigham Young's second wife, and Sandra
Tanner's great-great-grandmother. *Courtesy of the Church History
Library, The Church of Jesus Christ of Latter-day Saints.*

in the service of Roger Williams on a ship called the *Lion*.[68] However, there are gaps in the evidence. The *Lion* sailed from Bristol,
England, on December 1, 1630,[69] but Thomas's name is absent from
the passenger list.[70] When Roger Williams's newly formed convic-
tions made it necessary for him to depart Massachusetts and take
refuge with the friendly Indians of Narragansett Bay, Thomas is said
to have accompanied him.[71]

Thomas and twelve others signed the historic "Providence Com-
pact" on August 20, 1637, an early milestone in American religious
liberty due to its explicit assertion that government has no say in

68. Angell, *Genealogy of Descendants of Thomas Angell*, 9. Alternatively the name of
the ship is sometimes given as the *Lyon*.

69. According to John Winthrop's journal for Feb. 5, 1631, Winthrop, *Winthrop's
Journal*, 57–58. See also Governor Thomas Dudley, letter to the Countess of Lincoln,
Mar. 28, 1631, in *Collections of the Massachusetts Historical Society*, 1802, 36–47, esp. 44.

70. "New England Ship and Passenger Lists (continued)," *Boulder Genealogical Society Quarterly*, Aug. 1972, 2.

71. Lemon, *Baptists in Early North America*, 29; Stiles, *Literary Diary of Ezra Stiles*,
186. See the Angell Bible in the US and Canada Microfilm 0,945,224, Family History
Library, Church of Jesus Christ of Latter-day Saints, Salt Lake City.

religious things or in what people believe, but "only in civil things."[72] He may have attended the Baptist Church Williams founded and participated in for a short time. That church eventually ceased to exist. The oldest, continuously active Baptist Church in America was built in the 1770s on a piece of the original Angell allotment of land.[73] This is still obvious from the way that Providence's Angell Street comes to a sudden end in the middle of the back of the church.

Tracing the religious lives of Sandra's Angell ancestors is difficult and the evidence sparse. One early relative, John Angell, was a colorful character who dressed and spoke like a Quaker but insisted he was not one.[74] Instead he was a follower, the last follower, of the strange mystical teacher Samuel Gorton, a contemporary of Roger Williams, who had been tried for heresy in Massachusetts before coming to Rhode Island. Gorton had written a number of books, which John Angell proudly showed Ezra Stiles explaining that they had been "written in Heaven, & no Man could understand them unless he was in heaven."[75] (Some older works also make Jerald Tanner a direct descendant of Samuel Gorton by calling Jerald's seven-times great-grandfather, John Crandall, Samuel Gorton's son-in-law. More recent works maintain that it was John Crandall Jr. that married Gorton's daughter.)[76]

On one occasion, a certain Alexander Hamilton (a physician, not the Revolutionary statesman) breakfasted at John Angell's Providence establishment, the Sign of the White Horse, and when he asked if a certain Angell kept the house, John brusquely corrected him: "Hark ye friend ... Angell don't keep the house, but the house keeps Angell." Hamilton described Angell as "a queer pragmaticall old fellow pretending to great correctness of style in common

---

72. See, e.g., Hopkins, *Home Lots*, 15.

73. Hopkins, 36.

74. Stiles, *Literary Diary of Ezra Stiles*, 185.

75. Stiles. Nathaniel Morton described Gorton as "A proud and pestilent seducer, and deeply leavened with blasphemous and familistical opinions," Morton, *New-England's Memoriall*, 108. Roger Williams noted in a 1640 letter to John Winthrop that Gorton denied "all visible and externall Ordinances in depth of Familism," in Winslow, *Hypocrisie Unmasked*, 55–56.

76. That is to say, William Tanner's wife's uncle rather than her grandfather. Contrast Dexter, *As to Roger Williams, and his 'Banishment,'* 120, and *Baptists in Early America III*, lxxi–lxxii, n. 138.

discourse," who, while Hamilton waited for his breakfast, "gave me an account of his religion and opinions, which I found were as much out of the common road as the man himself."[77]

After John Angell, there were four more generations before Mary Ann was born to James Angell and his wife, Phebe. The two met while James traveled in New York, where they married and then returned to his home in Rhode Island. James was not a devoted husband and father; he abandoned his wife for an extended period, leaving her to support their seven children. Even when he was present, his conduct towards her was poor.[78]

Before Mary Ann converted to Mormonism, she was a Freewill Baptist. Like Methodists, Freewill Baptists insisted that the gospel offer of salvation was an open call and that anyone could embrace the gospel and be saved.[79] This non-Calvinist posture created a natural affinity between Freewill Baptists and the teachings in the Book of Mormon that declared human beings "free to choose liberty and eternal life, through the great mediation of all men, or to choose captivity and death" (2 Ne. 2:27). Mary Ann "testified many times that the Spirit bore witness to her when she took the Book of Mormon in her hands, of the truth of its origin, so strongly that she could never afterwards doubt it."[80]

Brigham and Mary Ann Young named their first son Joseph (b. 1834) after the Mormon prophet and their second son Brigham Jr. (b. 1836). Brigham Sr. and Mary Ann both outlived their first son, Joseph, (d. 1875) making Brigham Jr., Sandra's great-grandfather, their eldest living son when they both died. At the age of fifty-one Brigham Jr. married Sandra's great-grandmother, Abigail "Abbie" Stevens, then seventeen, who bore him seven children. Abbie lived until December 1954, when Sandra was thirteen years old. Sandra remembers as a small child visiting her great-grandmother who used to entertain her by crafting small dolls made by rolling up wads of cotton in a handkerchief and then creating a head, hands, and feet by tying it up in sections with thread. Sandra also

77. Hamilton, *Gentleman's Progress*, 149.

78. Thomas O. Angell, "Autobiography of Truman Osborn Angell," [1]. Also in Carter, *Our Pioneer Heritage*, 10:195–213.

79. See McGlothlin, *Baptist Confessions of Faith*, 318.

80. Wells, "Mary Ann Angell Young," 17.

Abbie Stevens Young, plural wife of Brigham Young Jr. and
Sandra's great-grandmother. *Courtesy of the Church History
Library, The Church of Jesus Christ of Latter-day Saints.*

remembers hearing stories about Abbie's experiences when her
husband was on the run from federal officers, forced underground
for practicing polygamy. On one occasion, Abbie had rescued him
by dressing him up in her own bed clothes and hustling him into
her bed before the officers arrived. She then invited the officers in
to search the house, asking only that they not disturb her very elderly ailing "mother." The ruse was successful, and Brigham Jr. was
spared from arrest. For Sandra, the story served as a great example
of the way God delivers his people.

Brigham Young Jr., Sandra's great-grandfather.

Brigham Jr. had no intention of obeying the anti-bigamy laws. The timing of his marriage to the teenage Abbie Stevens is indicative. The two wedded in 1887, shortly after passage of the anti-polygamy Edmunds–Tucker Act; nine months later, Sandra's grandfather, Walter Stevens Young, was born. One early anti-polygamous source claimed that Brigham Young Jr. married Abbie Stevens after the 1890 Manifesto, which was false.[81] So far as Sandra ever knew, Abbie was Brigham Jr.'s last plural wife. But more recently it has become

81. C. M. Owen, "Polygamous Mormons," *Northwest Christian Advocate*, Sep. 20, 1905, 13.

clear that he did take one more, a certain Kirsty Maria Willardsen, on August 8, 1901.[82]

After Brigham Jr. died in 1903, Abbie, a widow with seven children at age thirty-three, attended Ellis R. Shipp's School of Nursing and later moved to Provo so her children could attend Brigham Young Academy (today BYU). She eventually moved to a house in the Avenues in Salt Lake City. Those who remember her say that in her old age she almost never came downstairs. She loved playing Chinese Checkers, drying venison for jerky on her steam heater, making quilts, and paying children to dig out dandelions with their full roots so she could make dandelion tea and various other remedies. She died at the age of eighty-four.[83]

Sandra never knew her grandfather Walter Stevens Young, the first son of Abbie Stevens and Brigham Young Jr. He was a brick mason who traveled while working construction around the western states. Walter died in November 1935 at age forty-seven from complications of surgery intended to relieve empyema, the buildup of fluid between the lungs and chest wall.[84] Walter's wife was Sylvia Amelia Pearce Young. It was Sylvia who persuaded Sandra to drive her to the "fireside-like" meeting the night she first met Jerald. At some point Walter secretly took another wife, as is revealed by a postcard from some woman other than Sylvia that commenced "My Dear Husband," and was signed "your Dear Wife."[85]

After Walter died, Sylvia married Daniel Rogerson, and then, after he died, a Greek convert to Mormonism named Nicholas Philagios. She married Nicholas in 1959, ten days before Jerald and Sandra's marriage. They had met on the Mormon Tabernacle Choir's 1955 tour of Europe where both of them had traveled, not as singers, but as part of a group accompanying the choir. Afterward they kept in touch by correspondence.

---

82. Entry 23 of Matthias Foss Cowley's record "Marriages Solemnized" [5–6] MS 3420, CHL. Thanks to D. Michael Quinn for pointing me to this reference. Cowley gave her name as Kirsty, Quinn as "Kisty" (*Mormon Hierarchy: Extensions of Power*, 718).

83. Tanner, Recollections.

84. Walter Stevens Young, State of Utah Certificate of Death, no. 1971, Utah Death Certificate Index, 1905–1967, Utah Division of Archives and Records Service.

85. The date and signature on the postcard are illegible. Tanner and Tanner, Papers and Letters.

Walter and Sylvia Young family (Sandra's mother, Georgia,
stands behind and to the left of Walter).

Both came to the marriage four years later with unrealistic expectations. Nicholas was a retired locomotive fireman with a free
railway pass.[86] Sylvia loved to travel and had visions of train rides
with Nicholas all over the West visiting family and friends. But as
it turned out, the pass was only good on Eastern railway lines where
Sylvia had no family and friends. Nicholas, for his part, was looking forward to settling down in the Mecca of Mormonism with a
believing Mormon wife and entertaining old friends from the Mid-
west, staying with them while they toured the city and did temple
work. But Sylvia was always more relaxed, even liberal, in the way
she adhered to the faith. She drank coffee and chided her bishop
for not giving her a temple recommend when others, who she knew
drank coffee, had gotten theirs. "Yes," answered the bishop, "but they
don't tell me they do." "Oh," Sylvia responded, "so it's alright so long
as they lie about it to you!"

How the two avoided having their unrealistic expectations dis-
pelled beforehand is anybody's guess. But the contrast between Sylvia

86. On Philagios's job, see, "My Conversion," in Philagios, *Discourses*, 50.

Recently wed Sylvia Young Rogerson Philagios and
Nicholas E. Philagios at Jerald and Sandra's wedding.

and Nicholas resulted not in a bad marriage so much as in a comedy
of errors. Not only was Nicholas a more devout believer, he also had
a rather pontifical personality and would often preface his statements
by dramatically raising his right index figure and declaring: "I, Nicholas Philagios."[87] He used the expression no matter whether he was
cooking—"I tell you, I, Nicholas Philagios, *never* put cinnamon in
my lamb stew!"—or challenging the whole of Christendom to try
to refute the claims of his fiery little tracts—"I, Nicholas Philagios
challenge any Patriarch, Pope, Bishop, Priest, Minister or any one
else who knows the Greek Church History and Greek Philosophy...

---

87. Philagios, 5, 37, 41.

[to offer]…definite proof that the preceding statement be not true."[88] He even sent copies of his tracts, including the one just quoted, to the head of the Greek Orthodox Church, the Ecumenical Patriarch Athenagoras I, bishop of Constantinople himself, who sent his blessing and thanks, assuring Nicholas that "they will enrich our Patriarchal Library."[89] Nicholas's obituary described him as a "Regional missionary to Greeks," which was something of an understatement.[90] Sylvia complained that he stirred things up with the local Greek Orthodox community to such a degree that someone actually threatened to blow up his house, which was actually *her* house! She'd had it since she'd been married to Walter.[91]

Although Sylvia wasn't as orthodox as Philagios, she was proud of her Mormon heritage. She loved telling the story of her pioneer family, of her parents, James Pearce and Mary Jane Meeks, and how, along with other pioneers, they had "crossed the plains by team and wagon" and become established in Utah, and how they later became the first settlers of Taylor, Arizona.[92] But she never mentioned her father's and grandfather's participation in one of the darkest events in Mormon history, the 1857 Mountain Meadows Massacre. Sandra knew nothing of it until after she and Jerald reprinted a copy of the 1880 edition of the *Confessions of John D. Lee* in the early 1960s.[93] Sandra's uncle Marion Young, Walter and Silvia's oldest son, bought a copy and then, soon after, came back and asked whether they realized that "Grandpa Pearce" was included in the book's list of participants in the massacre.[94] Later it was discovered that Sylvia herself had once owned a copy of Lee's book, but a cousin had taken it and destroyed it lest someone in the family happened to flip through it and discover the mention of their kinfolk, James and Harrison Pearce, as participants in the Massacre.

---

88. Philagios, "Know Thyself," in *Discourses*, 5–6.

89. Athenarogas I to Nicholas Philagios, May 10, 1963, 1.

90. "Nicholas Philagios Obituary," *Salt Lake Tribune*, Nov. 24, 1965, 24.

91. See further on Philagios, "Greek Elder Translates Tracts," *Church News*, Apr. 22, 1961, 7.

92. "Jas. Pierce, Indian Fighter," *Deseret News*, Apr. 9, 1904, 15.

93. H. Michael Marquardt gives the date of this reprint as ca. 1963–64 in "A Tanner Bibliography, 1959–1983," *Restoration*, July 1984, 19. Updated and available online, utlm.org.

94. Lee, *Mormonism Unveiled*, 380 (nos. 34–35).

A story about Sylvia's father, James, only eighteen at the time of the massacre, and her grandfather Harrison would find its way into legend. The principal account comes from Brigham Young Sr.'s disaffected wife Ann Eliza Webb Young:

> To the honor of many of the men be it said,—the younger ones, especially,—they refused to join in this horrible work, and some of them made efforts to protect these helpless women from their fiend-like tormentors. I used often, while living in Payson, to see a man named Jim Pearce, whose face was deeply scarred by a bullet wound, made by his own father, while the brave young fellow was trying to assist a poor girl, who had appealed to him for succor.[95]

Georgia Young, Sandra's mother, was the third child of Sylvia Pearce and Walter Young. She was born on April 2, 1915, in Taylor, Arizona.[96] In 1936, she married Ivan McGee in the Salt Lake Temple and started a family.[97] Sandra McGee was born on January 14, 1941, the third of five children. She was named for Baby Sandy (Sandra Lee Henville), a toddler starlet famous for her strikingly large eyes, the quintessential cute toddler who served as the model for the then-popular Baby Sandy doll.[98] Sandra had an older sister, Carolyn (b. March 4, 1938), and a younger brother, Jon (b. February 22, 1949). Georgia and Ivan lost two other children in childbirth: a boy and a girl. In accordance with Mormon custom at the time, since the girl had taken her first breath, she was given a name (Laurna) and a funeral. However, the boy, not having taken a breath, was given neither. This was based on the belief that the child's pre-existent spirit sent from heaven bonded to its body only when taking its first breath. If the child dies before taking its first breath, the pre-existent

---

95. Young, *Wife No. 19*, 248. See also Bagley, *Blood of the Prophets*, 148; Brooks, *Mountain Meadows Massacre*, 90. Brooks, however, says that the story involved Harrison's son Tom rather than James. See further on Harrison's participation in Hawley, "Autobiography of John Pierce Hawley," 110.

96. Susa Young Gates and Mabel Young Sanborn, "Brigham Young Genealogy," *Utah Genealogical and Historical Magazine*, Apr. 1922, 89.

97. Ivan was born in Burley, Idaho, on December 18, 1912, and was one of six siblings (four boys, two girls). He was baptized in 1920.

98. She appeared in several Hollywood movies, including *Sandy Is A Lady* (1940), *Sandy Gets Her Man* (1940), and *Sandy Steps Out* (1942). She also appeared on the cover of the August 14, 1939, issue of *Life* magazine, and was chosen as the Baby of the Year in the May 1, 1940, issue of *Parents Magazine*.

spirit remains free to enter another body.[99] LDS temple proxy work is not performed for stillborn children.[100]

Early in their marriage, Georgia and Ivan moved their family to the San Fernando Valley in California, where they eventually opened two Pfaff Sewing Machine stores. Sandra has fond childhood memories of earning pocket money sitting at the Pfaff booth at the county fair and demonstrating, along with her sister, the flexibility of the machines by stitching designs of animals to whet the appetite of potential buyers. Later, Georgia and Ivan closed the stores and entered real estate.

Ivan McGee came from a strict, observant Mormon family. His father, William Henry McGee, was free from all doubt concerning the truth of his faith and expected the same from his children. As for Ivan, he didn't rebel against his father's religion but lacked the motivation to pattern his own life after it. He was inactive in the church during Sandra's childhood. Despite his lack of engagement with the religion, however, Ivan was not delighted with Sandra's marriage to Jerald. He was concerned that Jerald did not have the priesthood, and when he attended an Easter service at a non-LDS church with Jerald and Sandra soon after their marriage, he was horrified at Jerald's seeming lack of respect in not wearing a suit to church.

Sandra's mother, on the other hand, was more intellectually engaged with the church, busying herself (along with her sister Lucille) with hunting down original documents, studying the *Journal of Discourses*, and reading whatever she could get her hands on relating to Mormon history, including Fawn Brodie's controversial *No Man Knows My History*, trying to figure out what "really happened" in early Mormonism. Georgia considered herself a liberal, open-minded person, and, by the time Sandra married Jerald, had imbibed a substantial dose of the liberal Protestant view of scripture by

---

99. Lester E. Bush explains, "In practice, Mormon ritual has always distinguished between miscarriages or stillborn deliveries, and neonatal deaths. The former are not formally recorded in Church records; the latter are. Vicarious ordinance work, deemed essential for all humankind in Mormon theology, is never performed in the case of a miscarriage or stillborn delivery. It always is for a deceased infant." Bush, "Ethical Issues in Reproductive Medicine," 51.

100. "Temple ordinances are not performed for stillborn children ... memorial or graveside services may be held as determined by the parents," *General Handbook 2*, 194 (21.3.10). See also Val D. Greenwood, "I Have a Question," *Ensign*, Sep. 1987.

The McGee Family, left to right: Georgia, Carolyn,
Sandra, Ivan, and Jon in the center.

attending Pastor James Kepler's Bible studies, while personally moving in the direction of atheism. She was aware of Pauline Hancock's
group through her interest in seeking out early Mormon documents,
even before Sandra drove her grandmother to the meeting the night
she met Jerald.

Georgia knew Pauline and agreed with her about certain Book
of Mormon teachings, but she regarded her as too religious. Georgia
was furious with her mother after she introduced Sandra to Pauline's
group; it had resulted in Sandra's falling in love with one of their

most fervent disciples, Jerald Tanner. The romance had happened too suddenly and without any warning; Sandra had decided to quit college, and had fallen for Jerald too soon after breaking things off with her former boyfriend. But there was something more at stake: Jerald was also too religious for Georgia's tastes, and her concerns only increased after the marriage. "My concern for Sandra the last two or three years has over-shadowed everything else," she confided to LaMar Petersen in 1962. "Please understand, this is not criticism, only concern."[101] At the time, Jerald and Sandra had turned away from "worldly entertainments" to focus on the work of the Lord. They did not watch television or go to the movies. Sandra's giving up makeup, lipstick, and fancy clothes alarmed Georgia enough to fight to get Sandra back on track by getting her back into the "more normal" LDS Church. Looking back Sandra would describe her mother at the time as definitely on a quest for truth about Mormon origins but not, as yet, really on any sort of spiritual quest.

101. Georgia McGee to LaMar Petersen, Mar. 21, 1962, 1, in Wardle, Papers, box 34, fd. 1.

3

DIGGING INTO THE PAST

Anyone wanting to research Mormon history in the late 1950s or early 1960s sooner or later may have found themselves in a barbershop at 424 South State Street in Salt Lake City. As they passed the barber pole perpetually spiraling upward and entered, they would be greeted by the usual scents of hair tonic, hot clipper oil, and one smell that seemed out of place: old books. They would step back in time fifty years to Victorian woodwork and furniture, including two barber chairs, one filled with books and the other with a customer attended to by shop proprietor, barber, champion skater, and Groucho Marx look-alike, James D. Wardle. Wardle, a man whom one Salt Lake alternative newspaper called the "State Street Socrates," was colorful to say the least.[1] "A barbershop ... is more than giving a shave and a haircut," he once said. "It's a convention center for talking, discussing, and philosophizing."[2] "Before Facebook," Sandra remembers, "there was James Wardle."[3]

On the walls of his shop James hung various comical signs, one of which announced: "James D. Wardle: World Champion Secret Spreader."[4] With his signs and his jokes, James kept the atmosphere in the shop light, jovial, and relaxed, but with a serious purpose. James was very committed to the idea that Mormon history belonged to the Mormon people:

I have been in an environment where people did not want to tell me

---

1. Diane Olson Rutter, "State Street Socrates: A Barber by Vocation, a Philosopher for Free—James Wardle's Passionate Life Lives on in Collection of Books," *Catalyst*, July 1998, 16–17.

2. Vandra L. Huber, "Religious Fanatic (and Barber) Offers Humor, Nostalgia," *Salt Lake Tribune*, July 1, 1974, 10-A.

3. Tanner, Recollections.

4. Rutter, "State Street Socrates," 16.

something for fear it might hurt my faith; they wouldn't let me see a document because of how I might use it; and I was obsessed with the idea that things should not be kept a secret; especially things having to do with the church history, which I thought was the property of all Latter-day Saints, not just a church archive to keep them protected and nobody to look at them.[5]

Whenever Wardle got access to documents the church wasn't making available, his standing policy was to make it as widely available as possible. "Whenever I got hold of something," he said, "anybody that wanted it could get it; in fact, I always made sure that as quick as possible, anything that I got also had a copy in the hands of somebody else."[6]

Wardle had a vast collection of books in the back of his shop, which he categorized with the Dewey Decimal system supplemented by the Cutter–Sandborn Author numbering system. About half his enormous collection of books and documents related to the historical texts and documents of the various major and minor branches of Mormonism. As for the rest, his taste in collecting ran mainly towards titles and materials relating to the outer margins of religion, to the esoteric, the Kabbalistic, to witchcraft, the tarot, and the occult. He also had an enormous collection of material on UFOs. James never spent big money on books. He could not afford to pay the $500 going price for a first edition Book of Commandments someone once offered him. But he could spring for the $85 he paid for his first edition Book of Mormon, so that, by keeping his eye out, he'd managed little by little by 1979 to purchase for his library the first seventeen editions of the Book of Mormon.[7]

Jerald Tanner met Wardle around 1956 while he was investigating the RLDS Church of which Wardle was a prominent member. Jerald had heard of Wardle and approached him one Sunday at an RLDS service. Wardle encouraged Jerald to speak to the pastor,

---

5. Kent Walgren, Interview with James D. Wardle, Jan. 3, 1979, 21. Wardle, Papers, box 1, fd. 5.

6. Walgren.

7. Walgren, 5–6.

James D. Wardle, "World Champion Secret Spreader."

cautioning him that he "might hear a different story from me. If you want to talk to me," James said, "come to my barber shop."[8]

Jerald accepted Wardle's offer, and they grew close. One of the most significant moments in their friendship—indeed, in Jerald's life—came when Wardle handed him an 1887 tract entitled *An Address to All Believers in Christ*. It was written by David Whitmer, one of the original Book of Mormon Three Witnesses, and it disturbed Jerald. "Some of the revelations as they are now in the Book of Doctrine and Covenants," Whitmer wrote, "have been changed and added to. Some of the changes being of the greatest importance as the meaning is entirely changed on some very important matters; as if the Lord had changed his mind a few years after he gave the revelations."[9] Whitmer argued that the revelations first published in the Book of Commandments (1833) had been direct revelations from

---

8. Walgren, 22.
9. Whitmer, *An Address to All Believers in Christ*, 56.

Jerald Tanner in the late 1950s.

God and that Joseph Smith had no right to substantially modify them as a way of serving his own expanding prophetic aspirations.

As Jerald read Whitmer's tract, he was infuriated with Whitmer for making such outrageous claims against Smith. "I could not believe such a serious charge against the Prophet, and I tossed the pamphlet down in disgust." But then "[a]fter throwing it down …

I began to think that perhaps this was not the right way to face the problem. If David Whitmer was wrong in his criticism of Joseph Smith, surely I could prove him wrong. So, I picked up the pamphlet and read it through."[10]

In 1957, Jerald could not have compared Whitmer's claims about changes in the prophecies against an original edition of the Book of Commandments, since he had never seen one. We do not know whether he tried to access the copies in the possession of the LDS Church Historian's Office at the time, but had he done so, the kind of response he might have received can be surmised from a story told by the late Mormon historian LaMar Petersen. At some point in the 1950s, Petersen's well-meaning bishop persuaded him to accompany him on a trip to the LDS archives to examine a copy of the original Book of Commandments in order to lay to rest once and for all the accusation that Joseph Smith had changed the revelations as he went along. When they made their request, Earl E. Olson told them the Book of Commandments was never actually finished since the Missouri mobocrats had destroyed the press it was being printed on. In response Petersen listed off the names of several libraries where he had actually seen copies. "Oh," Olson said, "I didn't realize you'd actually *seen* the book," and then toddled off cheerfully to fetch a copy.[11]

But Jerald had no such previous-knowledge card to play so he began instead by comparing the latest edition of the LDS Doctrine and Covenants to the edition of the Book of Commandments published in around 1926 by the Mormon splinter group the Church of Christ (Temple Lot) and to an edition printed by the *Salt Lake Tribune* in 1903.

Since neither were photo reprints, both editions could be dismissed by members of the LDS Church as falsified to embarrass the church.[12] But they served Jerald's initial purpose of seeing if Whitmer was lying. Jerald concluded that Whitmer's "pamphlet,

---

10. Tanner, *Jerald Tanner's Testimony*, 5.

11. Sandra heard Petersen tell this story on several occasions over a number of years.

12. Earl E. Olson of the Church Historical Department later wrote to Sandra's mother to say the reprint was "exactly the same as the original as far as the method [i.e., in reset type] can be made accurate." Earl E. Olson to Georgia McGee, Aug. 13, 1959, 1, Tanner and Tanner, Papers and Letters.

in fact, proved to be very reliable with regard to historical facts."[13] He was unsatisfied with explanations like those offered later by Joseph Anderson of the LDS Church Historical Department that "Joseph Smith, being the one who received these revelations and had them recorded, likewise would have a right to add or to subtract from, or change, the revelations."[14] "Like David Whitmer," Jerald recalled, "I felt that it would be unthinkable for anyone to claim to have direct revelations from God and then turn around and alter those words."[15]

For Jerald, many of the revised revelations went to the heart of the church's organization and the divinely appointed boundaries of Smith's prophetic ministry. For example, as the revelation dated March 1829 had originally appeared, God told Smith that his prophetic calling was to end once the Book of Mormon was finished: "he [Joseph] has a gift to translate the book, and I have commanded him that he shall pretend to no other gift, for I will grant him no other gift" (Book of Commandments 4:2). Joseph later altered the revelation to say he would "pretend to no other gift *until my purpose is fulfilled in this*; for I will grant unto you no other gift *until it is finished*" (D&C 5:4, emphasis added).[16] Jerald reasoned that Smith altered the original revelation to justify his continuing status as a prophet following the completion of the Book of Mormon.

More striking to Jerald was Whitmer's claim that the "matter of the two orders of priesthood in the Church of Christ, and lineal priesthood of the old law being in the church, all originated in the mind of Sidney Rigdon," and that there were significant changes to priesthood offices.[17] Jerald once again compared the Book of Commandments to the Doctrine and Covenants and found that the sections dealing with the restoration of the Aaronic and Melchizedek priesthoods were either missing entirely (D&C 2 and 13) or

---

13. From Jerald's introduction to the Utah Lighthouse Ministry's photographic reproduction of Whitmer's *An Address to All Believers in Christ*.

14. Joseph Anderson to T. G. Whitsitt, July 29, 1974, 1, Tanner and Tanner, Papers.

15. From Jerald's introduction to the Utah Lighthouse Ministry's photographic reproduction of Whitmer's *An Address to All Believers in Christ*.

16. Originally Doctrine and Covenants 32:1 in the 1835 edition. See also MacKay et al., *Documents, Volume 1*, 20.

17. Whitmer, *An Address to All Believers in Christ*, 64.

were found to be in a primitive form to which crucial language had not yet been introduced (D&C 27).

Jerald still believed that Smith was the divine instrument to bring forth of the Book of Mormon, but he became convinced that Smith had become a fallen prophet after that. Jerald concluded that the Utah LDS Church, rooted in Joseph Smith's post-Book of Mormon prophetic career, had followed him into apostasy and perpetuated his errors. "While I felt that the Catholic and Protestant churches were all wrong," Jerald recalled, "I needed to know which of the churches ... based on Joseph Smith was the true church."[18] Jerald's next step showed the seriousness of his conviction and his search: he struck out for Zion.

Mormon Zion is in Missouri where Smith said the kingdom of God would rise. Jerald made his way to Richmond, the town where David Whitmer's tract had originally been published. He wanted to find the granddaughter of Book of Mormon witness Jacob Whitmer. Despite her advanced years, she recalled seeing David Whitmer just before he died lying in his bed and working on the tract that had inspired Jerald's journey. But she was one of the last two members of David Whitmer's church that he founded after his break from Smith. To Jerald's disappointment, she had no interest in seeing her church revived. From there, Jerald went to Independence where he visited two churches. The first was the Church of Christ (Temple Lot), named so because it owned the lot Smith had dedicated in 1831 as the site of the temple to which Christ was to eventually return (D&C 57, 86). At the Church of Christ (Temple Lot), Jerald was received warmly and a copy of the original edition of the Book of Commandments was brought out of the safe for him to see. But the Temple Lot church still represented a more developed form of Mormonism than the one Jerald found described in Whitmer's pamphlet.[19]

The second church Jerald visited in Independence was called the Church of Christ (Bible and Book of Mormon). Its most prominent member was its pastor, Pauline Hancock. Jerald had likely heard of the church from James Wardle; Pauline's father, J.W.A. Bailey, had

---

18. Tanner, *Jerald Tanner's Testimony*, 5.
19. Tanner, 6.

been Wardle's pastor at the RLDS Church in Salt Lake City during the late 1930s and early 1940s.

Pauline Hancock was raised in a faithful RLDS home. She and her husband, Silas, moved to the Independence area where she became superintendent of Sunday school in nearby Lee's Summit. Their timing coincided with a split within the RLDS Church after President Frederick M. Smith introduced the "Supreme Directional Control," which a significant number of members viewed as ecclesiastical overreach. A protest movement began under the leadership of RLDS Apostle T. W. Williams at the Kansas Street Church, and Pauline became its secretary. She was also asked to teach the Book of Mormon. She agreed to do so but with certain hesitations because she had never taught it before, and because someone had told her the Book of Mormon taught a doctrine of the Godhead that was different from the one she had grown up believing in the RLDS Church. They had actually cautioned her, she said, to "make light of it."[20] At some point, Pauline was given another tract by David Whitmer, this one titled *An Address to Believers in the Book of Mormon*. Whitmer repeated many of the same arguments that would later persuade Jerald, but especially emphasized that God had intended to build the Church of Christ "upon the Book of Mormon and the Bible alone."[21]

Whitmer wrote that, he, John Whitmer, and Oliver Cowdery, had been shown by the Lord in 1849 "that the Book of Doctrine and Covenants contained many doctrines of error, and that it must be laid aside," and that only when that happened would God be able to build up the "waste places of Zion" upon the proper foundation of "the two sacred books."[22] This does not mean that Whitmer believed the prophesies in their original form in the Book of Commandments had also been falsified. Rather they had been authentic prophesies but had never been intended to be published in a book and presented as Scripture.[23]

---

20. A typescript of Pauline's conversion story, presumably from a taped talk she had given, is in Wardle, Papers, box 22, fd. 10, 5–6. Hereafter cited as, "Pauline's Conversion." For more, see Williams, *Protest Movement*. Smith, "Pauline Hancock," 186.

21. David Whitmer, *An Address to Believers in the Book of Mormon*, 2, see also 1, 5, 7.

22. Whitmer, 1–2.

23. Whitmer, 5.

Pauline Hancock, pastor and leader of the Church of Christ (Bible and Book of Mormon), sometimes mislabeled "Lukites."

Having read Witmer's tract and been convinced by it, Pauline was no longer willing to subordinate the doctrines taught in the Book of Mormon to those current in the RLDS Church. She was henceforth determined "not to let anything come into my belief unless I could find it in the Bible and the Book of Mormon."[24] This conviction eventually led her out of both the RLDS reform movement and the Temple Lot church, which she had joined for a time afterward.[25]

Pauline became an antiques dealer for a time but felt called to teach and minister. She was approached by Ervin and Lois Luke to teach them in their home, which became a regularly held Friday

---

24. "Pauline's Conversion," 8.
25. Samuel Wood, "Biographical," *TM: An Independent Journal of Fundamental Religious and Social Reform*, Nov. 1963, 3.

night study group in August or September 1946.[26] Eventually they moved into a building at 723 S. Crysler in Independence that came to be called the "basement church" because they never finished the upper part of the building.

While traveling for her antiques business, Hancock said she heard the voice of the Lord asking her what she was doing, since antiques was not her true business.[27] Following this she reported other visions and communications from the Lord, though she never claimed to be a prophet, seer, or revelator in any special sense. Hancock taught her beliefs by appealing to scripture, sharing what she thought the Lord had communicated with her. She explicitly rejected the notion of "one true church," preaching instead the necessity of new birth (being born again) through faith in Jesus alone.

When Jerald visited Hancock's basement church in Missouri, he may have been drawn by his interest in early Mormon documents and Whitmerian doctrines. But time spent with Hancock and her small flock impressed Jerald more than theology. It was "not their research but the love they had towards each other and even people outside their group. ... They were different from any people I had ever met. It was almost as if I had stepped back into the first century and was meeting with the original disciples of the Lord. ... The joy in the hearts of this people was so obvious that I could not miss it. It was evident that they really loved the Lord and had dedicated their lives to serve him."[28]

Jerald wasn't the only one who felt there was something special, something unique about the little group. James Wardle had noticed it as well. "Pauline Hancock is one of the VERY FEW REAL CHRISTIANS that I have met in my whole life," Wardle wrote. "She is one of God's women, a child of Christ. As far as I am concerned, I've never met anyone quite like her."[29] He also had high praise for her basement church:

It is her group of people to whom she ministers. They have something that far exceeds anything I have ever felt in any church I've ever attended,

26. Pauline Hancock to James Wardle, Jan. 31, 1950, 2, Marquardt, Papers, box 9, fd. 1.

27. Hancock to Wardle.

28. Tanner, *Jerald Tanner's Testimony*, 6.

29. James D. Wardle to Mrs. S. G. Winholtz, Dec. 17, 1959, 1, Wardle, Papers, box 22, fd. 8.

Pauline Hancock's basement church, corner of Linden
and Crysler in Independence, Missouri.

including my own. They have the REAL fellowship.—If I were to judge
I would say that they have the real SPIRIT of Christ in their midst. They
LOVE one another … I wish we had more of that love in Salt Lake City.

Jerald was convinced that they had what he was seeking, but still
he resisted. He had come to Missouri to find the "true church," identifiable by the right set of divinely authorized doctrines making it
the "authentic" heir of the Restoration. "What I had learned in Missouri completely changed my way of thinking. Instead of focusing
on the errors of the Mormon Church and searching for the 'true
church,' I now had to take a hard look at my own heart and realize
how completely undone I was before God. I was a sinner in desperate need of a Savior."[30]

Jerald began to feel more keenly in himself "the depravity of the
heart of man." From a Christian perspective, his experience was
common and has been described by theologians such as Augustine

---

30. Tanner, *Jerald Tanner's Testimony*, 6.

of Hippo, John Wesley, and Charles Finney as an important stage leading to authentic conversion to Christ. According to Augustine the stages of salvation are fourfold: (1) *ante legem* (before law), (2) *sub lege* (under law), (3) *sub gratia* (under grace), (4) *in pace* (in peace).[31] The first three pertain to this life and the fourth to the life to come. Wesley and many others followed Augustine's basic pattern, though not always using precisely the same terminology. Wesley described the first three stages by saying that "The *natural* man neither fears nor loves God, one *under the law* fears, one *under grace* loves Him."[32] The natural man (*ante legem*) may be a person who dedicates his life to serving his religion, or a happy-go-lucky atheist who passes through life without ever troubling himself with realms beyond his immediate daily experience. But whatever their attitudes or views they share with others who are "before law" a basic insensibility to God. For this reason they are also sometimes described as "unawakened." By the same token those who moves to the next stage, "under law," are said to be "awakened." Whereas before they were more or less content with where they were with the God question, now everything changes. They are confronted with the reality that they are guilty before a righteous God who really exists. They come to understand that they are sinners, but they find themselves drawing back in fear. This is where Jerald now was.

But what does it really mean to be a sinner? Whereas Jerald had formerly thought of sin as some wrong thing you do as a result of temptation, traditional Christianity has taught that such a view underestimates the extent and seriousness of the fall of Adam on one's ability to love people and live for God. Jerald had discovered that he had a sinful nature, a nature prone and resistant to obeying and following God.

In contrast, LDS theology downplays the negative implication of the fall, instead viewing it as a part of God's Plan of Salvation. "The 'fall' of Adam and Eve," wrote LDS Apostle Joseph Fielding Smith, "was not a sin but an essential act upon which mortality depends."[33]

---

31. *Expositio quarundam propositionum ex epistula apostoli ad Romanos* 13:2–10. For English translation see Paula Fredriksen Landes, *Augustine of Romans*, 5, 7.

32. Wesley, *Wesley's Standard Sermons*, 1:194.

33. Smith, *Answers to Gospel Questions*, 5:15

From the LDS perspective, all Christendom was wrong when they said that humans have "inherited an evil, sinful nature from Adam and Eve."[34]

There was still snow on the ground when Jerald returned to Independence in the early part of 1958, intent on surrendering himself to the Lord. As soon as the people in Hancock's church learned he was in town again, he was invited to stay in the home of Gene and Barbara Moore who had recently lost a son in an automobile accident and welcomed him as "sort of a replacement for their son." He stayed a full month. It was during this visit that Jerald recalled, "I looked to Jesus Christ and my life was miraculously changed. I passed from a life of sin and misery to one of peace and joy."[35]

It is not surprising that Jerald did not immediately give up his belief in the Book of Mormon. Yet his embrace of the Book of Mormon hardly brought him into closer agreement with the religion of his youth, since, as Jerald came to believe "the Book of Mormon itself does not teach the unique doctrines which separate the Mormon church from other Churches"; that it is, in fact, "far closer to Protestant theology than it is to Mormonism."[36] Back in Salt Lake City, Jerald became the sole representative of the little Church of Christ (Bible and Book of Mormon).

Sandra's mother, Georgia, and her aunt Lucille often shared questions they encountered in their research, encouraging Sandra to bring them to her LDS seminary teacher. One question was the distinction between Elohim and Jehovah in the Old Testament, to which her seminary teacher offered, "Generally speaking, it's always Jehovah except in places where it's Elohim." It gradually became clear to Sandra that Mormonism's identification of Jesus as Jehovah and Heavenly Father as Elohim is a distinction that the Old Testament does not sustain.[37]

Sandra could not help but become aware of the things her mother

---

34. Daniel K. Judd, "Redeemed by the Savior from Fall," *Church News*, Nov. 27, 1993, 14; Bruce C. Hafen, "The Atonement: All for All," *Ensign*, May 2004, 97.

35. Tanner, *Jerald Tanner's Testimony*, 8.

36. Tanner.

37. "The Father and the Son: A Doctrinal Exposition by the First Presidency and the Twelve," *Improvement Era*, Aug. 1916, 934–42; "The Living Christ: The Testimony of the Apostles," Jan. 1, 2000, at churchofjesuschrist.org.

and aunt were discovering. Sandra's seminary teacher, Ina Easton, was a kind lady—a grade-school teacher whom Sandra felt did not have the training to answer the probing questions her mother and aunt were posing. Sandra felt sure, however, that the answers would become available once she graduated from seminary and moved on to institute, the college-age program of the LDS Church. She was wrong. "When I started asking questions the second year, [my teacher] got defensive and told me to stay after class. He then instructed me to not ask any more questions as I was disturbing a girl who was attending but wasn't a member yet." Ironically, it was Sandra who had been giving the girl a ride to the class.

Despite holding on to Mormonism at the time, Sandra is convinced that she would have eventually given it up even if she had never met Jerald. But meet him she did, and much of their time was spent doing research together. Early in their courtship, Jerald shared with Sandra the changes Joseph Smith had made to some of his revelations. Sandra purchased a current Doctrine and Covenants and a reprint edition of the Book of Commandments from Sam Weller's Zion Bookstore in Salt Lake City. She asked her grandmother to read passages of the Book of Commandments aloud while she followed along in the Doctrine and Covenants, noting the changes in the margins. She quickly learned that Jerald was right.

More impactful to Sandra, however, were the sermons of her great-great-grandfather Brigham Young. Jerald brought volumes of reprints of the *Journal of Discourses* along with actual photographs of pages from volumes not yet reprinted, pointing out some of Young's more shocking sermons and teachings.[38] One example was Young's prediction that the Civil War would not succeed in defeating slavery.[39] Others included Young's belief that Adam was God[40] and his insistence that only polygamists would achieve the highest heavenly exaltation.[41] Although Sandra could see the problem in each case, it did not seem to her that they were significant enough to

---

38. *The Journal of Discourses* is a collection of sermons by nineteenth-century LDS leaders, usually taken from discourses originally printed in the *Deseret News* and the *Millennial Star*. It is not a complete record of sermons.

39. *Journal of Discourses*, 10:250.

40. *Journal of Discourses*, 1:50.

41. *Journal of Discourses*, 11:269.

prove Mormonism wrong. What did prove more decisive to her was Young's blood atonement teaching, found in a sermon he preached in the Salt Lake Tabernacle on March 16, 1856: "Suppose you found your brother in bed with your wife, and put a javelin through both of them, you would be justified, and they would atone for their sins, and be received into the kingdom of God. ... The blood of Christ will never wipe that out, your own blood must atone for it; and the judgments of the Almighty will come, sooner or later, and every man and woman will have to atone for breaking their covenants"[42]

Sandra was shocked by Young's teaching that murdering someone does them a redemptive favor, and that the blood of Christ could not redeem all sins. In an instant, all of Sandra's illusions about Young being a true prophet fell away, as did her faith in the LDS Church.

Jerald was convinced that God had sent Sandra into his life, reasoning that "since she told me that she wanted to be a Christian, I felt that it would be pleasing to the Lord for us to be married."[43] For her part, Sandra contented herself to let the excitement of the marriage push thoughts about becoming a born-again Christian out of her mind. After they were married, Sandra's Bible reading began to slip despite Jerald's encouragement. He asked Sandra if she would like to travel to Independence to visit the people who had led him to the Lord. She left in September 1959, staying a week with the Moores.

Sandra recalled that "[w]hen she arrived in Independence, she found herself among some of the sweetest people she had ever met."[44] The light of Christ, "shown so bright that Sandra could not ignore it." Upon returning to California, she found herself in a similar condition to Jerald, convinced that she was a sinner, yet still resisting surrender to Christ. The matter was finally resolved a month later on Saturday morning, October 24, 1959. Sandra recalls:

> I was home alone and this minister came on and he was preaching from 1 John chapter 4:10, Herein is love, not that we loved God, but that he loved us and sent his son as a propitiation for our sins ... as he went through this ... it just hit me. "We love God because he *first* loved us. ...

---

42. *Journal of Discourses*, 3:247.

43. Tanner, *Jerald Tanner's Testimony*, 10.

44. Tanner, *Out of Darkness*, 1. In this tract Sandra describes her experience in the third person.

And that was such a revelation to me because I'd always assumed, Well, of course God loves me. I'm his child, you know. And so, here's this minister explaining, "No, you were in sin, hopeless, without the atonement of Christ. Christ loved you so much that *he first initiated* the step to make you reconciled to God. So, we love him because he *first* loved us. ... It was just such an amazing thought to me that I failed God every day and yet he loved me and made the move to me to bring me to reconciliation; and that it didn't have anything to do with going to church or paying tithing or any of those things. It was a matter of coming to God and accepting *His* forgiveness—accepting what he had done for me. And so, listening to that radio program that's when I had my conversion experience of accepting Christ as my savior. ... For me it was a shattering experience I sat on the couch and cried for an hour. [45]

Even though Jerald and Sandra had both now come to know Christ, they still believed the Book of Mormon and were careful to try to harmonize what they read in it about the doctrine of God with what the Bible said. There were certain implications to limiting what was to be accepted from Joseph Smith to the Book of Mormon. One was coming to a view of the Godhead that was different from both the trinitarianism of traditional Christianity and the plurality of gods doctrine of the Utah LDS Church, a view in which the Godhead consisted not of three divine persons, Father, Son, and Holy Ghost, but of one divine person manifesting himself in three different roles or modes, now as Father, now as Son, now as Holy Ghost. This view has traditionally been called *modalism*.

Pauline Hancock had embraced modalism more than a half century earlier when she was asked to teach the Book of Mormon as part of the Protest Movement of the RLDS Church in the late 1920s and early 1930s. She had come across a passage in the Book of Mormon which discussed Jesus becoming both the Father *and* the Son at the time of the incarnation:

God himself shall come down among the children of men, and shall redeem his people. And because he dwelleth in flesh, he shall be called

---

45. "Sandra (and Jerald) Tanner," interview by John Dehlin, *Mormon Stories*, 472, 54:00–57:25, mormonstories.org. In another context Sandra says "Nothing ever struck me with such force. I opened my heart to God and accepted Christ as my own personal Savior. The Holy Spirit flooded my soul with such joy that I wept for over an hour." Tanner and Tanner, *Mormonism: Shadow or Reality?*, 569.

the Son of God, and having subjected the flesh to the will of the Father, being the Father and the Son—the Father, because he was conceived by the power of God; and the Son, because of the flesh; thus becoming the Father and Son—and they are one God, yea, the very Eternal Father of heaven and of earth (Mosiah 15:1–4).

Hancock clung to the Book of Mormon until her death—even refusing baptism to those who did not believe in the book. She was convinced that God used its monotheistic doctrine to deliver her from what she considered to be a polytheistic background.[46] Taking her lead from the Book of Mormon, Pauline explained the Godhead:

> When the scriptures refer to the Father, it is *the Lord, that spirit*, which fills heaven and earth, our Creator, our God; when the word refers to the Son it is *that same spirit, the Lord*, our God, revealing Himself in a body to redeem man ... and when the scriptures refer to the Comforter which cometh into the heart of the true believer to give understanding, comfort, to fill with love and joy, it is *that same spirit, the Lord*, our God, in another one of His administrations or operations.[47]

A modalist view arose from reading both the Book of Mormon and Joseph Smith's Inspired Version of the Bible, which was the official scripture of the RLDS Church. Smith had changed the King James Version of Luke 10:22, "and no man knoweth who the Son is, but the Father; and who the Father is, but the Son," to read, "no man knoweth that the son *is* the Father, and that the Father *is* the son" (Inspired Version, Luke 10:23, emphasis added).

Hancock was not alone. Samuel Wood, who had been an apostle in the Temple Lot group but was later expelled for coming to a modalistic understanding of the Godhead, Jerald's friend James Wardle, and a Michigan RLDS pastor named Moroni Sherman all embraced modalism.[48] All three men wrote tracts or pamphlets supporting their beliefs, and enough came of it that other members

---

46. Pauline Hancock, "Does the Scriptures Teach A Trinity Concerning the Godhead?" *Independence Examiner*, Aug. 23, 1952. Pauline's struggle in accepting the Book of Mormon teaching that Jesus is the Eternal God is described in the rough transcription of a biographical sermon, Wardle, Papers, box 22, fd. 10.

47. Hancock, "Does the Scriptures Teach a Trinity," emphasis original.

48. Wood's trouble came after he published his views in *The Infinite God*.

of their respective faiths issued responses, and Wood and Sherman were censured by the Temple Lot and RLDS churches.[49]

Wardle ordered multiple copies of Sherman's *Who Is Jesus?* tract, presumably for distribution in his barbershop. Finding that he had an ally in Wardle, Sherman suggested getting together with others who were of one mind on the subject and asked if James might provide him with a list of people. This was in 1958. The list James sent was small but with significant names: himself, his son, Samuel Wood, Sylvia Rogerson, Georgia McGee, and Jerald Tanner.[50] Wardle told Sherman that "young Jerald is a member of Pauline Hancock's group and I consider him the local leader here." Wardle liked to use the phrase "Ethical Monotheism" to describe his views of the godhead, even though the name really didn't fit the teaching.[51] But it was the phrase that had been coined by Samuel Wood. So he described the names proffered on the list as "believers in Ethical Monotheism."[52]

Viewing Sandra's mother, Georgia, as potentially interested in "Ethical Monotheism" helps understand a letter she wrote to Earl E. Olson at the LDS Church Historian's Office on June 20, 1958. She requested information on changes in three Book of Mormon passages. Olson answered two days later with the texts of those passages in parallel columns as they appeared in the 1830 and 1840 editions:

1830 Edition	1840 Edition
And he said unto me, Behold, the virgin which thou seest, is the mother of God, after the manner of the flesh. [1 Ne. 11:18]	And he said unto me, behold, the virgin whom thou seest, is the mother of the Son of[53] God, after the manner of the flesh.

---

49. James Wardle to Moroni Sherman, May 9, 1958, Wardle, Papers, box 22, fd. 8; James Wardle to Samuel Wood, May 15, 1958; Wood to Wardle, Sep. 7, 1959, both in Wardle, Papers, box 30, fd. 6; Samuel Wood, "The Godhead: A Review," *TM: An Independent Journal of Fundamental Religious and Social Reform*, various issues, July 1953–Nov. 1955; James Wardle to V. H. Fisher, Oct. 30, 1953, Wardle, Papers, box 30, fd. 6. "The Matter of Silence Imposed Upon Moroni Sherman, Reese, Michigan (An Aaronic Priest of the Saginaw Branch)," June 9, 1956, Wardle, Papers, box 22, fd. 8; Wood, *The Infinite God.*

50. Moroni Sherman to James D. Wardle, Apr. 25, 1958, 1; Wardle to Sherman, Aug. 12, 1958, 4, both in Wardle, Papers, box 22, fd. 8.

51. Ethical Monotheism would seem to imply a number of divine persons united by a single ethical perspective, not the single divine person manifesting in three different modes.

52. Wardle to Sherman.

53. Underlining original; it is unclear whether Earl Olson or Georgia McGee underlined these lines for emphasis.

And I looked and beheld the Lamb of God, that he was taken by the people; yea, the Everlasting God, was judged of the world; [1 Ne. 11:32]	And I looked and beheld the Lamb of God, that he was taken by the people; yea, the <u>Son of</u> the Everlasting God, was judged of the world;
that the Lamb of God is the Eternal Father and the Saviour of the world; [1 Ne. 13:40]	that the Lamb of God is <u>the Son of the</u> Eternal Father and the Saviour of the world;

Olson added that these changes were also made in the 1837 edition of the Book of Mormon, where a preface said changes were due to "typographical errors." Although Olson did not directly claim that the words "Son of" had been inadvertently left out of the 1830 first edition of the Book of Mormon, that he included the 1837 preface suggests he probably intended it as an explanation.[54]

For Jerald and Sandra the idea of a modalist God challenged the very foundation of Mormonism: Joseph Smith's First Vision of 1820. The official account of the vision published in the Pearl of Great Price stresses that God and Jesus are two separate, distinct beings, and Mormons draw on the vision to support their anti-trinitarian theology. Today, differences found in the several accounts of Joseph Smith's vision are openly acknowledged by the LDS Church; but in the 1950s, anything but the official account was virtually unheard of.

Most of the Restoration proponents of "Ethical Monotheism," unwilling or unable to jettison their belief in Joseph Smith, went to great lengths to validate the later First Vision accounts while remaining faithful to modalist Book of Mormon teachings. One explanation was that even though two personages appeared, they only represented one person along the lines of the parallel between the spirit body and fleshly body of God in the brother of Jared

---

54. Olson at least might have known that the passage he quoted from the 1837 preface did not provide the true explanation of the situation because in the 1880s pages 3–20 of the Original Manuscript of the Book of Mormon, running from chapter 2 to 13, had come into the possession of the LDS Church. See Roberts, *New Witnesses for God II*, 129. Since the manuscript portion broke off at 1 Nephi 13:35, it does not include the third passage Georgia asked about, but it did include the original text for the two others. In both cases it was the 1830 Book of Mormon that faithfully reproduced the text of the Original Manuscript, and the editions from 1837 forward departed from it by adding "the son of" in each case.

vision (Ether 3:14–16). Both Moroni Sherman and James Wardle made this argument concerning the "personages" in Smith's account of his vision.[55]

Sandra was already aware of a different problem facing the traditional First Vision account. Her aunt and her mother had found a description in the *Historical Record* of the vision that called one of the personages who visited Joseph Smith "the angel."[56] If that were the end of it, the use of "angel" by LDS Church historian Andrew Jenson might have been forgotten. But the supposed facsimile reprint of the *Historical Record* Aunt Lucille obtained was a later printing, and in it she discovered that the language had been silently changed so that "the angel" was now "Holy Being" and "the Christ."

Historical Record, **Jan. 1888, 355–56.** Original	***Historical Record,*** **Jan. 1888, 355–56.** Reprint
"I saw two personages, whose brightness and glory defy all description, standing above me in the air. One of them spake unto me, calling me by name, and said (pointing to the other), THIS IS MY BELOVED SON, HEAR HIM. ... I asked the personages ... which of all the sects was right ... the **personage** who addressed me said that all their creeds, were an abomination in his sight. ...."	"I saw two personages, whose brightness and glory defy all description, standing above me in the air. One of them spake unto me, calling me by name, and said (pointing to the other), THIS IS MY BELOVED SON, HEAR HIM. ... I asked the personages ... which of all the sects was right ... the **personages** who addressed me said that all their creeds, were an abomination in his sight. ...."
The **angel** again forbade Joseph to join any of these churches, and he promised that the true and everlasting Gospel should be revealed to him at some future time. Joseph continues:	The **Holy Being** again forbade Joseph to join any of these churches, and he promised that the true and everlasting Gospel should be revealed to him at some future time. Joseph continues:

---

55. Sherman, *Who Is Jesus?* 6; James Wardle to Jasper O. Dutton, Feb. 23, 1944, 4, Wardle, Papers, box 4, fd. 2.

56. Andrew Jenson, "Joseph Smith the Prophet," *Historical Record: A Monthly Periodical*, Jan. 1888, 355–56.

"Many other things did he (**the angel**) say unto me which I cannot write at this time. ... [and later] I had actually seen a light, and in the midst of that light I saw two personages, and they did in reality speak unto me, **or one of them did**; and though I was hated and persecuted."

"Many other things did he (**the Christ**) say unto me which I cannot write at this time. ... [and later] I had actually seen a light, and in the midst of that light I saw two personages, and they did in reality speak unto me; and though I was hated and persecuted."

The description of the single personage that spoke in Jenson's original version as an "angel" suggested an interesting possibility. What if Joseph Smith had never intended the personages of the first vision to be identified with the Father and Son at all? If, as Sandra's mother, Georgia, suspected, explicit reference to the Father and Son was "notoriously missing from every [early] account," and "Angels were still taught and published in 1888," who were the personages anyway?[57] For most the New Testament phrase "This is my beloved son, hear him," spoken by the Father of the Son in Mark 9:7, was seen as sufficient to identify the two personages in the vision. But Georgia noticed that Mormon also regularly used the phrase "my beloved son" in reference to Moroni in the Book of Mormon. She concluded the personages must be Mormon and Moroni.[58] James Wardle viewed the interpretation as having "equal merit to this idea that it was God."[59] Sandra and Jerald never accepted the view, despite Georgia's unflagging attempts to persuade them.

The doctoring of Jenson's *Historical Record* was remarkable and troubling since it had been introduced into what was represented as a bound reprint of an old newspaper. It was like pretending to reprint old copies of the *New York Times* but carefully modifying something in the text to retroactively change or cover up an inconsistency. Those who lose their faith in Mormonism over historical issues often speak of being more troubled about being given deceptive answers about historical problems than they are about the historical problems themselves. "I was lied to" is not an uncommon

---

57. McGee, "Response to the First Vision Controversy," 9.
58. McGee, 10. Moroni 8:2, 9; 9:1, 6, 11.
59. Walgren Interview, 13 Wardle, Papers, box 1, fd 5.

refrain.[60] Long before the internet made discovery of such discrepancy's commonplace, Sandra Tanner and her family had stumbled on an LDS publication that was changed without warning or notice.

Six days after Sandra left Independence, she addressed a letter to Bishop Warren H. Kennedy in which she thanked him for an offer he had made during a "recent discussion" to send questions she might have to Apostle Joseph Fielding Smith, official LDS Church Historian. Sandra chose to ask the apostle about the changes to the *Historical Record*; she noted the discrepancy and asked for, among other things, "a photostatic copy of Joseph Smith's own account in his own hand writing," and any places where Joseph Smith or Brigham Young specifically identified the personages in the first vision as "God, the Father, and His Son Jesus Christ," or made any reference to the First Vision in a sermon.[61]

Sandra's letter was polite and deferential; the reply was not. Joseph Fielding Smith responded to Kennedy with little-disguised fury. "Those questions come from those who do not seek the truth, but rather are steeled against it. If this young lady would seek the Lord rather than the mouthings of enemies of the Church and obtain a testimony of the Gospel she would not be susceptible to the supposed arguments and mouthings of enemies of the Church." Smith seemed so irate at the question that he repeated himself again: "I tell you, Bishop, only those who do not seek to know the truth will quibble over this statement ... this kind of argument is contemptible. It is used only by those who are in opposition to the work of the Lord."

The apostle wasn't done. He accused Sandra of acting on behalf of a sinister conspiracy against the LDS Church:

> Now those who have concocted this plot have gone to considerable trouble to find other passages which seem to contradict this [i.e., the Church's official story of the First Vision]. If they had placed half of this diligent search in prayerful, faith, the chances are that the Lord would have given them a personal revelation that this is TRUE. But, NO! They must quibble over it!

---

60. See, for example, Laurie Goodstein, "A Top Mormon Leader Acknowledges the Church 'Made Mistakes,'" *New York Times*, Oct. 5, 2013, and Goodstein, "Some Mormons Search the Web and Find Doubt," *New York Times*, July 20, 2013, A1.

61. Tanner to Warren Kennedy, Oct. 1, 1959, 1, in Tanner and Tanner, Papers.

It is true that Andrew Jenson said the "Angel again forbade Joseph to join any of these churches.["] Who was the angel? MORONI! The holy being *again* forbade Joseph to join any of these churches, was Moroni.

Smith concluded that a photostatic copy of the official account of the First Vision in Joseph Smith's hand would not convince Sandra, then suggested that Kennedy direct her to the parable of the rich man and Lazarus, "If they hear not Moses and the prophets, neither will they be persuaded, though one rose from the dead" (Luke 16:31).[62]

When the response arrived, Kennedy invited Sandra to visit with him and read it to her. She was dumbfounded and asked if the bishop thought it was fair. He said he saw no problem with it. Sandra recalls her objection: "I told him either Joseph Fielding Smith didn't pay me the courtesy to look up the references or he was deliberately evading the real issue. ... I asked if I could have the letter, he said no. I asked if I could have a copy of [Smith's] letter, he said he would have to pray about it."[63]

Even though Sandra was young at the time, she did not internalize Smith's attack on her character. What's more, he gave away crucial information, though he may not have realized it. When he refused to provide Sandra with a copy of the First Vision in Joseph Smith's handwriting, insisting it would not convince her, he seems to have acknowledged that such a version exists.[64]

The only copy of the vision in Smith's hand dates from 1832, and it differs from the official account written in 1838.[65] Did Sandra hear whispers about the 1832 version of the First Vision that LaMar Petersen had heard about, but had promised not to share? In an early tract she seems to say she did. But today she feels convinced that she was simply assuming that the church would have preserved an account in the prophet's own hand.[66] She is sure Petersen didn't

---

62. Joseph Fielding Smith to Bishop Warren H. Kennedy, Nov. 3, 1959, 1, in Tanner and Tanner, Papers.

63. Tanner, Recollections.

64. Sandra interprets Smith's words as an admission. Jerald and Sandra Tanner to LeGrand Richards, Oct. 9, 1960, 5, as did her mother Georgia. McGee, "Response to the First Vision Controversy," 9, Tanner and Tanner, Papers.

65. See Davidson et al., *Histories, Volume 1*, 12–13; chapter eight, herein.

66. Tanner, Recollections. The question relates to interpreting a line Sandra wrote soon after: "Knowing that the church had an account of the First Vision in Joseph

tell her.[67] Thanks to Joseph Fielding Smith's disclosure, Sandra now felt more sure than ever that the church had an "account of the First Vision in Joseph Smith's own handwriting," Sandra remarked in a letter written not long after the incident, "I wrote to Joseph Fielding Smith and requested a copy. I was refused. There would be no reason to keep this from me if it read the same as the account the church releases today."[68]

As Jerald and Sandra's study progressed, it became evident that the official story of the First Vision, with its appearance of the Father and the Son to Joseph Smith, wasn't the version of the story most nineteenth-century Mormons knew. Instead, it was common for those who spoke of the vision to refer instead to an angel.

The young couple were ready to make their next step. One year after she first wrote to her bishop, Sandra replied to Joseph Fielding Smith, informing him that she intended to make mimeograph copies of both the contradictory passages in the *Historical Record* and his "explanation," asking him if he "wished to retract it." Smith never responded, but the Tanners were about to go into the publishing business.

Smith's own handwriting, I wrote to Joseph Fielding Smith, and requested a copy." Tanner, "Dear Friend I" 1.

67. Sandra met Petersen briefly for the first time on May 3, 1959, the day after her and Jerald's aborted elopement to Wendover. She went along with Jerald, her mother, and aunt. She didn't get to know Petersen well until after they returned to Salt Lake from California in the Summer of 1960, after writing to Joseph Fielding Smith. Petersen did not tell Jerald and Sandra about the 1832 account until after Levi Edgar Young's death in December 1963 (for details on this, see chap. 8).

68. Tanner, "Dear Friend I," 1959/1960.

4

"DEAR FRIEND"

It is not uncommon for those who go through a faith crisis or a powerful conversion to want to share their experiences with others. Today, anxious Mormons might post to Facebook or Twitter; they might send emails to family and friends; they might download podcasts and even attend support groups. In 1960, Jerald and Sandra Tanner bought a mimeograph machine from Sears. Both felt called to share their findings, to persuade others to come to Christ as they had done, and perhaps to justify their action to their friends and family. But while family and friends like Georgia McGee and James Wardle synthesized their new understandings of the Mormon past with their faith, Jerald and Sandra moved in a different direction.[1] They started by mailing letters and short tracts to family and friends.

It was Sandra who suggested they go into publishing since she knew how to work a mimeograph. Two of the first items they prepared focused on their recent experiences: research into the First Vision and their conversion to Christianity. One five-page tract reprinted quotes from several early Mormon leaders, including Brigham Young, George A. Smith, Wilford Woodruff, and others who referred to the First Vision involving angels.[2]

Another early mailing was a letter by Sandra explaining her reasons for leaving the LDS Church. Jerald had been inactive for some time, so no explanation of his departure was really needed.[3] Sandra recalls that, "I assumed, naively, when we first started out that

---

1. Walgren, Interview, Wardle Papers, box 1, fd. 5.
2. Tanner and Tanner, *The Father and the Son?* giving, among other things, quotations from a number of early Mormon leaders, including Brigham Young (*Journal of Discourses* 2:171), George Albert Smith (12:333–34 and 13:77–78), Wilford Woodruff (2:196–97), Orson Pratt (14:261–62 and 13:65–66), and Orson Hyde (6:335).
3. Sandra Tanner, email to Huggins, Dec. 9, 2019.

everyone in the church operated under the great moral standard I was raised to believe we operated under. We seek for truth and accept it when we see it. We can study our history and we don't run from it ... but as soon as you decide that you may have the capacity of determining truth on your own, then you're in trouble."[4]

On June 21, 1960, Sandra and Jerald began sending out her letter, "Dear Friend," giving her testimony and rational for leaving the LDS Church. Making the most of their new mimeograph machine, they sent copies to nearly everyone they personally knew, a handful of LDS scholars, and the general authorities of the church.[5] In it, Sandra listed a number of reasons for leaving. "I have found," she begins, "that since I accepted Jesus Christ as my personal Savior that I cannot reconcile the teachings of the church with those of Christ." The LDS Church "does not preach hard enough against sin," and is "too conformed to the world." Its focus, she said, is wrong as well: "too much 'church' and not enough 'Christ.'" The letter also discussed historical problems she had encountered, including that "the church doctrine and the doctrine contained in the Book of Mormon are exactly opposite," changes to the revelations, what she had discovered about the First Vision, and her experience with Joseph Fielding Smith.[6]

Jerald and Sandra moved to Salt Lake City on July 11, 1960, and their final days in California were marked by a significant event. In June, Sandra wrote to the bishop in their new ward requesting that her name be removed from the general membership records. At that time, a bishop's court (or disciplinary council) had to be held and the petitioner had to be found guilty of a spiritual crime worthy of excommunication—the only option available to a member who wished to resign from the church. Sandra's trial was held on Thursday, July 7, in the North Hollywood Ward. She was "found guilty" of "apostasy and engaging in activities contrary to the in[te]rests of the church."[7] Sandra had come to the trial loaded down with reference

---

4. Sandra Tanner, interview with James D'Arc, Sep. 10, 1972, in Faulring, "Oral History."

5. LeGrand Richards to William E. Barrett, Aug. 29, 1960, in Tanner and Tanner, Papers, speaks of Jerald and Sandra "sending literature to all of us General Authorities."

6. Tanner and Tanner, "Dear Friend 1," 1–2.

7. Reproduction of the letters announcing the result are in Tanner and Tanner, *Mormonism: Shadow or Reality?*, 575.

works to present her case. The bishop presiding over the court, Lyman P. Pinkston, would hear none of it: "It's you that's on trial here today, Mrs. Tanner. Not the Church." Still, Pinkston took no pleasure in the proceedings. As Sandra recalls, he "was visibly shaken by the proceeding. He was almost tearful. I was the first person he had excommunicated, and he very obviously believed he was sentencing me to spend eternity outside the presence of God. I tried to comfort him by telling him that I felt no sorrow about being excommunicated and I was fully ready to face God as an ex-Mormon since I was trusting in Christ, not church membership, to save me."[8]

Once settled in Salt Lake City, Jerald and Sandra continued researching the First Vision. They discovered another account while in James Wardle's barbershop that also called at least one of the personages who visited Joseph Smith "the angel."[9] Sandra recorded the version in a letter to her mother.[10] Also at the barbershop that day was Francis Kirkham, an LDS historian who edited the familiar two-volume standard collection of early historical documents relating to Mormonism titled *A New Witness for Christ in America*. Kirkham had come for a haircut and began chatting with James about having received a letter from a young woman who said the LDS Church was too conformed to the world. Kirkham had been sent a copy of Sandra's *Out of Darkness, into the "Sonlight"* tract.

Wardle had a little fun with the chance encounter, dragging out the conversation until finally asking Kirkham if he would like to meet the author of the tract. Kirkham said yes, so Wardle turned to Sandra, who had been in the shop the whole time. Sandra found Kirkham "nice and broad-minded," and they all talked for a long time.[11] That evening, Kirkham invited Jerald and Sandra to dinner and presented them with a copy of the new edition of the second volume of his compilation, which he inscribed, "To newly found friends and beleivers [*sic*] in the Book of Mormon. Mr & Mrs Jerald Tanner."

Among the LDS Church's general authorities, Apostle LeGrand Richards responded to Sandra's "Dear Friend" letter. While

---

8. Tanner and Tanner, 574.
9. Smith, *Young People's History*, vol. 1, 5–6.
10. Sandra Tanner to Georgia McGee, Sep. 22, 1960, 1, Tanner and Tanner, Papers.
11. Tanner to McGee, 2

Richards's six-page letter was more courteous than Joseph Fielding Smith's, the apostle could not resist trying to explain away Sandra's account of her leaving the church by casting her in a bad light. "You haven't found that the Church of Jesus Christ of Latter-day Saints is not the true church because that is absolutely impossible," writes Richards. "You have become infatuated with the man whom you married, and love is blind. You have not had the courage to stand out for what you knew to be correct."[12] Richards spent a few lines calling Sandra's assessment of the First Vision "absurd and untrue," and claimed to have a reference to the official vision dating from Joseph Lee Robinson's 1841 journal. But most of Richards's letter contained a series of anecdotes about Protestants becoming Mormons and Mormon girls who married non-Mormons only to find out that they could not stay away from the LDS Church because it was true. "Some day you will have to find your way back, if you leave the church, and the return trip, you will find much more difficult than you anticipate. My council and advice to you is that you start working on your husband and get him to join you in the true Church of Christ rather than to let him pull you away into the teachings of man."[13] Sandra arranged a meeting with the apostle with the understanding that he would show her Joseph Lee Robinson's 1841 account of the First Vision.[14]

When the day came, Sandra and Jerald went to the granite LDS Office Building on South Temple next to Brigham Young's Lion House. They mounted the steps, passed the stately fluted Ionic columns, entered the solemn precincts, and took the elevator up to meet Richards. Richards was dressed in a well-tailored suit of good material, and a white shirt and tie. The apostle seemed pleased when Sandra entered, but displeased when Jerald came in behind her. He motioned for them to sit down.

"Just what is it that this Jesus of yours has that the LDS Church hasn't got?" the apostle asked, addressing himself to Jerald.

---

12. LeGrand Richards to Sandra Tanner, July 12, 1960, 1, Tanner and Tanner, Papers.

13. Richards to Tanner, 5–6

14. Although Jerald recalls having this meeting in the fall of 1960 (Tanner and Tanner, *Mormonism: Shadow or Reality?*, 570), it took place by the end of August, since letters discussing the meeting in the past tense were written that month. See LeGrand Richards to William E. Barrett, Aug. 29, 1960; Georgia McGee to William E. Barrett, Aug. 30, 1960.

"Well," Jerald answered, "during my teenage years I began to fall into alcoholism and other sins, but thank God, Christ delivered me!"

This was no small matter in Jerald's case since the problem of alcoholism had plagued his family for generations, ensnaring his father George, his grandfather Caleb, and his great grandfather Myron Tanner and his wife Ann Crosby. But Jerald would remain free of it for the rest of his life.

Richards was not impressed: "I never drank," the apostle announced dismissively and asked: "What do you have to offer that this church doesn't have?"

"The love of Christ," Jerald said. "I want to show the Mormon people the love of Christ."

"If you think you've got more love than us," the apostle said, "you're crazy!"[15]

Before they were finished, Richards drew himself up and thundered, "*I am warning you, don't start anything against this church!*"[16]

The meeting had quickly become tense and awkward, so Sandra changed the subject to the account of the First Vision that they had come to see. The apostle produced a sheet of typed excerpts and laid it before Jerald and Sandra. They were astonished; he had to know they would not be satisfied with typed excerpts. The couple argued with the apostle until he agreed to accompany them to the library to show them the microfilm of the diary itself. On the way, two elderly Mormon women who found themselves riding in the elevator with the apostle, sputtered excitedly to one another. Used to this kind of treatment, Richards took it in stride, "Hello, Sisters," he beamed.

---

15. The incident provoked a flurry of phone calls, contemporary letters, and early references in tracts and books in which the essential pieces of the story are were told by Richards, Sandra's mother, Georgia McGee, and the Tanners themselves. See Jerald and Sandra [actual author] Tanner to LeGrand Richard, Oct. 9, 1960, 1–5; LeGrand Richards to Georgia McGee, Sep. 26, 1960, 2, and Nov. 28, 1960, 1; Georgia McGee to LeGrand Richards, Sep. 18, 1960, 2; Georgia McGee to William A. Barrett, Aug. 30, 1960, 1, Tanner and Tanner, *Excerpts from the Writings of Joseph Lee Robinson* (1960–1961), 1; Tanner and Tanner, *Suppression of the Records* (1961–1962), 2–3; Tanner and Tanner, *Who Censored the Joseph Smith Story?*, 3–4 (1962); Tanner, *Mormonism: A Study of Mormon History* (1963), 215, 238.

16. Tanner, *Jerald Tanner's Testimony*, 11, and Tanner and Tanner, *Mormonism: Shadow or Reality?*, 570, emphasis original.

The apostle led Jerald and Sandra out a side entrance and across to a building that in those days faced North Temple Street.

When the apostle entered with Jerald and Sandra, Sandra recalls the rush of hushed voices sweeping through the room like a tsunami as the patrons passed along the news of the apostolic visitation. Everyone watched as Richards walked through the large room to the help desk. After giving his instructions, the receptionist snapped into action looking the film up, then bringing it out and putting it on the machine.

Richards turned the crank on the microfilm viewer until he came to the page he wanted. He then let Jerald sit down to read it. Jerald read the page, and, sure enough, there was a passage very similar to the one on the typed sheet that Richards had given them. But it was not clear to Jerald *when* the passage had been written. Was it a contemporary passage in Robinson's journal, or was it a reminiscence? Jerald asked if he could turn back a few pages to try to get at that information. Displeasure furrowed across Richards's brow as he snapped the handle back one frame, and then another, and then yet another, each time manifesting an increasing air of impatience. Still, Jerald did not find what he needed and asked the apostle to keep flipping back or to let him look around in the document a bit himself until he could determine its provenance. With that Richards had had enough, he impatiently whipped the crank around until the film was back on its original reel and took it off the machine. He had gone to the trouble of showing Jerald and Sandra the microfilm of his own great-grandfather's journal in his own hand, and they still wouldn't believe.

Richards handed it back to the librarian, and Jerald asked her if he could come another time and view the microfilm. She said he could; Richards interrupted and told her that Jerald and Sandra were not to be permitted to see the diary again. Richards walked off to the elevators without them; Jerald chased after, asking, "Why won't you let me look at the microfilm? What is it you are trying to hide?" But Richards had gone.

This encounter with a beloved LDS apostle made a strong impression on Jerald and Sandra. The meeting further convinced them that the church was not just misguided, but that it had something to hide.

Jerald and Sandra have told the story several times as one of the key moments that caused them to start their work. Sandra was mortified that Jerald chased after Richards in the library, calling out to him, "What is it you are trying to hide?" Jerald was intimidated but not cowed: "While this meeting with Apostle Richards did cause me to grow somewhat weak in the knees," he later recalled, "it made me realize more than ever that the Mormon leaders had something to hide from their people and that I should become actively involved in bringing the truth to light. Since I am basically a cowardly sort of person, I entered into the work with fear and trembling."[17]

Were Jerald and Sandra determined to embarrass the LDS Church, as Richards seemed to believe? Anger and resentment are not uncommon among those who leave their religion. But this wasn't the case with the Tanners. They didn't leave because they were angry or disillusioned or felt lied to. They left because they firmly believed they had found something better. Something they now wanted to bring back and share with their own community. It was only afterward, through encounters like this one, that they became convinced from direct, personal experience that the church wasn't always being forthright and honest. In the meantime they had also shown, and would show in the future, a willingness to revise their thinking in light of new evidence. Sandra issued a follow-up version of her Dear Friend letter after discovering that LDS convert-turned-critic John Hyde had spoken of the Father and Son appearing to Joseph in his 1857 book, *Mormonism: Its Leaders and Designs*. But if they were not already convinced, the meeting with Richards solidified their conviction that the LDS Church was not just misguided, but wrong and keeping people from Christ.

The day after the apostle told the librarian not to share the microfilm with Jerald and Sandra, Sandra and her grandmother returned and put in a request for it. They were told that it was out for repair. The same excuse was given two more times. The fourth time was the charm. Sandra recalls that the "first time we went with L[eGrand] R[ichard] to the library there was a card for the diary in the card catalogue, which could be accessed by anyone in the library. The last

---

17. Tanner, *Jerald Tanner's Testimony*, 11, cf. Tanner and Tanner, *Mormonism: Shadow or Reality?*, 570.

time I went the card was no longer in the public card files."[18] Sandra had saved the number so she was able to fill out a request for the film. When she turned it in the woman at the desk said, "This film isn't available at all," and asked, "who gave you this number?" "I've had it a long time," Sandra answered. "Well that explains it," the woman said, noting that the film hadn't been available for a long time. Then she went and got the film and handed it over, apparently assuming that Sandra was doing family genealogy.[19]

She put the microfilm on the machine and started reading. As they suspected Richards's date was wrong. After reading the diary, Jerald and Sandra informed Richards in a letter that "the portion of the journal that you quoted in your letter to us was not written until 1883"—over forty years after the fact.[20] Whether Richards read the Tanners' letter or not is unclear, because soon after he repeated the same claim in a letter to Sandra's mother: "my grandfather Joseph Lee Robinson states in his journal published in 1842 when he first came to Nauvoo, that he had seen the prophet who had seen the Father and the Son and so it was common knowledge among the saints of that time that he had seen the Father and the Son."[21]

A year later, in his book *Just to Illustrate*, Richards again quoted the First Vision account from Joseph Lee Robinson's journal: "We have long since believed and known that Joseph Smith was a true and humble prophet of God *who had seen the Father*."[22] Jerald and Sandra knew better—and Richards had been provided with more accurate information. Richards's transcription had been sloppily done. In the letter they sent him the previous October, the Tanners explained that they compared his transcription with the microfilm of the original and found that the words "who had seen the Father" were not in the place Richards quotes it. It was actually part of a later statement in the original that was moved back and stuck in the wrong place.[23]

---

18. Sandra Tanner, email to Huggins, Jan. 18, 2020.

19. Dialogue based on Sandra's transcript of the interaction written down at the time, apparently on the back of a request form. Tanner and Tanner, Papers.

20. Tanners to Richards, Oct. 9, 1960, 2.

21. Richards to McGee, Nov. 28, 1960, 1.

22. Richards, *Just to Illustrate*, 205, emphasis added.

23. Tanners to Richards, Oct. 9, 1960, 2. The original read: "a Holy man of God who has seen the Father and the Son,"

In addition to the forty-one-year gap between the event and the time the account was written down, there were several passages of interest to Jerald and Sandra. One involved Robinson's sister-in-law Angeline telling Joseph Smith's wife Emma that the prophet had visited another woman behind her back. Emma "became very angry and said she would leave and was making preparations to go to her people in the State of New York. Emma came near leaving Joseph." When confronted by an angry Smith, Angeline, supported by her husband, was unrepentant, so the prophet "cursed her severely."[24] The LDS Church has long had an uncomfortable relationship with its polygamist past, simultaneously avowing that plural marriage was ordained of God while avoiding the topic as much as possible. Apostle Richards would likely have been embarrassed if Robinson's account of Joseph and Emma's marriage came to light. The diary also documents Brigham Young's Adam–God doctrine, with Robinson declaring that he "believed every word."

Jerald and Sandra put their new mimeograph to work and published *Excerpts from the Writings of Joseph Lee Robinson*. When Richards learned they were publishing material from Robinson's diary, he threatened legal action against them. "If any one descendant objects, no one has the right to copy and print anything from such journals."[25] Richards was wrong, and the Tanners knew it. After all, if the apostle were correct, Sandra (and hundreds of other descendants) could have sued the LDS Church every time they published materials by Brigham Young without her permission.[26]

At Richards's and Sandra's mother's request, BYU religion professor William E. Berrett wrote a lengthy letter responding to the Tanners' publications. Richards had written to Berrett on August 30 in the hope of coaxing Sandra back into the LDS Church. Georgia wrote, perhaps unaware of the irony, that she believed as Sandra studied LDS history she would have her doubts put to rest. However, "the opposite seemed to happen. The more she studied the more confusing it all became." Georgia told Berrett the story

---

24. Robinson, Autobiography, 27, Jul. 14, 1846. See also, Tanner and Tanner, *Excerpts from the Writings of Joseph Lee Robinson*, 1, and, Tanners to Richards, Oct. 9, 1960, 3.

25. LeGrand Richards to Jerald Tanner, Dec. 21, 1961, 1.

26. Tanner and Tanner, *Answering Dr. Clandestine*, 47.

of the experience in the genealogy library, the harsh letter from Joseph Fielding Smith, and insisted that Jerald and Sandra "radiate the spirit of Christ."[27]

Berrett was a welcome contrast to the two apostles who had corresponded with the Tanners. He was polite, courteous, and kind, and his letter was free of the kind of impatient rhetoric Jerald and Sandra had encountered from church leadership. Instead, Berrett used historical arguments against the evidence Jerald and Sandra had presented. He focused almost entirely on defending the official story of the First Vision with its clear identification of the two personages who appeared to Joseph as the Father and the Son. Berrett's thesis was that the official account of the First Vision, "which has been consistently used in the Church since 1838 is the account as written by the Prophet Joseph Smith," and that "when this account appeared … between 1838 and 1840 it did not come as a surprise to the membership of the Church; it created no stir and no denials, nor did the enemies of the Church at that time allude to it as a new approach."[28] In support of these claims, Berrett presented later recollections as well as some early accounts that were not, in his view, inconsistent with the official story of the First Vision.

The core of Berrett's time, however, was spent responding to the list of *Journal of Discourses* passages Jerald and Sandra had compiled in which the primary, and indeed, in some instances, the only figure mentioned was not the Father *or* the Son but an angel. First, Berrett stressed that he was familiar with the passages, claiming that they "have been available to scholars from the time they were first published."[29] He followed with two main points: First, he asserted that

---

27. Georgia McGee to William E. Berrett, Aug. 30, 1960, 2, Tanner and Tanner, Papers.

28. William E. Berrett to [J]erald and Sandra Tanner, Oct 7, 1960, 1–2, Tanner and Tanner, Papers.

29. Berrett to Tanner and Tanner, 4. The list of passages Berrett responds to corresponds with the tract Jerald and Sandra published around this time, *The Father and the Son?* Berrett's statement is somewhat misleading, at least in regard to the 26-volume set of the *Journal of Discourses*. See the statement historian LaMar Petersen once drew up for the Tanners: "In 1954 upon learning that the Deseret Book Company had a microfilm of the 26-volume *Journal of Discourses*. I asked for the privilege of reading from some of the volumes on their viewer. After checking 'across the street' [i.e., with the LDS Church Administration Offices] the management announced that the privilege of reading from the *Journals* could not be granted." Rpt. Tanner and Tanner, *Case Against Mormonism*, 1:44.

all of the passages that featured an angel likely referred to the 1823 visitation of the Angel Moroni, and not to the 1820 First Vision. He makes this claim even for unmistakable First Vision settings where it is an angel that brings the answer to First Vision questions, and *not* the Father and/or the Son.[30]

Second, he argues that the word angel applies to any heavenly visitor and could therefore be fairly used to refer to the Father and the Son.[31] Berrett appealed to Jerald and Sandra to stay in the church and extended an invitation to a face-to-face meeting.[32]

They met on October 26, 1960, and Jerald and Sandra found Berrett cordial and laid back, friendly, totally relaxed, and utterly unruffled discussing the problems they were having with the early LDS Church. When they raised the issue of the sermons in which Brigham Young taught that Adam was God, Berrett placidly asked for references. After looking at their list of passages he casually pushed it aside and said his list was "twice that long." "Just Brigham's opinion," Berrett observed cheerfully, "not official doctrine. Brigham said lots of confusing things. Just focus on what the current prophet says, that is the safest course."

Jerald and Sandra moved on to the issue of changes in the early revelations. Berrett nodded sympathetically, "Yes," he said, "there had been some small confusion there as well ... but God delivers his truth, as it were, 'line upon line and precept upon precept.'" Berrett informed them that a new edition of the Doctrine and Covenants was even then being produced that would clarify the changed revelations. Such an edition never materialized.

Berrett projected an air of contagious confidence. Jerald and Sandra much preferred his kindness to Richards's hostility. Still his approach to things could never be theirs. They wanted substance and found his responses lacking.

What played out among the three was a scene that would often repeat itself among those troubled by the LDS Church's past and those who had somehow made peace with it. Issues that concerned

30. See, e.g., Berrett's response to Brigham Young (*Journal of Discourses* 2:171), Wilford Woodruff (2:196–97), and George A. Smith (12:333–34); William E. Berrett to [J]erald and Sandra Tanner, Oct 7, 1960, 4–5.

31. Berrett to Tanner and Tanner, 4.

32. Berrett to Tanner and Tanner, 7 and 1.

Jerald and Sandra Tanner were minor curiosities to Berrett. He was no naïve family member or confident apostle doubling down on topics he knew little about. He was aware, untroubled, and confident he could ultimately make everything match up. Jerald and Sandra weren't so sure. They liked Berrett, but they had reached an impasse.

Was Berrett's approach to LDS history unreasonable? Was the Tanners'? Jerald and Sandra had not, as some critics would later charge, created an impossible standard for the church to abide by. They were raised in the faith; they had gone to church; Sandra had attended seminary daily in high school, and then institute. Both knew that the LDS Church revered its leaders, past and present, with a devotion that approached deification. Berrett could tell the Tanners that something was "just Brigham [Young's] opinion," but such an explanation would not be welcome in an LDS Sunday school or a college institute class. Suggesting that a prophet and president of the church was expressing an opinion, with the parallel implication that he could be wrong about something, would likely have been met with scorn and even anger in a church setting. Mormons like Jerald and Sandra had been taught their entire lives to follow the prophets and to take the words of past leaders as scripture. They were, in other words, only holding the church to the standard its leaders and members had created.

This formative chapter closed on November 25, 1960, when LeGrand Richards told Sandra's mother that he was bowing out of further interaction. "If I felt that your daughter and her husband really wanted to know the truth," Richards wrote, "I would put myself out to do most anything to help them but I am convinced … that they do not want to know that Joseph Smith was a prophet."[33]

---

33. Richards to McGee, Nov. 28, 1960, 2.

5

QUESTIONING THE BOOK OF MORMON

Jerald and Sandra Tanner had questioned the official LDS account of the First Vision and the changes to Joseph Smith's earliest revelations. They had been accused of impertinence by two of the most visible LDS apostles, LeGrand Richards and Joseph Fielding Smith. They had each experienced a powerful conversion to Jesus, something that had not happened in the LDS Church. They had published pamphlets questioning the veracity of Mormon foundations. It is therefore easy to forget that their doubts about the validity of the Restoration were not washed away by a sudden torrent, but by a constant, steady stream. It is easier still to picture Jerald and Sandra devoting all their time to poring over old documents, printing off tracts, and licking stamps and addressing envelopes. But they were a young married couple in love. Sandra had given birth to their first daughter, April, in the spring of 1960. Jerald and Sandra remained in California until July 1960, when they moved to Salt Lake City, but paused only long enough to drop off their belongings at the home of Jerald's parents and spend a few days before heading on to Missouri for a short visit with the little Basement Church group. On July 25, 1960, Jerald and Sandra, along with the two-month-old April and Jerald's sister Irene, traveled to Independence by train.

On August 2, Sandra was baptized by Pastor Hancock. Pauline had been hesitant to baptize Sandra unless she felt sure of her testimony of the divine origin of the Book of Mormon. Sandra did have doubts about the book, which Pauline had been able to answer to her satisfaction. Privately Jerald regarded Sandra's satisfaction with Pauline's explanations as a sort of sign to him that he should continue to hold on to his crumbling faith in the Book of Mormon's authenticity.

Jerald did not share his doubts with Sandra, but he had already expressed them to Pauline in a letter several months earlier. "I am really getting more faith in Christ," he wrote. "At the same time though I have lost faith in the Book of Mormon. It just won't seem to meet the tests like the Bible."[1] The questions in the letter reveal that Jerald was particularly having doubts in four areas.

The first was Joseph Smith's use of the same seer stone in his treasure digging to also translate the Book of Mormon and receive revelations published in the Book of Commandments.[2] In the *History of the Church* Joseph Smith tells of having both the gold plates and the Urim and Thummim taken away from him after Martin Harris lost the first 116 pages of the Book of Mormon manuscript in the summer of 1828. Although the pages were never recovered, Smith claimed that the plates were returned to him soon after, and "the former heavenly messenger appeared and handed to me the Urim and Thummim *again*."[3] The use of the word "again" seems to imply that the angel returned to Smith the same miraculous spectacles the prophet had found with the plates and had been using previously.[4] However, the only Urim and Thummim that witnesses to the translation process seemed to be aware of after the loss of the 116 pages were not the miraculous spectacles found buried with the gold plates, but the seer stones Smith had previously used in his treasure digging ventures. Pauline's group denied that Joseph Smith had used the same stone for divination and treasure hunting as he had for translating the Book of Mormon. Instead, they believed he used the stone that was given to him with the plates after the loss of 116 pages. But Jerald was now beginning to see that the evidence didn't support that. He wrote to Pauline: "Martin Harris talks of having the stone when he was scribe, (Historical Record) this was before the first 116 pages were complete."

Second, Jerald noticed that one of the Book of Commandment prophesies that came through the stone endorsed Oliver Cowdery's

---

1. Jerald Tanner to Pauline Hancock, ca. Dec. 1959, Tanner and Tanner, Papers.

2. That is, the 2nd through the 15th revelations. According to Whitmer: "The revelations in the Book of Commandments up to June, 1829, were given through the 'stone,' through which the Book of Mormon was translated," *An Address to All Believers in Christ*, 53.

3. Roberts, *History of the Church*, 1:20–23.

4. Smith gives the same impression in the Wentworth Letter in the *Chicago Democrat* (1842), *Times and Seasons*, Mar. 1, 1842, 707.

use of the divining rod: "You [Oliver] have another gift, which is the gift of working with the rod: behold it has told you things: behold there is no other power, save God, that can cause this rod of nature, to work in your hands, for it is the work of God."[5] This was in conflict with Deuteronomy 18:9–11, which led Jerald to ask Pauline, "is it possible that Joseph could have been inspired on the book of Mormon and then have false revelations of the same time," and through the same stone?

Third, there were contradictions between the Bible and Book of Mormon teachings, including, for example, their conflicting understandings of priesthood: "If High Priests don't continue after Christ; why then do priest continue in the Book of Mormon. I cannot find any reference to priest in the bible after Christ."

Then fourth, there was the extensive verbatim quotations of the King James Bible sown throughout the Book of Mormon. The problem, Jerald noted, extended to include even words added by the King James translators that hadn't been in the original Greek or Hebrew: "In the King James Bible where it says that charity is not easily provoked [compare 1 Cor. 13:5 to Moro. 7:45]. The word easily was added by the translators but it is also inserted in the Book of Mormon."[6]

At one point, historian LaMar Petersen recalled raising similar issues with Jerald:

> I would say to him, "Jerald, it seems to me that Mormonism is one package; I don't think you can split it down the middle. After all, the sequence of scriptural reference in the Doctrine and Covenants is an extension, you might say, of the Book of Mormon period, and you can't say that that's of the devil, as you're saying, and that the Book of Mormon is of God when obviously it's a continuation of the same line of thought. You've got to see Mormonism as a whole; not as two kinds of things."[7]

---

5. Book of Commandments, 7:3 (19). Beginning with the 1835 edition of the Doctrine & Covenants the references to the rod were replaced by the words "gift of Aaron" (see D&C 8:6–7).

6. Adam Clarke had written: "How the word *easily* got into our translation is hard to say; but, however it got in, it is utterly improper, and has nothing in the original to countenance it." Clarke's *Commentary*, 6:268). Jerald and Sandra bought a complete set of Clarke's Commentary at some point before they moved back to Salt Lake City from California in July 1960.

7. Petersen, "Memoirs of Lamar Petersen," 2:42.

But, as Jerald kept on promoting the Book of Mormon even after such conversations, Petersen concluded that he was sure it was "not my influence that changed his point of view." Jerald, he said, "is far too good a scholar to be led very far by anyone else. He does his own thinking; his own research; and I think in time he came to see the whole thing, the whole package of Mormonism, was indeed one and was misrepresented, i.e., it was not the one true church." Petersen was right. Jerald was not likely to easily fall under the sway of others, even those whom he respected highly like Pauline and Petersen. Nevertheless, questions like these showed that Jerald had been listening, whether Petersen realized it or not.

Pauline's response to Jerald's questions was kind and adhered to her group's belief that Joseph Smith was only called to reveal the Book of Mormon; she suggested that Jerald rely only on the Bible and the Book of Mormon and forget about the Book of Commandments, the Doctrine and Covenants, and anything that followed.[8] This was in line with their adherence to David Whitmer, who thought it inappropriate to publish any revelations: "Publishing the early revelations, or any of them, was contrary to the will of the Lord. ... The revelations in the Book of Commandments up to June 1829 ... are the only revelations that can be relied upon, and they are not law."[9]

Pauline's responses to Jerald were typical and followed a pattern he often heard from Mormon leaders. Jerald, she said, had experienced a profound feelings of acceptance and love in her group, so what did all of these issues matter? Jerald was certain, to the end of his life, that the love of Christ he'd experienced in such an unprecedented way in Pauline's group was real, but he would come to believe that it did not necessarily follow that the Book of Mormon was the divine word of God. "Actually I would like to believe the Book of Mormon is true," he told her. "My prejudice leans toward it instead of away from it. I pray about it all the time, but as yet I have received no answer." Jerald also enclosed some money and wrote, "Use the money to spread the good news. I think we could have given you

---

8. Pauline Hancock to Jerald Tanner, Jan. 20, 1960, Tanner and Tanner, Papers.
9. Whitmer, *An Address to all Believers in Christ*, 53.

Historian LaMar Petersen playing the organ at Jerald
and Sandra's daughter April's wedding.

much more, but we are not sure of the Book of Mormon, and I don't
really want to support a thing unless I am sure of it."[10]

Jerald's letter to Pauline marked the beginning of the end for his
and Sandra's belief in the Book of Mormon. Several factors over the
next two years contributed to this. Their ongoing conversations with
LaMar Petersen influenced them, but another person came into
their lives who had an equally significant impact: Wesley P. Walters,
a United Presbyterian pastor in Marissa, Illinois. Walters had contributed an article on Mormonism to the December 19, 1960, issue
of *Christianity Today*.[11] In two-and-a-half pages, Walters displayed a
remarkable grasp of Mormonism's teachings, history, and doctrines.

Though he doesn't pull any punches in stating historical and
theological difficulties, Walters's tone in the article was respectful,
and he described the Mormons as a people who "boast an extraordinarily well-organized welfare system and a love of culture and the

---

10. Jerald Tanner to Pauline Hancock, Feb. 27, 1960, Tanner and Tanner, Papers.
11. Wesley P. Walters, "Mormonism," *Christianity Today*, Dec. 19, 1960, 8–10 (228–30).

good things of life."[12] He even "flew to Salt Lake City for a week to substantiate facts with Mormon leaders." It's clear that LDS leaders were not the only people in Salt Lake whom he consulted with, since he also cites LaMar Petersen's *Problems in Mormon Text* (1957) and an "unpublished manuscript" by James D. Wardle. [13]

Walters had neither met nor consulted with the Tanners when he wrote the article, but at some point he learned of their work and visited them while in Salt Lake City in 1961. It became the basis for a lifelong friendship. They also never forgot something he said during that first visit: "I can see you guys love the Lord, but I just don't understand why you're still holding onto the Book of Mormon."[14]

Walters was not the only significant visitor the Tanners had that year. Pauline Hancock and her close friends, Olive Wilcox and Barbara Moore, traveled to Salt Lake City in September 1961. Sadly, Pauline was suffering from an illness that would kill her scarcely more than a year later. The problem had started three years before, or so Pauline imagined, at a church picnic. Some of the members decided to have a game of baseball, and a foul ball went astray and struck Pauline on one of her breasts, injuring it badly. Over time, the injury, rather than healing, formed a hard lump. When the lump showed no signs of improving, she consulted a doctor who told her she had breast cancer. By the time she visited Salt Lake City in the fall of 1961, the cancer had progressed to the point that a large festering wound had developed on the side of her breast. Wilcox and Moore nursed Pauline through her sickness, tenderly cleaning out the open wound and replacing the bandage each day.

Jerald and Sandra were deeply moved by the care Wilcox and Moore gave, which reflected the mutual love and support that characterized Pauline's little group. During their visit, Pauline called Jerald and Sandra to the motel where she was staying. She was eager that they see the open sore caused by the cancer. In their presence, with Wilcox and Moore assisting, she lifted her arm, and they uncovered just enough of the affected area for Jerald and Sandra to view the full extent of the ravages of the cancer. "I want you to see

---

12. Walters, 8.
13. Walters.
14. Tanner, Reminiscences.

Wes Walters in the mid-1980s with his grandson and Jerald.

this," she said, "so that if God heals me you will know it was real."[15] As Sandra reflects on this, she sees two motivations. First, that Hancock wanted Jerald and Sandra to be witnesses to her hoped-for healing, so that when she testified to it afterward she would have living witnesses; and second, that when she was healed, they would be strengthened in their own faith. "But you must remember," Pauline went on to say, "if I die, don't blame the Lord, blame my lack of faith!" She passed away on October 10, 1962, less than a month before her sixtieth birthday.

Pauline's pronouncement did not leave open a third explanation:

15. Tanner.

that death is no respecter of persons or faiths and eventually comes for us all. Pauline's small group was never of the health-and-wealth Christian variety that shunned medical care as a failure to believe. Yet Pauline apparently came to believe that if she died of cancer, it was due to a lack of faith. At the time Jerald and Sandra simply took her words at face value, with the result that when Pauline *did* die, it left them with a conundrum: If Pauline Hancock, the most authentically believing Christian they could imagine, did not have enough faith to be healed, what hope could there be for the rest of us?

As Jerald's faith continued to evolve, a particularly difficult point was the literary dependence of the Book of Mormon on the King James Bible. He became convinced that if the Book of Mormon were true, then the King James Bible had somehow been made miraculously available to the ancient pre-Christian Nephites.[16] Jerald's efforts to make this work didn't last long though, and he ultimately abandoned the whole enterprise of laboring to rescue the Book of Mormon.

Sandra held onto belief in the Book of Mormon longer than Jerald. She read both the Bible and the Book of Mormon every day, and she began to detect a puzzling difference in emphasis between the two. She found that the Bible had more to say about personal spiritual growth, while the Book of Mormon seemed to be more about the mechanics of religious practice.

It was, appropriately, a book that struck the final blow for Sandra's belief in the Book of Mormon. She read the Rev. Martin T. Lamb's *The Golden Bible: Or, the Book of Mormon: Is It From God?* (1887).[17] Lamb gave a series of four lectures in June 1884 in Salt Lake City, where he was serving as assistant pastor at the First Baptist Church. The lectures were so successful that Lamb's final address was moved to the large Walker Opera House.[18] The First Baptist Church voted unanimously to encourage Lamb to publish the lectures. Other

---

16. For more on King James English in the Book of Mormon, see Stan Larson, "The Historicity of the Matthean Sermon on the Mount in 3 Nephi," in Metcalfe, *New Approaches*, 115–63; Wunderli, *Imperfect Book*; Huggins, "Joseph Smith's 'Inspired Translation' of Romans 7," in Waterman, *Prophet Puzzle*, 259–87; and "Did the Author of 3 Nephi Know the Gospel of Matthew?" For defenses of King James English in the Book of Mormon, see Sperry, *Book of Mormon Compendium*, and Belnap, "King James Bible."

17. Lamb, *Golden Bible*.

18. Lamb, ix.

prominent local figures, including Utah Governor Eli H. Murray and Robert G. McNiece, pastor of Salt Lake City's First Presbyterian Church, also urged Lamb to publish.[19]

The handbills for the original lectures had promised "a calm, earnest discussion, entirely free from any abuse or slander or ill will," but, in print, Sandra found the book offensive. Still she braced herself with a determination to overlook Lamb's tone and focus on evaluating his arguments. By the time she reached the end of the book's 344 pages, she was finished with the Book of Mormon as well. Her belief in it had evaporated completely.

What Sandra found particularly eye-opening was Lamb's comparison of real ancient American writing with the alleged "Reformed Egyptian" characters transcribed from the Book of Mormon plates.[20] "They obviously bore no similarity," Sandra recalled.[21] She was also struck with Lamb's exposition of the difficulties in accepting the Book of Mormon proposition that the pre-Christian Nephites had been informed about all the intricacies of New Testament teaching and doctrine while the prophets and authors of the Hebrew Old Testament seemingly had not.[22] But the point that struck her most decisively related to a statement in Mosiah 2:3: "And they also took of the firstlings of their flocks, that they might offer sacrifices and burnt offerings according to the law of Moses." At first glance, the verse might seem benign, but Lamb explained,

> According to the law of Moses the *firstlings* of their flocks were *never* offered as *burnt offerings* or *sacrifices*. All *firstlings* belonged to the Lord, *de jure*, and could not be counted as a man's personal property—whereas, all burnt offerings, or sacrifices for sin of every kind, must be selected from the man's own personal property, or be purchased with his own money for that purpose, while all *firstlings* of the flock, as the Lord's property, came into the hands of the high priest, and by him could be offered up as a *peace offering*, not as a *burnt offering* or a *sin* offering,

---

19. Lamb, vii; McNiece later contributed the article on "Mormonism" to the famous series of religiously influential booklets issued during the second decade of the twentieth century entitled *The Fundamentals*.

20. Lamb, *Golden Bible*, chap. 8 and appendix B.

21. Tanner, Reminiscences.

22. Lamb, *Golden Bible*, chap. 5.

himself and family eating the flesh. (See Ex. 13:2,12 and 22:29,30; Numb. 3:13; 2d Sam. 24:24; Numb. 18:15–18 and other places.)[23]

This, she reasoned, was not the kind of error an ancient Jewish person, steeped in the traditions of the Law of Moses, would make. The principle of the firstborn's belonging to the Lord was bound up with the Exodus story, which was recited in the annual Jewish Passover Seder. On the night of the Exodus, God killed all the firstborn of Egypt but spared the firstborn of the Israelites who had sprinkled the blood of the Passover lamb on their doorposts. Henceforth, every firstborn of Israel, whether human or animal, belonged to the Lord. Among the many arguments put forward by Lamb that impressed Sandra, it was in this point in particular that Joseph Smith revealed himself as the author of the Book of Mormon.

In 1962 and 1963, Jerald wrote a number of longer tracts including a twenty-eight-page booklet, *The Facts about the Book of Mormon*, in which he first publicly questioned its validity. When the people at Pauline's church, now under the leadership of Eugene and Olive Wilcox, learned that Jerald had written on the Book of Mormon, they put in an order for multiple copies. Jerald and Sandra wrote back saying that perhaps they should start with only one copy, since they might not agree with the conclusions of the tract.

The timing between Pauline's death and Jerald's public rejection of the Book of Mormon suggests that Jerald might have postponed his open rejection of the book until after Pauline's death to spare the feelings of this woman who had meant so much to him. But Sandra is confident that if Jerald had rejected the Book of Mormon before she died, he would not have hesitated to tell Pauline.[24] When Pauline's church learned of Jerald and Sandra's rejection of the book, they grieved but did not reject them. On the contrary, their bond of affection and Christian fellowship were preserved.

Jerald's tract took a similar approach to his previous inquiries, asking questions and providing answers. But these answers were suggestive, not declarative; he aimed at persuasion more than defending his own reasons for giving up the Book of Mormon. He was

---

23. Lamb, 109, emphasis in original.
24. Tanner, Reminiscences.

especially sensitive in his treatment of the seer stone. Pauline's group was eager to deny that Smith had used the same stone for treasure digging that he did for translating the Book of Mormon, and the LDS Church was eager to deny that he had used anything besides the Urim and Thummim to translate the book. Jerald raised the possibility that Smith used the same stone for both, but does not mount a sustained case to prove the point.[25]

The Tanners still had difficulty admitting they no longer believed in the Book of Mormon. Giving it up was much more difficult for them than leaving the LDS Church. "Even when I had decided in my mind that I did not believe the 'Book of Mormon,' any longer," Sandra told the *New York Times* in 1965, "it was months before I could say it out loud."[26]

Jerald gave up the Book of Mormon in the same year that Kate Carter, president of the Daughters of Utah Pioneers, published her *Denominations that Base Their Beliefs on the Teachings of Joseph Smith*. She included a profile of Pauline's group and of Jerald. He had sent a list of beliefs to Carter who described the "youthful Jerald Tanner" as head of a Salt Lake City branch of the group, which she called the Church of Christ Independent. Jerald's first item of faith was, ironically, "We believe the Bible and the Book of Mormon to be the word of God." He accurately described Pauline's group and had not yet renounced his faith in the book when he sent his statement to Carter, showing how fluid his beliefs were during 1961 and 1962. His next statement of faith repudiated what he felt was too much of an LDS emphasis on church leaders: "We do not believe in holding up any man, but rather in holding up Christ."[27] Apart from the first line about the Book of Mormon, Jerald's declaration of faith was closely aligned to mainstream Protestant beliefs about grace, Christ, and salvation.

Reading Carter's pamphlet, one might assume that Jerald was the dynamic leader of a new restorationist sect. That assumption would be mistaken; he was only offering a brief explanation of the Hancock group's beliefs. While Jerald and Sandra never ceased their

---

25. Tanner, *Facts about the Book of Mormon*.
26. Wallace Turner, "Mormons Gain Despite Tensions," *New York Times*, Dec. 27, 1965, 18A.
27. Carter, *Denominations*, 51.

fellowship with Pauline's group, they could no longer think of themselves as primarily associated with them. With the birth of their second child, Dennis, on December 7, 1962, Sandra was feeling the need to settle their growing family in among a group of Christians.

It had never occurred to Jerald before becoming a Christian to seek the truth in ecclesiastical organizations with no connection to Joseph Smith. When he did find what he was looking for, it was not in an ecclesiastical organization, but in a person—Jesus Christ. He came to embrace mainstream Christian biblical beliefs about the church: it consisted of those who have been born again of the Spirit, joined to Christ, becoming a new creation in him. After their conversion, both Jerald and Sandra felt completely at ease meeting and worshipping with Christians anywhere.

Even before they gave up the Book of Mormon, the Tanners had visited a number of churches. They tried Bethel Baptist Church, and the legendary John Hornock's Church, where, despite his holding to a "once saved always saved" position, they enjoyed listening to his sermons and attending his Wednesday night Bible studies. They enjoyed the biblical preaching at the (Dutch) Christian Reformed Church on the corner of Ninth South and Eighth East but, coming from their LDS background, couldn't get used to the general practice of the men gathering on the front steps after service to enjoy the fellowship of having a smoke together. Being a dominantly ethnic Church (Dutch) even to this day, the Christian Reformed Christians did not include avoiding alcohol and tobacco in their definition of clean living, as Mormons and many conservative American Christians did both then and now. The Tanners also attended the Nazarene Church on Indiana Avenue, which was perhaps closest in its doctrine to where they were (when Pauline's group eventually disbanded, a large number of their members became Nazarenes). They ultimately found a connection with the little Gospel Assembly Church founded by the Greek Pentecostal Chris Christopulos at 1840 South 800 East in Salt Lake City. Christopulos's son, Bill, who usually preached on Sunday, greatly respected Pauline Hancock, counting her "a Mother in Israel." She had even preached in his church. Jerald and Sandra also became fast friends with the little Gospel Assembly's assistant pastor, Bob Sloan, and his wife, Margie.

On Sunday afternoons, several members from the church would go uptown to have a service at the old Salt Lake County jail. Sandra helped Chris Christopulos with preaching to the inmates, until he became too old and weak to carry on; then he turned the prison ministry over to her. Since they were ministering in the jail on behalf of a Pentecostal church, the gift of tongues, or rather Jerald and Sandra's lack of it, continued to be an issue. Sandra was often praised for her excellent teaching, but the praise was regularly followed up with an additional comment on how, if she could just get the baptism of the Holy Spirit, she would then be able to really preach! In the Pentecostal tradition, speaking in tongues (or glossolalia) was deemed to be the "initial evidence" of having received the Holy Spirit—often called the baptism of the Holy Spirit. If you didn't speak in tongues, you didn't have the baptism of the Holy Spirit.

Neither she nor Jerald had as yet grasped New Testament teachings on the distribution of spiritual gifts, but Sandra was open and desirous for the gift. Pentecostals taught that God would give the gift of tongues to anyone who sincerely asked for it. She asked for it but wasn't given it. She sometimes found herself thinking how easy it would be for her to simply fake it—to sputter out some disconnected sequences of syllables and be done with the problem; but the idea of faking the gift of tongues troubled her. She ultimately concluded (in agreement, as it happens, with the Apostle Paul in 1 Corinthians 12:29–31) that God gives some the gift of tongues in connection with their receiving the baptism of the Holy Spirit and others (including her and Jerald) the baptism of the Holy Spirit without tongues but with one or more of the other spiritual gifts mentioned in 1 Corinthians 12.

By the end of 1962, the Tanners could see that they would not ultimately make their home in the Pentecostal churches. In January 1963, Sandra visited a local Salt Lake City Christian bookstore, Tom and Nellie Constance's Northwest Books, and asked Nellie for her recommendations for good books on the deeper spiritual life. Nellie recommended A. W. Tozer, beginning with his classic, *The Pursuit of God*.

Sandra shared her thoughts about the issue of tongues, and Nellie pointed her to a poem by A. B. [Albert Benjamin] Simpson entitled

"Himself" that was especially meaningful to Sandra. The point of the poem was simple: Christians are not to be all taken up with the Lord's gifts, but with the Lord *himself.*

> Once it was the blessing,
> Now it is the Lord;
> Once it was the feeling,
> Now it is His Word;
> Once His gift I wanted,
> Now, the Giver own;
> Once I sought for healing,
> Now Himself alone.[28]

Nellie invited Sandra and Jerald to a Bible study she and her husband held every Sunday morning. The Constances' group grew, and the new church affiliated with the Christian & Missionary Alliance (C&MA) denomination founded by A. B. Simpson, and whose most prominent teacher was A. W. Tozer. In 1963, the year Jerald and Sandra first began to move in their circles, the C&MA stated its view on the gift of tongues in a little couplet that in the meantime has become standard to them: "Seek Not, Forbid Not."[29]

The Alliance is a relatively small denomination and, except for Tozer, is not in any sense as well known as the Presbyterians, Methodists, or Baptists. As a result, their views and teachings are often not well understood. Nowhere is this more apparent than when LDS writers have attempted to describe them while responding to the Tanners.[30]

Jerald and Sandra formally joined the Alliance church around 1969 or 1970. It was in any case soon after Bill Gaube came to serve as pastor in 1968 and before they were described as members by a BYU student paper by Robert R. Black in May 1970.[31] When

28. Thompson, *Life of A. B. Simpson,* 68.

29. Neinkirchen, *A. B. Simpson, and the Pentecostal Movement,* 139–40. The C&MA seeks a middle path between Christian denominations that over emphasize the gift of tongues and those that forbid it. In 1 Corinthians 14:39 the Apostle Paul actually forbids forbidding the exercise of the gift in the church: "do not forbid speaking in tongues."

30. See, for example, Durham Jr., "Institute of Religion Faculty Forum," 10, who erroneously identified the Alliance as "a kind of a liberal evangelical Christian group ... an offshoot of the Presbyterian Church." Durham was wrong on both counts.

31. Bill Gaube, email to Sandra Tanner, Apr. 20, 2015, in Tanner and Tanner, Papers; and Black, "Bibliography," iv.

they finally did present themselves, they were interrogated in the membership interview by a doctrinally astute old member named Brother Richard Rider. If you passed muster with Rider, you were in. He grilled them on their testimony of being born again and their doctrinal views; but interestingly the issue of the Baptism of the Holy Spirit as something subsequent to the New Birth, a standard part of C&MA teaching both then and now, never came up. Soon after they formally joined, Jerald raised an important concern. Pastor Gaube recalls an early encounter with Jerald:

> One thing that I remember vividly is Jerald coming to me after church with a very earnest, almost stern demeanor. … He told in no uncertain terms that he came to church to hear the Word of God and the moment I started to attack Mormons, or demean them, he would get up and walk out and never come back. This made a deep impact on me as I realized he really did love Mormons and it solidified my determination to focus on Christ in my preaching.[32]

Jerald would serve for many years on the governing board and as an elder in the Salt Lake Christian Missionary Alliance (now called Discovery Christian Community). Tom and Nellie Constance continued to run their bookstore and various other ministries until their retirement. Their daughter Connie married a Presbyterian named Jeff Silliman who went on to serve as pastor of numerous Utah churches and as president of the now-defunct Salt Lake Theological Seminary. He would eventually become the head of the Presbytery of Utah, retiring from the post at the end of 2020. The Tanners had centered their faith in Christ, and they had found a Christian community to support them along the way.

---

32. Gaube email.

6

THE STRUGGLE TO REPRINT
THE BOOK OF COMMANDMENTS

Today a quick internet search of terms such as "How do I leave the LDS Church?" finds numerous websites filled with answers. Write a letter, say the right things, send it to the right people, and within a certain amount of time confirmation arrives: You are no longer a member of the church. Before moving to California with Sandra, Jerald asked to have his name removed from the membership rolls and had been assured by a member of the stake presidency that it would be done. It wasn't until the Tanners returned to Utah and were living with Jerald's parents in his old ward that his sister, Irene, came home from the ward one Sunday and said he was still on the ward list.[1] So he wrote again, this time to the LDS Church president, and his request was referred to Bishop Alma E. Kehl of the Cannon Seventh Ward in Salt Lake City. But no letter would suffice; to be removed from the church, like Sandra before him, Jerald had to be formally excommunicated. He was summoned to appear with witnesses for a bishop's court on August 14, 1960. But when he arrived with Sandra and his mother, Helen, as witnesses, he was told they could not be present.

> I walked into the room alone, and they shut the door. They asked me if I would mind if they made a tape recording of the proceedings. I permitted them to make the recording but asked if I could also make a recording. The answer was no. They asked me if I wanted to plead guilty to the "alleged wrongdoing" of requesting my name to be removed from the Church records and teaching doctrines not in harmony with the Church. I replied that I did not believe my actions were "wrong" in these regards, and therefore could not plead guilty, but that I wanted my name

---

1. Tanner, Recollections.

removed without the use of the expression "wrongdoing." This caused a great deal of confusion among the members of the "Bishop's Court," and they did not know how to proceed. After conversing among themselves they decided to proceed without the admission of "wrongdoing" on my part.[2]

On August 28, 1960, Jerald received a letter informing him that he had been excommunicated from the Church of Jesus Christ of Latter-day Saints without mentioning that he had been found guilty of anything. "In accordance with your request your name has been removed from the records and you are no longer considered a member of the said Church."[3]

On Saturday, February 18, 1961, Hugh Nibley, the well-known BYU professor of religion, presented a lecture titled "The Suppression of the First Vision" at the BYU campus in the midst of a winter storm.[4] Nibley projected an aura of academic seriousness onto the study of LDS scriptures. In 1961 he was in his fifties, handsome, tall, thin, blue-eyed, and silver haired—he looked every bit the scholar, and many Mormons revered him. But this feeling was not universal, since he had the reputation of relying on mockery and ridicule to win arguments against his opponents rather than reasoned analysis based on the careful and respectful handling of evidence. Historian LaMar Petersen, for example, who served for eighteen years on the advisory board of the *Utah Historical Quarterly* and was an honorary life member of the Utah State Historical Society, echoed the opinion of many others when he wrote to Nibley damning his work as "shallow and facetious." "You have belittled the scholars," Petersen wrote, "and extolled fraudulence."[5] At the time Jerald and Sandra had yet to form a clear opinion of Nibley, and given their interest in the First Vision they were eager to attend Nibley's lectures.

---

2. Tanner and Tanner, *Mormonism: Shadow or Reality?*, 574.

3. Tanner and Tanner, 575, in which a copy of the letter appears.

4. This was the title Sandra used to refer to the lecture in a letter to her mother (Feb. 17–21, 1961), 6, which is consistent with the contents of the typescript of the speech. The typescript was likely made from a recording of the lecture by someone other than Nibley. The person who produced it was not able, for example, to make out the name of Nibley's great-grandfather. A rough-draft typescript of the presentation exists and was reproduced some years ago by FARMS in its Occasional Papers Series.

5. LaMar Petersen to Hugh Nibley, Feb. 17, 1968, 1.

To their surprise, the event cost $8 per person, which was a considerable amount of money in those days, and left them with too little for both to go. Sandra urged Jerald to attend Nibley's lecture while she read in the BYU library, but Jerald decided to go to the library with her to find out what it had in its collection. They discovered a gold mine of early sources on microfilm. The young student at the special collections desk did not know how to work the microfilm copying machine but, seeing that Jerald did, invited him to make whatever copies he wanted and pay for them after. Sandra and Jerald set to work, copying early Mormon newspapers, sermons, and books, including the Book of Commandments, addresses on blood atonement, the *Deseret News*, the *Millennial Star*, the *Elders' Journal*, the *Evening and Morning Star*,[6] the diary of Wandle Mace, reprints of early LDS scriptures, letters between general authorities on polygamy, and more. It was an embarrassment of riches, and their only regret was they did not have more money to make even more copies.[7]

Copying the first forty-one pages of the Book of Commandments that day would lead to their first photomechanical reprint of an early Mormon document. As for Nibley's lecture, they got to read it when it became the basis of a series of articles in the 1961 July through November issues of the LDS Church-owned *Improvement Era* magazine, titled "Censoring the Joseph Smith Story." Nibley wrote about his great-grandfather, Alexander Neibaur, and claimed he had recorded the First Vision in his journal. He argued that Neibaur did not share the story "because it was a sacred and privileged communication; it was never published before the world and never should be."[8]

Nibley's comments tantalized the Tanners and others trying to track down sources on the First Vision. The story sounded suspicious and too convenient. The passage from Neibaur's journal, May 24, 1844, twenty-four years after the traditional dating of the First Vision, did eventually become available despite Nibley's stated

---

6. The *Deseret News, Millennial Star, Elders' Journal,* and *Evening and Morning Star* are all early Mormon newspapers, valuable to researchers for their contemporary content, reprinted journal excerpts, recollections of church leaders, early accounts of Mormon origins, and histories of the church otherwise unavailable to researchers at LDS Church archives at the time. Today, they are available online.

7. Sandra Tanner to Georgia McGee, Feb. 17–21, 1961, 6–7, Tanner and Tanner, Papers.

8. Hugh Nibley, "Censoring the Joseph Smith Story," *Improvement Era*, July 1961, 522.

conviction that it was too sacred for publication. It largely conformed to the official 1838 account.[9]

Jerald and Sandra had sought access to Neibaur's journal for some time, since this was not the first time Nibley had written about it. In his 1954 *The World and the Prophets*, Nibley said that Neibaur "cross-examined Joseph Smith on every minute detail of the First Vision and of how the Prophet satisfied him promptly and completely. From that day he never doubted the calling of the Prophet."[10] Nibley's writing portrayed his great-grandfather as a tough-minded skeptic, when he actually was more of a mystic and student of the Kabbalah. He joined Mormonism after he believed a supernatural dream directed him to be baptized.[11] Sandra, anxious to read Neibaur's account, wrote to Nibley on January 4, 1961, a little more than a month before his lecture at BYU. "I am quite interested in your grandfather's [*sic*] diary ... and I wonder if it would be possible to obtain a copy of it? If this is not possible, do you have a copy of his diary that I could read?"[12]

Nibley responded: "my great-grandfather heard that remarkable account of the First Vision ... and for 40 years after he never mentioned it to a soul. Therefore, when I came across the story unexpectedly I handed the book over to Joseph Fielding Smith and it is now where it belongs—in a safe."[13] Armed with this information, the Tanners sent $10 to Joseph Fielding Smith requesting a microfilm of the Neibaur journal. On March 13, 1961, Smith returned the money and responded, "Private journals are filed in this office with the understanding that they will be available to members of the family, but not to the general public."

Sandra wrote another request to Nibley, who replied on March 21: "I believe I said in my [first] letter to you that the Neibaur journal now reposes in a safe in the Church Historian's Office, *where it belongs*" (emphasis in original). In the same letter he also claimed that "the last time [he] asked permission to see the Journal, [he]

---

9. Neibaur, Journal, May 24, 1844.

10. Nibley, *World and the Prophets*, 21.

11. See the account of Neibaur in Owens, "Joseph Smith and the Kabbalah," 173–78, 191–94 (esp. 174).

12. Tanner and Tanner, Papers.

13. Hugh Nibley to Mrs. Jerald Tanner, Mar. 8, 1961, Tanner and Tanner, Papers.

was refused."[14] LDS Church historian Leonard Arrington wrote that Nibley's account was not entirely accurate. Nibley did ask to see the diary and was denied by assistant historian William Lund, but "he explained that he had gone to the president of the church, who instructed Lund to let him use it."[15]

Jerald and Sandra were growing savvier in their pursuit of documents. They realized that as church leaders became aware of them, they could ask other people to try to gain access to records they would probably be denied. At times, this approach proved effective. In the Tanners' files is a letter from Joseph Fielding Smith to "Sister Christine Sweet" dated August 29, 1961, responding to a question about the First Vision account in the Alexander Neibaur journal. Smith revealed that the passage contains the words "this is my Beloved Son harken ye him."[16]

After Jerald and Sandra copied and started to publish their treasure trove from BYU, they learned that repercussions had been swift. Jerald explained what happened in an early tract, "They [the LDS Church Historian's Office] became very upset and informed the BYU Library that they were not to allow us to have access to these microfilms of rare documents. Two women [probably Sandra's mother, Georgia, and her aunt Lucille] who went to the BYU Library after this had happened were informed that the Church Historian's Office had instructed the library to make a list of the microfilms they had, so that they would know just what we had access to."[17] Jerald wrote to Chad Flake at BYU Special Collections in early April 1961 for photocopies of the remainder of the Book of Commandments, since they had earlier only obtained the first

---

14. A photocopy of the letter is in Tanner and Tanner, *Mormonism: Shadow or Reality?*, 12.

15. Arrington, *Adventures of a Church Historian*, 16. Sandra would later have occasion herself to test the policy that allows family members to view records penned by their ancestors. But when she requested material written by Brigham Young, she was turned away.

16. It was a number of years before the First Vision passage in Alexander Neibaur's diary was made public. Although it is unclear precisely when the account became available, the entire passage was reproduced in appendix H, Backman, *Joseph Smith's First Vision*. As of 2021, visitors to the LDS Church History Museum can read Alexander Neibaur's First Vision account along with several others at one of the museum's displays.

17. Tanner, *Suppression of the Records*, unpaginated, last page in tract.

forty-one pages. Flake answered, "You would need to secure the permission of the Church Historian's library," since BYU's copy had come from the LDS Church. Flake alluded to their previous success in obtaining copies and hinted that he knew what lengths they were willing to go to: "Unfortunately, none of our professional staff, either in the Special Collections or microfilm area, are on duty on Saturday; and our student assistants are instructed not to make any photocopies. This policy is for their protection, so that they will not be held responsible for copyright violations."[18]

Flake's reasoning was suspect. The Book of Commandments, published in 1833, was long in the public domain and therefore copyright law no longer applied to its reproduction. But it was reasoning Flake used with others, including Pauline Hancock. Flake's explanation—that the church requested that BYU not provide copies of the book—appeared to be genuine.

Jerald recruited the help of William E. Berrett, who had been gracious to both Tanners and their questions. Berrett wrote that he had the same luck with BYU that they did; he was told he would have to go through the Church Historian's Office. Berrett quickly learned that the church was on to the Tanners. Assuming it could not be a coincidence that Berrett was requesting the same document as Jerald and Sandra, the Historian's Office wrote back and told him they could not provide a copy unless he disclosed why he wanted it and whom it was for, mentioning Jerald and Sandra by name. "Apparently," Berrett told them, "the feeling is that you have only one desire in using a copy and that is to attack the Church. I regret that you should have given any cause for them to feel that that is the case."[19]

The Tanners were nothing if not tenacious. They wrote first to Joseph Fielding Smith, who replied, "Private records are sacred to the individual." The Book of Commandments was, of course, not a private record, and when Sandra wrote the letter, she was careful to note that she was requesting copies of the printed book, not the original handwritten manuscript revelations. Next they tried assistant historian A. William Lund, son of deceased First Presidency

---

18. Chad Flake to Jerald Tanner, Apr. 11, 1961, 1. Tanner and Tanner, Papers.

19. William E. Berrett to Jerald and Sandra Tanner, Apr. 24, May 5, 1961, Tanner and Tanner, Papers.

member Anthon H. Lund. He refused her request in a letter dated June 5. They then went all the way to the top, but President David O. McKay also refused to provide any assistance.[20]

The Tanners fared no better with the Reorganized Church of Jesus Christ of Latter Day Saints. RLDS Historian Charles Davies declined them twice.[21] Finally, Jerald and Sandra put in a request with Yale University Library, which saw no difficulty in giving them what they asked for.

One of the more bizarre episodes in the ongoing saga of the Tanners' efforts to reprint an early Mormon text was the apparent attempt by somebody to instigate the destruction of the photocopies of the Book of Commandments copies Jerald and Sandra had obtained that Saturday at BYU.

These copies had originally been printed in the negative, i.e., the print was white and the background black. In order to have this reversed prior to being able to take them to a printer, Jerald and Sandra took them down to John A. Spencer Jr.'s Universal Microfilm Company, then at 141 Pierpont Avenue in Salt Lake City. At the time Universal was the only microfilm company in the Salt Lake Valley and thus had the LDS Church as one of its clients.

As the story was told to Jerald and Sandra by Spencer himself, one day someone from the LDS Church came in and asked Spencer whether someone had recently brought in copies of some pages from the Book of Commandments. Spencer answered that he didn't really pay much attention to what people brought to him, only what they wanted him to do, but that he thought someone might have brought in some Book of Commandments pages. The person then said something to the effect of, "Well, don't you use some sort of chemicals around the shop that might, say, spill 'accidentally' and destroy some copies someone might have brought in for you to work on. I mean, you couldn't be blamed if some chemical 'accidentally' spilled." Spencer, realizing that he was being asked to destroy the Book of Commandments pages Sandra and Jerald had brought to him, tried to laugh it off, saying something to the effect of, "Look, I'm just a business man. I could hardly afford having it get around that I

---

20. Tanner and Tanner, *Case Against Mormonism*, 1:135–37.
21. Tanner and Tanner, 1:86.

have those kind of accidents." But Spencer had realized what he was being asked to do, or at least imagined he did. When Jerald and Sandra went to pick up their order, Spencer told them about the visitor, hinting they might need to be careful whom they did business with.[22]

Once the preparations for their reprint edition of the *Book of Commandments* was complete, the Tanners took it to Woodruff Printing Company. It was a small volume, 5 1/2 by 8 1/2 inches, the first photo reprint edition of the Book of Commandments ever produced. On the original title page was the signature of Wilford Woodruff. Underneath the picture of the title page, they explained, "The first forty-one pages are reproduced from the Wilford Woodruff copy at the Brigham Young University. Pages forty-two through one hundred sixty are reproduced from the Yale University copy." No preface or introduction was bound into the volume, but they did add a four-page insert. The first page gave a brief account of the Tanners' attempts to gain access to the original,[23] the second reproduced Chad Flake's April 11 letter denying access, the third copied the revelation that was Book of Commandments 4 and showed how it had been altered in D&C 5, and the fourth did the same with Book of Commandments 28 (D&C 27).

Jerald and Sandra approached the *Salt Lake Tribune* and the church-owned *Deseret News* about advertising. Both refused to sell them an ad.[24] One of the employees of the Newspaper Agency Corporation told the Tanners that the insert was "too controversial."[25]

Adding insult to injury, Chad Flake in *Brigham Young University Studies* attacked the quality of Jerald and Sandra's reprint of the Book of Commandments, complaining that "it has pages which are

---

22. Tanner and Tanner, *The Case Against Mormonism*, 1:51–52; Tanner, Recollections.

23. Including an early account of the shakeup that followed their making photocopies during their February visit to BYU: "When the L.D.S. Church Historian's Office found out that we had obtained these photographs, they immediately sent word to the Brigham Young University to keep us from obtaining any more photo-copies of these rare documents."

24. Although the *Tribune* and the *Deseret News* differed in ownership and editorial content, both papers had founded the Newspaper Agency Corporation, a joint operating agreement to share printing and advertising costs. It gave the corporation some control over what kind of ads were accepted by both newspapers.

25. Tanner and Tanner, *Case Against Mormonism*, 1:52.

completely unreadable."[26] Left unsaid, of course, was how Flake or the LDS Church's cooperation could have greatly improved the print quality of the Tanners' reprint. It is the first forty-one pages that are the worst quality: the pages obtained from BYU. Although they could have used the Yale copy for their entire reprint, Jerald felt it was important to use a copy in the church's possession.

Even after the Tanners produced their photographic reprint, there were those who cast doubts on its authenticity. One Mormon woman, when finding out that part of it came from the Yale library, dismissed it saying: "Yale! Don't you know that there was a communist plot there in the 1930s bent on undermining the LDS Church? Nope you can't trust anything from Yale. No doubt the document has been doctored."[27]

A better reprint of the Book of Commandments appeared in early 1962 by Mormon antiquarian Wilford C. Wood. It was titled *Joseph Smith Begins His Work, Vol. II,* and the copy was made from one owned by Wood. *Joseph Smith Begins His Work, Vol. I,* had been published a few years earlier and was a photo reprint of the 1830 Book of Mormon. Although the books were self-published by Wood, they were printed for him by the LDS Church-owned Deseret News Printing company.

Wood was a lifelong believing Mormon with a passion for collecting early Mormon documents and artifacts. Some of the highlights of his collection included the original death masks of Joseph and Hyrum Smith, the magical Jupiter talisman that Joseph Smith reportedly had on him when he was killed, and Joseph Smith's sandy-colored seer stone. In his capacity as an LDS history hunter, Wood provided invaluable service to the LDS Church by buying up historic sites with his own funds and then selling them at very reasonable prices to the church. Wood bought the land where the Nauvoo Temple sat; "the Liberty Jail at Liberty, Missouri; Aaronic Priesthood property at Harmony, Pennsylvania; Adam-ondi-Ahman in Missouri; the Masonic Lodge at Nauvoo, Illinois; the John Johnson home at Hiram, Ohio, and a store in Kirtland, Ohio."[28]

---

26. Flake, "Mormon Bibliography 1963," 242.

27. Tanner, Recollections.

28. Berrett, *Wilford C. Wood Collection*, i.

When Wood wanted to print his own editions of the 1830 Book of Mormon, the 1833 Book of Commandments, and 1835 Doctrine and Covenants, not only did church officials refrain from discouraging him, some representatives of the Deseret News Publishing Company offered sworn statements lest anyone doubt the authenticity of the texts he was reprinting. One of the statements came from future apostle and LDS president Thomas S. Monson.[29]

The Wilford Wood reprints were made available for sale at LDS Church-owned Deseret Book and other stores. Advertisements for the book were placed in the same newspapers that had refused to run ads for Jerald and Sandra's reprint. Jerald and Sandra speculated that the "leaders of the Mormon Church evidently felt that by using reverse psychology they could make the Mormon people believe that they were glad that the Book of Commandments had been reprinted."[30] But on October 9, 1964, Jerald and Sandra learned that the Wood's reprints had been pulled from Deseret Book. The next day, Sandra asked at the store and was told, "President David O. McKay won't let us sell that anymore." On October 11, Jerald and Sandra wrote to Wood himself about it. Wood replied that he had plenty of the books available and asked if they would permit him "to use your letter to show it to President McKay or those responsible for stopping the sale of the book at Deseret Book Company."[31]

Wood blamed the stoppage on Joseph Fielding Smith. McKay was known to be influenced by those who were able to see him and speak to him, and Smith may have convinced him to have the books pulled. Or Smith may have acted on his own. Wood explained to the Tanners, "The man who is supposed to answer all of the questions about the Church in the *Improvement Era* [Joseph Fielding Smith] is the man who stopped Deseret Book from selling the book. . . . President McKay has told me more than once that he would see to it that the Deseret Book sold Volumes one and two."[32] However,

29. Wood, *Joseph Smith Begins His Work, Vol. I*, unpaginated affidavits at the beginning of the book.

30. Tanner and Tanner, *Case Against Mormonism*, 1:52.

31. Wilford C. Wood to Jerald Tanner, Oct. 27, 1964. See Tanner and Tanner, *Case Against Mormonism*, 1:54.

32. Tanner and Tanner, *Case Against Mormonism*, 1:55; Wood to Edmond C. Gruss, Mar. 22, 1967, Tanner and Tanner, Papers.

sixteen years passed before the Wood's reprints again became available in Deseret Book.

The Tanners, not beholden to the church, continued to sell Wood's reprints independently. When the Reorganized Church produced their own reprints of the 1830 Book of Mormon (1970), 1835 Doctrine and Covenants (1971) and 1833 Book of Commandments (1972), Jerald and Sandra decided to continue to sell the Wood reprints because the pedigree (originally published by the Deseret News Publishing Company) remained impeccable despite the fact that Joseph Fielding Smith had blacklisted the reprints from official church stores.

7

SHADOW OR REALITY?

For three years, through new discoveries about the LDS past, through questions about the Book of Mormon, through the births of two children, and through the loss of one of their dearest friends, Pauline Hancock, Jerald and Sandra Tanner had diligently printed tracts, broadsides, and pamphlets. They were earnest about their beliefs and what they discovered. Now, they were certain, it was time to synthesize their work.

In 1963 they upgraded their troublesome Sears–Robuck hand-cranked mimeograph to a German motor-driven Gestetner mimeograph machine. Not only was the Gestetner faster and more reliable, Jerald and Sandra could make stencils of diagrams and photographs. The new machine cost $500 and was financed through Zions Bank. With the new mimeograph ready, Jerald felt he needed a microfilm machine. From there sprang the idea of going into business for themselves as a microfilm and photocopy business. They hoped "people would bring in rare books, letters and journals for copying and that they might allow us to have a microfilm copy of these documents if we gave them a discount on the work."[1]

They learned that the Universal Microfilm Company was selling one of its microfilm cameras for $1,200.[2] Universal Microfilm wanted $300 down, money the Tanners did not have. Jerald shared his plan with his coworkers at the machinist shop where he was still employed, and one of them became interested in helping. He had also lost his father and ate just one meal a day to send more money home to his mother. He was hardly the kind of person Jerald would

---

1. Tanner, *Jerald Tanner's Testimony*, 13.
2. This would have been as much as $10,000 in 2020 dollars. See, for example, measuringworth.com.

feel right about taking money from—if he had money to give. But the young friend had applied for a program to become a meat cutter, and his uncle had loaned him a lump sum of money to attend. The school accepted monthly payments, so he and Jerald worked out an arrangement: the young man would give Jerald the lump sum his uncle had loaned him and Jerald would pay his monthly tuition. Jerald took him up on the offer and was appreciative of the trust his coworker put in him. Shortly after Jerald paid off the debt, the young man was electrocuted and killed on a construction job. Jerald never forgot his kindness.[3]

Jerald and Sandra had upgraded equipment and were ready to tackle bigger projects besides reprints. One of the first was a work that, as it grew over the years, became their best-known book: *Mormonism: Shadow or Reality?* The original title when it was first published in 1963 was *Mormonism: A Study of History and Doctrine.*[4] Sandra drew the cover illustration in ink by copying a photograph of a sunstone from the Nauvoo Temple that she found in Fawn Brodie's *No Man Knows My History.*[5]

The book was 239 pages, printed on both sides, and subdivided into twenty chapters. There was an introduction by the Tanners, and an appendix tacked onto the end consisting of a reprint of a pamphlet on parallels between the Book of Mormon and Ethan Smith's *View of the Hebrews* by Mervin B. Hogan, a professor of mechanical engineering at the University of Utah with an interest in LDS history. Because the book was mimeographed and not mass printed, Jerald and Sandra could make changes, edits, and additions as they needed. On May 4, 1963, they added a page that showed the salaries of church officials.[6]

Sandra's Aunt Lucille, when she saw the large book the young couple had produced, quipped, "Well, I guess this proves that an uneducated young man can produce a very big book!" Jerald Tanner and Joseph Smith were both twenty-four when each of them

---

3. Tanner, *Jerald Tanner's Testimony*, 13.
4. Marvin Hill incorrectly dates the work "before 1961" in "New Mormon History," 117; Lawrence Foster to 1962 in "Career Apostates," 40. Marquardt, "Tanner Bibliography," lists Jerald as the author.
5. Brodie, *No Man Knows My History*, photograph opposite page 291.
6. Marquardt, "Tanner Bibliography," 5.

Advertisement for *Mormonism: A Study of History and Doctrine* (1963) using the same cover art as the book. The title was changed in later editions to *Mormonism: Shadow or Reality?*

published his first book.[7] The section on the Book of Mormon was identical to the tract Jerald had written and published the previous year.[8] The rest, though based on things they had worked on earlier, for the most part appear to have been rewritten and reshaped for inclusion in the book. The original chapter list provides an overview

---

7. Jerald's book was already out when he turned twenty-five on June 1, 1963 (as is seen in the March 8, 1963, date of LaMar Petersen's congratulatory letter quoted below). For his part Joseph turned twenty-five on December 23, 1830, and the first edition of the Book of Mormon was published on March 26, 1830.

8. Tanner, *Facts about the Book of Mormon.*

of the issues the Tanners had explored by 1963: 1) Change, Censorship, and Suppression; 2) The Doctored Covenants (Changes in the Revelations); 3) The Book of Mormon; 4) The Arm of the Flesh; 5) Mormonism and Truth; 6) The First Vision; 7) The Godhead; 8) The Adam–God Doctrine; 9) Blood Atonement; 10) Avenging Blood at Mountain Meadows; 11) Old Testament Practices in Mormonism; 12) The Danites; 13) Mormonism and Plural Marriage; 14) The Noblest Spirits; 15) The Mormon Priesthood; 16) The Word of Wisdom; 17), Mormonism and Money; 18) Temple Work; 19) The Apostasy; and 20) Miscellaneous Mormon History and Doctrine.

The work swelled as it passed through subsequent editions. The number of chapters would nearly double by the present edition. But most of the chapter divisions and titles in the first edition would be retained in later ones. Only two chapters would not be obviously carried over after the first edition: chapters 14, The Noblest Spirits, and 19, The Apostasy. Some chapter titles were changed, including the flippant sounding "The Doctored Covenants," which was renamed "Changes in the Revelations," from the second edition forward.

In the preface of the first edition Jerald acknowledges several sources of help but expresses a particular debt to James Wardle and LaMar Petersen. When Petersen got the book, he wrote a letter of encouragement and congratulations to Jerald, praising the work, and its author, in hyperbolic terms, even comparing it to Martin Luther nailing his 95 theses to the door of the Castle Church at Wittenburg. "There will be many who will question your right to do this type of inquiry. Yours is not the soft approach; it is the style of the sledgehammer. But 'if such a policy, perchance, shall change some of our beliefs—then so be it.'" Petersen thought Jerald's "restraint in quoting from harsh anti-Mormon critics whose purposes were more often to defame than to enlighten" was a masterstroke. Instead, the Tanners appealed to "those who have had deep stakes in Mormonism, who were personally involved and whose opinions must be carefully considered."[9]

The book had all the hallmarks of what would become recognizable in Tanner publications: a homemade appearance; an overuse of underlining, all-capital letters, and tediously long quotations; *and* an

---

9. LaMar Petersen to Jerald Tanner, Mar. 8, 1963, 1, Wardle, Papers, box 34, fd. 1.

overtly evangelical Christian perspective. It also delved into topics sacred, even taboo, to Mormons, such as the temple ceremony. Nevertheless, it brought forward mountains of new evidence with an eye for accuracy. Plenty of Mormons dismissed the book as a pack of lies, but in hindsight, there is little in the book in terms of bare facts that faithful Mormon historians have not subsequently acknowledged. Believers may insist some of the claims are sensationalized, or they may disagree with Jerald and Sandra's conclusions about what the evidence means for the church, but they cannot say that *Shadow or Reality?* made up any sources or facts.

When the first edition was published, the Tanners' friends the Constances, as local Christian booksellers, approached Moody Press, a prominent Chicago-based Christian publisher with the suggestion that they formally publish it. Moody was unenthusiastic and responded that there wouldn't be more than "250 to 300 people in the U.S. who would be sufficiently interested in a work of this kind to buy it."[10] During its first year, however, sales of the book exceeded Moody's prediction by some 2,000 copies.[11]

In early 1964 Jerald and Sandra upgraded their equipment again. A new technology had been developed that allowed masters to be made from microfilm. The masters could then be run on a press for a fraction of the cost of what was previously possible. Despite recently purchasing new equipment, Jerald and Sandra decided to get an offset press. After doing some research, Jerald settled on the Multilith Model 1000 as the best option, except that they had no money for it. He approached Sandra and suggested that if their tax refund arrived the next day, he would take it as a sign of God's approval and use it as a down payment for the new press. Sandra was not enthusiastic but agreed because she felt certain that there had not been enough time for the government to have processed their taxes. The tax return arrived the next day.

Jerald took the money and headed to get his new offset press, only to find that his and Sandra's means at the time were too slender for the company to sell it to him. It was suggested he approach a bank

10. E. H. Thompson to Mr. Tom M. Constance, May 14, 1963, 1, compare, Tanner, *Jerald Tanner's Testimony*, 16. Even in this first letter Moody suggested that they might consider publishing a work that had been rewritten for a more popular audience.

11. Preface to the second edition.

for a loan, but the only bank he had built up any credit with was the LDS Church-owned Zions Bank, which he felt sure would not be willing to give him the needed loan. Nevertheless, he decided to go and make his pitch anyway. He went in and described the new technology and how it worked. But it was when Jerald shared his idea of providing inexpensive reprints of out-of-print Mormon books that the man became interested, even excited. Normally, he said, he would not approve a loan request to someone with Jerald's unsteady income. But in this case, he felt so certain the plan would succeed that he gladly loaned Jerald the nearly $2,000 he was asking for. The vice president apparently felt that every good Mormon would love reading the old books, and even said he would like to drop in once Jerald had gotten up and running. Their home on Center Street, he said, was on his usual route home.[12] But he never did.[13]

With their new equipment set up, Jerald and Sandra produced the second edition of their book, this time with a new title: *Mormonism—Shadow or Reality?* (1964). Sandra's drawing of the sunstone was now replaced with the familiar graphic of the Salt Lake Temple that has been on its cover ever since, which they bought from John L. Smith, the Southern Baptist founder of Utah Missions Inc., and publisher of the *Utah Evangel*.[14] At the time he bought the press, Jerald had no idea how to use it. He learned in fits and starts, through trial and error. On the first edition, he learned that trying to print on both sides of the paper on a mimeograph machine was difficult. Jerald tried to solve that problem in the second edition by shrinking the pages, rotating them 90 degrees, then doubling them up putting two pages on one sheet. Perhaps it was easier for Jerald to print, but it was awkward for readers who had to hold the book horizontally to read it. That format was abandoned in subsequent editions. The new edition ran 431 pages and grew from twenty to twenty-seven chapters.

The thirty-eight chapter, 587-page third edition of 1972 was entirely retyped in the familiar two-column format followed in all

---

12. The Tanners moved to their West Temple home on June 14, 1964.

13. Tanner, Reminiscences; Tanner, *Jerald Tanner's Testimony*, 13–14.

14. Tanner, Reminiscences; For the second edition being produced on the new press, see Tanner, *Jerald Tanner's Testimony*, 12.

Jerald printing on his new Multilith Model 1000 offset press (1964).

subsequent editions, and apart from the disappearance of the second appendix from subsequent editions, this edition would become the basis for all later ones. The Tanners were eager to keep the page numbers the same in all subsequent editions so that references to it in their writings as they went along would all be standard and stay current. For the 1982 fourth edition, they innovated a new pattern of pagination in new "Updated Material" sections added after the various chapters that did not change the original page numbering of the rest of the book.[15]

In 1984 Michael Briggs prepared an index to *Shadow* that the Tanners printed. The fifth and final edition appeared in spring 1987.[16] After Jerald's death in 2006, Marlene Reeves, who had worked for the Tanners since 1979, retyped and reformatted the fifth edition. She managed to retain the pagination, and finally, with a digital copy

15. For example, the updated section on Joseph Smith's money digging is numbered 49-A, 49-B, 49-C, and 49-D, etc.
16. The date given in the preface is March 4, 1987.

in hand, the manuscript could be turned into a fully searchable edition, with Briggs's index included as well. This reformatted version was published in 2008 and is the last form the book will take.

Seventeen years after its initial prediction that *Shadow* would sell at most 250–300 copies, Moody Press published a "condensation and revision" edition titled *The Changing World of Mormonism*. It first appeared in 1980 and ran just under 600 pages. By the time the Moody edition hit bookshelves, *Shadow* had already sold over 32,000 copies.[17]

Jerald and Sandra wanted their friend Wesley Walters to write the introduction to *Changing World*. But Moody Press, far removed from Mormonism and unaware of Walters's reputation, wanted the introduction done by their preferred expert on Mormonism: Gordon H. Fraser. "You and we have differing perspectives," Moody editor Leslie H. Stobbe wrote to Jerald. "Wesley Walters is … probably well-known in research circles. But the average church member has never heard of him—whereas Gordon Fraser's books have sold in the tens of thousands."[18] The Tanners were less than enthusiastic. The book Fraser published with Moody Press in 1975, *Is Mormonism Christian?*, was a small, general-market title, and Fraser was not an expert on Mormonism. He had spent most of his time as a Christian missionary and educator among Native Americans, and had studied Mormonism only after he had encountered LDS missionaries also proselytizing Native Americans. A compromise was reached: Fraser wrote the foreword and Walters the introduction.

Moody agreed to publish *The Changing World of Mormonism* largely thanks to the efforts of Jerry Urban, an airline pilot who supported the Tanners' work. Urban had connections at evangelical schools in Illinois, and he knew several of the professors from these institutions because he attended the same church. Urban introduced these influential acquaintances to the Tanners and urged them to help him convince Moody to publish it.

Moody asked the Tanners to gather permissions related to the sources quoted, and to drop or modify sources where necessary. In

---

17. The details derive from "Changing World of Mormonism," *Salt Lake City Messenger* 41, Dec. 1979, 1.

18. Leslie H. Stobbe to Jerald Tanner, Sep. 8, 1978, 1, Tanner and Tanner, Papers.

a few cases, Moody relented with sources where permission was refused where no legitimate ownership claim or appeal to copyright could be made. A major editorial challenge Moody wanted was to eliminate the overuse of underlining, bolded fonts, and capitalization the Tanners used for emphasis. Text could be italicized, but any attempt to insert individual "italics mine," notes in each case would not only be a mammoth undertaking, but would also swell the footnotes unduly. The solution settled on was to include a single note at the bottom of the book's copywrite and printing history page that solved the problem in one stroke: "Certain words that appear in quote sections were italicized by the authors of the book for emphasis."[19]

Moody did well with *The Changing World of Mormonism.* It was reprinted several times, usually in batches of 1,500 copies,[20] and ultimately sold 29,686 copies—nearly as many copies as *Shadow* had sold by the time *Changing World* first appeared.[21] More than half the total sales were during its first four years in print. Moody declared *Changing World* out of print in September 1995.[22]

Ironically no sooner had *Changing World* appeared than changes in the world of Mormonism made it necessary for the Tanners to update one section during the first year of the book's existence, with the result that the second printing of 1981 was also the second, or "revised" edition. The issue had to do with the Book of Abraham

---

19. This is from the second printing. The first printing had put it in slightly different words: "Many italicized words that appear in quoted sections were added by the authors of this book for emphasis." Jerald insisted this be changed in the second edition. Presumably he noticed the way it was put in the first printing implied the Tanners actually *added* italicized word to certain quotations, rather than that they italicized words that were already there *in* the quotations. Jerald's correction to the proof of the page was sent with a letter, Jerald Tanner to Bill Cridden, Oct. 21, 1980, Tanner and Tanner, Papers.

20. Ella K. Lindvall to Jerald and Sandra Tanner, July 13, 1990, 1, Tanner and Tanner, Papers.

21. The back cover of *Changing World* says that *Shadow* "sold more than 30,000 copies without the benefit of an advertising campaign." The number comes from Wesley Walters's foreword (16). As noted, the month prior to the publication of *Changing World*, *Shadow* had already sold over 32,000 (see "Changing World of Mormonism," *Salt Lake City Messenger* 41, Dec. 1979, 1).

22. Email of letter of Ann Hackler, Manager, Moody Publishers Customer Service to Huggins, June 17, 2016. The detail of the book's selling more than half the final number in the first year comes from an incidental remark in a May 9, 1984, letter to Jerald from Ella K. Lindvall that by that time they'd sold 17,020 copies.

and the part played in the story by a gifted and colorful imposter (or partial imposter) named Dee Jay Nelson (see chapter 10).[23]

In November of 1964, the year the second edition of *Shadow* came out, Jerald began to suffer persistent and sometimes intense stomach pains. These had been ongoing, and he had surgery in the fall of 1963 on the assumption that he was suffering from appendicitis. But that had not solved the problem. This time the doctors suspected it might be his gall bladder. When Jerald was wheeled in for surgery, what Sandra assumed would be solved with a simple operation became complicated and scary. Jerald's gall bladder wasn't the problem, but he had adhesions that prohibited normal function. When the adhesions were removed, the gall bladder worked perfectly, but there was another issue. Seventeen feet of Jerald's small intestines had a mysterious matting growth. The doctors had no idea what it was.

Sandra got the news over the telephone while she stood at the nurses' station: the problem was not the gall bladder or cancer, but it might have been tuberculosis. Sandra's mind whirled as she could not keep worst-case scenarios at bay. Would she be left to raise their three small children as a single mom? She called the Constances, and they rushed to the hospital to pray with her.

The matter was turned over to specialists, but it was such a strange case they also didn't know what it was. Finally, one of the specialists had a flicker of recognition. He was sure he had seen a case like Jerald's that was caused by contact with poultry. But even that was only speculative, and the specialists agreed that it was likely neither curable nor life threatening. Jerald would need to discover on his own what might aggravate the condition, from foods to exercises to sleep patterns. His parents remained so concerned that they wanted the doctors to give a referral to the famed Mayo Clinic in Minnesota. But the doctors reassured them, and over time Jerald came to live with the condition. Young as the Tanners were, the scare gave them a sense of urgency and a greater dedication to their work.

---

23. Robert and Rosemary Brown took credit for the 1981 second edition of *Changing World*, insinuating that they influenced Moody Press to insist the Tanners change the information on Dee Jay Nelson in the book. Brown and Brown, *They Lie in Wait to Deceive*, 1:161. It simply wasn't true. See Charles E. Phelps, General Editor of Moody Press, to Jerald and Sandra Tanner, Mar. 17, 1981, qtd. in Tanner and Tanner, *Can the Browns Save Joseph Smith?* 18.

Jerald had given up being a machinist to work full time to build Modern Microfilm. But within two years, it was floundering. The books sold, but there was not enough revenue to keep everything afloat and support a family. The November 1965 issue of the Tanners' newsletter, the *Salt Lake City Messenger*, announced a 10 percent discount on their books.[24] The Tanners were candid with their readers: "We hope that by selling these books we will be able to pay off our loans, and, if it is possible, to keep our equipment. ... The Lord may call us to some other work, or we may even continue Modern Microfilm Co. on a part time basis."[25]

They planned to continue the sale through the end of June 1966, but "things have taken a turn for the worse," Jerald and Sandra announced in July, as they offered a 20 percent discount on everything.[26] They made an appeal for loans to the company at 8 percent interest, suggesting thousand-dollar advances paid off over two years with monthly payments of $48.34. They insisted there was no fear of bankruptcy, but Jerald was working on a new book and was eager to finish it without seeking outside employment. A few readers responded with money, mostly family and friends, and it became a method that the Tanners used into the early 1980s until they became a non-profit organization in 1983.

During these difficulties, Jerald and Sandra's visibility was bolstered by Wallace Turner's 1966 book, *The Mormon Establishment*. Turner, a Pulitzer-Prize-winning journalist with the *New York Times*, featured the Tanners and their work, including their testimonies of how they had become Christians. "The most important thing I have found," Jerald was reported as saying, "was not that the [LDS] Church was in error, but that I myself was in error. I found that I was a sinner and needed a Savior."[27] Not everything Turner said about the Tanners was positive, but he called Jerald "one of the most influential apostates of the 1960s."[28] Turner also shared how, as he interviewed one member of the church and Jerald's name was mentioned, the

---

24. *Salt Lake City Messenger* 5, Nov. 1965, 1.
25. *Salt Lake City Messenger* 6, Jan. 1966, 3.
26. *Salt Lake City Messenger* 8, Jul. 1966, 1.
27. Turner, *Mormon Establishment*, 158. Turner is actually quoting here from Jerald's testimony in the back of *Shadow*, 568.
28. Turner, *Mormon Establishment*, 155.

man's "face darkened." "Yes, I know of him," the man told Turner. "My wife is in his clutches—intellectually speaking, of course."[29]

Turner described *Mormonism—Shadow or Reality?* as an "intricate weaving of arguments from many sources against the fundamental precepts of the Saints' doctrine." He even delved into Mormon theology and reprinted a selection of early Mormon quotations that said Jesus was born through the sexual union of God the Father and the Virgin Mary, a teaching, he noted, that the Tanners said, "conflicts with the Bible and the Book of Mormon."[30]

The Tanners could not have hoped for a better advertisement. Turner even told his readers how much *Shadow* cost and printed the Tanners' address so those interested could place an order. Jerald and Sandra believed that Turner's encounter with them was divinely appointed. When Turner was in Salt Lake City in the summer of 1965 working on a series of articles on Mormonism for the *New York Times*, he stopped by the Tanners' living-room bookstore. He had no particular interest in Jerald and Sandra as a potential story; he had needed to clarify information on the church. But while he was in the store, he got to see first-hand "an apostasy … in the making."[31] A young convert from California who had fallen in love with a Mormon girl and married her on the promise that he would be a Mormon was in the store at the same time. He had read the Tanners' *Changes in Joseph Smith's History*, published some months before, which catalogued changes in Smith's history as it had originally been reported in early Mormon newspapers.

Sitting in the store that day, the curious convert remarked that he had wanted to check out some of the things in the book against the original manuscripts, had gone to the Church Historian's Office, and had asked to see them. He had been told that they would be happy to let him see them, but he needed to wait until they had been microfilmed since the originals were too fragile to handle. He had no reason to doubt what he had been told, but the Tanners had some bad news for him. "Those manuscripts have already been

---

29. Turner, 162.
30. Turner, 160–62.
31. Turner, 155–56; Tanner, *Jerald Tanner's Testimony*, 15–16; Tanner and Tanner, *Falsification of Joseph Smith's History*, 4.

microfilmed."[32] The microfilm in question, of Joseph Smith's history through 1834, was produced by the LDS Church Genealogical Society on January 27, 1942.[33]

The visitor was disinclined to believe the Tanners and expressed confidence that the Historian's Office would not have lied about such a thing. Jerald fetched a copy of Paul R. Cheesman's master's thesis from BYU, opened it to page 77, and handed it to the young man, pointing to the place where it said, "Joseph Smith started officially to write the History of the Church ... sometime near May 2, 1838. ... This handwritten copy of the history is in possession of the Church Historian's office. A microfilm has been made from the original and from this film the following copy was made."[34] Turner watched the man's reaction. "In an agitated voice he exclaimed: 'That does it! That's all! I can still get out of it and I will ... I can still get out of [the marriage] because it wasn't consummated,' he said as he left the house."[35]

The young man's reaction was in every way bizarre, not least his remark about his marriage not being consummated. But when the man was confronted with the idea that the Historian's Office had lied to him, he reacted strongly. His intensity gave Turner the idea to formally interview the Tanners. While he conducted the interview, a polygamist man entered the shop, and Jerald suggested to Turner that he interview him as well. It was rapidly becoming clear to the reporter that this was an important place to be to learn about the facets of Mormonism he might not get from more official sources.

Thanks largely to Turner, the Tanners came to have their names in reporters' Rolodexes as the go-to people for "the other side" of the story on Mormonism. The Tanners began to be mentioned in Turner's *New York Times* articles, and when he finished *The Mormon*

---

32. Tanner and Tanner, *Falsification of Joseph Smith's History* 4, and Tanner and Tanner, *Mormonism: Shadow or Reality?*, 128.

33. This official history has gone by many names, including History of Joseph Smith (and later History of Brigham Young, after Smith's death), the History of the Church, and most commonly, the Manuscript History of the Church. Today it is catalogued as Historian's Office, History of the Church, CR 100 102.

34. Cheesman, "Analysis of the Accounts," 77, and *Keystone of Mormonism*, 129.

35. Turner, *Mormon Establishment*, 155–56. As it would turn out, the young man apparently did remain with the girl, but did not return to Mormonism; Tanner and Tanner, *Mormonism: Shadow or Reality?*, 128.

Establishment, he asked Jerald and Sandra to read it and give feedback. Jerald was now working full time on Modern Microfilm with Sandra's help, even as she juggled raising their children. They were no longer dabblers, but professional publishers. To these labels Latter-day Saints would add the slur: professional anti-Mormons.

In August 1965 Sandra's parents, Ivan and Georgia McGee, got a divorce.[36] It was a tragic story but one that had a happy ending. When Sandra was in high school her parents gave up their sewing machine businesses and went into real estate. Georgia focused on the San Fernando Valley and did well. Ivan had his eye on land in the desert out in Hesperia, hoping that it would take off and make them a fortune. It didn't. Some desert areas did do well, but not Hesperia. Ivan began to take out loans until almost everything he and Georgia owned was burdened with debt. But this was only the beginning of troubles.

In 1964, when Sandra and Jerald's third child, Teresa, was born, Sandra's parents and her younger brother Jon made the trip up from California to see the baby. When they got back home, Ivan found that the car they'd left in the driveway wouldn't start. He had Jon sit in the driver's seat while he put some gas into the carburetor hoping it would turn over. When Jon turned the key and the starter began to crank the engine, the gas Ivan was pouring ignited, injuring him badly, incinerating the skin on his hands all the way up his arms, leaving only two strips of unburned skin in the crooks of his elbows. He never fully recovered. It was at this time, Jon recalls, that the troubles began that would end in Ivan's and Georgia's divorce.

The frustration caused by Ivan's crippling injuries added to his financial disappointments and led to increasing anger and frustration, which he sometimes took out on Georgia. In the latter half of 1964, Ivan attempted suicide. He was found in senseless semi-consciousness at home in the TV room. He was taken to a psychiatric unit in Los Angeles, where they were told that if he checked himself in it would be much easier getting him released later. Sandra's sister Carolyn took a writing implement, put it in Ivan's hand, closed his

---

36. The details of Ivan and Georgia's divorce and subsequent events comes from Tanner, Reminiscences.

hand around it, and made an X on the form. Sandra was able to visit her father a couple of times. In hindsight, she feels she and her mom caved to pressure to get him released too early.

Despite all of this, Sandra, who was largely out of the loop living in Utah, was shocked to get the call from her mother announcing that she was divorcing Ivan. He'd become violent, she said, if she locked herself in a room, he would break down the door; she'd become afraid for her life, she said. Sandra found the news hard to process, hard to believe. Her dad had been strict when she was growing up, but this didn't sound right. But it was true, her father had changed. It is unclear even to this day the extent to which an ongoing series of mini-strokes Ivan was later discovered to be suffering from might have been contributing to his change in personality at that early stage.

When they divorced, Georgia took on most of the debt-laden property herself. Ivan was left with a car and just a few other things. Georgia was eager to pay off the debt so that she and Ivan could have good credit for their future lives. She knew that if it were left to Ivan they would soon have to file bankruptcy. She approached this with great determination, taking on an additional job while continuing to sell real estate, and after some years managed to pay off everything. She became quite bitter though when Ivan, who was still working in the same real estate office as she was, spread it around that she had taken him for everything he had. In the midst of all this Georgia also had to raise their teenage son, Jon.

After the divorce Ivan drifted north to San Francisco where his brother-in-law Orval L. Ostler, husband of Ivan's sister, Cleoma, helped him to get work. His first job was a night watchman in a shipyard where he was assigned to doing the rounds on a ship from China. He was required to carry a gun to keep anyone who tried to leave the ship from doing so. Following this job he worked another as night watchman on property associated with Howard Hughes.

Neither job struck Sandra as particularly suitable for a potentially suicidal man. If Ivan began feeling despondent, he could easily jump into the open hold of the ship, which was several stories deep, or shoot himself with the gun. And as for the latter position, working through the night, and then returning to his little apartment all alone to sleep by day, seemed to Sandra too lonely a job for a man of Ivan's personality and mental state. She suggested to Jerald that they invite her father to come and stay with them. Her mother, she assured him, being as dominant a personality as Georgia was, would be impossible to bring into the house; she'd simply take over. But her dad, she said, should be a piece of cake. Famous last words.

The Tanners had never had a television until Ivan brought one with him. It soon became clear that Ivan was suffering from serious psychological and behavioral problems. He exhibited typical symptoms of manic-depression; great bursts of energetic enthusiasm followed by deep valleys of crushing depression. He arrived with a rope in the trunk of his car, which frightened Sandra. Would she, or worse yet, the children, come home one day to find he'd hanged himself?

Ivan was getting unemployment checks, but he spent most of them on new door-to-door money-making schemes that required him to put up money for product, training modules, or sample displays. On one occasion he purchased an electroplating machine intending to start a business coating baby shoes in bronze, but the fad had passed. Next he invested in a de-icing product that was supposed to serve as an alternative to salting icy walkways. Jerald and Sandra's house was filled with bags of it. But Ivan struggled to find buyers because it was more expensive than salt. He tried to sell shoes, socks, toilet bowl cleaner, indoor/outdoor carpeting, and plastic polymer paint to seal roofs. He had always been an easy target for presentations of the come-on-down-to-the-Hiawatha-Room-at-the-Red-Tiger-Inn-by-the-Raceway-and-let-me-tell-you-how-I-made-my-first-million-dollars-in-only-three-months variety. But now he was getting roped into a new one nearly every month. Predictably all of his schemes came to nothing. When he'd start pursuing a new one he would be full of hope and optimism, which would soon be disappointed and leave him devastated. Jerald and Sandra found both moods difficult to cope with.

Georgia was remarried in 1969 to Bill Lamb. When Sandra and the kids were planning a trip to go down and see them Ivan became so upset that he ran out in front of an oncoming car. His injuries weren't severe, but he was badly bruised. When Sandra felt he was

Sandra's mother, Georgia, and her new husband Bill Lamb (1969).

blaming her for making him do it, she told Jerald she *had to* take the trip, lest she give in to what felt like her father's emotional blackmail. And so they did.

Georgia's marriage only lasted a year because Ivan's problems were still too much of an ongoing presence in her life—calls in the middle of the night and crises of one sort or another on an ongoing basis. Finally, her new husband said he couldn't live like that and that Georgia would have to choose between him and Ivan. Georgia felt she couldn't abandon Ivan, so the new marriage came to an end.

In the meantime, Ivan's increasing difficulties caused by the series of mini-strokes made things worse. He became meaner and increasingly prone to threatening suicide. By 1969 it became necessary to put him in a nursing home. Every day a cheerful resident of the nursing home would wheel himself down the hall in the morning, calling out some positive message such as, "Hey everyone, it's a wonderful day!" This irritated Ivan to no end. One day, when the man was passing by with his usual upbeat greeting, Ivan took hold of the man's wheelchair and dumped him out onto the floor.

Ivan also lost all interest in being an observant Mormon. He wanted to go to one of the lower kingdoms where he felt sure his friends would be rather than to the Celestial Kingdom, which, he said, would be full of self-satisfied stuffed shirts.

While in the home, Ivan somehow decided to start counseling with Pastor Thomas H. Miller of the Anchor Baptist Church.[37] People from the church also came on Sundays and picked him up to take him to the service. It was then that Sandra witnessed a marvelous change in her father. At a service Ivan went forward and accepted Christ as his savior. He surrendered all the anger, the resentment, and the failures and bitter disappointments of his life to God, and in their place the lost sweetness of his original personality returned, only now made even better. Before this happened, Sandra could hardly stand to visit her father. He would invariably let loose his anger and frustration on her the way he used to do to her mother: "How can you do this to me?" he would say. "You know how I hate this place. The food's terrible. Anyone who could do this to their father must be the most hateful person in the world." Every visit was a deeply painful experience for Sandra. But she continued to go because she knew someone had to check up on him. She'd usually make the dreaded trip out to see him on Saturdays. But then one day she got a call early in the week from Pastor Miller asking if she'd been out to see her dad yet that week.

"No, I haven't," she said, "Why?"

"Well," he said, "I'd rather not be the one to say, just go."

The pastor later told Sandra he hadn't wanted to tell her about Ivan's coming to Christ, lest she disbelieved it. He wanted her to see the change in Ivan for herself.

When she arrived and saw him in his wheelchair it was like he was a different man. His eyes filled with tears and he apologized to

---

37. The church was at 1880 East 5600 South, Salt Lake City.

Sandra for what he'd become and how badly he'd treated her, and then he told her, "I just want you to know how much I love you." That comment from his lips, Sandra recalls, was "overpowering." She had no recollection of his ever telling her he loved her before. It wasn't that she felt he hadn't cared for her. It was just that he'd always been so fixated, so wrapped up in his wife, that Sandra had always felt that she and the other children were tagalongs. Her father's humility, his remorsefully reaching out in a loving way, after all these years, came as a total shock.

Nor was Ivan's new attitude short lived. By finding Christ, Sandra recalled, Ivan really had become a new man. "He was at peace, he wasn't mad at the world anymore. It was like seeing the dad I knew as a child." As Sandra tried to describe the change in attitude she seemed to be grasping for the right words. Ivan had become "companionable, amenable, pleasant. He'd been an angry old man, now he was a pleasant man."

Georgia and Ivan had always loved each other. But the relationship had become so toxic, with Ivan so dependent on Georgia, so absolutely devastated, hopeless, and lost in the world without her, and yet so unable to avoid making her the brunt of his anger and frustration when they were together. And with all the unfairness on his part associated with that, Georgia was convinced she simply had to get him out of her life, even though she continued to care about him. As she once confided to Sandra, "I love your dad, but at a distance." She was also dealing with a lot of unforgiveness herself over the way he had treated her and how he had demonized her after the divorce. Apart from the radical change in Ivan, it would have been unimaginable to think that Georgia would have ever taken him back. Eventually, however, through seeing the new Ivan on visits to Salt Lake City, Georgia arranged to take him back to California in 1971, where she placed him in another care center and moved into an apartment just around the corner so that she could look in on him every day. A happy ending to a very difficult story. Ivan and Georgia never formally remarried. Georgia kept the last name Lamb for the rest of her life. Yet, when Ivan's father, Grandpa McGee— the "Joseph Fielding Smith" of the family—died several years later, his children graciously honored Georgia with Ivan's portion of the

Ivan (front) with (left to right) Carolyn, Georgia, Jon, and Sandra (1972).

inheritance for her loving care of their brother in his final years. Ivan died on February 24, 1976, and Sandra's uncle Orval L. Ostler, a stake president in the LDS Church, officiated at his funeral service, which took place on Friday, February 27, in the chapel at the Glen Haven Memorial Park, where Ivan was laid to rest.[38]

---

38. Ivan McGee Funeral Program, Tanner and Tanner, Papers. Sandra recalls that her uncle, a Mormon, "did a nice, non-partisan job, without making any issue of Mormonism." Tanner, Reminiscences.

120

8

THE FIRST VISION REVISITED

In the summer of 1965, when Jerald showed the copy of Paul R. Cheesman's BYU master's thesis to the young shop visitor in Wallace Turner's presence, he had only recently obtained it himself.[1] A BYU student sent them a photocopy of the main body of the thesis, but without the appendices. As Jerald began to read the thesis, he quickly saw that it was dynamite. Somehow Cheesman had been granted unprecedented access to sources the Tanners and others had been trying to get hold of for years. In the thesis Cheesman quoted a small excerpt of the First Vision account from Alexander Neibaur's journal, the same journal the Tanners had played cat and mouse with Hugh Nibley over in 1961. What was more, Cheesman stated in the thesis that appendix D, which the student hadn't copied, contained a never-before-released account of the First Vision. The Tanners wondered whether it might be the very document that Levi Edgar Young had described to LaMar Petersen more than a decade earlier (1953), calling it a "'strange account' ... written in Joseph's own hand ... that ... did not agree entirely with the official version."[2] Jerald contacted the student and asked for the appendix. The student obliged, and when it arrived, Sandra saw it was exactly what they'd hoped: the long-suppressed First Vision account by Joseph Smith. She was so excited she phoned Jerald from the post office. In it, as LaMar Petersen had remembered Levi Edgar Young saying, "Jesus was the center of the vision, but God was not mentioned"[3]:

> The Lord opened the heavens upon me and I saw the Lord and he spake unto me saying Joseph my son Thy Sins are forgiven thee, go thy way

---

1. Cheesman, "Analysis of Accounts."
2. Petersen, *Creation of the Book of Mormon*, xii.
3. Petersen.

walk in my Statutes and keep my commandments behold I am the Lord of glory I was crucifyed for the world ... I come quickly as it is written of me in the cloud clothed in the glory of my Father.[4]

When Sandra got home from the post office, she and Jerald pored over it. They were holding the earliest written account of the First Vision, penned by Joseph Smith himself in 1832.[5] It had never been published anywhere until Cheesman printed it as an appendix to a master's thesis only a few people would likely ever see.[6] The account was written in 1832, between July 20 and November 27,[7] and it alternates between the hand of his scribe, Frederick G. Williams, and Joseph Smith himself. But the lines about the divine visitation are in Smith's handwriting alone.[8] As in many of Joseph's revelations and other writings, Jesus says little here that is not quoted or paraphrased from the King James Bible.

In many respects the 1832 account differed significantly from the official version in the Pearl of Great Price. The issue that drove the narrative of that later account, the whole reason Joseph had gone out to seek the Lord in the first place, was his desire to "know which of all the sects was right, that I might know which to join."[9] In that account the Lord informed Joseph that he "must join none of them, for they were all wrong." In the 1832 account the issue does not come up during the vision because Joseph had already concluded they were all wrong beforehand after "Searching the Scriptures."[10]

---

4. Chessman, "Analysis of Accounts," D-4. Jesus's name isn't mentioned, but the figure identifies itself as Jesus by saying he "was crucifyed for the world," and will come "in the glory of my Father."

5. This account has since been reprinted many times, including in Davidson et al., *Histories, Volume 1*, 12–13.

6. Cheesman, "Analysis of Accounts," 3–4: "It is also notable that Joseph Smith evidently attempted to dictate an account of these experiences as early as approximately 1833. This was never corrected, completed, or published. It is found in Appendix D of this thesis."

7. Williams began his duties as Smith's scribe on July 27, and November 27 is the date of the first letter to be included in the repurposed Letter Book, from which the account had been excised. See, Smith, *Personal Writings*, 640n6.

8. Davidson et al., *Histories, Volume 1*, 10–12.

9. JS-H 1:18–19.

10. Chessman, "Analysis of Accounts," 128: "by Searching the Scriptures I found that mankind did not come unto the Lord but that they had apostatized from the true and living faith and there was no society or denomination that built upon the gospel of Jesus Christ as recorded in the new testament."

Joseph had initially written that a pillar of "fire" rested on him, then crossed it out and wrote "light." In the 1832 account God the Father isn't present at all. Chessman sought to minimize the latter by remarking that Joseph "writes briefly of the vision, he does not mention the Father, as being present; however, this does not indicate that he was not present."[11]

Cheesman dated the "Strange" account to around 1833,[12] and he does not identify who wrote it beyond saying that "Joseph Smith wrote it or he dictated it. From handwriting comparisons it would appear that the latter supposition is the more likely one."[13] By 1969 the scribal hand was positively attributed to Frederick G. William by Dean Jessee, an expert in early Mormon handwriting.[14] By 1971, however, Jessee had come to believe that Smith's writing was present as well.[15] Jessee's assessment continues to be followed.[16]

In a way it is strange it took so long to identify it as Smith's handwriting in the document since Levi Edgar Young, who had seen the document long before, was under the impression that it had been written in Joseph's own hand.[17] In any case, once the Tanners had the document, they quickly moved to publish it in a booklet entitled *Joseph Smith's Strange Account of the First Vision* (1965). The book consisted of two parts: a general overview of issues related to the First Vision, and a photocopy of the typewritten "Strange" account from Cheesman's thesis. The cover of the booklet proclaimed: "Important Document Suppressed for 130 Years Now Comes to Light. This document dictated by Joseph Smith reveals that he did not see the Father and the Son in 1820."

The idea that Joseph did not see the Father and the Son in 1820

---

11. Chessman, 63.

12. Cheesman, 3, 126.

13. Cheesman, 126.

14. He expressed this view, for example, in Jessee, "Early Accounts," 277.

15. Jessee, "Writing of Joseph Smith's History," 462n78, and Jessee, "How Lovely Was the Morning," 86.

16. See, e.g., Faulring, *American Prophet's Record*, 3; Vogel, *Early Mormon Documents* 1:26. The Joseph Smith Papers project dates it to summer 1832.

17. Petersen, *Creation of the Book of Mormon*, xii. Petersen incorrectly gives 1952 as the date of his visits with Young. They actually met in 1953. The notes he took at the first two of the six interviews mentioned in *Creation of the Book of Mormon*, can be found in a bound volume in his papers entitled "Book Reviews and Letters, Vol. 1," 138–40, box 1, fd 1. The date of the first interview is given as "Tuesday, Feb. 3, 1953 from noon to 1:15."

was not particularly new since the same conclusion had suggested itself to a few researchers prior to this document's coming to light. In 1953, LaMar Petersen had asked Levi Edgar Young how to reconcile Joseph's report of drawing widespread persecution against "himself by openly reporting his vision of the Father and the Son in 1820 with the fact that in the hundreds of articles and affidavits denouncing the Prophet the visit of the Father and the Son is never alluded to?"[18] Fawn M. Brodie in her 1945 biography of Smith likewise noted that "between 1820 and 1840 Joseph's friends were writing long panegyrics; his enemies were defaming him in an unceasing stream of affidavits and pamphlets, and Joseph himself was dictating several volumes of Bible-flavored prose. But no one in this long period even intimated that he had heard the story of the two gods."[19]

The Tanners' description of the account as "suppressed for 130 Years" stands in stark contrast to the language of fortuitous discovery traditionally employed by faithful LDS scholars. Cheesman speaks of it as having been "found in a journal ledger in the Church Historian's office Salt Lake City."[20] Cheesman concluded from the fact that the "account was never published or referred to by any of the authorities of the church as far as the writer had been able to determine," that the document must not have been very important.[21] Speaking of the account a year later, James Allen, who had served on Cheesman's thesis committee, grants its importance but again using the language of fortuitous discovery. The manuscript, he says, "has apparently lain in the LDS Church Historian's office for many years, and yet few if any who saw it realized its profound historical significance."[22] When we ask whether the Tanners' language of suppression or Chessman's language of fortuitous discovery is more correct, there can be no doubt as to the answer.

The importance of the document had not simply been missed, people had known about it for some time, and had tried to see it, but they failed. Others came close to fortuitously discovering it but were put off. When Fawn M. Brodie, niece to then LDS President David

---

18. "Book Reviews and Letters, Vol. 1," 139, box 1, fd. 1.
19. Brodie, *No Man Knows My History*, 25 (1945, 1st ed.).
20. Cheesman, "Analysis of Accounts," 126.
21. Chessman, 64.
22. Allen, "Significance of Joseph Smith's 'First Vision,'" 35.

O. McKay, asked to see Joseph Smith's 1832 diary along with other material relating to Nauvoo polygamy in 1943 for *No Man Knows My History*, Joseph Fielding Smith refused, noting that "There are things in this library we don't let anyone see."[23] Brodie recalls Smith's demeanor toward her being "most unfriendly."[24] When McKay found out about her request, he went to where she was staying later that day and angrily confronted her, forbidding her to do any more research in the library and archives. Later, however, McKay thought better of it, and sent her a note granting permission to see the materials.[25] But in order to spare him "further embarrassment," she turned instead to the less restrictive venues of the University of Utah and the Utah State Historical Society, both of which followed the more standard guidelines with regard to both access and appropriate courtesy toward researchers. Brodie never consulted materials in the LDS Church archives again. It is not known whether Brodie had heard of the 1832 account when she asked for the Joseph Smith's 1832 diary, nor whether Joseph Fielding Smith had it specifically in mind when he told her there were things he didn't let anyone see. It is therefore unclear in this case whether Smith was directly intending to suppress the 1832 account or had something else in mind.[26]

If Levi Edgar Young had thought the account was in the handwriting of Joseph Smith, then Joseph Fielding Smith probably knew as well. He may have imagined that when Sandra had earlier passed along a request through her bishop for a "photostatic copy of Joseph Smith's own account in his own hand writing of this first vision,"[27] she had somehow learned of the existence of the 1832 account, which she had not. But in his response, Smith seemed to admit its existence: "This young woman asks for a 'photostatic copy' of the

---

23. Bringhurst, *Fawn McKay Brodie*, 84. In fact, the 1832 First Vision account appears not in the 1832 diary of Joseph Smith, but in what became Letter Book 1.

24. Qtd. in Bringhurst, "Biography of a Biography,"16.

25. Bringhurst, 17.

26. Smith also told Brodie that "a revelation on polygamy came as early as 1831 but has never been printed because it would be misinterpreted by the bulk of church members," qtd. in Bringhurst, "Biography of a Biography," 16. It is interesting to speculate whether Brodie's request and David O. McKay's finally granting it might have provided the occasion for the 1832 account being cut out of Letter Book 1 at some point between 1930 and 1965. See "History, circa Summer 1832," josephsmithpapers.org.

27. Sandra Tanner to Bishop Kennedy, Oct. 1, 1959, Tanner and Tanner, Papers.

Prophet's statement in his own handwriting. Well, if we furnished it would that convince her?"[28]

One of the excuses for denying the Tanners access to church archives over the years was that they were not "qualified researchers." It is an excuse they might even have been inclined to believe themselves, given their lack of academic credentials. But even Levi Edgar Young, the head of the Seven Presidents of the Seventies, confided to LaMar Petersen that he had "quit going down with his questions to Brother Joseph Fielding (Smith) because he was laughed at and put off."[29] When Young was finally granted access to the documents he was "told not to copy or tell what they contained,"[30] a directive he didn't fully obey, since he told Petersen about the existence of the "Strange" account and bid him not to tell anyone else until after he (Young) had died. LaMar did as Young asked. He did not tell the Tanners about the document until after Young died on December 13, 1963, at which time they in turn sent a letter to Joseph Fielding Smith asking for a copy and enclosing a dollar to pay for it. Smith never responded; it looked as though they might never see the "Strange" account at all.[31] But now scarcely a year later they suddenly found it in their hands. They published it sometime between June and October 1965.[32]

How did it happen that a document hidden away out of the view and reach of more qualified scholars came into the hands of a BYU student working on his Masters of Religious Instruction degree? And why, given that Cheesman's thesis dealt with analyzing various accounts of the First Vision, didn't the church grant him access as well to the account of the vision Joseph gave to Robert Matthews ("Joshua the Jewish Minister") on November 9, 1835?

LaMar Petersen suggested in a letter to the editor of *Dialogue*

---

28. Joseph Fielding Smith to Bishop Kennedy, Nov. 5, 1959, 2, Tanner and Tanner, Papers.

29. "Book Reviews and Letters, Vol. 1," 138. box 1, fd. 1.

30. "Book Reviews and Letters."

31. Tanner and Tanner, *Strange Account*, 4; Tanner and Tanner, *Shadow or Reality?*, 165.

32. On the front inside cover of Jerald's copy someone has penciled in the date as "Before Oct. 1965 / After May 1965." This is probably because the thesis is referred to in the booklet as being dated May 1965, and the first clear external reference to the booklet is in the Oct. 1965 *Messenger* (2), where part of a letter from California is reprinted expressing appreciation for the booklet. The May date, however, appears to be incorrect because the copy of the thesis sent to Jerald by the BYU student was dated June 1965.

that was never printed that the "Strange" account was shared with Cheesman because the Levi Edgar Young account had gotten out and been referred to in the Tanners' *Changes in Joseph Smith's History* (January 1965), which, Petersen said, had "provoked considerable discussion at that time."[33] The problem with this explanation is that the Tanners' *Changes* came out the month before Cheesman's thesis was approved on February 15, 1965, possibly too narrow a window for seeing Chessman (and the church through him) responding to *Changes*. On the other hand, Petersen, himself an influential figure in the Utah historical community, had been freed from his promise of silence for more than a year since Levi Edgar Young's death. And surely he would have been talking about the "Strange" account. He had after all told the Tanners. One thing we do know is that LDS historian James B. Allen, who was on Cheesman's thesis committee,[34] is on record as saying he didn't learn about the later November 9, 1835, First Vision account until June 1966.[35]

When Cheeman's thesis mysteriously (though perhaps predictably) went missing from the BYU library, a rumor spread that the Tanners had stolen it. The claim wasn't true. The Tanners' copy is conspicuously not the original but a photocopy. The fingers of the BYU student who made it are clearly visible on the copies. A BYU student told Sandra that it was Cheesman's wife who was spreading the rumor. Sandra wrote assuring her they were not responsible for the alleged theft of her husband's thesis and that her statements amounted to slander.[36] Jerald wrote to his friend Jerry Urban in 1969, some five years after the publication of the "Strange" account, saying it was "hard ... to believe that he [Cheesman] would make such a statement," suggesting that "perhaps he meant that we did not get his permission to use it."[37] Urban had gotten wind of the rumor from a student who had allegedly heard Cheesman himself allude to the theft in class. The fact that Urban had heard it so long after the fact and in another part of the country suggests the false accusation had

---

33. LaMar Petersen to Manuscript Editor of *Dialogue*, Nov. 9, 1966, "Book Reviews and Letters, Vol. 1," 158, 1, box 1, fd. 1.
34. Tanner and Tanners, *Strange Account*, 11.
35. Allen, "Significance of Joseph Smith's 'First Vision,'" 35n11.
36. Jerry Urban to Jerald Tanner, undated, 1, Tanner and Tanner, Papers.
37. Jerald Tanner to Jerry Urban, rec'd, Apr. 21, 1969, 1, Tanner and Tanner, Papers.

circulated far and wide. Without mentioning names, Urban wrote to Cheesman asking about what he'd allegedly said in class and for "comment as to *who* and *why* would steal your work."[38] Cheesman's undated response, written at the bottom of Urban's letter, was: "As to the thief—we have it back now & you can get it through interlibrary loan." Urban wrote a second time specifically asking if Jerald had been the one he accused of stealing the thesis in class.[39] In his response, Cheesman declined to say who the thief was.[40]

When the Tanners published the 1832 First Vision account in 1965, they could little imagine the wealth of new information concerning the First Vision that would emerge in the latter half of that decade. First, James Allen published "The Significance of Joseph Smith's First Vision in Mormon Thought" in the third issue of *Dialogue*. Allen's article included both the 1832 account and a previously unknown 1835 account given by Smith to "Joshua the Jewish Minister" (Robert Matthews).[41] *Dialogue* claimed that Allen's article published "for the first time substantial portions of two early accounts by Joseph Smith of his First Vision."[42] LaMar Petersen sent a correction; the Tanners had published one of the accounts "more than a year ago."[43] At the time, the Tanners' *"Strange" Account* booklet had sold approximately six hundred copies.[44]

In explaining where his newly published 1835 account came from, Allen again resorted to the language of fortuitous discovery. It had come to his attention in June 1966, he said, after having been "brought to light by a member of the staff at the Church Historian's office."[45] It was not the original account that appeared in Smith's 1835–36 diary, which would be edited by H. Michael Marquardt

38. Jerry Urban to Paul R. Cheesman, Apr. 15, 1969, 1, copy in Tanner and Tanner, Papers.

39. Jerry Urban to Jerald Tanner, undated, 1, Tanner and Tanner, Papers.

40. Jerry Urban to Jerald and Sandra Tanner, June 20, [1969], 1, Tanner and Tanner, Papers.

41. The other two are the 1838 official account, canonized in the Pearl of Great Price, and the well-known 1842 account published in the Wentworth Letter.

42. "In This Issue," *Dialogue: A Journal of Mormon Thought* 1, no. 3 (Autumn 1966): 2.

43. Petersen, "Letter to the Editor."

44. This from a portion of the first page of Petersen's letter to the editor that did not appear, in "Book Reviews and Letters," Petersen, Papers, box 1, fd. 1.

45. Allen, "Significance of Joseph Smith's 'First Vision,'" 35.

and published for the first time by the Tanners in late 1979. It was rather a later transcription of it in the back pages of the first volume of the Manuscript History.[46]

Allen described the document as "curious," partly because "it was apparently written in 1835 by someone other than Joseph Smith, for it records the day-to-day events in the prophet's life in the third person, as if it were a scribe recording them as he observed them."[47] But, as would become clear later, someone had actually recast Joseph Smith's first-person narrative in the third person in the version Allen had access to.

Allen admitted that it was "unusual that someone had not found it earlier and recognized its significance," but suggested that "few if any people" were aware of it because "the use of the 'Manuscript History' is highly restricted, due to its extremely high value, and ... any research done in it is done through a microfilm copy." When one sees where the account appears in the larger context of the Manuscript History, it is easy to see how it might have been overlooked. The Manuscript History runs chronologically through several volumes. At the end of August 1834, where the chronological record of the first volume ends, the reader is directed to pick up the thread of the story for September 1834 in the beginning of the second volume. But after that the first volume goes on to include various historical odds and ends, among which was the version of the account Allen published. It is certainly plausible that the account may have been fortuitously discovered, but it raises the question why Allen was not given access to the version recorded in Joseph Smith's original 1835–36 diary.

The 1835 version of the First Vision was not noted in the Tanners' 1965 *Changes in Joseph Smith's History*, which only traced changes made in printed editions, because it had already been excised from all of those printed editions and replaced by a statement in which

---

46. In the Joseph Smith Papers the volumes of the Manuscript History referred to here are called "History, 1838–1856, volumes A-1 and B-1. They are also commonly cited as Church Historian's Office, History of the Church, A-1 and B-1 (CR 100 102). The document used by Allen appears separately in the Joseph Smith Papers as "History, 1834–1836."

47. Allen, "Significance of Joseph Smith's 'First Vision,'" 36. Thanks to H. Michael Marquardt for help in identifying Warren Cowdery as the scribe of the account available to Allen.

Smith gives Joshua the Jewish Minister "a relation of the circumstances connected with the coming forth of the Book of Mormon, *as recorded in the former part of this history.*"[48]

In contrast to the 1832 account, Allen's newly published account does say that two personages were present, just like the canonized 1838 version and the 1842 version that Smith provided to John Wentworth, editor of the *Chicago Democrat.*[49] But it gives no indication as to who they are. Instead of one personage pointing to the other and saying, "This is my beloved son, Hear Him," as in the canonized version, the 1835 account only reports that the personage "testified to me that Jesus is the Son of God." Allen had noted that one of the "most unusual" statements in the 1835 account "is Joseph's declaration that he saw many angels in this vision."[50] The question is, were the personages angels too? A possible answer lay in a brief account of Smith to Erastus Holmes five days after talking to Joshua the Jewish Minister.

The Tanners had learned of the Holmes account from Sandra's grandmother Sylvia, who discovered it in early 1961 while perusing old microfilm copies of the *Deseret News* at the Utah State Historical Society, then located in the Governor's Mansion on South Temple. She was surprised to discover the different version of Smith's First Vision account and ordered a 32 x 24 inch poster-size copy of the page.[51] Sylvia later noticed it had also appeared in the *Millennial Star.*[52] The version of the Holmes account Sylvia had found contradicted the familiar one in the *History of the Church* published by the LDS Church, which rewrote it so that the words of Smith, who had originally said, "Up to the time I received the first visitation of Angels," were changed to read instead, "Up to the time I received

---

48. This change had already been made where Smith encounters Joshua the Jewish Minister in the main text of the Manuscript History's second volume. Manuscript History, Nov. 9, 1835, B-1, 637.

49. Jessee, Ashurst-McGee, and Jensen, *Journals, Volume 1*, 88.

50. Allen, "Significance of Joseph Smith's 'First Vision,'" 41.

51. Sandra recalls the copy being made at Spencer's Universal Microfilming Corporation at 141 Pierpont Avenue. Spencer's had many historic Mormon and Utah newspapers in their collection from which they could make copies or films.

52. "History of Joseph Smith," *Millennial Star*, July 2, 1853, 424; see, also, e.g., Tanner and Tanner, *Changes in Joseph Smith's History*, 29.

my first vision."[53] If Smith had been thinking of the two personages mentioned in Allen's account as the Father and the Son, as the canonized version has it, why would he sum that experience up five days later as a "visitation of Angels?" Had the idea of identifying the two personages with the Father and Son occurred to Smith by 1835?

Another development in First Vision scholarship was an article by Wesley P. Walters published late in 1967 in the *Bulletin of the Evangelical Theological Society* titled "New Light on Mormon Origins from Palmyra (N.Y.) Revival."[54] Walters, on the basis of extensive research in a wide array of contemporary ecclesiastical records, argued that the 1820 Palmyra revival featured in the canonical version of the First Vision story never happened, a conclusion that accorded with the recollections of Smith's own family and other early observers, which pointed instead to a revival in 1824 and 1825. Walters's article provided a new starting point for all subsequent discussions of the First Vision.

It was an exciting time to be interested in Mormon studies, but by the time Allen and Walters wrote their articles, Jerald and Sandra were looking into a forgery.

---

53. Contrast Jessee, Ashurst-McGee, and Jensen, *Journals, Volume 1*, 100, and Roberts, *History of the Church*, 2:312.
54. Walters, "New Light on Mormon Origins."

9

THE BOOK OF ABRAHAM
AND THE EGYPTIAN ALPHABET

The Tanners had published a fake, they just didn't know it yet. Nobody did. Around 1962, Jerald and Sandra printed *Revealing Statements by the Three Witnesses of the Book of Mormon*.[1] It included Oliver Cowdery's *Defence in a Rehearsal of My Grounds for Separating Myself from the Latter Day Saints*. Jerald was especially interested in the statements of Book of Mormon witnesses David Whitmer and Oliver Cowdery, because they both affirmed the Book of Mormon but held that Joseph Smith became a fallen prophet after translating it. In his pamphlet, Cowdery even claimed to have had "an open vision" in which Jesus said Latter Day Saints had "permitt[ed] their President, Joseph Smith, Jr., to lead them forth into errors, where I led him not, nor commanded him."[2]

At the time, it did not occur to Jerald and Sandra to doubt the authenticity of the Cowdery tract. It was treated as authentic by Mormon historian B. H. Roberts in *Comprehensive History of the Church*, in which he referred his readers to the 1906 printing of the tract by R. B. Neal.[3] Fawn Brodie also accepted it in the original edition of *No Man Knows My History*, but noted that "apparently there are no copies of the original extant."[4] Cowdery's tract had supposedly been published in 1839, but the earliest available reprints date from after 1900. This naturally represented a challenge to Jerald and Sandra's circle of friends and fellow researchers to see if they could find an original copy.

---

1. Tanner and Tanner, *Revealing Statements*.
2. Cowdery, *Defence in a Rehearsal*, 4.
3. Roberts, *Comprehensive History of the Church*, 1:163n11.
4. Brodie, *No Man Knows My History*, 471.

In late 1960 Pauline Hancock had received a letter from Susan Kallenbach of the Yale University Library's Western Americana Collection announcing that they did not have the original but a copy of it, which they were willing to photocopy or microfilm. They stressed however that they had no information "as to the location of the original copy."[5] Before long Wesley P. Walters managed to trace the original from which the Yale copy was made to a certain Mr. Fulk, who allowed him to examine it in his home. Walters was disappointed to discover that it too was not an original but only made to look like one.[6] Evidently Walters's discovery occurred prior to the publication of the Tanners' *Revealing Statements* where they make mention of it.[7]

The following April (1961), Jerald requested a copy of the Cowdery document from the LDS Church Historian's Office, but was promptly refused.[8] So he and Sandra would eventually publish the Yale copy.[9]

By the summer of 1962, Richard Lloyd Anderson of Brigham Young University was also trying to determine whether the *Defence* was authentic. He sent a copy of the Cowdery *Defence* that he had managed to obtain to Yale and received a letter back recommending he contact Ernest Wessen of Midland Rare Book Company in Mansfield, Ohio. He did so no later than October 1963.[10] Wessen responded that there was no press in the town where the tract was supposedly printed (Norton, Ohio) in 1839 and that the typeface used in it came from a later period.[11]

---

5. Susan Kallenbach to Pauline Hancock, Nov. 15, 1960, Tanner and Tanner, Papers.

6. Wesley P. Walters to Jerald Tanner, Apr. 25, 1967, 1, Tanner and Tanner, Papers.

7. Although the Tanners' statement does not make this explicit: "In a letter dated Nov 15, 1960, an employee of the Yale University Library stated that they had 'a copy of the original.' Wesley P. Walters ... stated that he examined the copy and that he believed it to be the 1906 reprint. After examining we are inclined to agree with Mr. Walters." Had Walters already seen Fulk's copy of the *Defence*, or did he merely come to that conclusion by examining the Yale photocopy?

8. Earl E. Olson to Jerald Tanner, Apr. 24, 1961. A photocopy of this letter is in Tanner and Tanner, *Revealing Statements*, 3.

9. Tanner and Tanner, *Critical Look*, 7.

10. The date is derived from Ernest J. Wessen to Richard L. Anderson, Oct. 21, 1963, who speaks of "yours of the seventh." There may have been letters before this. The tone of Wessen's letter is at least consistent with it being his first response, but not decisively so.

11. Wessen to Anderson, Oct. 21, 1963.

When the Tanners set out to make a case against the *Defence*, they expressed many of the same concerns as Walters, Anderson, and other early investigators, namely, that the tract was never quoted anywhere prior to its appearance in the early twentieth century, that a first edition could not be discovered anywhere, and so on. But, as with much of his work, Jerald's most decisive argument was a textual one in which he showed that the *Defence* had been cobbled together from published Cowdery writings, especially the series of letters he wrote on the history of the church in the LDS newspaper *Messenger and Advocate*. It was impressive work that may have given a few of their critics pause: The Tanners were arguing that a broadly received document written by one of the three witnesses to the Book of Mormon but painted the LDS Church in a bad light was a fake.

In 1968, a year after the Tanners published their pamphlet, Richard Lloyd Anderson wrote an article on Oliver Cowdery for the *Improvement Era* in which he discussed the *Defence* and the likelihood of its being a forgery.[12] He did not mention the Tanners' efforts from the previous year. Other historians had read the Tanners' tract but were not convinced. Juanita Brooks wrote to Sandra and said the pamphlet had the opposite effect on her: "You have convinced me that the item is genuine and that it was really written by Oliver Cowdery."[13] Fawn Brodie similarly rejected the Tanners' arguments. "I regret very much to say that I cannot agree with you about the Cowdery 'Defence.' After the most careful reading, I still believe it to be genuine."[14] But, over time, most historians would come around to the Tanners' and Anderson's views and abandon Cowdery's *Defence* as a forgery.

The time the Tanners spent chasing leads and writing *A Critical Look* paled in comparison to the work they put into the Book of Abraham. For Egyptian scholars and critics of Mormonism, the Book of Abraham had long been pointed to as proof that Smith was not a prophet but a fraud.

In 1835 Smith bought four Egyptian mummies from Michael

---

12. Richard Lloyd Anderson, "The Second Witness of Priesthood Restoration, (Part 1)" *Improvement Era*, Sep. 1968, 21.

13. Juanita Brooks to Sandra Tanner, Jul. 13, 1968, 1, Tanner and Tanner, Papers.

14. Fawn M. Brodie to Jerald and Sandra Tanner, May 10, 1967, 1, Tanner and Tanner, Papers.

Chandler, who was touring the U.S. and displaying the artifacts. Included with the mummies were some papyri that Smith said contained the writings of the ancient prophets Abraham and Joseph. Smith set to work translating the papyri and produced the Book of Abraham, a now-canonized part of LDS scripture. The slim book is Mormonism's most esoteric scriptural book, discussing a plurality of gods, the eternal nature of matter, and "Kolob," the star nearest to where God resides.

But it is not only the book's strangeness that made it interesting. The Joseph Smith Papyri from which it was allegedly translated were long thought lost in the Great Chicago Fire of 1871, but in 1966 several fragments resurfaced in the New York Metropolitan Museum of Art. The next year the LDS Church obtained the fragments, and, as pictures of them began to circulate, it became clear that the papyri Smith "translated" had nothing to do with Abraham or any other biblical characters. Instead, they were familiar Egyptian funerary texts.[15]

In early 1965 a student from BYU told the Tanners that he had a copy of a document called the Egyptian Alphabet and asked whether they would be interested in reprinting it. They said they would, only to find out it was a typescript and not a copy of the original document itself.[16] Later that same year, James Wardle gave them a very poor microfilm of the original document, from which Sandra painstakingly produced a transcription. In April 1966 they were finally able to print the material on the microfilm, along with the transcription Sandra had made from it, under the title *Joseph Smith's Egyptian Alphabet & Grammar*. The significance of this document is hard to overstate since it reveals the very process by which Joseph attempted to translate character by character the Egyptian materials he had bought from Chandler in 1835 in order to produce the early part of the Book of Abraham.

This "Grammar & Alphabet of the Egyptian Language," as the title is given to the document itself, has thirty-four pages of text,

15. The Joseph Smith Papyri is the name given by scholars to the Egyptian materials purchased by Smith. For more on the history of the fragments, see Ritner, *Joseph Smith Egyptian Papyri*, and Jensen and Hauglid, *Revelations and Translations, Volume 4*, Introduction. Peterson, *Story of the Book of Abraham*, is a devotional history of the papyri.

16. Tanner and Tanner, *Joseph Smith's Egyptian Alphabet & Grammar*, 2.

interspersed with blank pages.[17] There are five sections labeled "degrees," and each degree is divided into two parts. Each degree repeats the same list of supposed Egyptian symbols/letters/characters in the left-hand margins, followed by the same fanciful English transliterations, and then "translations" that are expanded and supplemented through the degrees. The earliest versions of these translations appear in the first degree and the latest in the fifth.

The microfilm Wardle lent the Tanners contained other items as well on pages organized by letters of the alphabet. Scattered among these papers are three additional significant manuscripts related to the Alphabet and Grammar in its beginning stages—rough drafts, as it were.

On July 5, 1835, two days after he bought the mummies from Chandler, Smith along "with W. W. Phelps and O. Cowdery as scribes ... commenced the translation of some of the characters or hieroglyphics."[18] Consistent with this statement, the three rough drafts previously mentioned consist of one in the hand of Smith and Oliver Cowdery, one in the hand of W. W. Phelps, and one in the hand of Cowdery alone.[19]

Phelps was also the scribe for the whole of the first part of the five degrees of the Alphabet and Grammar itself. Phelps was later joined in writing out the section on the second part of the degrees by Warren Parrish, who came to the project apparently on November 14, 1835.[20] Each of these drafts is in much of the same state of completeness/incompleteness. Wardle's microfilm also contained two partial copies of the handwritten manuscript of the Book of Abraham—one written by Phelps and the other by Parrish.[21] Both manuscripts were headed "sign of the fifth degree of the second part," connecting them directly with the Grammar and Alphabet. Each

---

17. Jensen and Hauglid, *Revelations and Translations, Volume 4*, 111–90.

18. "Manuscript History B-1," 596.

19. Smith and Cowdery's pages were numbered as B, T, U, V, and W on the microfilm, Phelps's pages were numbered C, D, E, and F, and Cowdery's alone were A, X, I, and an unlettered page marked page 4. Marquardt, *Egyptian Papers*, 83–112; Jensen and Hauglid, *Revelations and Translations, Volume 4*, 55–109.

20. Marquardt, *Egyptian Papers*, 3.

21. Phelps's were lettered pages J–M (Abr. 1:4–2:6; Marquardt, *Egyptian Papers*, 175–83; Jensen and Hauglid, 191–201), and Parrish's were pages S, R, Q, P, N, and O (Abr. 1:4–2:2; Marquardt, *Egyptian Papers*, 185–97; Jensen and Hauglid, 203–15).

also included in its margins, next to its "translations" of the Book of Abraham text, the same set of character clusters. These had been created by taking over and joining together the individual characters in the Grammar and Alphabet. Thus, it becomes possible to trace the translation process from its inception and development through the five degrees culminating in the final wording of the Book of Abraham text.

None of this would have been immediately apparent to someone looking at the Tanners' reprint of the microfilm. This is because the five degrees appeared in reverse order, and the rest of the material on the microfilm is in a state of general disarray making it difficult to follow. It was left to H. Michael Marquardt to put the pages in their proper order and make sense of them in his book *The Joseph Smith Egyptian Papers* (1981). Despite the fact that the microfilm the Tanners and Marquardt used was of a very poor quality, making it extremely difficult to read the reproductions of many of the pages, theirs were the only reprints of the Grammar and Alphabet available to researchers for a half-century, until an edition with high-quality photos was finally made available online by the Joseph Smith Papers in 2012–13, followed by a hard copy edition in 2018.[22]

There had been a significant amount of discussion of the Grammar and Alphabet before the Tanners came out with their edition. Decades before, LDS Scholar Sidney Sperry, having encountered references to the Grammar and Alphabet in historical documents, eventually found it in 1935 in the LDS archives.[23] Permission was granted to Sperry and his colleague James R. Clark to photograph the document, which was brought to BYU from the Historian's Office by A. William Lund and photographed by Wayne B. Hales of the physics department.[24]

Clark made the Grammar and Alphabet a focus of special study, mentioning it often in his writings and explaining its characters, layout, and content.[25] It was he who apparently first realized the

22. Jensen and Hauglid, *Revelations and Translations, Volume 4*.

23. Clark, *Story of the Pearl of Great Price*, 156.

24. The details were given by Sidney B. Sperry in an interview aired on KBYU-FM on the Evening of December 11, 1967, and printed in Christenson, *Mummies, Scrolls*, 16–24.

25. Clark, *Story of the Pearl of Great Price*, 103.

true connection between its characters and the text of the Book of Abraham: "Abraham 1:23–24 is condensed in the translation for the fifth degree of Iota toues zip zet [*sic*]."[26] So earnest was Clark in discovering what Joseph Smith was doing in the process of translating the Book of Abraham that he wrote down each of the characters from the Grammar and Alphabet along with their various translations onto 350 5x8 inch note cards to help him in the process of deciphering them.[27] Approaching things this way was natural for a believing Mormon who took at face value Smith's claims about translating the Egyptian papyri to make the Book of Abraham. It was this same motivation that would cause another believer to face excommunication for studying the Grammar and Alphabet. Grant Stuart Heward, James Wardle's postman, would make a significant contribution to Book of Abraham studies. Heward would, in time, become friends with the Tanners and part of the Tanner/Wardle circle of researchers. His journey from faithful believer to excommunicant would highlight the primary issues surrounding the Book of Abraham, and why it represented a serious challenge to Joseph Smith's prophetic translations.

Heward had a "happy and united home" in which he and his wife rose early every morning to "worship and pray" and to "discuss spiritual topics and try and get our spiritual bearing for the day."[28] When he heard about the Grammar and Alphabet, he was very excited. Here, he thought, would be clear and concrete evidence that Joseph Smith succeeded in translating Egyptian, and therefore prove that he was a true prophet of God. In pursuit of this goal, between delivering letters and packages, Heward studied Egyptian. The published LDS scriptural canon provided examples of Egyptian texts in the form of the Pearl of Great Price's three Book of Abraham facsimiles that he could use to test Smith's prophetic ability. Little did Heward know at the time that others had gone that way before him, and that he was about to step into a deep hole of disappointment.

By late May 1965, Heward reported that his studies had progressed to the point where he was "beginning to recognize some of

---

26. Clark, *Study Guide*, 43.
27. Clark, "History and Translation," 60.
28. Grant S. Heward to Murray, May 4, 1967, Tanner and Tanner, Papers.

the characters on the Hypocephalus [Book of Abraham, Facsimile 2] myself."[29] A hypocephalus is a circular piece of papyrus or other material covered with inscriptions and incantations that was traditionally placed under the heads of mummies. Smith had numbered various images on the copied hypocephalus and provided explanations and translations of what he represented to be Egyptian words, but two of which were actually Hebrew words he apparently cribbed from the second edition of Joshua Seixas's *Manual Hebrew Grammar for the Use of Beginners* (1834). Smith took a two-month Hebrew course from Seixas in early 1836.[30]

The previous year (1964) the Tanners had already made available a reprint of *Why Egyptologists Reject the Book of Abraham*, a booklet originally published in 1912 by Salt Lake City Episcopalian bishop Franklin S. Spalding.[31] Heward may have had access to this booklet, as he compared his own work to the collected opinions of the early Egyptologists.[32] Spalding's eight prominent scholars, some of the most distinguished in the world, unanimously agreed that while Joseph Smith had some knowledge of Hebrew words, he knew nothing about Egyptian.[33]

None of this would have been clearly understood by Heward when he first undertook the study of Egyptian in 1965. As for the supposed Egyptian terms, one of the few places beside the Book of Abraham where relevant parallels could be found was in a letter

---

29. Grant S. Heward to Earnest C. Conrad, May 22, 1965, Tanner and Tanner, Papers.

30. "Certificate from *Joshua* Seixas, 30 March 1936," in Rogers et al., *Documents, Volume 5*, 214–16.

31. The Spalding/Mercer reprint was advertised on page 3 of the first issue of the *Salt Lake City Messenger*, Nov. 1964.

32. Grant S. Heward to Murray, May 2, 1967, 2. The Tanners reviewed the scholars' testimony in the article they wrote to accompany the release of their edition of the Egyptian alphabet, "Hidden Document Revealed," *Salt Lake City Messenger* 7, Apr. 1966, 1–3.

33. According to them, Smith was "absolutely ignorant of the simplest facts of Egyptian writing and civilization" (James S. Breasted, University of Chicago, Haskell Oriental Museum, in Tanner and Tanner, *Why Egyptologists Reject*, 27); "knows nothing" of Chaldean or Egyptian (John Peters, University of Pennsylvania, 28); and "knew neither the Egyptian language nor the meaning of the most commonplace Egyptian figures" ([S]. A. B. Mercer, University of Toronto, 29). Mercer also remarked that "the author either knew Hebrew or had some means of arriving at, at least, an elementary knowledge of that language" (29).

from Smith to James A. Bennet in the 1843 *Times and Seasons* in which he displayed his knowledge of different languages.[34]

Smith appears to have intended the Egyptian words as real words with meanings similar to words he presents in other languages, as seen in the other stock phrases he quotes, like the Latin *Dominus regit me* ("The Lord is my Shepherd" [Psalm 23:1]), the Hebrew *Haueloheem yerau* ("Fear God" [Ecclesiastes 5:6,12:13]), and the Greek "God is Light" (*O theos phos esi* [*sic*]1 John 1:5).[35] As for the Egyptian, he translates for the words "Jah-oh-eh, Enish-go-on-dosh, Flo-ees-Flos-is-is" as "O the earth! the power of attraction, and the moon passing between her and the sun." He does not specifically explain how these supposed Egyptian words, which were also used in Facsimile no. 2 with similar meanings, connect to the particular English words in his translation.

When the Egyptian Grammar and Alphabet became available it allowed scholars to cross-check Smith's work. There Heward, the new student of Egyptian, could view what were supposed to be Egyptian characters along with their translations. While many of the characters in the margins of the Grammar and Alphabet had been inartfully copied from hieratic script, there were still a few items that Heward would have been able to compare with the characters he was learning from standard Egyptian grammars and lexicons. Except none of the accompanying transliterations and meanings matched up.[36]

Heward could now identify the exact characters that the words from Facsimile 2 were supposedly derived from. Ja-ho-eh ("earth") was represented by a circle with a cross in it,[37] Flo-ees ("moon") as a circle with a line drawn down its middle,[38] and Flos-is-is ("sun")

---

34. *Times and Seasons*, Nov. 1, 1843, 373. The letter is dated November 13, 1843. But see Brown, "Translator and Ghostwriter," 46–47.

35. The Greek is wrong: *esi* should be *esti*

36. E.g., the character transliterated "Ho-oop-hah," found on pages 3, 9, 13, 17, and 21 of the Egyptian Alphabet (Marquardt, *Joseph Smith Egyptian Papers*; Jensen and Hauglid, *Revelations and Translations, Volume 4*) and translated as a "crown," but which Heward could have found to represent M in, for example, Budge, *Easy Lessons in Egyptian Hieroglyphics*, 11, 31, along with an additional phonetic value of *ḳes*, with its meaning as an ideogram or determinative given as "side" (75).

37. Alphabet and Grammar, 24, 27, 29, 31, 33.

38. Alphabet and Grammar, 25, 27, 30, 31, 34.

as a black circle.[39] But again, neither the characters nor the translit-erations were right. In the course of his letters, Heward mentioned some of the Egyptian reference works he was using, including Alan Gardiner's *Egyptian Grammar* and E. Wallace Budge's *Egyptian Hieroglyphic Dictionary*.[40]

The closest that the Egyptian Grammar and Alphabet came to translating something correctly in relation to these three symbols was the moon: the circle with a line through it. It was not the most commonly described hieroglyphic character for the moon, but Gardiner did include in his grammar a character of a circle with a line through it as representing the moon. But even in that case there was a problem. In Gardiner's symbol the line ran not vertically as in the Egyptian Grammar, but horizontally.[41] Furthermore, the pho-netic value of the character was *psḏ*, nothing at all like "Flo-ees." Heward was additionally troubled to discover how the translations of what could only represent at most a letter, syllable, or word in Egyptian hieroglyphics expanded into whole paragraphs that even-tually took shape as Book of Abraham text. By the time it reached the fifth degree, the translation of the word "Ja-ho-eh" extended to 144 words[42]; "Flo-ees" ran eleven words but no longer referred to the moon alone, but to "the moon, the earth, and the sun in their annual revolutions."[43] Finally, the translation of "Flos-is-is" blossomed to 114 words by the time it reached the fifth degree.[44]

When Heward first came into contact with the Egyptian Gram-mar and Alphabet, he was "really excited and tackled it with a perfect confidence in Joseph Smith."[45] He was certain that if Smith

---

39. Alphabet and Grammar, 25, 27, 30, 31, 34.

40. Gardiner, *Egyptian Grammar*, and Budge, *Egyptian Hieroglyphic Dictionary*. He names these two sources (along with others) in Grant S. Heward to I. E. S. Edwards, Mar. 4, 1968, 1, Tanner and Tanner, Papers; Heward, *What About*, 1.

41. Gardiner, *Egyptian Grammar*, 486. Described as representing "half-full moon" in Selden, *Hieroglyphic Egyptian*, 363, with a phonetic value of *psḏ*.

42. Or 114, if you accept the commas dividing the Egyptian names of the fifteen moving planets. The commas only admit twelve names.

43. Alphabet and Grammar, 25; Jensen and Hauglid, *Revelations and Translations, Volume 4*. It referred primarily to the moon through the preceding four degrees (27, 30, 31, 34).

44. Alphabet and Grammar, 25; Jensen and Hauglid, *Revelations and Translations, Volume 4*.

45. Grant S. Heward to Brother Miller, Apr. 9, 1969, 2, Tanner and Tanner, Papers.

"took part in the translation, it would without a doubt, match the Egyptian meaning it was taken from."[46] But his hopes were quickly dashed when "I started studying the [Egyptian] grammar [and Alphabet], but to my dismay, I soon found it was full of nonsense." Heward was shocked. "The document must not be authentic," he reasoned. "Someone was trying to make Joseph Smith look bad!" He had to find out if the document was real, and to discredit it if possible. He spoke by telephone with one of the heads of the Historian's Office, who denied any knowledge of the Grammar and Alphabet's existence. He then discovered that James R. Clark had written about the document in his 1955 book *The Story of the Pearl of Great Price*. He telephoned Clark.

Clark assured him that the document did exist and was authentic. Clark also told Heward that the Historian's Office employee who had denied knowledge of the document's existence to Heward over the telephone was one of two people who had originally brought it to BYU to be photographed.[47] Clark suggested that Heward go the Historian's Office in person. Heward did so and was told that he could not see the original, but he might be able to see the microfilm if he got permission from Church Historian Joseph Fielding Smith. He had already been troubled by being lied to, but he was now even more distraught after being grilled by William Lund and Joseph Fielding Smith. "After a session of inter[r]ogation, I was granted the permission I sought; but their cynical questions left me with the dismal impression that they had no confidence in Joseph Smith's translating ability and a fear of honest, open research."[48]

Heward examined the Church Historian's copy and became convinced that it was the same document he had been working with, concluding that it must therefore not be a forgery created to embarrass Joseph Smith. Even more troubling to Heward was the conviction that LDS general authorities also knew (and had likely known for years) what he had just discovered. "I realized then," Heward wrote, "that if they had anywhere near the confidence in

46. Heward to Miller, 3
47. Sidney B. Sperry identified A. William Lund as the one who brought the Egyptian alphabet to BYU to be photographed, in an interview aired on KBYU-FM on December 11, 1967, and printed in Christenson, *Mummies, Scrolls,* 16–24.
48. Heward to Miller, 3.

Joseph Smith they pretended to have, they would have proudly published it [the Egyptian Grammar and Alphabet] years before, instead of keeping it quietly hidden away."[49]

Heward, now convinced he could not rely on the church to give him accurate information, sent a copy of the Egyptian Grammar and Alphabet to Professor Klaus Baer at the University of Chicago's Oriental Institute. In response, Baer focused on a document from the microfilm purporting to present "Egyptian Counting" from one to thirty-nine. Baer contrasted the symbols found there for one through ten with what they really were in both Coptic and Old Egyptian, concluding, "Further comment needed?"[50] Heward would learn of other Egyptologists equally dismissive of the Book of Abraham.[51]

The following January, Labib Habachi, of Cairo, Egypt, who had recently visited Salt Lake City and had received a very kind reception from LDS leadership, responded to Heward somewhat hesitantly:

> Now you are sending me a [micro]film, an Egyptian Grammar, some quotations about Egyptians and coloured people. These, I have to say, are simple imaginations and no scholar at all can ever approve anything in these documents of the Mormons. ... I would not like to shake your faith. There is no question that the Mormons have planned a wonderful organization, but I have to tell, you, as an Egyptologist, that their claim to understand hieroglyphics is mere imagination.[52]

Heward felt certain that his fellow Mormons needed to hear what he had discovered and came up with the idea of producing leaflets to hand out at the LDS semi-annual general conference. These consisted of at least two sheets, one entitled "Why Would Anyone Want to Fight Truth?" and the other "What About Joseph

---

49. Heward to Miller, 4.

50. Klaus Baer to Grant S. Heward, Sep. 20, 1966, 1, Tanner and Tanner, Papers.

51. See, for example, I. E. S. Edwards, Keeper of Egyptian Antiquities at the British Museum, to "Dear Sir," Dec. 22, 1965; John A. Wilson, University of Chicago, to Marv Cowan, Mar. 16, 1966; Richard A. Parker, Brown University, to Marv Cowan, Mar. 22, 1966, in Tanner and Tanner, Papers.

52. Habachi was an Egyptologist who worked for the Egyptian government to help protect national antiquities. Labib Habachi to Grant S. Heward, Jan. 15, 1967, Tanner and Tanner, Papers. See also, Kamil, *Labib Habachi*.

Smith's Egyptian Grammar?"[53] Heward asked Jerald if he thought this plan would get him into trouble. Jerald felt it was unlikely, reasoning that the church would not want to draw attention to the Book of Abraham problems. So Heward moved forward with his plans and distributed his leaflets at general conference in April 1967. One of the leaflets was particularly well conceived. Heward spelled out in a simple way the problem raised by Joseph's translating many words from single Egyptian characters in the Grammar and Alphabet: "Suppose someone showed you a round black dot on a piece of paper and said that it was writing. That it told the story of 'Little Red Riding Hood'; the whole story–Little Red Riding Hood, her mother, her grandmother, the wolf, the woodcutter, the forest, the basket of cookies and all–everything! The whole story was there! Could a single round dot carry that much meaning?"

On the other side Heward brought home his point by reproducing the actual Egyptian alphabet, describing how his readers could use it to write their own names, how the drawing of an owl represents "m," and of a foot, "b", and so on. He then explained how a single Egyptian character in the Egyptian Grammar and Alphabet had become the source of the seventy-six words that make up Book of Abraham 1:13–14.

It was a good argument, making plain the problem of taking the Book of Abraham seriously as an actual translation from Egyptian, and it seems to have played a part in motivating BYU professor Hugh Nibley to try to come up with a way of denying that Joseph Smith was responsible for the "translation" process observed in the Egyptian Grammar and Alphabet. "[W]e nowhere find mention of Joseph Smith engaged in translating the Book of Abraham itself," Nibley insists, "before October of 1840." And he goes on to assure his readers that "none of [the Egyptian Grammar and Alphabet] could ever have been used even as an imaginary basis for constructing the story of Abraham."[54]

---

53. Nibley refers to Heward's Little Red Riding Hood illustration, noting that "In 1967 a Mr. Heward passed out Handbills at a general conference." "Meaning of Kirtland Egyptian Papers," 374.

54. Nibley, "Meaning of Kirtland Egyptian Papers," 355, 365. Some authors still argue along Nibley's lines, see, e.g., John Gee, *Introduction to the Book of Abraham*, 33–34; Bushman, *Joseph Smith: Rough Stone Rolling*, 290. Increasingly, however, Heward's approach is being recognized as the correct one and Nibley's as primarily apologetic in nature.

In any case, as it would turn out, Jerald was wrong about Heward not getting into trouble. There was no way the LDS Church could ignore one of its members passing out leaflets at general conference challenging a canonized book of scripture. The church reacted quickly; Heward was tried for his membership on June 21, 1967, for the "alleged circulation of literature challenging the validity of the translation of a standard work of the Church of Jesus Christ of Latter-day Saints" and excommunicated.[55] The charge against Heward had come down from Joseph Fielding Smith himself, then a counselor in the First Presidency.[56]

---

55. The wording comes from the summons issued by the Midvale Stake (June 14, 1967), and signed by S. A. Hutchings, Lloyd Gardner, and R. Kent King, Tanner and Tanner, Papers.

56. In a circular letter that Heward prepared to explain his excommunication to his friends, he writes that "both [i.e., the bishop and stake president] stated that the charge came from the office of Joseph Fielding Smith." Tanner and Tanner, Papers.

10

DEE JAY NELSON AND
THE JOSEPH SMITH PAPYRI

Just as they had with the earliest account of Joseph Smith's First Vision, indications began to reach the Tanners and their circle that some of the original papyri that Smith had purchased from Michael Chandler in 1835 still existed. This was big news; it was one thing to have the Egyptian Grammar and Alphabet, recorded by Smith and his scribes. It was another entirely to have the original papyri Smith used in his translation of the book of Abraham.

In August 1966, University of Chicago Egyptologist Klaus Baer wrote to Grant Heward that "there is good reason to think that some, at least of the papyri are still in existence, despite the persistent stories about their having been destroyed in a fire around 1871."[1] In September, Baer more explicitly referred to a "lot of eleven papyri from the Joseph Smith collection that will probably make a reappearance in the not too distant future."[2] The New York Metropolitan Museum of Art, however, was asking Egyptologists to keep the location of these papyri confidential. In a letter Baer wrote to Jerald later, he speculated, "It may very well be that the Metr[opolitan] Mus[eum] was dropping hints about the papyri to everyone they could think of … in the hope that they'd do something about it—and we all took the request to keep the matter confidential too seriously."[3]

One day Glen W. Davidson, a writer and professor of religion at the University of Chicago, was visiting his colleague Klaus Baer, who showed him photographs of the Joseph Smith Papyri. Davidson

---

1. Klaus Baer to Grant S. Heward, Aug. 9, 1966, 1. Unless otherwise noted, all letters cited in this chapter come from Tanner and Tanner, Papers.
2. Klaus Baer to Grant S. Heward, Sep. 20, 1966, 1.
3. Klaus Baer to Jerald Tanner, Aug. 16, 1968, 1.

noticed that the pictures were each marked with a number, which he took to be catalog numbers. Davidson memorized as many of the numbers as he could and wrote them down after leaving. He wrote a letter to Jerald and Sandra and gave them the numbers, saying that Hugh Nibley had already obtained a set of the photos through the mediation of a "Prof. Aryah (?), Arabic Studies, of the U. of Utah." The Tanners recognized that "Prof. Araya" probably referred to Aziz S. Atiya.[4] Heward called Atiya and asked him for help to match the catalog numbers with the institution that used them, but Atiya feigned ignorance, suggesting only that "he'd heard the papyri had been burned years ago in the Chicago fire."[5] Atiya, who had already seen the fragments, also sought to put Heward off the scent by suggesting he write to the University of Michigan. The numbers were then passed along to Wesley P. Walters, who, on November 23, 1967, wrote to the Metropolitan Museum of Art in New York City. Henry G. Fischer, Curator of Egyptian Art, responded in a letter dated November 28, saying, "It is curious that you should inquire about these fragments just now, for they were turned over to the Mormon Church yesterday."[6]

According to the official story, Atiya, a non-LDS professor of Middle Eastern studies at the University of Utah, had visited the Met in May 1966 in pursuit of his own research. In the process he stumbled upon a set of papyri that he recognized at once to be related to the facsimiles in the Pearl of Great Price. Over the next year he played a key role in negotiating the transfer of the eleven papyrus fragments to the LDS Church, "made possible" by an anonymous donation to the museum.[7] Baer wrote to Jerald explaining that

the Metr[opolitan] Mus[eum] photos were shown to Nibley in 1965 (at which time he did not know where the originals were). Atiya's story about "discovering" the papyri is obviously mistaken. He "discovered"

4. Glen W. Davidson to Jerald and Sandra Tanner, Oct. 10, 1967, 1. See also Tanner and Tanner, *Case Against Mormonism*, 2:136.

5. Grant S. Heward to Klaus Baer, Jan. 8, 1968, 1. Atiya says that he had promised the Metropolitan Museum that he would "not divulge the whereabouts of these documents until the whole deal is concluded" (Atiya, "Discovery and Date," 41).

6. Henry G. Fischer to Wesley P. Walters, Nov. 28, 1967, qtd. in Tanners, *Case Against Mormonism* 2:137.

7. "Interview with Dr. Fischer," 64.

them because the Metr. Mus. wanted them "discovered." It is also pretty clear to me that the Metr. Mus. didn't want anyone to find out about the papyri before the Mormon Church did, at least not publicly, and that they took their own sweet time about it. To me this is tantamount to suppression.[8]

The museum had acquired the documents in 1947.[9] Within six years, Mormon historian Dale Morgan had heard of their existence.[10]

The LDS Church only allowed select individuals to see them between the time the Met had handed the papyri over on November 27, 1967, and when the church published pictures of them in a last-minute insert in the February 1968 issue of the *Improvement Era* magazine.

Copies of the photos were already leaking out by then. James Wardle, who had once been considered for the post of Church Historian of the RLDS Church, tried to get copies from Richard P. Howard, the current occupant of that office. But to his dismay, his request was denied.[11] He still somehow managed to acquire a full set of the pictures, though of poor quality. The Tanners and their friends wondered whether the only reason the LDS Church suddenly decided to publish the pictures in the *Improvement Era* was because copies had already begun to circulate. Grant Heward had taken his own set to the church-owned *Deseret News*, hoping to obtain the church's clearer photos; if he already had them, he reasoned, why shouldn't they give him the clearer copies? The *News* turned him down, and, shortly after, the church announced it would publish photos of the papyri in its magazine.

With photographs of the Joseph Smith Papyri in hand, it was now possible to solve further mysteries by comparing them with the material on the Egyptian Grammar and Alphabet microfilm. In this way Heward was able to identify the particular Joseph Smith Papyri document that had actually been used as the "source" for the

---

8. Klaus Baer to Jerald Tanner, Aug. 13, 1968, 1–2.

9. Peter F. Dorman, Assistant Curator, Egyptian Dept., Metropolitan Museum of Art, to Jerald Tanner, June 26, 1981, 1.

10. Morgan, *Dale Morgan*, 199.

11. Richard P. Howard to James W. Wardle, Jan. 15 and 29, 1968; James D. Wardle to Richard P. Howard, Jan. 27 and 31, 1968.

characters "translated" to become the text of the opening part of the Book of Abraham down to chapter 2 verse 12.

The characters in the left margin of the Book of Abraham translation manuscripts taken down by W. W. Phelps and Warren Parrish in the Egyptian Grammar and Alphabet were the same characters *appearing in the same sequence* as they are found in Joseph Smith Papyrus XI. Because the sequence of characters was retained, it could now be determined that when Smith encountered holes or gaps in Papyrus XI, he attempted to "restore" the missing Egyptian characters from revelation or some other source. These "restored" characters turned out not to be Egyptian characters at all. This explained why non-Egyptian characters had been interspersed with Egyptian ones in the margins of the Phelps/Parrish Book of Abraham translation manuscripts.

The comparison also solved another mystery. The Egyptian Grammar and Alphabet microfilm included an ink sketch of the hypocephalus that served as basis for the Book of Abraham's facsimile 2. The sketch revealed that the hypocephalus was apparently already extensively damaged when it came into Joseph Smith's possession. It was missing several pieces, including one substantial pie-shaped piece out of one side. Where the hypocephalus was extant, facsimile 2 got it generally right, but where pieces were missing, facsimile 2 got it all wrong. Heward discovered that Papyrus XI had also been the source of the characters used to fill in the missing gaps in the hypocephalus in order to create facsimile 2. They were taken from lines 2–4 of the papyrus's right-hand column, but whoever had done it mistakenly copied the characters from line 4 upside down.[12]

On the very same day that Grant discovered this, Jerald had also been studying the documents and also noticed that the section numbered 14 on the right side of facsimile 2 had been taken over from Joseph Smith Papyrus XI.[13] Jerald and Grant further noticed that the fill-in material was in a different script from that was used in the original document. The original hypocephalus had been produced using *hieroglyphic* script, whereas the fill-in material, relying as it did on the Joseph Smith Papyrus XI, used *hieratic* script. Consequently

---

12. Tanner and Tanner, *Shadow or Reality?*, 339.
13. Grant S. Heward to Brother Miller, Apr. 9, 1969, 1. For Jerald's account of the joint discovery, see "Facsimile's Altered," *Salt Lake City Messenger* 21, Nov. 1968, 2.

the material added from Papyrus XI, even if some of it had not been copied upside down, would still be foreign to the document, not only in thought but also in script. Grant and Jerald also noticed that not all of the fill-in material came from Papyrus XI. The god in the boat in the upper-right of the picture, for example, was copied instead from Joseph Smith Papyrus IV.

Once Jerald and Heward discovered all this, they collaborated on an article that appeared in the 1968 summer issue of *Dialogue: A Journal of Mormon Thought* under the title "The Source of the Book of Abraham Identified."[14] Klaus Baer praised the article, "which seems to be factual and uncontrovertable [*sic*] in every detail."[15] Predictably, LDS scholar Hugh Nibley disagreed, and asserted instead that Joseph Smith Papyrus XI did not pose any problems to Facsimile 2: "We must recognize that there are sections of hieroglyphic text in Facsimile 2, that present-day Egyptologists read without too much trouble," Nibley stated in the September 1968 *Improvement Era*, "since these legible portions are found to be correct and conventional Egyptian, it is perfectly plain that nobody has falsified or jumbled them, as was charged."[16] But Jerald and Heward's conclusions were accepted by Baer and later Egyptologists.[17]

Yet even some early faithful LDS authors tacitly granted the legitimacy of Grant and Jerald's evidence, as is seen for example in Richley Crapo's contribution to an April 3, 1970, Book of Abraham Symposium at the University of Utah Institute of Religion, where Crapo comes close to taking credit for the Heward/Tanner discovery himself, without mentioning their names at all.[18] He even

---

14. Heward and Tanner, "Source of the Book of Abraham Identified."

15. Klaus Baer to Jerald Tanner, Aug. 16, 1968, 2; see also Baer, "Breathing Permit of Hôr," 111–12n11, where Baer cites Grant and Jerald's article to support his claim that it was "now certain" that "Joseph Smith thought that this papyrus contained the Book of Abraham," 2.

16. Hugh Nibley, "A New Look at the Pearl of Great Price: Facsimile No. 1, A Unique Document (Part 5)," *Improvement Era*, Sep. 1968, 74, qtd. in "Facsimile's Altered," 2.

17. Ritner, "Breathing Permit of Hôr," 98n4.

18. Crapo writes: "In December of 1967, I was able to examine the original papyri in the vaults of the BYU library and obtain one of the first released sets of photographic copies for extended study. A more careful examination of these revealed the startling fact that one of the papyri of the Church collection, known as the Small Sen-Sen Papyrus, contained the same series of hieratic symbols, which had been copied, in the same order, into the Book of Abraham manuscript next to verses of that book!" Richley Crapo, "Emic and Etic Studies," 27. The question is, who made the "more careful examination?" Crapo or somebody else?

seems to have redrawn their illustration and presented it as his own, again without giving credit.[19]

In 1968 Jerald received a call from an LDS man named Dee Jay Nelson, who said he was working on a translation of the Joseph Smith Papyri and wanted to come to Salt Lake City to discuss the possibility of having the Tanners publish it. Jerald agreed at least to meet and talk. Nelson sounded legitimate, impressive even, but did he really know what he was doing, and could he really translate Egyptian?

Jerald had been studying Egyptian with Heward. To test Nelson's abilities, he devised a set of questions about the papyri. Nelson's answers satisfied Jerald. As it happened, Nelson had been one of the few who had been granted access to the photographs of the papyri before they were made public. Hugh Nibley had expressed confidence in Nelson's abilities five months earlier when he told him he could "see no reason in the world why you should not be taken into the confidence of the brethren if this thing ever comes out into the open; in fact, you should be enormously useful to the Church."[20]

In the early days of their acquaintance, Nelson wrote to the Tanners using a letterhead that described him as "Prof. Dee Jay Nelson, Lecturer and Egyptologist," which included, in addition to his home address, a "Field Address" at Cairo's Nile Hilton.[21] A second letterhead that he also often used described him not as a professor but as Dee Jay Nelson, "Explorer and Naturalist, President of the Explorers' League and Member of the Los Angeles Adventurers' Club."[22] A third gave his address as the National Audubon Society's New York 5th Avenue Audubon House, describing Nelson as a "Film Lecturer."[23] And a fourth, decorated with hieroglyphics, does not include his name at all, but simply the English words "Keepers

---

19. See Crapo, "Emic and Etic Studies," 34. Compare Crapo's Fig. 1 with Heward and Tanner, "Source Identified," 96, which dates to the summer of 1968, and the earlier "Fall of the Book of Abraham," *Salt Lake City Messenger* 17, Mar. 1968, 1; Tanner and Tanner, *Is the Book of Abraham True*, 4; and Grant S. Heward, "The Book of Abraham Papyrus Found" (undated single-sheet leaflet, late 1968?), reverse side.

20. Hugh Nibley to Dee Jay Nelson, June 27, 1967, 1.

21. See, e.g., Dee Jay Nelson to Jerald Tanner, Apr. 17, 1968, 1.

22. See, e.g., Dee Jay Nelson to "Beloved Friends" [Sandra and Jerald Tanner], Nov. 18, 1968, 1.

23. Dee Jay Nelson to "Friends," Nov. 6, 1972, 1.

of Truth."[24] Such an array of letterheads might well raise suspicion, but if you had asked Nelson for proof of his credentials, he would provide it in one form or another. Yet when the Tanners first considered publishing Nelson's translation, he had stuck mostly to the first letterhead: "Prof. Dee Jay Nelson, Lecturer and Egyptologist," who could be reached in either Billings or Cairo.

Why would a man trusted by Nibley and LDS Church authorities want to publish his work through Modern Microfilm? Nelson may have believed that, given the contents of the papyri, the church would refuse to publish a translation that revealed the disconnect between the papyri and the Book of Abraham. And so it happened that Dee Jay Nelson and Modern Microfilm would produce the first translation of the Joseph Smith Papyri. By the end of March 1968, one thousand copies of Nelson's *The Joseph Smith Papyri: A Translation and Preliminary Survey of the T-shirt-Min & Ter Papyri* were printed and ready for sale at seventy-five cents a copy.[25]

As part of the book's launch, the Tanners arranged with the Newspaper Agency Corporation for ads in the *Salt Lake Tribune* and the *Deseret News*. They took the Tanners' money, but when the time came for the ad to appear, the *Tribune* ran it, but the *Deseret News* refused.[26] The Tanners discussed the matter with N. Eldon Tanner, a counselor in the First Presidency, but he also refused to help in any way. The money taken for the ad in the *Deseret News* was never returned, and the refusal provided additional fodder for an article announcing the release of Nelson's translation in the next issue of the *Salt Lake City Messenger*.[27]

Nelson's *Joseph Smith Papyri* was the first of four booklets he produced for the Tanners offering translations of the Book of Abraham facsimiles and the rest of the Joseph Smith Papyri. The first booklet, among other things, included a discussion of the creation of the Book of Abraham's Facsimile 1. This was followed by the

24. Dee Jay Nelson, open letter "to friends," Dec. 1, 1977, 1.

25. The sales were noted on the sheet on which Jerald kept track of Nelson's royalties, in Tanner and Tanner, Papers.

26. See the advertisement in the *Salt Lake Tribune*, Apr. 6, 1968, A-2. The Tanners were informed of the refusal to print on the part of the *Deseret News* on April 3, 1968. See "Papyri Not about Abraham," *Salt Lake City Messenger* 18, Apr. 1968, 1.

27. "Papyri Not about Abraham."

simultaneous release of Nelson's *Joseph Smith's "Eye of Ra: A Preliminary Survey and First Translation of Facsimile No. 2 in the Book of Abraham* and *The Joseph Smith Papyri Part 2: Additional Translations and a Supplemental Survery of the Ta-shert-Min, Hor and Amen Terp Papyri*, which included extensive discussion of Smith Papyri XI, the sensen text that had served as the source of first part of the Book of Abraham.[28] Nelson's fourth and final contribution, *A Translation of Facsimile No. 3 in the Book of Abraham*, appeared in February 1969.[29]

Even though Nelson chose to publish with the Tanners, some LDS scholars were willing to overlook the partnership. Hugh Nibley, after disparaging Heward's work, said, "It is a different story when we come to Mr. Dee Jay Nelson's work, the *Joseph Smith Papyri*. This is a conscientious and courageous piece of work . . . the first step in a serious study of the Facsimiles of the Pearl of Great Price ... a usable and reliable translation of the available papyri that once belonged to Joseph Smith."[30] Others echoed Nibley, and even compared Nelson favorably to Klaus Baer.[31]

Nelson kept his credibility firmly in place with Latter-day Saints because of his devout belief in the Book of Mormon.[32] He impressed others because, before the second of his four booklets became available, well-known Egyptologists had weighed in on the Joseph Smith Papyri with results that tended to affirm Nelson's work.[33] Indeed, although his work was far from perfect, if Nelson had been content to write his booklets and gone on to pursue other interests, things might have turned out differently for him.

By 1972, Jerald began to hear "rumors from different people who have talked to you [Nelson]. They claim there is more to the story

---

28. Both advertised for the first time in the *Salt Lake City Messenger* 20, Sep. 1968. Starting with a printing of 1,000 copies each (according to Jerald's handwritten royalty record for Nelson's booklets).

29. First advertised in the *Salt Lake City Messenger* 22, Feb. 1969, 1.

30. Nibley, "Getting Ready to Begin," 247.

31. See, for example, Tvedtnes, "Critics of the Book of Abraham," 70, and Crapo, "Emic and Etic Studies," 27.

32. Nelson made such arguments in a number of his letters to the Tanners during their early association. See, e.g., his letters to them dated Nov. 18, 1968, Nov. 23, 1968, Jan. 1, 1969.

33. Wilson, "Joseph Smith Egyptian Papyri", 65–85; Parker, "Joseph Smith Papyri: A Preliminary Report," 86–88; Parker, "Book of Breathings," 98–99.

about you and Church leaders. For instance, it has been claimed that [N. Eldon] Tanner asked you to change the translation and that the Church had originally agreed to publish the translation."[34] Nelson hadn't mentioned these things to Jerald in 1968 when he had approached the Tanners about publishing his work. Nelson responded to Jerald with a bizarre story. He admitted it was "true that the Church agreed to publish my translation ... before I did it. At that time there was no question among Church fathers that I was the only Mormon capable of the task." Then he explained that

> a little over a year ago [in 1971] six persons (3 men and their wives) contacted me and arranged for a meeting at a big hotel here in Billings (not at my home mind you ... very suspicious). At the appointed time I joined them in the hotel restaurant. The man who dominated the group introduced himself as James Baker but during the course of the evening (in the cafe and later in the lob[b]y) he was twice called Bill by one of the other men. I noticed that when he paid the dinner bill with a credit card he signed it with a much longer name than James Baker. I was not close enough to read it but I counted 23 distinctive upward strokes of his pen. Later in my office I practiced writting [sic] James Baker counting only 15 or 16 upward motions. ... I really believe that they were sent by the Church to sound me out. [N. Eldon] Tanner himself has avoided me at every turn and has relegated the answering of letters to a secretary so that the "Great Man's" signature would not appear on them.[35]

Reading the above gives more credence to Nelson's claim that in the mid-1940s he had made ends meet by writing pulp fiction under the pen name Nugget Lance[36] than it does to his being asked by N. Eldon Tanner to change the text. But in telling the tale, Nelson avoided giving Jerald a direct answer. All that was shared was a story of a mysterious man with a fake name who had "very suspiciously" taken him to dinner in an unnamed "big hotel" in Billings, Montana.

Some years later, however, Nelson would be much less hesitant in making the charge that N. Eldon Tanner had directly asked him to change the text. In one telling, he wrote in the third person that

---

34. Dee Jay Nelson to Jerald Tanner, probably, Nov. 6, 1972, 1, ellipsis in original.

35. Nelson to Tanner, 1–2.

36. Dee Jay Nelson, "Published Papers, Books, Booklets, Articles and Still Photo Credits," Oct. 1977, 1. Nelson says he wrote pulp science fiction.

"Tanner commissioned him to do the work and supplied 8x10 photographs [of the papyri]. Within six weeks the annotated translation was sent to Tanner who subsequently expressed much displeasure with it. ... On threat of excommunication he privately published his translation."[37] In another telling, he wrote that Tanner "suggested that maybe I could have slanted it a little bit more toward Mormon ways, but he did it very diplomatically. He promised me the Church would publish the work and I, in exchange, promised that I would not editorialize."[38]

Nelson's work published by the Tanners was reserved and descriptive; his booklets contained professional-looking facsimiles and illustrations. They all had an air of seriousness and credibility that was only belied by the grandiose biography of Nelson included in one of the pamphlets, supposedly written by his business manager, Reed Neuberger. Sandra thought Nelson was self-absorbed, but she did not initially doubt him. Looking over his career with the benefit of hindsight, however, one sees that the signs (and not a few red flags) were there all along. Dee Jay Nelson was an imposter.

Reed Neuberger, Nelson's business manager, almost certainly did not exist. Instead, he was probably one of Nelson's inventions,[39] created so Nelson could promote himself in the third person. Not only was Neuberger's address the same as Nelson's in Billings, but his letters were typed on the same typewriter and his signature bore a resemblance to Nelson's wife's signature.[40]

Unable to confine himself to the Joseph Smith Papyri, Nelson portrayed himself as a "recognized authority" on the Dead Sea Scrolls.[41] On April 28, 1968, Nelson promised to send Jerald pictures

---

37. Press release info sheet attached to "Dee Jay Nelson to Mr. and Mrs._____ (Jan 1979)."

38. Nelson, "Book of Abraham Papyri," (transcript, [1975], 5), cf. Dee Jay Nelson to John Fitzgerald, May 25, 1973.

39. For samples of Neuberger's letterhead, see Reed J. Neuberger to N. Eldon Tanner, June 15, 1968, Reed J. Neuberger to Jerald Tanner, May 3, 1968, 1, and Dee Jay Nelson to Jerald and Sandra Tanner, July 17, 1969, 1.

40. Rosemary Brown to Sandra Tanner, Sep. 12, 1980, 1; Brown and Brown, *They Lie in Wait*, 1:87–95. A sample of Mrs. Nelson's signature appears on an undated letter whose content suggests a date in the mid-1970s. Neuberger's signature appears on the business card Nelson left with N. Eldon Tanner (N. Eldon Tanner to Wilber Lingle, May 18, 1977), and in a letter sent to Jerald Tanner on May 3, 1968.

41. "Reed Neuberger" to N. Eldon Tanner, June 15, 1968, 1.

of himself with the Dead Sea Scrolls "in a few days,"[42] which he did through his Neuberger persona. "Neuberger" explained that the pictures, supposedly taken in 1958 or 1959 at the Hebrew University Shrine of the Book, showed Nelson with a number of fragments and an infrared light and the caption: "Dee Jay makes special photographs to bring out dim and damaged writting [sic]."[43] Neuberger stressed that "very few have been allowed to handle and study the scrolls this way." Jerald and Sandra included this picture in the September 1968 *Salt Lake City Messenger*. It would be odd if Nelson were granted access when he did not know the languages of the Dead Sea Scrolls: Hebrew, Aramaic, and Greek.[44] There is no evidence that Nelson was ever granted access, and the evidence he provided the Tanners was faked. He appears to have cut photographs out of a book and used a flame to singe around the edges and around cut-out holes in the pictures to try to make them match the damaged, fragmented originals. As a result, the pictures Nelson faked ended up being more damaged than the originals from which they were taken.[45]

Which of Nelson's many claims were false and which real? Untangling them is difficult, as one incident demonstrates. Neuberger's glowing biography of Nelson states, "In 1958 Prime Minister David Ben-Gurion (whom Dee Jay calls Dave Green, his real name) invited Professor Nelson to come to Israel and make the first motion picture of the Dead Sea Scrolls" which Neuberger claims was shown in two different episodes of the *Seven League Boots* television series.[46] When Robert and Rosemary Brown, two well-known LDS apologists, wrote their book discrediting Nelson, they dismissed the

42. Dee Jay Nelson to Jerald Tanner, Apr. 28, 1968, 1.

43. Notice that both Neuberger and Nelson misspell "writing" as "writting," cf. this letter with Dee Jay Nelson to Jerald Tanner, Nov. 6, 1972, 1.

44. Dee Jay Nelson to Jerald and Sandra Tanner, Jan. 1, 1969; Dee Jay Nelson to Jerald and Sandra Tanner (undated, c.1972); second undated letter from Dee Jay Nelson to Jerald and Sandra Tanner, c.1972, 4.

45. Nelson likely used E. L. Sukenik's *The Dead Sea Scrolls* (1955). Most notably, he appears to have cut out Plate 37, a picture of a portion of the famous Thanksgiving Scroll (1 QHa) from Qumran Cave 1, singed it around the edges and around a hole in the middle. In the process, he destroyed portions of the photograph that are still intact in the original scroll itself. In Nelson's faked picture the singed cutout of Plate 37 appears as a single separate page of text, but in actuality it is and always has been part of a scroll. A more recent photograph of the Thanksgiving Scroll is online at imj.org.il.

46. Neuberger, "About the Author," in *Joseph Smith Papyri Part 2*, iii.

Dee Jay Nelson creates a fake picture of himself allegedly studying the Dead Sea Scrolls, which he made in part by cutting out a picture of the Thanksgiving Scroll, probably from E. L. Sukenik's *The Dead Sea Scrolls* (1955), and burning it around the edges. In reality the page is still connected on both sides in the original scroll.

validity of this claim by asserting that "ABC in New York has never heard of the films of Nelson."[47] But they did not dig deep enough.

Nelson actually was in Israel for a film on the Dead Sea Scrolls, but he went neither as a scholar nor as a friend of Prime Minister David Ben-Gurion. He was a member of the film crew.[48] When these episodes of the series were to be shown on KOOK-TV Billings,

47. Brown and Brown, *They Lie in Wait*, 1:93.
48. Dee Jay Nelson to Jerald and Sandra Tanner, Jan. 10, 1970, 1.

the station's weekly *TV Preview* did a cover story on Nelson.[49] Dee Jay Nelson mixed routine occurences in his life story with fantastical tall tales. His claim to be well acquainted with the Prime Minister of Israel was just the sort of strange pretense he would often make. Nelson also numbered among his "personal friends ... two kings, two prime ministers, three ex-presidents, bishops, royalty and movie stars." He boasted of enjoying braised duck with King Hussein of Jordan[50] or taking a break from his research in the Vatican Library to join Pope Paul VI in his private apartments for an intimate cup of tea and private conversation.[51] Given the outlandishness of these assertions, it is surprising that Nelson's fraud did not come to light sooner.

In the years after the publication of his four booklets with Modern Microfilm, Nelson's credibility began to unravel. Nelson often called himself "professor"; the title appeared on the business card he gave to N. Eldon Tanner[52] and on the letterhead he used when calling himself an Egyptologist. He would speak of himself as a "Professor of Egyptology," usually in connection with Rocky Mountain College in Billings, using the title "Professor of Egyptology at Rocky Mountain College"[53] or "New Horizons Professor of Egyptology at Rocky Mountain College."[54] New Horizons was the name of Rocky Mountain College's continuing education program where Nelson regularly taught a non-credit introductory class on Egyptology.[55]

It all caught up to Nelson when he began referring to himself as "Dr." In January 1978, Nelson had written to the Tanners announcing that he was spending time "in Washington [state] working on my doctorate. I'll have it within 4 or 5 months. The thises [*sic*] has been done and only some required class credits remain." [56] Edward Ashment, an LDS student of Egyptology, mentioned to Jerald that

49. "Local Man Films Dead Sea Scrolls to Be Seen on 'Seven League Boots,'" *TV Preview*, July 23, 1959, 45.

50. Brown and Brown, *They Lie in Wait*, 1:93.

51. Dee Jay Nelson to Jerald and Sandra Tanner and Grant Heward, Oct. 24, 1970, 2.

52. N. Eldon Tanner to Wilber Lingle, May 18, 1977, 1.

53. Nelson and Coville, *Life Force of the Great Pyramids*, vi.

54. Handwritten by Nelson into the Tanners' copy of Dee Jay Nelson to Mr. and Mrs. _____, Jan. 1979, 3, in Tanner and Tanner, Papers.

55. Described, for example, in the Spring 1976 New Horizons Course Program.

56. Dee Jay Nelson to Jerald and Sandra Tanner, Mike Marquardt, and John Fitzgerald, postmarked, Jan. 9, 1978, 1.

Dee Jay Nelson in a few of his other assumed roles as expert bird trainer, Audubon naturalist and lecturer, Middle Eastern wanderer, and ship captain.

there was something fishy about Nelson's credentials. At the time Jerald didn't take it seriously, because, as he said, "people have started many false stories about me (such as that I am a polygamist, have sclerosis of the liver, etc.)."[57] He was troubled, however, when Sandra and he attended a lecture in Brigham City, Utah, on February 13, 1980, during which Nelson was introduced as Dr. Dee Jay Nelson. At the lecture, Nelson stated he had a PhD in anthropology but did not say from where. In the meantime, Sandra was skeptical of a large mummy case Nelson claimed belonged to an Egyptian Army officer named *Tener-Hormaches* "the head-splitter."[58] Sandra thought it looked fake and modern. She was not alone; one newspaper account commented that the markings on it looked "very much like felt-tip pen writings."[59]

When Nelson arrived in Mesa, Arizona, to give a lecture, Robert and Rosemary Brown, the LDS apologists who would later question Nelson's work with the Dead Sea Scrolls (see above), were waiting for him. They had been contacting people to verify Nelson's various claims. Nelson seemed to give contradictory information about his PhD. When asked about it as a guest on a talk show, he said, "I took some of my studies at Northwestern and was given my PhD from the Oriental Institute at the University of Chicago." However, in

---

57. Jerald Tanner to Dee Jay Nelson, 1, Mar. 11, 1980, 1. See also Tanner and Tanner, *Can the Browns Save Joseph Smith?*, 2.

58. Nelson claimed he discovered this mummy case during his alleged 1976 excavations and had for some reason been allowed to bring it back with him. Dee Jay Nelson to Jerald and Sandra Tanner, Dec. 6, 1976, 1.

59. Mike Padgett, "Ask His Mummy: Lecturer's Credentials Are Disputed," *Mesa Tribune*, Feb. 24, 1980 (clipping).

a *Mesa Tribune* interview four days later, he reversed the two and said that "he got his doctorate from Northwestern and attended the Oriental Institute."[60]

The Browns learned from both the registrar's office at the University of Chicago and from Klaus Baer himself that Nelson had neither studied at nor gotten a degree from the Oriental Institute.[61] Checking into his claim about Northwestern was another matter, since Nelson apparently did not mean the well-known school north of Chicago. In a lecture on February 22, Nelson said that Northwestern was "near Seattle," but no one could find it.[62] Jerald called Nelson asking for clarification, but he got no solid answers.

On the third of March Jerald received a mailgram from Nelson saying the school, which always was small, had apparently been sold and its name changed but that he had been unable to contact the registrar over the weekend, and that it was a "matter of little importance anyway as I had no doctorate when [I] did [the] translation."[63] Jerald disagreed. He waited a week, ample time for Nelson to contact the registrar and provide proof of his degree. When he heard nothing from Nelson, Jerald wrote a letter informing Nelson that their business relationship had come to an end. "I am enclosing a check for $55.00 to pay in full the royalties I owe on your books. Even though I still believe in the general accuracy of your translation and conclusions concerning the Joseph Smith Papyri, I will not be reprinting any of the books."[64] Nelson responded by finally sending a copy of his doctoral certificate awarded on May 10, 1978, from Pacific Northwestern College, an unaccredited school. He claimed to have attended lectures and done correspondence work and to have been told that the school was coming very near to being accredited and that he would be informed when it was. He claimed that he had been duped.[65]

---

60. Padgett.

61. Brown and Brown, *They Lie in Wait*, 1:33–34.

62. See Jerald Tanner to Dee Jay Nelson, Mar. 11, 1980, 1; and Tanner and Tanner, *Can the Browns?*, 2.

63. The text of Nelson's mailgram is quoted in Jerald Tanner to Dee Jay Nelson, Mar. 11, 1980, 2, and reproduced in *Can the Browns?* 3. The original also survives.

64. Jerald Tanner to Dee Jay Nelson, Mar. 11 and 12, 1980, 1; Tanner and Tanner, *Can the Browns?*, 7.

65. Dee Jay Nelson to Jerald and Sandra Tanner, Mar. 16, 1980, 1.

The day after the Tanners received a copy of Nelson's doctoral certificate, Sandra called Sterling McMurrin to ask for his help discovering whether the Pacific Northwestern College was a degree mill. McMurrin was a professor of philosophy at the University of Utah and a former US Commissioner of Education. He agreed to help and called James Bemis, executive director of the Higher Education Commission of the Northwest Association of Schools and Colleges, who confirmed that the school was a "degree mill of the worst kind"; it sold degrees and even provided fake transcripts.[66] Jerald wrote to Nelson with the information and told him "it would not be right for us to continue selling your books."[67] One week later, the *Ogden Standard-Examiner* contacted the Tanners and Sandra informed the reporter of what they had found—that the school had been "shut down recently by the federal government as being a diploma mill."[68] It would later come out that Nelson had for years been exaggerating his previous education as well—including that he had attended UC–Berkeley. He exaggerated his previous employment too. Since he had no degrees in biology, it would also seem to follow that his claim of having been a biology professor at Tulane in New Orleans must have also been untrue. [69]

Once his credentials were proven to be fake, Nelson claimed it was all a diabolical plot hatched by the LDS Church to silence him:

---

66. Sterling M. McMurrin to John Fitzgerald, Mar. 20, 1980, 1.

67. Jerald Tanner to Dee Jay Nelson, Mar. 20, 1980, 1, rpt. in Tanner and Tanner, *Can the Browns?*, 9. Jerald cross-checked McMurrin's information by contacting John Mohr of the US Postal Service in Seattle, and the King County Attorney's office.

68. Charles F. Trentelman, "No Doctor's Degree: Egyptologist's Credentials Questioned," Ogden Standard-Examiner, Mar. 29, 1980 (clipping). At some point the Tanners provided Robert and Rosemary Brown with some of the material they used in their exposé of Nelson, including a copy of Dee Jay Nelson's bogus doctoral diploma from Pacific Northwestern College. The Browns afterward claimed that they had been the ones who informed the Tanners of Nelson's bogus degree and that the Tanners had attempted to cover it up. The sequence of unfolding events, however, make it clear that the Tanners publicly exposed Nelson's phony doctorate months before the Browns obtained their copy. Compare the dates given above with Brown and Brown, *They Lie in Wait*, 1:6.

69. Brown and Brown, *They Lie in Wait*, 1:4, 39, 42–43; for his claim that he attended Berkeley, see Nelson and Coville, *Life Force*, vi. For his claim that he taught at Tulane, see "Educational Interlude: Winslow School Youngsters Hear Experts in Lecture on Adventures in Falconry," Jan 25, 1964 (clipping from unnamed Flagstaff paper). Holly K. DiDomenico of the Registrar's Office at Tulane also confirmed that Nelson had never been a student there (email to Huggins, Feb. 10, 2017).

The iron-clad evidence I came up with to debunk the Book of Abraham is the strongest evidence against the Church since Joe Smith's time. I had to be silenced at any cost. Over a two year period they set up a very complicated deal in Seattle ... luring me out there with the promise of an easy doctors degree. I was suspicious but could see no harm in it and certain limited advantages. As a matter of fact I was completely taken in. It even involved a group of Mormons who were paid to play the part of fellow students. Letters I wrote to a few of them, who befriended me, were either unanswered or they flatly denied ever having met me. It was a great set up and it served its purpose very well indeed. The Tanners are now angry with me. I thought that they would see through the whole thing before anyone else but such has not been the case.[70]

Nelson's misrepresentations about his educational background raised questions as to whether he ever had formal training in Egyptian. He had claimed to study it under experts and to have visited Egypt.[71] Wherever he learned it, he did have some knowledge of the language, perhaps self-taught. He had translated the Joseph Smith Papyri, though as an amateur might, according to Egyptologists. In 1980, even when Nelson's lies were catching up with him, Baer stated that Nelson had "a good amateur knowledge (let's say at the level of a solid undergraduate major)."[72]

As the last step in his alleged role of a renowned Egyptologist, Nelson said he had unlocked the power of pyramids, and he had remarkable studies that provided "a logical reason (within the framework of the scientific method) for some of the unaccountable crib deaths of babies, and an easily corrected cause for some (perhaps 80%) cases of breast cancer."[73] So remarkable were his discoveries, he claimed, that he had no problem convincing the American Medical Association team that had come to investigate; and even the Stanford University Research Institute had become

70. Dee Jay Nelson to Jim (n.d., but c.1980), 1.

71. Sometimes claiming his visit was before entering the military (see Mike Dixon Talk Show on K.O.Y. Phoenix, Feb. 20, 1980; Brown and Brown, *They Lie In Wait*, 1:33; sometimes during his military service, implied in "Press Information: Dr. Dee Jay Nelson, Ph. D., [Anthropology]," 1980, 1, and sometimes after getting out of the military, Reed J. Neuberger, "About the author," in Nelson, *Joseph Smith Papyri Part 2*, iii.

72. Brown and Brown, *They Lie in Wait*, 1:37.

73. Dee Jay Nelson to Jerald and Sandra Tanner, Sep. 1, 1977, 1.

keenly interested in his results.[74] Dee Jay Nelson died on Wednesday, June 7, 1989, at his home in Billings from heart failure at the age of sixty-three.[75]

---

74. Dee Jay Nelson to Jerald Tanner, Mike Marquardt, and John Fitzgerald, Jan. 9, 1978, 1.

75. "Dee Jay Nelson #664 Leaves on the Great Adventure on June 7th, 1989," *Adventurers Club News*, Aug. 1989, 20.

11

WATERGATE AND WIRETAPPING

By the 1970s, Jerald and Sandra Tanner had become well-known purveyors of LDS historical documents. Through their circle of friends, they shared their own findings and learned of more. When a new discovery did not merit its own publication, it was added to the Tanners' newsletter, the *Salt Lake City Messenger*. The *Messenger*, first published in 1964, appeared sporadically, with as many as six issues some years and only one in others.[1] When Wesley Walters wrote to the Tanners in the summer of 1971 with astonishing news, Jerald and Sandra prepped another issue of the *Messenger*.

Fawn Brodie and others had written that in 1826 Joseph Smith was brought before a court and found guilty of being a "glass looker"—one who used a seer stone, or magic stone used for divination, to find buried treasure. Most LDS-friendly sources as well as members of Pauline Hancock's group had dismissed the account out of hand.[2] But Wes Walters and Fred Poffarl found direct evidence in a bundle of old bills in the Chenango County dead storage, which was in the basement of the county jail in Norwich, New York: the actual bills submitted by the constable and the judge in the case.[3]

The bills did not detail what happened at the trial, but by confirming that a trial happened at all, the discovery lent credence to

---

1. As of 2020, there are 133 issues of the *Messenger*, with two issues printed each year since 2001.

2. A transcript of the account was published in Anonymous, "The Original Prophet," *Fraser's Magazine* n.s. 7, Feb. 1873, 229–30. For LDS writers who dismissed the account, see Kirkham, *New Witness to Christ*, 1:385–86, 389; "Appraisal of the So-Called Brodie Book," *LDS Church News*, May 11, 1946, 6; Widtsoe, *Joseph Smith*, 78.

3. That is, their requests to Chenango County for payment for overseeing the trial; "New Find Undermines Mormonism," *Salt Lake City Messenger* 32, Aug. 1971, 2. In the same issue they offered a booklet on this subject as well: *Joseph Smith's 1826 Trial*. For the chronology of the discovery and initial publication, see Walters, "Joseph Smith's Bainbridge Trial," 129n11, 154.

the existing transcript of the hearing (first published in 1873). The day after they found the bills, Walters dispatched Xerox copies of them to Jerald. Jerald and Sandra reproduced them within a few days as part of a lead article in the August 1971 issue of the *Salt Lake City Messenger*. Once again, Jerald and Sandra were part of a circle breaking Mormon news. The significance was not lost on the Tanners. Smith was brought to trial for using a seer stone to find buried treasure. A year later, using the same stone, he claimed to have unearthed an ancient record written on gold plates. He would also use seer stones to translate the Book of Mormon. Latter-day Saints familiar with Smith's treasure seeking often dismissed it as youthful indiscretion. But Jerald and Sandra were fully aware of Smith's use of the stone in the translation of the Book of Mormon as well. For a time Francis Kirkham persuaded Jerald that since he had repented of the misuse of the stone, God could use the stone to bring forth the Book of Mormon.

It was this discovery of Walters and Poffarl that finally led the Tanners' beloved friends in Pauline Hancock's group to give up the Book of Mormon. The fact that the Tanners had rejected the Book of Mormon more than a decade before in 1962 had not caused a rift in fellowship between them and Pauline's group, but it did not convince the group to abandon the Book of Mormon.

Unlike the LDS Church, Pauline's group always admitted that Smith used a seer stone in translating the Book of Mormon. What they had denied was that he had formerly used the same stone to practice divination. Jerald had already realized the problems with that position in the late 1950s.[4] Now Walters's and his associate's discovery became the tipping point for Pauline's group. They made a number of calls to the Tanners to discuss it, until they were ready to announce that, in view of the implications of the discovery, they were formally giving up the Book of Mormon. They made the announcement on November 24, 1973, in an article in the *Independence Examiner* entitled "Attention Book of Mormon Believers." The day

---

4. Jerald asked Pauline, "Can you explain why the Book of Mormon would come forth by the same means that was used to find treasures?" Jerald Tanner to Pauline Hancock, Nov./Dec. 1959, Tanner and Tanner, Papers; Jerald Tanner, *The Facts about the Book of Mormon*, 13.

Olive Wilcox and Pauline Hancock

after the article appeared, the group's pastors, Olive and Gene Wilcox, sent a clipping of it to the Tanners, along with a brief note that read: "Dear Jerald and Sandra—thought you folks would be happy and pleased with this. Would love to see you. Gene and Olive."

The same August 1971 issue of the *Messenger* that published Walters and Poffarl's glass-looker bills also announced a new book Jerald had written entitled *A Look at Christianity*. This is one of the works Sandra says Jerald wrote mainly for his father, George, an outspoken atheist who had boasted of the superiority of his MIT education. Jerald had very little formal education. His grades in high school were so bad as to be almost comical.[5] Then he had one year at the University of Utah, with remedial English, before going to trade school. That was all. Jerald's mother, Helen, too had been forced to

---

5. To take the first semester of the 1954–55 school year at Salt Lake City's West High School as an example, Jerald got a D in English (absent fifteen times), a D+ in Utah State History (also absent fifteen days), a D in General Shop (absent sixteen times), a C- in Auto Mechanics 1 (absent thirteen times), a C- in Auto Mechanics 2 (absent another thirteen times), and a B- in Physical Education (absent twelve times).

leave school early after barely surviving an airplane crash. She had become a Christian in the early 1960s while listening to the local Evangelical Free Church pastor Wilber Nelson's *Beams of Blessings* radio program.

Jerald and his mother always felt that George held his MIT education over their heads as proof that the only reason they had become Christians was because they were uneducated. In reality, George's boasting about his MIT education was greatly exaggerated. He hadn't been a stellar student himself during his undergraduate years at BYU.[6] And he only went to MIT for a short time later because he was a meteorologist, and during World War II the US Army Air Corp and the Weather Bureau had jointly developed a short-term program for meteorologists run through MIT from July 1, 1941, to February 7, 1942, in order to train them on potential roles they might be called upon to play during the course of the war.[7] So far as we know neither Jerald nor his mother ever knew the true extent of George's study at MIT.

At one point LaMar Petersen, who at the time was much inclined toward negative assessments of the historicity of Jesus,[8] offered Jerald a copy of Charles Guignebert's five-hundred-plus-page, densely printed and markedly skeptical volume *Jesus*. LaMar didn't remember exactly when this was, but he thought it was in about 1970 or 1971[9]—in other words just around the time Jerald was working on his *A Look at Christianity*. LaMar recalled that in giving the book to

---

6. A grade sheet tucked in George's calculus notebook gave the following examples of George's college performance: For 1926–27 Hist.—D / Drafting—D / Phys. Ed.—A / Theol.—D / Inst.—B- / Eng.—C- and D. For 1927–28, Theol.—C and D / Math—B and C / Chem.—C+ and B / Physics—C / Eng.—C. For 1929–30 Rel. Ed.—C and B / Math C+ and B / Pol. Sci.—C / Physics—C and B and A / Phys. Ed.—B / Astron.—D. Below these are more grades handwritten showing no improvement: Hygene—C/ Botany—C/ German—D and C/ Bacteriology—C/ Zoology—C/ Geology—C. Certainly grades like these would scarcely have made George an obvious candidate for acceptance at MIT.

7. A report card issued on October 14, 1941, shows George doing quite well at MIT.

8. For example, LaMar listed as books he owned George Guignebert, Maurice Goguel, David Friedrich Strauss, and Alvin Boyd Kuhn, all of which were very skeptical of the miraculous elements of the New Testament account, but none of whom, except the last (who was a Theosophist and not a Bible scholar), doubted that Jesus existed. Still in his verbal comment on them, LaMar seems to have thought that they all denied Jesus existed. "Memoirs of Lamar Petersen," book 2, 77.

9. In March 1978, LaMar recalled that he had given the book to Jerald seven or eight years before. "Memoirs of Petersen," book 2, 77.

Jerald's father, George Tanner.

Jerald, "I'm afraid I frightened him. He did look into it, but he shook his head rather sadly and returned it to me and he said he wasn't ready for that. He didn't wish to pursue it."[10] In this LaMar singularly misjudged Jerald, who had worked through materials much more critical than Guignebert, not least in *A Look at Christianity*.

In *A Look at Christianity*, Jerald addressed sensational theories about Jesus that the vast majority of qualified scholars had never taken seriously, but of the sort that have always found ready audiences among atheists, and often among Mormons who no longer

---

10. "Memoirs of LaMar Petersen."

believe. In short, books of the sort his father George would have read and considered credible.[11] Jerald took four popular views to task: 1) the solar myth theory of eighteenth-century writer Constantin Volney, which claimed that the story of Jesus, who likely never existed, represented a common dying and rising solar savior myth that was paralleled in the stories of many other ancient heroes and saviors including Krishna, Attis, Adonis, Osiris, and Mithras;[12] 2) the Essene swoon theory of the eighteenth- and nineteenth-century authors Karl Friedrich Bahrdt and Karl Heinrich Venturini, which claimed that Jesus's body had been removed from the tomb, either alive or dead, by fellow members of the Essene order;[13] 3) the Jesus went to India theory of nineteenth-century writers Nicolas Notovitch and Hazrat Mirza Ghulam Ahmad, which claimed that Jesus either spent the "Lost Years" of his youth in the East or traveled there after surviving the crucifixion;[14] and 4) Bertrand Russell's argument that Christ probably never existed.[15] Ironically, had Jerald read or had access to the book LaMar had offered to loan him by Charles Guignebert, he would have found in him a powerful ally in countering the views he was trying to answer.[16]

Jerald's section on Jesus represented only a small part of *A Look at Christianity*, which also included discussion of early New Testament manuscripts and a survey of biblical archaeology dealing with the most important secular parallels to biblical history. Leading up to *A Look at Christianity* were the Tanners' earlier works *Archaeology and the Book of Mormon* (1969) and *Mormon Scripture and the Bible* (1970). A second book Jerald wrote for his father came a couple years later, titled *Views on Creation, Evolution, and Fossil Man*

---

11. The sort, in fact, that Guignebert himself roundly denounces in the book LaMar offered to loan Jerald, *Jesus*, 63–64.

12. Volney, *Les Ruines, ou méditations sur les révolutions des empires,* 1791. Jerald's foils in this case were Oray, *An Analysis of Christian Origins* 48, 58–59, and Massey, *The Historical Jesus and the Mythical Christ,* 43.

13. See Schweizer, *Quest for the Historical Jesus,* 38–47. Jerald's foil in this case was Larson's *The Religion of the Occident,* 1959.

14. Nicolas Notovich, *Unknown Life of Jesus,* 1894; Mirza Ghulam Ahmad, *Jesus in India,* 1899. Jerald foil in this case was Al-Haj Khwaja Nazir Ahmad's *Jesus in Heaven on Earth,* 218, 312, 365–77. This work is an apologetic for the Ahmaddiya movement in Islam, whose founder was Mirza Ghulam Ahmad.

15. Russell, *Why I Am Not a Christian,* 16.

16. Guignebert, *Jesus,* 63–64.

(1975). It ran 332 pages and tackled the creation/evolution debate and digested an enormous amount of literature on both sides of the subject.[17] It was one of the very few books that didn't include Sandra's name as one of the authors.

Between 1965 and 1971, Jerald and Sandra published numerous books and pamphlets, reprinted other books, and continued to distribute the *Messenger*. In 1972 they published the third edition of *Mormonism: Shadow or Reality?* By 1973 they slowed down and only released one issue of the *Messenger*. But they did publish an editorial in the *Salt Lake Tribune* that would foreshadow a growing preoccupation. They responded to Verle A. Workman's October 21, 1973, essay in the *Tribune*, which argued that the LDS Church "does not cover up like the Watergate affair."[18] Jerald and Sandra's response was titled "Mormon Records, Like Watergate, Embarrassing." Workman had made himself a ready target for refutation by asserting things easily disproven, such as that instances of post-Manifesto polygamy were consistently punished with excommunication, that there had been no changes made in Mormon scriptures, and that the LDS Church's doctrines had never changed. The Tanners' response mostly consisted of material they had been presenting for years.

Then Hugh Nibley jumped in, rebutting the Tanners' rebuttal.[19] Jerald approached the *Tribune* about responding to Nibley, but they were unwilling, even after he asked if he could do it as a paid advertisement. So instead the Tanners produced their own booklet, *Mormonism Like Watergate?* offered for sale in the May 1974 *Messenger*. The same issue also featured as its lead article a piece entitled *Mormonism and Watergate* that printed the July 1831 prophesy of Joseph Smith that promised that in time Mormons would intermarry with the Lamanites (Indigenous Peoples) in order "that their posterity may become white, delightsome and just." H. Michael Marquardt

---

17. Tanner, *Views on Creation*. Jerald found the subject intriguing enough to try to start a regular newsletter on the subject later titled *The Compass*. The first issue appeared in July 1982. A second issue was promised, which was to feature the dispute between Richard Leaky and Donald Johanson, but it never appeared.

18. Qtd. in Jerald and Sandra Tanner, "Mormon Records, Like Watergate, Embarrassing," *Salt Lake Tribune*, Nov. 11, 1973, 6-B.

19. Hugh Nibley, "Author Defends Image of Joseph Smith as Prophet," *Salt Lake Tribune*, Nov. 25, 1973, G-2.

Ogden Kraut *Courtesy Anne Wilde*   H. Michael Marquardt

had only recently managed to obtained a typed copy of the prophesy, after its having been kept under wraps by the church for 140 years. Perhaps then Mormonism *was* a bit like Watergate after all. But the analogous use of Watergate—accusing the LDS Church of covering up its past—was about to take an unexpected turn.

In three different conversations between March 5 and June 20, 1974, independent LDS fundamentalist Ogden Kraut told Jerald and historian H. Michael Marquardt that his home and work telephones had been tapped prior to his excommunication two years earlier.[20] He said that his boss at Dugway Proving Ground, west of Salt Lake City, had warned him beforehand that his telephone was going to be bugged, and that a higher up at his work, along with a security official, discussed the matter with him. A tape several hours long of Kraut's conversations was purportedly compiled and listened to by Kraut's Stake President Kenneth C. Johnson and First Counselor Max L. Shirts. Shirts allegedly confided to Kraut's wife that the tape existed and that he had listened to it. Kraut also claimed that he

---

20. Unless otherwise noted, information or this section is derived from notes taken by H. Michael Marquardt of these conversations (Mar. 6, June 8, 20, 1974), photocopies in my possession. See also Kraut, *Complaint Against Ogden Kraut*, 63–64.

knew of three instances in which people had their personal journals stolen prior to their being excommunicated, including a portion of his own, which he had been dictating to his plural wife, Anne Wilde, and was taken from her home.[21]

Kraut was convinced that it was not the police or any government agency behind the telephone taps or break-ins. He also did not believe the institutional LDS Church was the culprit, but that LDS Apostle Mark E. Petersen had done so on his own using private detectives. Kraut had learned this, he said, from someone he trusted who worked in LDS Church security. After his excommunication, Kraut wrote to church leaders, "I had heard rumors, but now have received confirmation, that Mark E. Petersen has, with his own money, hired private detectives to gather information and evidence against members who might attend a Fundamentalist meeting, associate with a polygamist, or harbor any Fundamentalist ideology so that he could have them excommunicated from the Church."[22]

A counselor in Kraut's stake presidency said he heard a tape, but details are scant. Could the counselor have been bluffing to intimidate Kraut and his wife? But Kraut and Wilde both insisted that pages from his diary were stolen from Wilde's home, and nothing else was taken. On their own, Kraut's allegations may sound conspiratorial, yet he certainly wasn't the only suspected polygamist targeted by Mark E. Petersen. A letter exists from Petersen himself from the summer of 1974 in which he instructs stake presidents in Provo to "quietly make some inquiries" about the activities of a new polygamous group that had split off from Rulon Allred's group.[23] In 1971 someone at the post office where H. Michael Marquardt worked the overnight shift apparently accused Marquardt of advocating plural marriage at work. Petersen wrote a letter to Don R. Earl, president of the Liberty Stake in Salt Lake City, accusing Marquardt of

21. The theft was confirmed and described to me by Anne Wilde in an email to Huggins, Mar. 26, 2017: "I don't like to use the term 'burglarized' as only one item was taken; but yes someone did break into my house in Sandy through the basement door and took the part of Ogden's journal that we had been working on the previous day (at the most about 10 pages)." Wilde became Kraut's plural wife in 1969 (Bennett, *Gospel Tangents*, 56).

22. Ogden Kraut to the general authorities of the LDS Church, Sep. 18, 1972, rpt. in Kraut, *Complaint Against Ogden Kraut*, 68.

23. Mark E. Petersen to Wayne A. Mineer, Jul. 26, 1974, 1: "I am writing to you presidents in the Provo area," Marquardt Papers, box 455, fd. 4.

"evidently having a good deal to do with some of the polygamous cult people" and calling for an investigation.[24] When Marquardt was told that Earl wanted to see him, he assumed it was to discuss a church calling. Instead he found himself confronted with Petersen's accusations by Earl, his two counselors, and the clerk. Flabbergasted, Marquardt strongly affirmed that he had and wanted only one wife, and that he had absolutely no connection with, nor sympathy for, any polygamous body. Happily, in this case his stake president believed him, and reported back to Petersen that Marquardt "strongly sustained the president of the church."[25] When Marquardt and Jerald spoke on the phone after that, they'd often make a joke of greeting not only one another, but also Mark E. Petersen, just in case he happened to be listening in on the line!

Petersen was not the first high-ranking LDS leader to spy on members he suspected of being polygamists. J. Reuben Clark oversaw some surveillance activities and received intelligence from Salt Lake City's police department to spy on those he suspected of fundamentalism.[26] Whatever transpired, Kraut's blaming Petersen in a letter to other church leaders suggests he believed these accusations.[27]

After Jerald learned of Kraut's allegations, he set to work trying to get to the bottom of them. Jerald himself had spoken by phone to Kraut during the period in question. Had his private conversations been taped as well? In this age of Watergate, US Attorney General William B. Saxbe had invited Americans who felt they had been victims of illegal electronic surveillance to file a report.[28] On July 1, 1974, Jerald sent a letter with a package of evidence to Saxbe telling him that Kraut's telephones had been illegally tapped. Jerald would also

---

24. Mark E. Petersen to Don R. Earl, May 26, 1971, 1; Marquardt Papers, box 445, fd. 4.

25. Don R. Earl to Mark E. Petersen, Jun. 23, 1971, 1; Marquardt Papers, box 445, fd. 4.

26. Quinn, *Elder Statesman*, 251–54.

27. Brent Metcalfe, who once worked for LDS Church Security, confirmed that Petersen spied on polygamists, but was skeptical that it involved wiretapping. Metcalfe recalled that "two of the female guards would occasionally attend fundamentalist gatherings." Others "would collect license plate info off vehicles in the vicinity with the intention of turning them into church security. ... [I] never saw any tapes [of conversations]. ... Whatever church security or Petersen's ad hoc committee were involved in, it was very low tech." Metcalfe, emails to Huggins, Mar. 16–17, 2018.

28. "Mormons and the Watergate Scandal: Justice Dept. Warns Church About Illegal Tapping," *Salt Lake City Messenger* 37, Jan. 1975, 7.

send copies to the FBI, Senators Sam Irvin, Howard Baker, Lowell Weicker Jr., Utah District Court Judge Willis Ritter, and *New York Times* reporter Wallace Turner.[29] Jerald's response highlighted a fundamental aspect of his nature: a love of justice coupled with naiveté. Jerald was troubled by what had happened to Kraut and wanted justice, so he acted. But if he expected justice for Kraut, it never came. Still his efforts may have had a positive effect. The LDS Church-published *Priesthood Bulletin* for the third quarter of 1974 included the following notice on the use of tape recordings in church courts:

> The United States Department of Justice has notified the Church that federal law can be violated by the illegal use of an oral communication in connection with a Church court. The law is violated when anyone willfully and knowingly uses a recorded communication when he knows or has reason to believe that the recording was obtained by interception without the consent of the parties involved in the conversation. All priesthood authorities are advised to refrain from using any tape-recorded communication unless the party whose conversation was recorded clearly has given express consent in writing to its use.[30]

That the church felt the need to warn leaders not to use electronic surveillance as evidence in a church court might be interpreted as suggesting it had happened at least once before.

Another result of Jerald's naïve efforts may have been drawing unwelcome scrutiny upon himself. Did he really expect the intelligence community, which employed several Mormons, or the government, which had its share of very powerful Mormons too, to be able to dispassionately address the concerns of the likes of an Ogden Kraut or a Jerald Tanner? And would they not be even less likely to do so when the charge involved the activities of a member of the Quorum of the Twelve Apostles of the LDS Church? When Jerald wrote to Attorney General Saxbe, he didn't yet know that the FBI already had a file on him and Sandra that included a report, dating back to April 30, 1970,[31] accusing them of being "trouble makers and Communists."[32]

---

29. Jerald Tanner to William B. Saxbe, July 1, 1974, in Tanner and Tanner, Papers.
30. *Priesthood Bulletin*, Fall 1974, 2.
31. Reproduced in "Communists in Zion? FBI Documents to Be Sought in Court," *Salt Lake City Messenger* 45, Feb. 1981, 3b.
32. "Communists in Zion?" Memorandum reporting the accusation dated May 7, 1970.

Jerald's letter did spur a federal investigation, though it was listlessly pursued. The US intelligence community, not least the FBI, was famously comprised of a significant number of Mormons.[33] Many Latter-day Saint men had experience living in other countries and learning other languages as missionaries, making them candidates for intelligence work. One LDS writer explained the appeal of Mormons to rigid law enforcement groups: "[Mormons] are more loyal and honest, and less likely to succumb to the temptations that might interfere with their job, such as alcohol abuse, gambling, sexual promiscuity, blackmail, and other such activities."[34] But there was also a darker side to the question of what made Mormons good spies. Questions of blind obedience, a black-and-white view of what distinguishes right from wrong and good guys from bad, and a failure to grasp what constitutes legitimate and illegitimate appeals to loyalty. This darker aspect was reflected, for example, in BYU president Ernest L. Wilkinson's recruitment of students to spy on their professors and fellow students. Already on September 21, 1951, he wrote to Associated Student Body president Keith Orme, saying it would be "a most excellent thing if the students as part of their civic responsibility ... check on 'dives' [i.e., places where alcohol is served illegally]," in order that they might be "reported and eliminated." Wilkinson goes on to suggest that Orme "might talk to one or two in whom you have complete confidence and have them make some observations."[35]

In the mid-1960s this approach led to difficulties for Wilkinson when it was found that students had been recruited to report on professors, a number of whom were then fired. On one occasion in 1966, for example, Wilkinson delivered a strongly worded speech in support of conservative politics and then encouraged student spies to report back to him on certain professors.[36] In one sense Mormons spying on Mormons could be described as students fulfilling their "civic duty," or of being "loyal" to the church and the college, and no doubt that was how the actions were represented to the student

---

33. See, for example, McPheters, *Agent Bishop*.
34. Johanson, *What Is Mormonism*, 44.
35. Ernest L. Wilkinson to Keith Orme, Sep. 21, 1951, copy in author's possession.
36. Bergera, "1966 BYU Student Spy Ring," 183.

spies. Yet it is precisely here that we see the darker side referred to earlier fully expressed.

Jerald and Sandra's involvement in Kraut's claims led them down an unexpected road. They began reporting on the Mormon connections to Watergate.[37] This would lead to their writing a book unlike any they had produced thus far: *Mormon Spies, Hughes, and the CIA* (1976). As they worked on this project it became clear what the Tanners had really been all along: investigative reporters. They spent a great deal of money keeping abreast of the testimony in the various Watergate hearings by ordering photocopies from the official court reporter in Washington, DC, at fifty cents a page.[38]

An early hint for Jerald and Sandra of a Mormon connection to the Watergate break-in was the name Robert R. Mullen. Mullen had owned a prominent public relations firm, and Jerald remembered a sympathetic book written by the non-Mormon Mullen titled *The Latter-day Saints: The Mormons Yesterday and Today.*[39] Mullen was not a scholar writing objectively about the church; the LDS Church had been one of his clients since they had hired his firm to help promote the Mormon Tabernacle Choir's world tour in 1955.[40] Mullen wrote his book as part of his PR efforts for the church.[41] In 1971, the Mullen company had been bought by Robert "Bob" Bennett.[42]

Bennett was the son of US Senator Wallace Bennett (R-Utah). The younger Bennett had met Mullen in 1955 when Bennett was on a mission in Scotland for the LDS Church.[43] Bennett had also worked in the Nixon administration. He brought one primary client

---

37. The Watergate scandal encompassed years of unethical and criminal behavior and involved hundreds of people, nearly fifty of whom were found guilty of criminal conduct. I do not delve into the complexities of Watergate here and trust readers to consult other sources for more details. See, for example, Bernstein and Woodward, *All the President's Men*; Kutler, *Wars of Watergate*; and Graff, *Watergate*.

38. See, for example, Nicholas Sokal to Jerald Tanner, Apr. 29, 1975, 1, in Tanner and Tanner, Papers. In the case of this letter the Tanners paid $100 for the testimony of a single witness.

39. Mullen, *Latter-day Saints*.

40. Haws, *Mormon Image in the American Mind*, 25.

41. James A. Everett to Jerald Tanner, Oct. 15, 1974, 1, in Tanner and Tanner, Papers.

42. Bob Bennett was also a grandson of Heber J. Grant, LDS Church president from 1918 to 1945.

43. "Robert Bennett, Interviewed by Peggy Fletcher," *Sunstone*, Jan.–Feb. 1978, 17.

with him when he purchased the Mullen company: Las Vegas billionaire recluse Howard Hughes. In 1972 the vice president of the Mullen company was a former CIA officer named E. Howard Hunt. It was in Hunt's office in spring of 1972 that he and G. Gordon Liddy planned the Watergate break-in.[44] In other words, Bob Bennett, Mormon, son of a US senator, and former Nixon administration official, was the boss of one of the primary instigators of the Watergate break-in.[45]

These tangled connections spurred Jerald's interest. He had heard a reference in US President Richard Nixon's White House audiotapes to Bennett. It was alleged that Bennett was using his relationship with Hughes to arrange for Hunt to break into the safe of Hank Greenspun, publisher of the *Las Vegas Sun*.[46] According to claims by Hunt, Bennett believed the safe contained information that would "blow [Edmund] Muskie out of the water," meaning it would destroy Muskie's chances of becoming the Democratic presidential nominee running against Nixon in 1972.[47] Greenspun later said that the safe did not contain information about Muskie, but rather documents related to Hughes. Whatever the purpose of the plan to raid Greenspun's safe, Hughes clearly was involved as it was his people who provided logistical support for the operation.[48] The plan was for Hunt and Liddy to break in with a team, crack the safe, remove its contents, then board a private jet provided by Hughes to fly to a Caribbean location controlled by Hughes, where the documents could then be divided up among the interested parties. Apparently Hughes got nervous at the eleventh hour and the plan fizzled.[49] Greenspun himself told a different story. The break-in attempt wasn't called off, it had failed,

---

44. Testimony of James W. McCord, in Select Committee on Presidential Campaign Activities, *Hearings before the Select Committee*, 142. On Hunt's position in the Mullen Company, see Hunt, *American Spy*, 159.

45. J. Anthony Lukas, "The Bennett Mystery," *New York Times*, Jan. 29, 1976, 32.

46. Brinkley and Nichter, *The Nixon Tapes*, 414.

47. Testimony of E. Howard Hunt, in Select Committee on Presidential Campaign Activities, *Hearings before the Select Committee*, 3686.

48. Hunt described Ralph Windt as "head of security for either the Hughes Tool Co. or one of its many subsidiaries." Testimony of E. Howard Hunt, 3686–67.

49. Liddy, *Will*, 205; Testimony of E. Howard Hunt, 3687; Dean, *Blind Ambition*, 390.

the "office window ... had been jimmied and ... the safe bore the marks of heavy tools."[50]

Bennett denied playing the part Hunt said he did, pointing instead at Hunt as the one who had raised the issue of damaging material on Muskie.[51] Some suspected Bennett's part in the political intrigue of the time ran much broader and deeper than he ever admitted, a belief reflected, for example, in Charles Colson's remark to John Dean as they sat together in prison when it was all over: "It's unbelievable to me that Bob Bennett has waltzed through this thing. He's got the answers to a lot of unanswered questions."[52] Hughes apparently had more to gain from the break-in than the Nixon campaign, and this pointed suspicion at Bennett.[53] Over time, suspicions around Bennett (if they were known at all) abated enough that he was later elected to the US senate from Utah. Whatever Bennett's ultimate role was in the Watergate scandal, he was close enough to some of the primary players that it was later rumored he may have been Deep Throat, *Washington Post* reporter Bob Woodward's secret source of information. Woodward later said he did get information from Bennett, but Deep Throat was associate FBI director Mark Felt.[54]

The Tanners vaguely recalled that they had been contacted by someone from the Mullen company at some point in the past. Jerald finally unearthed a letter dated January 20, 1965, from James A. Everett, a representative of Mullen living in Sweden. It was a friendly letter, so Jerald decided to contact him. They learned that Everett had moved to Lee's Summit near Independence, Missouri.[55] On October 7, 1974, Jerald was finally able to speak with Everett by telephone and had a long, informative conversation about the

50. Tom Buckley, "Greenspun says Hughes File Was Sought," *New York Times*, May 23, 1973, 30.

51. Anthony Ripley, "Burglary Plans Aimed at Muskie in 1972 Laid to Hunt," *New York Times*, Apr. 28, 1973, 15. Another account credits Bennett with putting Hunt in touch with Hughes's people, see *Report to the President*, 196.

52. Dean, *Blind Ambition*, 391. See also Colson, *Born Again*, 218, but especially Senator Howard Baker in *Final Report of the Senate Select Committee on Presidential Campaign Activities, June 1974*, Washington, DC: U. S. Government Printing Office, 1974.

53. Lukas, "The Bennett Mystery," 32; idem, "Why the Water-Gate Break-In?" *New York Times*, Nov. 30, 1987, A-19.

54. Felt and O'Conner, *G-Man's Life*, xii; Woodward, *The Secret Man*, 56.

55. Everett was RLDS. H. Michael Marquardt, telephone conversation with Huggins, Mar. 25, 2017.

relationship between Mormonism and the Mullen Company. Jerald followed up with a letter posing several questions, which Everett answered in detail. Everett, Jerald felt, seemed "very open and willing to discuss this matter."[56]

Everett had remarkable inside information. He had returned to Washington, DC, on Saturday, June 17, 1972, the very night that the Watergate break-in occurred. He was in Mullen's Washington office the following Monday to observe Howard Hunt's reaction to the first telephone call from Bob Woodward and Carl Bernstein, who would become famous for their investigation of Watergate.

But Everett made no mention that the Mullen Company had served as a CIA front since 1959, nor of his own position as the Mullen company's "Vice President, Europe," nor that he had been on the Mullen company's payroll for nine years, the whole period of which his employment had been a cover for his CIA work.[57] Everett placed the blame for Watergate at the feet of Hunt and implied that Bennett played no part whatsoever.

Everett's portrayal of Bennett as innocent may have been sincere, or it may have been loyalty of friendship, but it was not entirely accurate. Bennett may have had no role in planning the break-in or the subsequent cover up, but he apparently did work with the CIA on damage control. Jerald had read Senator Howard Baker's report in which he said Bennett "was keeping the CIA informed while withholding evidence from the FBI and the Watergate grand jury."[58]

Surprisingly, all this circled back to the issue of Mark E. Petersen's surveillance of Ogden Kraut and other potential polygamists. Bob Bennett had testified that Howard Hunt told him about a device that was "very, very sophisticated in the realm of electronic surveillance": voice-activated bugs that could be attached to furniture and were invulnerable to traditional means of detection.[59] Bennett had

---

56. "Mormonism and the Watergate Scandal: Justice Dept. Warns Church About Illegal Taping," *Salt Lake City Messenger* 37, Jan. 1975, 2.

57. For Mullen company as a CIA front, see Senator Howard Baker in *Final Report*, 1121. For Everett's position, see Everett, *The Making and Breaking of an American Spy*, 131. For the length of Everett's association with Mullen, see, "Testimony of Robert F. Bennett," July 2, 1974; *Inquiry*, 1084.

58. Annis, *Howard Baker*, 76.

59. Deposition of Robert Foster Bennett, in the Democratic National Committee v. James W. McCord, rpt. in Edwards, "Watergate Hearings," 6.8.

apparently offered to make these bugs available to his clients, which included both the Hughes organization and the LDS Church. How easy would it be, Jerald reasoned, for Petersen, who was the church's liaison with the Mullen company, to access from Bennett the kinds of technologies he felt he needed to spy on polygamists.[60] Jerald also noticed that Donald Segretti, another key Watergate figure who had been hired by the White House to sabotage various Democratic campaigns, and who was handled by Hunt and Liddy, was in Salt Lake City between March 2–5, 1972, just a few months before Kraut was excommunicated.[61] In this era of intrigue and paranoia, little seemed too far-fetched.

Jerald was curious whether Segretti's visit had anything to do with the tap on Kraut's telephone. Everett said he doubted Segretti had such skills.[62] A local FBI agent, Harry L. Lee, who had been assigned to the Kraut case, told Jerald that his agency had no record of wiretapping Kraut, which meant that whoever was doing it was acting illegally.[63]

In view of certain unusual developments during that period, it might seem that Jerald had indeed drawn unwanted government scrutiny on himself after all. He was rattled after picking up the telephone on November 6, 1975, to call a friend, but heard other voices. As he wrote to the friend afterward, "I tried to call your number at your home. No one answered, but in between the rings I heard the voice of a woman say, 'They're trying to call out.'"[64] Jerald later read a passage from Howard Hunt's memoir that said, "I was telephoning attorney Bittman from my home when I heard a whisper just after my attorney had spoken. The intruder voice said, '*That's Bittman*,' as though to identify the person to whom I was talking. This slipup by the monitors convinced me—if I needed further convincing—that my phone lines continued to be tapped."[65] To Jerald, what had

---

60. James A. Everett to Jerald Tanner, Oct. 15, 1974, 2.

61. Hunt, *American Spy*, 260, 263; Jerald Tanner to Wallace Turner, Oct 11, 1974, 3, Tanner and Tanner, Papers.

62. Tanner to Turner.

63. Tanner to Turner, 1. Lee's full name is given in an FBI Report SU 139–69 Cover Page D (11/21/74).

64. Jerald Tanner to Preston Truman, Aug. 26, 1976, 1, Tanner and Tanner, Papers.

65. Hunt, *Undercover*, 273. On October 12, 1972, E. Howard Hunt, G. Gordon Liddy, and James W. McCord, three defendants in the case, filed affidavits complaining

happened to Hunt's telephone seemed to demonstrate that such glitches might indeed occur during the course of phone surveillance.

In view of their new understanding of how advanced spying technology was becoming, Sandra recalls a reporter around this time asking if they would be willing to let him leave his typewriter with them while he made a quick trip to California. They agreed, but as she and Jerald sat there in their living room together looking at the typewriter case, one of them said to the other, "Why don't we just put this out in the garage?"

It was in the April 1976 issue of the *Messenger* that the Tanners announced the publication of their work on Watergate, *Mormon Spies, Hughes, and the CIA*. But that same month, the Howard Hughes angle burst open in another direction. Hughes died on April 5 while being rushed by airplane from Acapulco to Houston and, remarkably for a billionaire, he apparently left no will. An extensive search was made, but nothing was found. Then three weeks later, on April 27, a three-page handwritten document purporting to be Hughes's will mysteriously appeared. It wasn't found among papers in his estate, but on a desk on the twenty-fifth floor of the LDS Church office building in Salt Lake City. The document was in an old envelope showing "the yellowing stains of time." It had been stuffed into another envelope from the LDS visitor's center, addressed to President Spencer W. Kimball, and marked "Personal."[66] If the Tanners thought the news about Watergate was curious, this was something else entirely, and they reported on it in their newsletter and ultimately in its own booklet.

The will divided up Hughes's estate among his medical institute

---

that they were being tailed and that their phones were being tapped. In his affidavit Hunt told the story of the same experience. This was reported on the following day, as follows: "Mr. Hunt's affidavit says that during a Sept. 22 [1972] telephone conversation from his home in Potomac, Md., with his attorney William O. Bittman 'I heard someone on the line make the statement, "That's Bittman." At the time of the conversation, no one was on any of the telephone extensions in my home.'" Carl Bernstein and Bob Woodward, "Four Top Nixon Associates Refuse to Testify," *International Herald Tribune*, Oct. 13, 1972, 3.

66. Hal Knight, "Who Delivered Hughes Will? 'Mystery Woman' Is One Guess," *Deseret News*, May 1, 1976, 8-A; Peter J. Scarlet, "Howard Hughes 'Will' Gives LDS 16th Split," *Salt Lake Tribune*, Apr. 30, 1976, A-1; "Hughes Will Found in SLC," *LDS Church News*. May 8, 1976, 3.

in Miami, several universities, his ex-wives, and his cousin William R. Lummis, who had taken charge of the Hughes Corporation. Of special interest, the will bequeathed a sixteenth portion of his estate to the LDS Church and another sixteenth to his personal aids at the time of his death. The remainder was divided among key men in his various companies. One unusual item in the will was the bequest of a sixteenth of his estate to a Melvin Dummar, who operated a gas station in Wilber, Utah.[67] According to Dummar, he was driving toward Las Vegas in early 1968 and gave a ride to an injured man on the side of the road. Dummar asked whether the man wanted to go to the hospital. The man said he'd rather be dropped off instead at the back entrance of the Sands Hotel. As he got out of the car the man asked Dummar to loan him a quarter, which he did. The man asked Dummar his name and then said he was Howard Hughes. Dummar, who believed the man to be an old tramp, drove off thinking, "Howard Hughes? Oh sure!"[68]

Although no one could explain how the will ended up at LDS Church headquarters, it was not that surprising that Hughes would leave so much money to the church. Sometime before, Hughes's executor, Noah Dietrich, stated that Hughes would leave a substantial portion of his estate to the faith. Hughes enjoyed employing Mormons; 30 percent of employees of Hughes's Summa Corporation were members of the LDS Church.[69]

A few spoke out quickly in support of the authenticity of the will. Signature expert Charles Hamilton of New York declared it genuine as well as Hughes handwriting expert Henry Silver of Los Angeles.[70] (Jerald would cross swords with these two experts later). The will's executor, Noah Dietrich, said he had no doubt that the will had been written by Hughes, feeling sure that "Nobody could imitate his writing for three pages like that."[71] Others were not so sure.[72] Hank Greenspun, who intimated he had writing samples dating around

---

67. For the full text of the will, see Wallace Turner, "Purported Will of Hughes Found at Mormon Office," *New York Times*, Apr. 30, 1976, A-17.
68. "Hughes Will Found in SLC," *LDS Church News*, May 8, 1976, 3 and 12.
69. "Hughes Document Found," *Deseret News*, Apr. 29, 1976 (clipping).
70. "More experts Authenticate Hughes Will," *Deseret News*, May 1, 1976, A-1.
71. "More experts Authenticate Hughes Will," A-8.
72. "More Experts Authenticate Hughes Will," A-1.

the time the will was purportedly written, felt certain that Hughes was not its author.[73] The Summa Corporation, led by William Gay, leader of Hughes's "Mormon Mafia," hired its own writing expert— an ex-FBI document examiner—who declared the will a forgery.[74] Jerald and Sandra followed the case closely, and on May 25, 1976, they published a nine-page booklet concluding that "the more we study it the more we become convinced it is a forgery."[75]

Jerald continued to follow the story for a time as additional details arose. Dummar, who had originally said he knew nothing about the will until after its discovery, suffered a hit to his credibility when his fingerprints were found on the envelope. He then claimed that the will had been given to him by a mysterious stranger to deliver, which in turn sounded absolutely absurd until the actual alleged Hughes delivery man, LeVane Forsythe, came forward himself.[76] Eventually the document was declared a forgery by the court, which settled the matter legally if not actually.[77]

After being drawn into the Watergate scandal, Jerald became intrigued with other mysterious events possibly involving some of the same people as Watergate—the Kennedy assassination, for example. Did Watergate figures like E. Howard Hunt, for example, play into the equation there?[78] These questions intrigued Jerald and, like many other Americans at the time, trying to answer them became a hobby. As was his usual habit, Jerald gathered materials from all sides. A portion of a manuscript survives suggesting he intended to write on the topic, but then events took yet another strange turn.

It started one day when a man named Gerald Evans Tuckett, who claimed to be a musician from Chicago, stopped by the Tanners'.

---

73. Hank Greenspun, "Where I Stand," *Las Vegas Sun*, May 1, 1976, 1–2.

74. Rick Hackman, "Expert Claims Will a Forgery," *Las Vegas Sun*, May 19, 1976 (clipping).

75. Tanner and Tanner, *Howard Hughes*, 9.

76. Barlett and Steele, *Howard Hughes*, 604

77. In 2005 Gary Magnesen, a former FBI Agent, sought to vindicate Dummar in his book *Investigation*.

78. Some of Hunt's children later claimed their father gave a deathbed confession admitting to a role in the Kennedy assassination, but other family members dispute this. Erik Hedegaard, "The Last Confessions of E. Howard Hunt," *Rolling Stone*, Apr. 5, 2007. For a detailed review of the Kennedy assassination and a rebuttal of the major conspiracy theories, see Bugliosi, *Reclaiming History*.

By the 1970s, the Tanners were quasi-famous LDS critics. They published books and pamphlets with contact information, and their names regularly appeared in local and national newspapers. Visitors of all kinds were not unusual, from outlandish ex-Mormon conspiracy theorists, to reporters and journalists, to faithful Mormons determined to call the Tanners to repentance.

Tuckett started to talk about various conspiracy theories with Jerald including, especially, the mysterious December 8, 1972, crash of United Airlines flight 553 from Washington to Chicago, which had on board E. Howard Hunt's wife, Dorothy, who for some reason was carrying $10,000 in cash.[79] Jerald had read enough about the players in the Watergate scandal along with the spin off conspiracy theories about them to have a feel for what was generally known and what was not. He was amazed at the depth of Tuckett's knowledge. "You're not just a musician form Chicago," Jerald said, confronting Tuckett. "What are you then, CIA?"

Tuckett admitted that he "used to be CIA," but was now retired. Tuckett claimed he had become disgusted with both the intelligence services and the LDS Church. Then Tuckett brought up another topic. Unprompted, he told the Tanners that Robert Foster Smith, a man whose snide but well-informed missives about Mormon topics had periodically appeared in the Tanners' post box, had been interviewed for the CIA.

Smith was something of an enigma. He was a self-proclaimed non-Mormon Mormon apologist. Even given Smith's claim that he was "not a member of the Mormon Church," he was nevertheless tied closely to Mormonism in some way. Long before denying being Mormon, he served as the first editor of the Foundation for Ancient Research and Mormon Studies (FARMS) Book of Mormon Critical Text Project (1979–87)[80] and wrote apologetic books and articles on

---

79. Dorothy Hunt's death is still a matter of interest to conspiracy theorists. See Howard Hunt's son St. John Hunt, *Dorothy, "An Amoral and Dangerous Woman."* E. Howard Hunt himself claims the $10,000 was his and his wife's nest egg which they planned to invest in her cousin-in-law Hal Carlstead's company (Hunt, *American Spy,* 263). Hunt gives no credence to any of the conspiracy theories and claims no knowledge of them. But he does leave a little window open for the curious by saying that perhaps "Dorothy was an extremely resourceful individual, and it is possible that she could have taken matters into her own hands without my knowledge" (267).

80. Smith, "If There Be Faults," 203.

Mormonism.[81] H. Michael Marquardt recalled Smith attending the same LDS ward as Marquardt in San Francisco in the early 1960s.[82]

When Smith learned the Tanners were talking to Tuckett he reacted strongly, setting out immediately to discredit him. He passionately insisted that no matter what Tuckett might say, he himself was *not* CIA.[83] Yet despite Smith's denials, in the interactions that followed he did show himself to be a man who, like Tuckett, "knew things." Even the previously mentioned CIA operative James Everett apparently thought Smith was a fellow member of the intelligence community.[84] Smith had a national security clearance that he didn't apparently get from the FBI.[85] So *where* did it come from? Smith produced, as proof of his non-association, a letter from the CIA stating that it had no information on him. He claimed that Tuckett was CIA and that he may have been recruited by either Ray C. Hillam of the political science department at BYU or by a Russian teacher there named Pëtr Lysenko.[86] Smith and Tuckett had studied Russian and roomed together at BYU.[87] They had been together in Jerusalem at one point as well.[88] Smith contradicted Tuckett's claim about having retired from the agency, saying he was either on a two-year leave of absence or simply acting undercover.[89] This appears to be confirmed by information about Tuckett available at the Wikileak's ICWATCH site, which has Tuckett working for the government until June 1987.[90]

---

81. E.g., Smith, "Some 'Neologisms,'" "Assessing the Broad Impact," *Oracles & Talismans,* and Sorenson and Smith, "Once More: The Horse,"

82. Marquardt, telephone conversation with Huggins, Jan 11, 2020.

83. Even providing two letters from Gene F. Wilson at CIA headquarters to Smith (May 18 and June 9, 1977) and one from B. C. Evans (June 28, 1977) saying they had no information about him. Along the bottom of the May 18 letter Smith has written, "So much for Mr. Tuckett's fake claim that I had once been interviewed for employment by the CIA."

84. Robert F. Smith to Jerald and Sandra Tanner, May 15, 1982, 1, Tanner and Tanner, Papers.

85. Or at least he once claimed he had one when writing to the FBI. See Clarence M. Kelly, Second Director of the FBI, to Robert F. Smith, Sep. 20, 1977, 1

86. Robert F. Smith, Dossier on Tuckett: PR I, U.S. National, C-3, Addenda 2, 2. n.d.

87. Robert F. Smith, Dossier on Tuckett: PR II, U.S. national, C-3, [1]. Sent with note dated Nov. 15, 1977.

88. J. Tuckett to Robert F. Smith, postmarked Feb 3, 1971, 1.

89. Robert F. Smith to Richard Sprague, Chief Counsel of the House Assassination Committee, Mar. 13, 1977, 1.

90. See Wikileaks: icwatch.wikileaks.org.

In addition, Smith also embarked on an energetic letter writing campaign calling for an investigation of Tuckett at the highest levels of government, insisting that "his most recent conduct is in violation of [CIA] regulations."[91] He took his appeal all the way to US President Jimmy Carter, who passed it on to Attorney General Griffin B. Bell.[92] Smith also wrote to the FBI, the CIA, and copied Vice President Walter Mondale on his letters.[93] He wrote to Richard A. Sprague, chief council of the House Select Committee on Assassinations,[94] insinuating that Tuckett may have been involved in Dorothy Hunt's death or at least knew something about it.[95] He warned the Tanners that Tuckett's motive for getting into contact with them was because they had become "primary objects of a CIA 'preventative action,' operation designed to prevent or delay your damaging publication of information not damaging to US national security, but very damaging to the reputation and credibility of the CIA and of one or more of its employees."[96] Smith accused Tuckett of feeding Jerald and Sandra disinformation to save himself from scrutiny. He told them that Tuckett had attended the same ward in Washington as Bob Bennett, implying a possible connection.[97] Smith continued to link Tuckett to the plane crash that had killed Dorothy Hunt.[98] And he finally sent the Tanners what amounted to a remarkable dossier on Tuckett that included a detailed description of Tuckett's entire intelligence career.[99] The dossier included letters between Smith and Tuckett and evidence

---

91. Smith to Sprague, 1.
92. Griffin B. Bell to Robert F. Smith, Aug. 18, 1977, 1, Tanner and Tanner, Papers.
93. Robert F. Smith to Charles E. Savige, May 22, 1977, 2. Tanner and Tanner, Papers.
94. The House of Representatives Select Committee on Assassinations was formed in 1976 to re-investigate the deaths of John F. Kennedy and Martin Luther King Jr. Due to the Vietnam War and Watergate, public trust in government was at an all-time low and conspiracy theories flourished in the 1970s. The House committee hoped to reassure the American public.
95. Smith to Sprague.
96. Robert F. Smith to Jerald and Sandra Tanner, July 3, 1977, 1.
97. Robert F. Smith to Alex J. Bottos Jr., May 22, 1977, copied to Jerald and Sandra Tanner.
98. Alex J. Bottos Jr. to Robert F. Smith, Apr. 11, 1977, 1, Tanner and Tanner, Papers.
99. Document PR II, U.S. national, C-3 [4], sent with note dated Nov. 15, 1977, in Tanner and Tanner, Papers.

of clippings and leaflets meant to prove that Tuckett had been a racist years before at BYU.[100]

What on earth had they been dragged into, the Tanners wondered. How were two people with a small printing business in Salt Lake City suddenly in the middle of charges and counter-charges by two men who may or may not have been CIA agents? Why were they being copied onto letters to prominent investigators/conspiracy theorists?[101] And why was Smith telling the Tanners all this in the first place? The Tanners wondered if Smith was the one trying to misinform them. They liked Tuckett even though they assumed that, as a CIA man, he was often lying to them about something or other, and they tended to trust him. They even remained friends long afterward, with Tuckett stopping by to see them whenever he happened to be in town.

Robert Smith had warned Jerald that he was right to assume his telephone was being tapped and urged him to register a complaint about it and make an application demanding whatever information the government had collected on him through the Freedom of Information Act. Smith seemed to hint darkly that part of the reason for doing so was to produce a paper trail, just in case one day Jerald and Sandra mysteriously fell off the edge of the earth. Despite their suspicions, this was one piece of advice the Tanners followed. They did make a Freedom of Information Act request, and, as it turned out, they would have to pursue it in court to get the justice department to comply.[102] The government eventually turned over twenty-nine pages in which everything except what the Tanners already knew or had provided themselves was redacted. Eighteen more pages on the Tanners were withheld completely, with their descriptions briefly listed in the court papers as relating to the Ogden Kraut wiretapping investigation.[103]

It was all very disorienting, troubling, and even a little scary. Jerald was, for all his intensity in writing about Mormonism, a shy, private man. The thought that his and Sandra's names had been bandied

---

100. For example, Jerry Tuckett, "Who's Rights" *BYU Daily Universe*, May 7, 1964, 2.
101. Robert F. Smith to Alex J. Bottos Jr., May 22, 1977. Copied to Jerald and Sandra.
102. Jerald Tanner v. the United States Department of Justice.
103. The withheld pages related to documents designated for the court case as HQ4, HQ5, HQ8, all three of which related to the Ogden Kraut wiretapping investigation. Jerald Tanner v. the United States Department of Justice, 6.

about by the CIA or the FBI or the US attorney general was incomprehensible. Could their inquiries really be inviting the kind of trouble Smith suggested? Jerald felt called to investigate Mormonism, not the US government. So one day he announced to Sandra, "I'm done. I have decided that henceforth I *don't want* the answers to my questions about the Kennedy assassination or the crash of United Airlines flight 553." No sooner had the excitement stirred up by Robert F. Smith started to settle down than a covert operation of another, more amateur variety was just being put into effect.

Jerald and Sandra had one more spy to unmask. Steve Mayfield regularly attends Mormon studies conferences, such as the Sunstone Symposium, the Mormon History Association, and the John Whitmer Historical Society. He is a pleasant, stocky balding man with a mustache that makes him look a bit like one of the Mario Brothers. He often volunteers at these conferences, taking photographs and facilitating audio recordings of sessions. Mayfield also has an enormous body of materials at BYU's Harold B. Lee Library that he started compiling in the 1970s.[104] While Mayfield's collection will no doubt be of significant benefit to future researchers and historians, a substantial portion of it was compiled when he began monitoring and infiltrating dissident Mormon and "anti-Mormon" groups under the false name Stan Fields. At the time Mayfield was employed by the FBI in San Francisco, making his alias and tactics seem all the more menacing.

Mayfield would pretend sympathy with the groups he wanted to monitor and, if possible, infiltrate them. Using the Stan Fields name, Mayfield was a regular member of feminist Sonia Johnson's Mormons for ERA at the time Johnson was excommunicated in December 1979.[105] Mayfield once boasted to Sandra of having compiled the largest file on Sonia Johnson anywhere.[106] He also presented himself to evangelical Christians as a born-again ex-Mormon, complete with an inspiring testimony that he often repeated.[107] At other

---

104. See Mayfield, Papers.
105. Tanner and Tanner, *Unmasking a Mormon Spy*, 13;
106. See, e.g., Tanner, "Statement on Mormon Spies," [2].
107. "Stan Fields" to Paul [Carden], July 13, 1979, 3; "Stan Fields" to Dear Brother in Jesus, Feb. 2, 1980, 1–2.

times he claimed he had been disfellowshipped on "drummed up charges" or that he had been "excommunicated."[108]

Mayfield traveled extensively in order to ingratiate himself with almost all of the counter-cult leaders who specifically featured Mormonism, and accepted donations for his "mission" in order to keep traveling and distributing literature.[109] He also said he had passed out literature and proselytized Mormons; today he denies distributing tracts.[110] Mayfield compiled lists of Mormon dissidents and "anti-Mormon" Christian groups, and he seemed interested in stirring up division within the groups.[111] Jerald later felt that this made sense in light of Mayfield's work in the FBI, which actively encouraged agents to infiltrate the New Left and sow conflict.[112]

Mayfield always claimed to have worked alone, but at least some in LDS Church Security were aware of his masquerade. Brent Metcalfe, who worked for church security at the time, knew about Mayfield's imposture, recalling that Ron Francis, director of security, "gave Steve kudos for collecting data, which encouraged him all the more."[113]

While some were taken in by Mayfield's fake persona, others were skeptical. Chris Vlachos, pastor of Calvary Fellowship in American Fork and a professor at the Salt Lake Theological Seminary, saw through Mayfield.[114] "It was so obvious he was a mole," Vlachos remembered. "He would use a lot of superficial Christian lingo but

---

108. "Stan Fields" to Dear Friends in Christ [Mission to Mormons], May 7, 1979, 2; "Stan Fields" to Paul Carden, Feb. 8, 1980, 1; and "Stand Fields" to Melanie [*sic*] Layton, Apr. 14, 1977, 1; Paul Carden to Jerald Tanner, July 15, 1980, 1.

109. Undated Associate Staff Member Application, Mission to Mormons [3–4]; Tanner and Tanner, *Unmasking a Mormon Spy*, 13; "Stan Field" to Dear Friend [Maurice Barnett?], Sep. 10, 1979, 1.

110. "Stan Fields" to Melanie [sic] [Layton], Oct. 6, 1977, 4, 7–8; Mayfield, interview with Scott Faulring, 41–42; Tanner and Tanner, *Unmasking a Mormon Spy*, 8. Mayfield repeated his denial to me in a conversation at the Utah Lighthouse bookstore in March 2017.

111. Tanner and Tanner, *Unmasking a Mormon Spy*, 11.

112. *Intelligence Activities and the Rights of Americans Book II: Final Report of the Select Committee to Study Governmental Operations with Respect to Intelligence Activities* (Washington, DC: U.S. Government Printing Office, 1976), 89, referred to in Tanner and Tanner, *Unmasking a Mormon Spy*, 9.

113. Metcalfe, email to Huggins, Apr. 4, 2017.

114. Vlachos was also involved in His Place Bookstore in Provo and today teaches at Wheaton College.

Steve Mayfield (left) as "Stan Fields" at the time of his infiltration
of Mormon dissident and Ex-Mormon Christian groups.

never the right lingo ... I was onto him for quite some time and
played along for months," Vlachos further recalled, "talking about
baseball and changing the subject." He also remembered Mayfield
gossiping to try and "pit me against others by saying, 'Did you hear
what so and so said about you?'"[115]

Jerald was also suspicious. The kind of questions "Stan Fields"
asked and the materials he sought from the Tanners didn't seem
to match the person Fields presented himself to be. Sandra, on the
other hand, took Fields's account of himself more at face value. At
one point before Mayfield's exposure, Jerald expressed his doubts

115. Vlachos, emails to Huggins, July 28, 2016, Mar. 26, 2017, and Apr. 19, 20, 2021.

191

about him to Brent Metcalfe, who in turn warned Mayfield to drop the charade.[116] Mayfield didn't.

The phony persona unraveled when someone who knew Mayfield ran into him as he was pretending to be Stan Fields around Jerald and Sandra. When a man named Michael George Marquart crashed his truck through the gates at Temple Square, insisting to police that God made him do it, Mayfield insinuated to a number of people that it was historian H. Michael Marquardt who had been arrested. Even after he was corrected, Mayfield reportedly continued to implicate the wrong Marquardt.[117]

H. Michael Marquardt already knew Mayfield before the Temple Square incident. After they were introduced, Mayfield—as Mayfield, not as "Stan Fields"—visited H. Michael Marquardt in Marquardt's home on March 18, 1980, spending five hours with him.[118] Because Marquardt knew the Tanners, and also knew who Mayfield was, time was running out for Stan Fields.

On the morning of Thursday, July 10, 1980, Edward H. Ashment, who worked at the LDS Church Translation Department, visited the Tanners.[119] Stan Fields had arrived just before Ashment, but when Ashment walked in, Fields turned away and looked at books until Ashment left. According to Mayfield, Ashment knew him by his real name and he was trying to avoid being caught.[120] After Ashment left and Fields turned back around, Jerald noticed he seemed uneasy. He wondered whether Fields was there to spy on Ashment.[121] But now with Ashment gone, Fields continued to converse with Jerald, who was more than a little suspicious of him. They spoke for some time until around 2:00 p.m., when H. Michael

---

116. Metcalfe, email to Huggins, Apr. 4, 2017.

117. Vlachos, email to Huggins, Apr. 20, 2021; Tanners, *Unmasking a Mormon Spy*, 11.

118. During this visit, Marquardt retrieved a phone number for Mayfield from his address book, then later that day noticed the book was missing. He never found it again (Marquardt, email to the author, Apr. 28, 2017). Mayfield told me he knew nothing about its disappearance (conversation with Mayfield, July 28, 2016).

119. At the time Ashment was working on a PhD in Egyptology at the University of Chicago and had already made significant scholarly contributions to Mormon studies relating to the Book of Abraham. See, for example, Ashment, "Facsimiles of the Book of Abraham."

120. Mayfield, interview with Faulring, 29.

121. Tanner and Tanner, *Unmasking*, 3.

Marquardt approached the house. Fields, panicking because he knew that if Marquardt came in, he would be recognized as Steve Mayfield, rushed to the door and literally ran away from the store.[122] Marquardt watched in amazement.

"What's Steve Mayfield in such a hurry about?" he asked.

"No, that was Stan Fields, not Steve Mayfield," Jerald replied.

"No it wasn't" Michael answered back, "that was Steve Mayfield, his name is Steve Mayfield, not Stan Fields." Mayfield's career as Stan Fields was over.

Six days later Jerald and Ed Decker went to the Church Office Building, confronted Mayfield, and taped an interview with him. Mayfield admitted he had worked for the FBI from July 1973 to July 1977, but that even though he took on his alias while still working for the agency, his Stan Fields persona had nothing to do with them.[123] Nor, he claimed, was he spying on behalf of the LDS Church or was otherwise funded by them.[124] In another interview with historian Scott Faulring, Mayfield admitted he had concocted the Stan Fields alias and that people fell for it "hook, line and sinker."[125] And for the most part they did.

In the end it didn't matter whether Mayfield was acting on his own or not. That he came along at the height of the wiretapping scare, and as an FBI employee no less, made it appear as if his activities were somehow tied to the other spies the Tanners had been coping with. A year later, Mayfield moved to Denver and got a job working for the local sheriff's department. He would return to collecting "anti-Mormon" materials again for his massive collection, and he occasionally confronted ex-Mormons or those he perceived as critical of the church, including Jerald and Sandra, and A. J. Simmonds, Curator of the Special Collections and Archives at Utah State University's

---

122. From this point I rely on the verbal recollections of Sandra Tanner and H. Michael Marquardt repeated in my presence on a number of different occasions.

123. See "Unmasking a Mormon Spy," 2. Mayfield began communicating with the Tanners using his alias on November 11, 1976. Jerald Tanner to Roger S. Young, US Department of Justice, July 26, 1980, in Tanner and Tanner, Papers.

124. Jerald, unceasingly thorough, wrote to the US Justice Department to learn if Mayfield's story was true. It apparently was; Mayfield worked as a clerk for the FBI for four years. Tanner to Young, and Young to Tanner, in Tanner and Tanner, Papers.

125. Mayfield, interview with Faulring, 10.

Merrill library.[126] He eventually returned to Salt Lake City and joined the police department, working as a forensic photographer.

Sometime after Stan Fields was exposed, Sandra asked Mayfield what he really thought he could have gotten from them under false pretenses that he couldn't have gotten by simply honestly asking? His response was "nothing," but that he didn't realize that at the time. He still regularly drops by the Lighthouse bookstore to look around, buy new books, and pick up the latest newsletter. I even encountered him there one day while working on this chapter.

126. Steve Mayfield to Jerald and Sandra Tanner, Jan. 21, 1983; A.J. Simmonds to Jerald and Sandra Tanner, Aug. 14, 1987, 2.

12

DR. CLANDESTINE

Wilfrid Clark, an employee of Salt Lake City's venerable Sam Weller's Zion Bookstore, was driving down Redwood Road, a north–south street lined with dilapidated industrial buildings running the length of the city. Locals knew it as something of a rough dividing line between the city's blue-collar westside and the vast salty wastes to the west. It was December 1977 and there was little hope for a white Christmas. The weather was overcast and dreary, with temperatures stuck in the low 40s. As he drove, Clark kept his eye out for an address given to him by his boss, Sam Weller. Clark spotted the building, turned off the road in front of a nondescript self-storage company, and began searching. He was hunting for a numbered door that matched the key he held—the key that had mysteriously arrived with instructions in an anonymous letter sent to Weller.

Clark found the door, turned the key, and stepped inside. The light outside revealed the room's contents: a pile of boxes. The bookseller dutifully loaded them into his vehicle and drove back to Zion Bookstore. They opened the boxes and found 1,800 copies of a booklet, *Jerald and Sandra Tanner's Distorted View of Mormonism: A Response to* Mormonism: Shadow or Reality? The booklet listed Salt Lake City as its printing location and its author as "a Latter-day Saint Historian." A note on the inside cover stressed that the booklet "has not been copyrighted, so that it can be reproduced and distributed freely by others, if they feel that the contents have value."

Five days before Christmas, the sky cleared and the temperature plummeted to near zero, and Weller put the anonymous booklets on display. It was the same day that, according to one student who witnessed it, LDS Church Historian Leonard J. Arrington was seen distributing copies of the booklet at BYU.[1]

Before the New Year, the tract had made its way to other places as well, such as Bloomington, Minnesota, where the mission president gave a copy to Jack Hallman, who read it and then wrote to the Tanners asking if they knew about it.[2] The mission president would say only that a friend had sent it to him, but refused to identify the friend. Hallman said that, "from what he told me, that 'friend' was probably the Church Historian's Office in Salt Lake."[3]

The Tanners were naturally curious to discover who wrote the pamphlet. To find out, they first asked Weller where he sent the payment for the booklets. Weller told them that instead of paying, he was asked to reprint the pamphlet with any profits.[4] When the Tanners asked to see the original anonymous letter, Weller declined.[5]

No one in the burgeoning Mormon historian community admitted to knowing anything about *Jerald and Sandra Tanner's* [sic] *Distorted View of Mormonism.* Arrington claimed he was in the dark until it mysteriously appeared.[6] However, there had been rumors of a forthcoming response to their work for more than a year. The 1970s were a unique era in Mormon historiography. The once-closed LDS Church archives had become more accessible—not to everyone, and certainly not to Jerald and Sandra Tanner. But certain professional historians and favored graduate students could call at the archives in the east wing of the new Church Office Building on North Temple Street and ask to see documents long inaccessible. It was not a free for all; some collections remained restricted, and historians employed by the church had more access than outsiders. But it seemed to represent a positive shift in how the LDS Church approached

---

1. Tanner and Tanner, *Answering Dr. Clandestine*, 5. Arrington was the first academically credentialed person to be set apart as official LDS Church Historian. Prior to Arrington, the post was filled by LDS general authorities, as it is today.

2. Jack Hallman to Jerald and Sandra Tanner, Jan. 7, 1978, 1, in Tanner and Tanner, Papers. In his letter Hallman says that he had been given the booklet "a little over a week ago."

3. Jack Hallman to Jerald Tanner, Jan. 24, 1977, 1, Tanner and Tanner, Papers.

4. Tanner and Tanner, *Answering Dr. Clandestine*, 2.

5. Tanner and Tanner, 2, and "Ambushing the Tanners," *Salt Lake City Messenger* 39, July 1978, 8.

6. Tanner and Tanner, *Answering Dr. Clandestine*, 4.

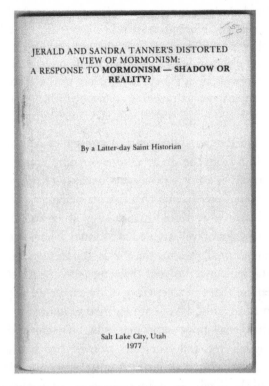

JERALD AND SANDRA TANNER'S DISTORTED
VIEW OF MORMONISM:
A RESPONSE TO **MORMONISM — SHADOW OR
REALITY?**

By a Latter-day Saint Historian

Salt Lake City, Utah
1977

"Dr. Clandestine's" (D. Michael Quinn's) anonymous tract.

and handled its history, and more people, especially students, were getting involved. But it was all still very fragile and tenuous.

A senior project by Richard Steven Marshall, a student at the University of Utah, submitted the previous May, inadvertently shed some light on the booklet. Marshall's paper, "The New Mormon History," included several interviews with Mormon historians and others (including the Tanners) as part of the project. Marshall interviewed Reed C. Durham Jr., a historian and former director of the University of Utah Institute of Religion:

> [Durham] said that due to the large number of letters the Church Historian's Office is receiving asking for answers to the things the Tanners have published, a certain scholar (name deliberately withheld) was appointed to write a general answer to the Tanners including advice on how to read anti-Mormon literature. This unnamed person solicited the

help of Reed Durham on the project. The work is finished but its publication is delayed, according to what Leonard Arrington told Durham, because they can not decide how or where to publish it. Because the article is an open and honest approach to the problem, although it by no means answers all of the questions raised by the Tanners, it will be published anonymously, to avoid any difficulties which could result were such an article connected with an official Church agency.[7]

Jerald found the possibility of a committee of Mormon scholars shooting at him from the shadows of anonymity under the pretense of a letter written by a single person disconcerting because of the level of deception involved. "Inasmuch as we are being attacked from ambush," Jerald wrote, "we would like to know if we are up against one individual or a team of well-trained marksmen."[8] Jerald used the word *ambush* to intentionally mirror the words of Mormon historian B. H. Roberts, who had once insisted that engagement in debate "would certainly require that the acceptance of the challenge should be otherwise than from ambush … I am entitled to know the name of my opponent that I may judge somewhat of his character and standing."[9]

Jerald vaguely recalled a conversation he had had a year prior during which he learned about a potential response. He could not remember all the details, including whom he had spoken to, but the name Michael Quinn stood out. Leafing through Quinn's published works did not prove helpful, but when the Tanners studied his 1973 University of Utah master's thesis and his 1976 Yale doctoral dissertation, they detected similarities to *Jerald and Sandra Tanner's Distorted View of Mormonism*.

The author of the booklet included Latin fallacy phrases such as *post hoc ergo propter hoc* (after this, therefore because of this). Who but Quinn, Jerald reasoned, would employ a phrase like that in a document purporting to be written to a layperson with questions? Quinn, Jerald noticed, had previously used *post hoc ergo propter hoc* in both his thesis and his dissertation.[10] There were other similarities, such as footnotes containing the same references to the same sources

7. Marshall, "New Mormon History," 61–62.
8. Tanner and Tanner, *Answering Dr. Clandestine*, 6.
9. Roberts, *Defense of the Faith*, 1:328; Tanner and Tanner, *Answering Dr. Clandestine*, 1.
10. Quinn, "Organizational Developments" and "Mormon Hierarchy."

in the same order in the booklet as in the thesis and the dissertation. Quinn's work and the booklet quoted from a rare anti-Mormon manuscript in the Oliver H. Olney Papers in Yale University's Beinecke Library where Quinn had worked on his doctorate.

By the time Jerald had finished working through Quinn's master's thesis, he felt sure he had enough evidence to get an admission from Quinn that he was the anonymous "Latter-day Saint Historian." When he called and presented his evidence, Quinn emphatically denied that he had anything to do with the matter. It was this that had caused Jerald to work his way through Quinn's doctoral dissertation as well, which only further solidified what he suspected.

Jerald finally confirmed the authorship when, digging through a drawer, he found his handwritten notes of the previous year's conversation when he had first heard that a response was in the works. Quinn's name had been mentioned. The conversation, according to the notes, had taken place almost a year to the day before the booklet was put on sale at Sam Weller's Zion Bookstore. The notes, consisting of only a few words and phrases in Jerald's scrawl, "confirmed that the author was 'Michael Quin[n],'" that the work was written 'For [the] Historians Office,'" that "it was a '50 page paper,'" and that the Church 'may not publish it.'"[11] But it also included the name "David Mayfield" written in a box along with the line "had been done."[12] So Jerald picked up the phone and gave Mayfield a call, but apparently did not identify himself, or, if he did, Mayfield missed it. One of the first things he asked was if Mayfield had seen Quinn's paper before it came out in the form of a booklet. Mayfield, apparently assuming he was speaking with someone at the LDS Church History Department, admitted that he had. But when he discovered it was Jerald he was talking to, he quickly backed away from his earlier statements. After hanging up, Jerald called Arrington and confronted him with Mayfield's admission. Arrington recalls his response:

I vehemently denied that this was true, and had a considerable argument with him, completely denying everything. We got into a little bit

---

11. Tanner and Tanner, *Answering Dr. Clandestine*, 4; "Ambushing the Tanners," 9.

12. Mayfield was an LDS Church employee who was later director of the Family History Department. The note, still in the Tanners' papers, says that "someone phoned on Dec. 12, 1976."

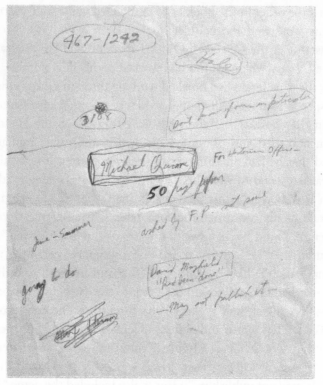

Notes from a phone call that warned Jerald of the forthcoming
"Dr. Clandestine" tract a year in advance.

of a shouting match. I then telephoned Dave, who said that Jerald had
telephoned him and asked if he had seen a paper by Mike Quinn which
was a response to the Tanners. He said he was "caught off guard," and
did admit he had seen such a paper. Pretty soon, Jerald Tanner telephoned me again and apologized for becoming angry with me for my
denial. I re-denied the whole business again. Tanner said he was going
to publish the complete story, and no doubt he will publish what he
believes to be the true story. But he said he would publish that I denied
it. I telephoned Mike Quinn to tell him this.[13]

After a conversation with Mayfield, Arrington told Jerald that
Mayfield had said he had made a mistake and had been thinking about a different paper. When subsequently asked about this,

---

13. Arrington, *Confessions of a Mormon Historian*, 2:453–54.

Mayfield refused to say one way or the other. When Jerald confronted Quinn with what he now knew, Quinn no longer denied he had been the author, but adopted a neutral position that he would neither affirm nor deny being its author.

In the meantime Jerald had found the historical scholarship in Quinn's dissertation to be excellent: "Although Dr. Quinn has almost nothing good to say about us," Jerald wrote, "we feel that he is probably one of the best historians in the Mormon Church. His dissertation written for Yale University is a masterpiece."[14] But the quality of scholarship in the booklet was mixed, suggesting to Jerald that other scholars besides Quinn might be involved.[15] "Since we do not think it fair to give Michael Quinn all the blame for this pamphlet," Jerald wrote, "we have decided to christen the 'author or authors' as 'DR. CLANDESTINE.'"[16]

The Tanners spent nearly half of their *Answering Dr. Clandestine* unmasking the author. The thing that made *Distorted View of Mormonism* interesting, after all, was not what it said, but its anonymity and the absurd carnivalesque series of events that accompanied its birth.

The two dueling publications, Clandestine's on the one side and the Tanners' on the other, provoked different responses. Chad Flake, director of Special Collections at BYU's Harold B. Lee Library, understood the Tanners' frustration. "Here's a man who's writing to evaluate the Tanners, yet he doesn't have enough gumption to put his name on it. The credibility of the pamphlet, as far as I am concerned, is nil."[17] Non-Mormon historian Lawrence Foster, on the other hand, saw the Tanners' preoccupation with the anonymous author as thin-skinned: "How could anyone who had unleashed the volume of invective that the Tanners have on the Mormons react with such outrage and seeming surprise to a generally fair, if critical, analysis of their own efforts?"[18]

---

14. Tanner and Tanner, *Answering Dr. Clandestine*, 5.

15. But it also may reflect Quinn's being stronger in some research areas than others.

16. Tanner and Tanner, *Answering Dr. Clandestine*, 6. Quinn identifies himself as the author of the tract in "The Chosen Path of a Conflicted Mormon Historian, 1944–2009." D. Michael Quinn Papers, WA MSS S-2692, Special Collections, Beinecke Library, Yale University. Cited in Arrington, *Confessions of a Mormon Historian*, 2:453n12.

17. Flake interview, Jan. 18, 1978, in Bergera, "Dissent in Zion," 7.

18. Foster, "Career Apostates," 51–52.

But Foster got it wrong. Far from being motivated primarily by anger, Jerald was also energized by it, excited to engage it. If anything angered Jerald, it wasn't the response. It was the subterfuge, the anonymity, the cloak and dagger. As Sandra recalls, "He would have been glad to see someone give a serious review of the issues, but why such a cowardly process? We were always in the phone book, put our name and address on everything. If the church was going to put out a rebuttal why not own their defense? It was like the anonymous phone calls we would receive telling us off."[19]

Although convinced that Quinn had written at least a substantial portion of the booklet, the Tanners were left in doubt over the extent of Arrington's involvement. As it would turn out Arrington had to have known about the booklet before its release because he had sent a copy of an earlier draft to a friend along with a cover letter dated September 6, 1977, which eventually came into the Tanners' hands.[20]

The Tanners probably didn't need to write an entire book in response to *Distorted View of Mormonism*. A newsletter establishing its connection with the Church History Department would have probably sufficed, after which they could have watched the booklet sink under the burden of the problems it had created for itself: It was too honest. "We certainly do not believe that Apostle [Ezra Taft] Benson would approve of the rebuttal," Jerald and Sandra wrote. "[I]t makes far too many admissions concerning historical problems in the Church."[21] Some LDS apostles were in fact at that moment taking steps to rein in Arrington and his department, which they felt had been too secular in their historical writing.[22]

In the process of making his case, the anonymous author admitted that Joseph Smith had a violent temper, drank alcohol after revealing the Word of Wisdom, took plural wives before the polygamy revelation, retroactively changed revelations, quoted from the King James Bible in the Book of Mormon, and was tried as a glass looker in 1826. The pamphlet argued that church leaders had

---

19. Email to Huggins, Jan. 14, 2020.

20. The letter is reproduced in Tanner and Tanner, *Answering Dr. Clandestine*, 24. Arrington actually knew of the pamphlet and spoke about it more than a year prior to that (Arrington, *Confessions of a Mormon Historian*, 2:453n12.

21. Tanner and Tanner, *Answering Dr. Clandestine*, 7.

22. Arrington, *Adventures of a Church Historian*, 143–56.

the "limitations of all men" and might err in their teaching due to misunderstandings of scripture and history. It acknowledged that the LDS temple endowment may have borrowed from Freemasonry. It chided "many of our writers (including nearly all of our apologist–defenders)" on the ground that they "ignore or even deny the weaknesses, fallibility, and humanity of our prophets and apostles." The author frankly acknowledged the issues surrounding the First Vision and embarked on a lengthy but idiosyncratic argument in support of its historicity.[23]

An anonymous historian refuting the Tanners by not only admitting that many of their criticisms against Smith and the church were true, but also challenging the veracity of the First Vision as recounted in the LDS canon, was not a strategy that was likely to warm the hearts of a majority of LDS Church leaders. Then to have the booklet traced directly to the LDS Church Historical Department within a month of its publication represented a particularly bad bit of luck for Arrington, who was already sensing that his position as church historian was becoming increasingly untenable. On the same day Jerald called him to confront him over the booklet, Arrington recorded in his diary

> my job as Church Historian is an impossible assignment. Consider the following.
> 1. The anti-Mormons (Jerald and Sandra Tanner, Michael Marquardt, Wesley Walters, John W. Fitzgerald) seek to use every advantage to get information. If one is truthful and "open," they destroy me by citing you, by declaring I permitted them access, by tripping me up on inconsistencies. They're out to injure the Church by injuring me.
> 2. The highly orthodox, cautious people, such as Elders [Ezra Taft] Benson, [Mark E.] Petersen, and [Boyd K.] Packer, are alert for every misstep; they want to discredit me.
> 3. [Church employee] Tom Truitt (and also Lauritz Petersen at an earlier stage) is a spy for Elders Benson and Petersen. He reads everything I do or say that he can get his hands on, underlines statements which, out of context, will be objectionable to Elders Benson and Petersen, and sends these on to them....
> I feel very despondent today, pessimistic about my future, feel that I

---

23. Anonymous, *Jerald and Sandra Tanner's Distorted View*, 29–46.

do not have the support of the brethren, and also that I do not have the support of the fellow historians I have a right to expect support from.[24]

For years the Tanners had argued that the LDS Church suppressed documents and was squeamish about its past. If it publicly began to look as though things were changing as Arrington and his team produced honest, if sympathetic, LDS history, church leaders privately proved Jerald and Sandra right. In the previous five years, apostles had complained publicly about Arrington and his team's work. Within a few years, Arrington and his department would be moved to BYU, and the previous open access to the LDS archives would be curtailed.[25]

Jerald and Sandra Tanner's Distorted View of Mormonism had strengths and weaknesses in its challenge of the Tanners' work, but one claim rings especially hollow: That the LDS Church archives functioned as all other professional and academic institutions throughout the world. The Tanners "berate the LDS for Suppression of Records," the anonymous author said, but other "prestigious manuscript libraries throughout the world ... have long refused permission to photocopy manuscripts, or have restricted the photocopying of manuscripts—but this is not mentioned by the Tanners."[26] The issue, however, was not simply restrictions on photocopying, but access itself. In addition, the other archives Clandestine refers to have not tended to restrict materials as a way of controlling the outcome of historical research.[27]

One Mormon historian asked the Tanners "not to expose the role of the Historical Department in the[ir] rebuttal lest it cause unsurmountable [*sic*] problems for Leonard Arrington."[28] The Tanners were convinced, however, that the general authorities would have already seen Richard Steven Marshall's thesis and that Arrington would have more than enough trouble because of disclosures made in it. Arrington would later describe Marshall's paper as a "land mine

---

24. Jerald called Arrington on January 14, 1978. Arrington, *Confessions of a Mormon Historian*, 2:452–53 (Bergera's brackets).

25. Prince, *Leonard Arrington*, 328–71.

26. Anonymous, *Jerald and Sandra Tanner's Distorted View*, 13.

27. Prince, *Arrington*, 205.

28. Tanner and Tanner, *Answering Dr. Clandestine*, 43.

... that later exploded."[29] Marshall had been summoned to Mark E. Petersen's office, questioned, and asked to provide a copy of his paper. Copies were made and subsequently distributed among the Twelve Apostles, and several Mormon scholars suffered the consequences.[30] The Tanners felt sure that whatever they published about the booklet could not get Arrington into any more trouble with the church than he already was. Rumors were spreading that Arrington's days were numbered.

The Tanners published their twenty-two-page edition of *Answering Dr. Clandestine* in February 1978, less than two months after the booklet appeared. On February 24 Arrington was called into the office of his supervisor, G. Homer Durham, and informed that the First Presidency had decided to bring the Historical Department under its direct control, with Apostles Gordon B. Hinckley and Boyd K. Packer reporting to the presidency on the department's actions. Arrington was also informed that he was no longer the official Church Historian, but would now be called Director of the History Division. Arrington was not to publicize this change in title.[31]

29. Arrington, *Adventures of a Church Historian*, 154, without naming Marshall.
30. Prince, *Leonard Arrington*, 298–99.
31. Arrington, *Confessions of a Mormon Historian*, 2:474–81.

13

JERALD'S OTHER MINISTRY:
THE RESCUE MISSION OF SALT LAKE

One day in 1978 Jerald's car broke down in front of Kramer's Used Car Lot on Main Street Salt Lake City. Don Kramer was there talking to the director of the Rescue Mission of Salt Lake.[1] He called Jerald over to introduce him, and the man told Jerald they were in need of "fishers of men." Jerald felt this was the Lord's calling, but he resisted for a time.

From their early days as Christians, the Tanners had sponsored children from developing countries through World Vision, peaking in 1987 sponsoring one hundred children.[2] But this new calling was more up close and personal. Jerald came from a family that had struggled with alcohol at least as far back as his great-grandparents Myron and Ann Tanner.

On May 19, 1866, Myron married Ann Crosby as his second wife, and first plural wife. His first wife, whom he married a decade earlier, was Mary Jane Mount, a woman he'd described as "a very refined and intelligent woman of literary tastes and poetic instincts ... just the opposite of my own rugged, untempered and uncultivated nature."[3] Ann was a young British convert in her late teens.[4] Married to a man twice her age, with a sister wife who was significantly older, more refined and educated, and singularly unsympathetic towards her, Ann did not thrive. Myron was kind and attentive to both his wives and their children. At first both women

---

1. Don Kramer and his father, Dan, were on the mission's board.
2. *Salt Lake City Messenger* 62, Mar. 1987, 10.
3. *Biography of Myron Tanner*, 16–17. They married on May 22, 1856.
4. Tanner, 20. Ann's death certificate indicates that she was born in 1847. For the date of the marriage George S. Tanner, *John Tanner*, 284.

lived in the same house, but eventually Myron provided each with her own home, where she could live and raise her children. But at some point Ann slipped hopelessly into alcoholism.

By the early 1880s Ann's addiction had brought things to the point of crisis, and Myron felt it best to take Ann's children away from her. On January 9, 1883, he brought Jerald's grandfather Caleb into his and Mary Jane's home to be raised there, sending Caleb's brothers, Willie and Freeman, to live with his brother in Payson.[5] After that, things went from bad to worse for Ann, who was sometimes even arrested and put in jail for public intoxication.[6]

Mary Jane attributed Ann's alcoholism to her mother and sister, who "were used to drink in the old country. They led her into it and she is gone in spite of all Myron could do to save her."[7] Mary Jane fails to mention, however, that when Ann married Myron, she entered a household where there "was always a barrel of liquor of some kind in the cellar."[8] Alcohol was always present. Myron, though never intoxicated, was nonetheless addicted for most of his life to "the use of liquor, tobacco, tea and coffee." Myron's son Joseph Marion recalls that it was his father's "custom every morning before breakfast and every noon before dinner, to take a bowl of what was commonly called sling, that was drunk perhaps as freely as tea or coffee are drunk today. He not only drank this sling, or toddy, himself, but he gave it to his family if they cared to use it."

This was the norm until George A. Smith, to whom Myron was always especially attached, came to Provo one time and gave "a very spirited address in the old Cluff Hall" on the importance of strict adherence to the Word of Wisdom, the Mormon health code. Myron determined to quit cold turkey. He removed all liquor and tobacco from his house. The extent of his addiction at the time is seen in his physical reaction to quitting. It was "perhaps three months" before he could "keep a breakfast upon his stomach or be free from

5. Mary Jane Mount Tanner Diary Vol. II, 10–11; Mary Jane Mount Tanner Papers, box 3 bk. 2.

6. Mount Tanner Diary Vol. II, 74–75 and Vol. III, 209.

7. Mary Jane Mount Tanner to Aunt Mary, Oct. 7, 1883, in Tanner, *A Fragment: The Autobiography of Mary Jane Mount Tanner*, 199.

8. Tanner, *Biography of Myron Tanner*, 26.

The Rescue Mission of Salt Lake.

hours of nausea."[9] He began going blind and had to remain in dark rooms to avoid the "painful effects of sunshine." The doctors eventually persuaded him to take some snuff for his condition, which he continued to use until he died. Twice he tried to give up his snuff, "only to learn that as a consequence his eyes each time became bad." Myron's son Joseph Marion Tanner tells how living in his father's house, he himself "had learned to enjoy the liquor that was taken before meals," and recalled "his own personal inconveniences when told that there was to be no more liquor, no more tea or coffee served in that home."[10]

Jerald's grandfather, Caleb, though rescued from his alcoholic mother and brought into Mary Jane's home in his mid-teens to be raised, nevertheless became an alcoholic himself. Caleb's wife Esthma (Curtis) Tanner, however, would always remain a strict teetotaler.

Whenever Jerald told of his own struggles with alcohol, he always

9. Tanner, 27.
10. Tanner, 26.

Jerald's great-grandmother, Ann Crosby Tanner,
first plural wife of Myron Tanner.

Myron and Mary Jane Mount Tanner

Jerald's grandparents Caleb and Esthma (Curtis) Tanner.

concealed the fact that his parents too had both been alcoholics for a time. Helen's parents had opposed her marriage to George because he was already known to be a drinker. For a long time Helen, who struggled throughout her life from the injuries she suffered in a plane crash that killed her first fiancé, fought against George's alcoholism, sometimes very dramatically. On one occasion she broke all the bottles she discovered in one of George's secret stashes. But in the mean time she became addicted to the pain medication she needed to live an active life. Eventually she succumbed to alcoholism herself, while George, having sustained some rather serious injuries, became addicted to pain medicine on top of the alcohol. Eventually things came to a point where it became necessary for Jerald to commit first his father and then his mother for treatment. Happily they both managed to kick their addictions.

Jerald's sister Irene also tells a story of a struggle with alcohol and, like Jerald, of her deliverance from it when she became a Christian.[11]

---

11. Irene Bonner to Fay, Sep. 16, 1974.

On the other side of the family, Myron and Mary Jane Mount Tanner's great-granddaughter, the former Episcopal Bishop Carolyn Tanner Irish, has also openly and frankly discussed her own struggles with alcohol.[12]

One would think given this background that Jerald would have had sympathy for men whose lives had been ruined by alcohol. He now had to face a shameful fact about himself. Far from feeling sympathetic he was actually repulsed by them, even though he knew he was really just like them, and might have ended up where they were had things been different. This bothered Jerald until one day he felt the strong conviction that "if I didn't answer the call soon I never would. ... I ... went to the old mission which was on Second West at the time. It was a total disaster. I disliked the place and had a difficult time adjusting to the situation. Miraculously, God gave me great peace; and I began to love both the mission and the people who came in from off the street."[13]

For the rest of his life, six days a week, Jerald would leave home by 9:00 a.m. to walk the mile and a half to the rescue mission, memorizing verses of the Bible from homemade scripture memory cards along the way. He would begin his day helping out in the office, then at around ten or eleven he would go down to a little room in the basement, put up a "Prayer Room Open" sign, and go in and pray. Other men would join him, sometimes to pray, other times to talk. Jerald would go home for lunch from 12:00–12:30. After lunch he would be ready to plunge into his research for the day.

In his early days at the mission Jerald was on the board of directors. Then the mission hired a man named Ed Brotherton to promote the ministry, whom Jerald (and unfortunately only Jerald) very quickly suspected wasn't what he claimed to be. Although Brotherton seemed very active on behalf of the struggling mission, the dismal financial situation wasn't improving. A little research on Jerald's part began to uncover problems. Brotherton's stories didn't hold up under scrutiny. Jerald discovered that he had been in prison and that his résumé made false claims about previous employment.

---

12. Amanda Piece, "Bishop Carolyn Tanner Irish Becomes First Woman to Win Giant in Our City Award," *Deseret News*, May 21, 2010, B1, B5.

13. Rescue Mission/Rescue Haven of Salt Lake Newsletter, Apr. 1998.

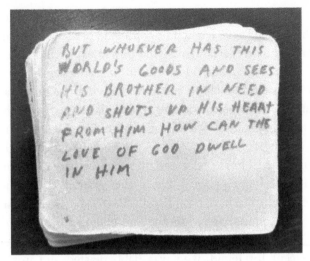

Jerald Tanner's scripture memory cards.

Brotherton traveled to other cities on behalf of the mission and came back full of glowing reports of substantial funding to be donated from the companies he had contacted. But the money never came and the companies denied ever speaking with Brotherton or even knowing who he was. Brotherton had talked a woman into making a donation of $1,000, which he told her he would spend buying airplane parts to sell at a substantial profit, and then refund her money, keeping the profits for the mission. Neither the woman nor the mission ever saw a dime.

Jerald learned that the Ogden, Utah, police wanted to arrest Brotherton for stealing a car off a lot and that they strongly suspected him of robbing a house on the same night. But they hadn't been able to put together a case because the owner of the car lot had moved out of state.

Jerald approached the director of the mission with the evidence he had compiled and strongly suggested that Brotherton be fired at once. The director agreed and Brotherton was dismissed on July 17, 1981. Three days later, however, the board met and fired the director, generally blaming him for the poor financial state of the institution, and rehired Brotherton. The president of the board promised Jerald his accusations would be thoroughly investigated. If they proved true, he said, Brotherton would be dismissed permanently. For his part, Brotherton threatened to sue Jerald if he continued pressing his accusations.

"I had really underestimated the power of the individual I was dealing with," Jerald would later recall. "It seemed as if he had some type of supernatural help to extricate himself from almost any type of situation."[14] Brotherton defended himself very persuasively before the board. He claimed that the accusation about his stealing a car was all a misunderstanding, and that it really had to do with something unrelated (Jerald later saw the felony charge for auto theft filed with the Ogden police). He further granted that some of his activities might not have been handled in the best way possible. He also seemed appropriately humble and apologetic. When the vote was taken the decision was unanimous in favor of keeping Brotherton, except for Jerald, who was flabbergasted and immediately resigned from the board. He intended to continue at the mission, but strictly as a volunteer. Then the board took a further step. They hired Brotherton as the new mission director.

Once that happened it was only a matter of time before Jerald became persona non grata. On the morning of October 1, 1981, Jerald was met at the door by a big beefy guy who informed him that he had been banned from the mission, and that Jerald's daughter April, who had also served faithfully there for a long time, was also banned. It was, Jerald recalled, "one of the saddest experiences I ever had in my Christian life."[15]

But Jerald had been right about Brotherton, and as a result of his warning being ignored, things went from bad to worse at the mission. Brotherton also got rid of the mission chaplain and shut down the prayer ministry, lest it become some sort of subversive cell. Finally, after studying the way the mission was legally organized, Brotherton managed to undermine the board of directors itself, on one occasion even having the police come and remove one of them from the premises.

Jerald wanted to save the mission, and he knew he could probably succeed in taking Brotherton down by going public with the

---

14. *Jerald Tanner's Testimony*, 23. Most of the details given here comes from pages 23–26. Jerald did not refer to Brotherton by name.

15. *Jerald Tanner's Testimony*, 25.

evidence he had gathered, but he also knew the scandal might bring the mission itself down, putting all the men getting help there back out onto the street. One morning while reading the Bible, Jerald came across the promise in John 14:13–14 where it says, "Whatever you may ask in my name this I will do, that the Father may be glorified in the Son. If you ask me anything in my name I will do it." Jerald reminded the Lord that it had been a year since he had first asked that the mission be delivered from Brotherton, and so far nothing seemed to be happening. Later that afternoon he got a call asking him to come to the mission and help print the newsletter, something he had taken part in before Brotherton arrived but that he did not participate in after Brotherton had taken over.

When he arrived, he was warmly greeted with the news that Brotherton had finally been dismissed and a new director was on his way from California. Not long after this a policeman came to the mission looking for Brotherton, explaining that he was wanted in two states. By 1987 news arrived that the mission's old director had finally been apprehended and was serving a prison term in an adjacent state.

No one ever apologized to Jerald or April for treating them the way they did, but perhaps this is understandable given that before it was all over most everyone had been alienated by Brotherton in one way or another. Jerald was received back warmly but declined ever serving on the board again. He continued to go to the mission for years, even after Sandra feared that his Alzheimer's might keep him from finding his way there and back safely. He always walked even in the worst weather. His family still laughs about how absurd he looked all bundled up to go in the most severe winter weather, in big boots and ridiculously enormous ear-muffs protecting extremely cold-sensitive ears, six days a week, summer, winter, rain or shine, memorizing Bible verses from his homemade memory cards, working on newsletters, bulk mailings, tallying up incoming donations, updating mailing lists, and praying with the men.

It wasn't always easy for Jerald and Sandra's children growing up with such well-known, and some might say notorious, parents. Tanner is a good old Mormon family name that can incline fellow Mormons to look on the bearer with favor the moment they hear it.

But then that might suddenly change when they find out you aren't just the child of *a* Tanner, but of *the* Tanners.

A couple years after he graduated from high school, Dennis decided it was time to get out from under the shadow of his parents and find somewhere he could just be himself. Todd Price, a Mormon friend from high school, suggested they go to Southern Utah State College (now Southern Utah University) in Cedar City. Dennis agreed, naively thinking that it was far enough away to escape the stigma of being Jerald and Sandra's son. They both enrolled in the fall of 1983.

It quickly became clear that he had not traveled far enough away to experience the kind of blessed anonymity he was seeking. On a Monday before classes began, Todd had left to run errands and planned to attend the LDS single's ward that evening. Dennis was bored, so he paged through the campus newspaper to see if there might be something interesting for him to attend. He saw an ad for a Bible study in the home of Professor Ron Aden. Since the ad called it a "Bible study," Dennis felt sure it likely wasn't a Mormon thing. What was more, it was only two blocks away, and started at six that evening. Plenty of time for him to attend. But what happened when he arrived left him baffled: "I rang the doorbell and a pretty young woman answered the door. Heidi smiled and said to me, 'Hi Dennis.' I just stood and stared at her. Heidi then thought she had made a mistake. 'You're not Dennis?' I said, 'Yes, my name is Dennis.' Heidi smiled and said 'Dennis Tanner? We have been expecting you.'"[16] Dennis never did discover how they knew he was coming; Jerald and Sandra assured him they hadn't done anything to connect him with Christians in Cedar City.

About three weeks into the semester, Dennis was driving past the LDS Institute of Religion and saw an announcement for a "Talk on the Tanners" lecture. Ron Thompson, who led the Bible study and whose church Dennis had started attending, suggested they go. And so, when the time came, they went and sat in the back.

The speaker was Van Hale, a well-known radio host and defender of Mormonism, but Dennis recalls less about what Hale said about his parents than about how controversial his own view was on the

---

16. Dennis Tanner, email to Ron Huggins, Apr. 4, 2018.

"We knew you were down here!" Todd Price and
Dennis Tanner leaving for college in Cedar City.

Book of Mormon, which Hale apparently took to be something less
than history. This sidetracked the evening, and led afterwards to a lot
of Mormon students getting up and bearing their testimonies of the
church, Joseph Smith, and the truthfulness of the Book of Mormon.

At the end, Thompson urged Dennis to go up with him so they
could introduce themselves to Hale and to the head of the LDS
Institute. They found Hale very friendly and respectful, but Dennis
was nonplussed when the "head of the Institute looked at me and ar-
rogantly told me, 'We knew you were down here,' and indicated this
was the reason they had Mr. Hale speak."[17] How in the world had
they discovered he was "down here"? And how was it that his mere
presence was viewed as such a threat in some people's mind that it
was felt necessary to schedule a special event at the LDS Institute.
Cedar City was definitely not far enough away.

Eventually Dennis married Sherry Brush on August 4, 1990, and
moved to California. Sandra and Jerald's daughters would also move
away; April would settle with her husband and family in western
Washington, and Teresa moved to southern Idaho. Only Dennis
would eventually return to Utah in 1995.

17. Tanner to Huggins.

Jerald's mother, Helen, died on October 26, 1984, and his father, George, four years later on September 6, 1988. In the interim Jerald's oldest sister, Ruth, and her husband, who were still both faithful Mormons, moved in with George to care for him. Jerald served as executor of his parents' estate, which was finalized by 1989. In addition to all their other engagements with Mormon and evangelical critics in the 1980s, the Tanners were also able to update *Mormonism: Shadow or Reality?* twice, with a fourth edition in 1982 and a fifth in 1987.

In 1981, the same year that Jerald was barred from the rescue mission, he and Sandra became the inspiration of two characters in a book of pulp fiction. Peter Bart, a reporter and columnist for such papers as the *New York Times* and the *Wall Street Journal*, turned his hand to writing a scary novel about the Mormons, or particularly one very powerful Mormon named Dana Sloat, a member of the First Presidency, who was in charge of the church's vast financial and political empire. Sloat had a crippled son who was the head of a fundamentalist Mormon sect. The book was titled *Thy Kingdom Come*. The two characters Bart modeled after Jerald and Sandra were named Hiram and Augusta "Gussie" Cobb, and are described on the fly leaf as "two young dissidents who strive to enlighten the Mormons about the darker secrets of their history, the corruption of their present leadership, the exotic rituals of polygamy, the violent persecution and the ruthlessness behind the façade of benevolence."[18] Eventually Hiram's research gets him in a little too deep and he is murdered.[19]

---

18. Bart told the Tanners he had patterned the Cobbs after them.
19. Bart, *Thy Kingdom Come*, 267–69, 312.

14

RACE AND PRIESTHOOD

The first tract the Tanners published was Jerald's *Does the Book of Mormon Teach Racial Prejudice?*[1] It was printed in 1959, and was one page long. No copies are known to exist. It showcased what was to become a repeating theme in the Tanners' work over the coming decades: an occupation with issues of race. Even authors who were otherwise critical of Jerald and Sandra noted their "opposition to Mormon racism."[2] Jerald's tract was followed by several other publications by the Tanners on race which had always been an issue in the LDS Church.

Racism and discrimination against Blacks went back to the beginnings of Mormonism. In the spring of 1836, an abolitionist by the name of Alvord had visited Kirtland, Ohio, and founded an anti-slavery society.[3] Seeking to discourage church members from participating, Joseph Smith, Warren Parrish, and the anonymous editor (presumably Oliver Cowdery) of the Mormon newspaper the *Messenger and Advocate* all contributed anti-abolitionist pieces, each specifically endorsing the unwarranted connection between Black slavery and the curse of Ham and Canaan.[4] Cowdery's article was the most strongly worded:

> Where can be the common sense of any wishing to see the slaves of the south set at liberty, is past our comprehension. Such a thing could not take place without corrupting all civil and wholesome society, of both the north and the south! Let the blacks of the south be free, and our community is overrun with paupers, and a reckless mass of human beings, uncultivated, untaught and unaccustomed to provide for themselves the necessaries of life—endangering the chastity of every female

---

1. Tanner, *Does the Book of Mormon Teach Racial Prejudice?*
2. Foster, "Career Apostates," 39.
3. "Anti-Slavery Intelligence," *The Philanthropist*, Apr. 22, 1936, 2.
4. *Messenger and Advocate*, Apr. 1836, 291–93, 300, 302.

who might by chance be found in our streets—our prisons filled with convicts, and the hang-man wearied with executing the functions of his office! This must unavoidably be the case, every rational man must admit, who have ever travelled in the slave states, or we must open our houses, unfold our arms, and bid these degraded and degrading sons of Canaan, a hearty welcome and a free admittance to all we possess! A society of this nature, to us, is so intolerably degrading, that the bare reflection causes our feelings to recoil, and our hearts to revolt. ... The idea of transportation is folly, the project of emancipation is destructive to our government, and the notion of amalgamation is devilish!—And insensible to feeling must be the heart, and low indeed must be the mind, that would consent for a moment, to see his fair daughter, his sister, or perhaps, his bosom companion, in the embrace of a NEGRO![5]

Utah would retain the South's peculiar institution until 1862 when Congress emancipated all slaves in US territories. Yet the state, like most of the country, remained barely tolerant of Black Americans, expecting them to conform to unwritten Jim Crow norms. At least three Black men were lynched in Utah between 1865 and 1925: Thomas Coleman, who had a sign posted with his body in Salt Lake City warning Black men to "leave white women alone"; a black man who was shot and hanged in Uintah in Weber County in 1869 because he was "a damned Nigger"; and Robert Marshall, murdered in Price in 1925.[6] There may have been more. The Salt Lake chapter of the NAACP was founded in 1919 after "a group of soldiers committed an act of brutality against a group of [Black] young ladies" from the congregation of Reverend George W. Harts, pastor of the Calvary Missionary Baptist Church in Salt Lake City. Attorney David H. Oliver, whom the Tanners knew, reported having been beaten in 1933 by the police and booked into jail as "Joe Doe, Nigger–Lawyer." His crime? When he went to the jail to visit an incarcerated client, the police captain commented that he didn't know there were any "nigger lawyers" in Utah. Oliver made the mistake of quipping, to his own harm, "I didn't either." The beating he got for his "impertinent" reply caused permanent damage to his right eye.[7]

5. [Cowdery], "The Abolitionists," *Messenger and Advocate*, Apr. 1836, 300.
6. O'Donovan, "Let This Be a Warning"; May, *Utah*, 145; Brunsman, "From Lynchings to Legal Rights," 24.
7. David H. Oliver, *A Negro on Mormonism*, 11.

As the Civil Rights movement slowly spread through the 1950s and 1960s, Utah, like other northern and western states, made progress in fits and starts. Utah's US senators and congressional representatives voted for the Civil Rights Act of 1964 and the Voting Rights Act of 1965.[8] However, Blacks—even prominent ones—had difficulty finding accommodations when visiting Utah. World-famous opera singer Marian Anderson was only allowed to stay at the LDS Church-owned Utah Hotel on the condition that she not eat in the dining room and that she use the freight elevator. She, at least, managed to obtain lodging; Harry Belafonte, Ella Fitzgerald, and Lionel Hampton were denied lodging as late as the 1960s.[9] Two Black men, David Martin and Ted Fields, the latter a friend of the Tanners' son, Dennis, were gunned down by Joseph Paul Franklin while jogging with two white women in Salt Lake City's Liberty Park in 1980.[10] In fairness, the shooter, though a Mormon since 1974, was not from Salt Lake City.[11] Still Utah, even with its small number of Black residents, was not immune to racism.

Neither was Sandra's own family immune. When Sandra was young, the McGees were cordial with a Chinese family who lived next door, giving Sandra a false impression about her parents' tolerance. An Italian man from the neighborhood asked her parents to sign a petition aimed at "getting the foreigners out," and Sandra remembers her father telling the man, "When you get a petition together aimed at getting rid of *all* the foreigners, bring it back and I'll sign it." For years Sandra assumed this was her father's way of noting the man's hypocrisy. Later, when Sandra recounted the story of the petition to her mother, Georgia laughed and corrected her daughter: If the man had brought a petition aimed at getting rid of

---

8. One representative, Sherman Lloyd, abstained from voting for the 1964 Civil Rights Act, but did not vote against it.

9. Davis, *Light in the Midst of Zion*, 23; May, *Utah*, 145.

10. Ayton, *Dark Soul*, 106–09.

11. Ayton, 181, 6–13. He was a Southerner, a racist killer who had committed some twenty-two racially motivated murders in various states across the country. It was he who shot and paralyzed Larry Flynt, the porno king, on March 6, 1978, after seeing a spread in *Hustler* magazine featuring a Black man and white woman, and late Civil Rights leader Vernon Jordan on May 29, 1980, in Fort Wayne, Indiana, who survived and went on to serve as an advisor to President Bill Clinton.

all foreigners, including Italians, Georgia assured her, Ivan would have happily signed it.

Sandra recalls that it never crossed her youthful mind that racial issues might represent a problem for the LDS Church. She remembers a teenage boy in the same stake who had received the priesthood only to be stripped of it when his family's genealogical research discovered that they had a black ancestor. Sandra and her friends all felt terrible for the boy, but it had not led her to question the church.[12]

In Jerald's family, there was a suspicion that his great-grandmother, Ann Crosby, second wife to Myron Tanner, had African blood. The possibility that she did is rendered especially plausible by photographs of both her and her son (Jerald's grandfather) Caleb. As if to flaunt this tradition, Jerald's grandfather Caleb named his first child, who died very young, "Cain."[13] Jerald's oldest sister, Ruth, feared that her sons might be kept from serving missions expecting that if the rumor were true church leaders would spiritually discern it. She was so worried that she went to a leader and stated her fears plainly; somehow she came away from the meeting reassured that her sons could indeed go on their missions. Jerald did not record his reaction to all this, but when he left the LDS Church and joined Pauline Hancock's group, he was eager to prove that the Book of Mormon was not racist.

Jerald's first publication, *Does the Book of Mormon Teach Racial Prejudice?*, was not a denunciation of the book, but a defense of it. Although there are no known surviving copies of the tract, it probably survives at least in part in a section of Jerald's 1963 book *Mormonism* under the heading "The Book of Mormon and Racial Prejudice."[14] There we find highlighted passages in the Book of Mormon that promoted racial equality, including 2 Nephi 26:27–28, which taught that God offered salvation "free for all men," and that "all men are privileged the one like unto the other, and none are forbidden." 2 Nephi 26:33 was even more explicit: God "denieth none that come unto him, black and white, bond and free, male and female;

---

12. Tanner, Reminiscences.
13. Cain Tanner lived 1898–1902. Caleb was sealed to his wife Esthma posthumously on April 16, 1969.
14. Tanner, *Mormonism*, 177.

Jerald's grandfather Caleb named his first son Cain, as if to flaunt the family rumor that his mother (and therefore he himself) had African blood.

and he remembereth the heathen; and all are alike unto God, both Jew and Gentile."[15]

By the time Jerald published the tract, he no longer accepted the LDS Church teachings on priesthood and race. At that stage he and Sandra were being guided by David Whitmer in trying to peel back the layers to discover which parts of Joseph Smith's prophetic ministry and calling were legitimate and which were not. When they became convinced that Joseph Smith's only prophetic calling had been to produce the Book of Mormon, it had given them a whole new perspective on the issue of Blacks being banned from the priesthood, since, as Whitmer had claimed, priesthoods were an aberration introduced as a result of Sidney Rigdon's leading Joseph astray.[16] At the same time the Tanners were coming to terms with the New Testament teaching that in addition to Christ—the only Melchizedek priest—all Christian believers are priests, and that the

---

15. Tanner.
16. Whitmer, *An Address to all Believers in Christ*, 64.

Old Testament Aaronic priesthood, with its animal sacrifices and offerings, its need for an earthly physical temple where the sacrifice took place, had been rendered obsolete in the cross of Jesus (Heb. 7–8; 1 Pet. 2:9). This was one of the points where Jerald was beginning to see the Book of Mormon coming into conflict not only with later Mormon scripture and practice, but with the Bible as well. In the same year that Jerald published his tract on the Book of Mormon and racism, he had also privately expressed doubt about this point in a letter to Pauline Hancock: "If High Priests don't continue after Christ; why then do priest[s] continue in the Book of Mormon. I cannot find any reference to priest in the bible after Christ."[17] But in the letter, which expresses a number of other doubts about the Book of Mormon, the race issue hadn't come up.

Had Jerald missed the problem? Was this another case of what LaMar Petersen had been talking about when he told Jerald, "You've got to see Mormonism as a whole; not as two kinds of things."[18] It was the very same Book of Mormon teaching that white skin meant righteousness and black skin wickedness that Joseph would carry over into the Book of Moses by asserting that the Mark of Cain (compare Gen. 4:15 to Moses 7:22) and the curse of Canaan (Gen 9:25 to Moses 7:8) were being made black.[19] In doing this Joseph provided seeming scriptural validation for the baseless and "often refuted" Southern interpretation of Genesis passages used to support Black slavery.[20] Which explained as well why Joseph Smith and other early Mormon leaders had explicitly endorsed the erroneous Southern readings.

Smith does not specifically mention priesthood or Blacks in his two scriptural accounts of the war in heaven in the pre-existence

---

17. Jerald Tanner to Pauline Hancock, ca. Dec. 1959, Tanner and Tanner, Papers.

18. Petersen, "Memoirs of Lamar Petersen," 2:42.

19. See, 1 Ne. 12:23, 2 Ne. 5:21, 2 Ne. 30:6, 3 Ne. 2:15–16. The 1981 edition of the Book of Mormon replaced "white" with "pure." See Skousen, *Book of Mormon*, 148 and 754, and Campbell, "'White' and 'Pure.'"

20. The words in quotation marks come from Noll, *Civil War as a Theological Crisis*, 56. The interpretation was not widely endorsed by historic Protestantism, because there is no indication in the Bible that Cain, Ham, or Canaan were Black. Popular Protestant commentaries, including Adam Clarke's, often contained extensive notes summarizing possible interpretations of what the Mark of Cain might have been, but seldom reflected awareness of anyone suggesting it had anything to do with being Black.

(Moses 4:1–4, Abr. 3:24–27). But he does connect the curse of Ham and Canaan to priesthood in Abraham 1:21–27, the passage LDS Apostle David O. McKay would refer to in 1947, when he said, "I know of no scriptural basis for denying the Priesthood to Negroes other than the one verse in the Book of Abraham."[21]

The Tanners insisted that the LDS Church, which avoided proselytizing in nations with large numbers of Black citizens, could not be the true church of Jesus Christ because it did not obey Jesus's final "Great Commission" at the end of the Gospel of Matthew: "Go ye therefore, and teach *all* nations, baptizing them in the name of the Father, and of the Son, and of the Holy Ghost" (Matthew 28:19–20).[22] The "proof text" often adduced for the church's exclusionary practice was Moses 7:12, where Enoch calls all the people to repent "save it were the people of Canaan," because of the curse that fell upon them a few verses earlier (v. 8).[23]

At some point early on the Tanners' circle learned of the ordination during Joseph Smith's time of African American Elijah Abel.[24] In 1960 Sandra's step-grandfather, Nicholas Philagios, wrote a letter asking Joseph Fielding Smith whether "Negro[e]s were ordained Elders in the early church." Smith wrote a terse response in red on the same letter: "Negroes were *not* ordained in the early church."[25] Bob Phillips, a friend of James Wardle and the Tanners, discovered that Abel's son Enoch and grandson Elijah had all been ordained elders.[26] Joseph Fielding Smith soon adopted a new explanation after Abel's ordination became more publicly known: The only reason Abel was ordained, Smith now claimed, was because it happened "before the

---

21. David O. McKay, Letter of Nov 3, 1947, rpt. in Lund, *Church and the Negro,* 91.

22. Tanner and Tanner, *Solving the Racial Problem in Utah,* 7 (emphasis mine). Jerald points, for example, to statements by Bruce R. McConkie, that "the message of salvation is not carried affirmatively to them" ("Negroes," *Mormon Doctrine,* 477), and William E. Berrett, that "no direct efforts have been made to proselytize among them," in "Church and the Negroid People," 65.

23. McConkie, "Negroes," *Mormon Doctrine,* 477; Petersen, "Race Problems," 14; Smith, *Way to Perfection,* 107.

24. Abel (sometimes spelled Able, Abels, and Ables) was ordained an elder on March 3, 1836, and a seventy on April 4, 1841. For more on his life, see Andrew Jenson, "Abel, Elijah," *Latter-day Saint Biographical Encyclopedia,* 3, 577, and Stevenson, *Black Mormon.*

25. Nicholas Philagios to Joseph Fielding Smith, June 8, 1960, Tanner and Tanner, Papers.

26. Tanner and Tanner, *Negro in Mormon Theology,* 14–17, and *Curse of Cain?,* 38–41.

matter had been submitted to the Prophet Joseph Smith."[27] In other words, rogue priesthood holders had ordained Abel without Joseph Smith's permission, which, according to Joseph Fielding Smith, the Prophet would have certainly forbidden had he known about it.

With the information provided by Phillips, Sandra searched the records of the LDS Genealogical Library to see if she could find the ordinations of Abel's kin. She eventually found the record for his grandson, whose name was also Elijah. When she asked for a copy to be made, her request was refused.[28] So Sandra and Jerald got creative. Using a special photosensitive paper, they could copy images projected from microfilm. Sandra went to the genealogy library with several cut sheets of the paper in her purse and made copies. The document became a prominent feature of a new book they published called *Joseph Smith and the Curse upon the Negro*.[29]

As the Tanners and others researched, the LDS Church struggled to find its footing. The Civil Rights movement had begun to apply indirect pressure to the church as more and more people began to ask why it discriminated against Black members. Contradictory statements regarding race emerged among LDS leaders. President David O. McKay declared in 1954 that there "is no doctrine in this church and there never was a doctrine in this church to the effect that the Negroes are under any kind of divine curse."[30] This statement, however, was contradicted by the explicit use of the word "curse" in that connection in Mormon scripture in Moses 7:22, 9:25 and Abraham 1:26–27. These, after all, were the go-to verses traditionally cited for justifying the denial of the priesthood to Blacks. This was why other church leaders at the same time did not hesitate to speak of Blacks as being under a curse.[31]

Joseph Smith had provided the pieces from which the Mormon teaching on race was later assembled, but he had not joined

27. Joseph Fielding Smith to Joseph H. Henderson, Apr. 10, 1963, rpt. in Tanner and Tanner, *Curse of Cain?*, 114–15.

28. Tanner and Tanner, *Joseph Smith's Curse*, 8.

29. Tanner and Tanner, between pages 8 and 9.

30. "Educator Cites McKay Statement of No Negro Bias in LDS Tenets," *Salt Lake Tribune*, Jan. 15, 1970, B-9. As recollected by Sterling M. McMurrin, the comment from McKay was said to have been made in 1954.

31. Smith, *Way to Perfection*, 106; Petersen, "Race Problems," 14, 17–18; Dyer, "For What Purpose," 2; McConkie, *Mormon Doctrine*, 107

them together into a coherent system. In the process of correlating them later, the LDS Church eventually came up with both a justification for denying the priesthood to Blacks and a comprehensive, karma-like sliding-scale explanation as to why some were born privileged, white, and Mormon, and others disadvantaged, non-white, and of some other religion. On March 18, 1961, Alvin R. Dyer, then president of the European Mission and later a counselor to David O. McKay,[32] addressed this topic at a Missionary Conference in Oslo, Norway. In the talk Dyer spells out both the supposed implications of the Mormon teaching:

> Why it is that you are white and not colored? ... Who had anything to do with your being born into the Church and not being Chinese, Hindu or a Negro? Is God such an unjust person that He would make you white and free and make a Negro cursed under the cursing of Cain that he could not hold the Priesthood of God?"[33]

God was not arbitrary, Dyer explained, people got just what they deserved. When they "left the Spirit World, they had already been judged by what they had done in the Spirit World and in their previous life." [34] Dyer went on to stress that given the race, time and religious context in which his listeners were born, there could be no doubt as to their having behaved well in the pre-existence:

> You were a person of nobility in the pre-existence. If you were not, you would have been born into one of these other channels [i.e., races, divisions of humanity, religions], and you would not have been born in this day and age, because the Lord has withheld the choice spirits of the pre-existence to come forth in this, the last dispensation.[35]

Dyer's presentation wasn't anomalous for the time, but was in line with other descriptions in those days.[36] Often the way of describing the alleged bad behavior of Blacks in the pre-existence

---

32. On Dyer's relations with McKay, see Bergera, "Tensions in David O. McKay's Presidencies."

33. Dyer, "For What Purpose," 2.

34. Dyer.

35. Dyer, 9.

36. See, for example, Bruce R. McConkie's, *Mormon Doctrine* entries on "Cain" (102), "Negroes" (447), and "Perdition" (512). See also the same entries of the 1966 second edition, 108–09, 526–27, 566–67.

was to say that they had not been sufficiently "valiant" in defending Jesus's plan of salvation during the war in heaven. Dyer, however, insisted that Blacks had actually rejected the priesthood of God in the pre-existence.[37]

Despite whatever moderate remarks McKay might have made about the church's teaching on the matter, he was outnumbered at the time by others in LDS leadership, with people like Alvin Dyer, Joseph Fielding Smith, Mark E. Petersen, and Bruce R. McConkie advocating for the traditional doctrine, with Hugh B. Brown pressing for change as the "sole voice of moderation on the subject of civil rights within McKay's inner circle," and "a lone voice among the General Authorities."[38]

In 1963, Jerald predicted that if "the pressure continues to increase on the Negro question, the leaders of the Mormon Church will probably have another revelation which will allow the Negro to hold the priesthood."[39] This prediction, though cynical about the divine source of Mormon revelation, scarcely came out of nowhere. The matter was being openly discussed by the LDS leadership.[40] In 1963, the church announced plans to send missionaries to Nigeria.[41] Prior to this, the LDS Church had avoided missions to predominantly black African nations, although they did send missionaries to whites in South Africa. The announcement came just at the time the issue of Blacks and the priesthood was coming into the spotlight in the eyes of both the nation and the world as a civil rights issue. There was immediate pushback. A Nigerian named Ambrose Chukwu, a student at California State Polytechnic, saw the announcement in *Newsweek* and was so disturbed by it that he wrote a piece for the *Nigerian Outlook*, entitled

---

37. Dyer, "What Purpose," 4: "Why is the Negro a Negro? ... You have heard this answer. 'Well, they must have been neutral in the pre-existence or they must have straddled the fence.['] That is the most common saying—they were neither hot nor cold, so the Lord made them Negroes. This, of course, is not true. The reason that spirits are born into Negro bodies is because those spirits rejected the Priesthood of God in the pre-existence. This is the reason why you have Negroes upon the earth."

38. Prince, *David O. McKay*, 65–66.

39. Tanner, *Will There Be a Revelation?*

40. Wallace Turner, "Mormons Weigh Stand on Negro: May End Ban on Complete Membership in Church," *New York Times*, Western Edition, June 7, 1963, 1, 4.

41. Turner, 4. See also Bush, "Writing 'Mormonism's Negro Doctrine,'" 233.

"They're Importing Ungodliness."[42] The article featured quotations from John J. Stewart and William E. Berrett's *Mormonism and the Negro*, and explained to his countrymen back home that anyone who read the book could see "that such a collection of madmen have no right to go under the name Christians." Chukwu's article was introduced by a separate piece entitled "Evil Saints" that openly described the LDS Church's racial teaching using the Nazi term *Herrenvolkism* (Master Racism).[43] The article had its desired effect—the Nigerian government decided not to grant visas to Mormon missionaries.[44]

In the meantime, Mormonism was being reported as a good alternative for racists in other denominations who disliked the increasing emphasis on racial equality they were hearing from their churches, who had become, to quote one racist convert to Mormonism, "fed up with being told by some preacher that these nigras are equal to me."[45]

Criticism of the LDS ban on Black members continued to intensify. At its annual meeting in Denver, Colorado, in 1965, the NAACP formally declared the LDS Church a racist organization and urged all non-white nations, including countries in Asia, South America, and Africa, not to open their doors to LDS missionaries.[46] By the end of the 1960s, the church was faced with a serious problem, and it came to a head in college athletics via BYU's membership in the Western Athletic Conference (WAC). On November 30, 1968, seven Black athletes at San Jose State refused to play in a basketball game against BYU in protest of the LDS Church's racial policy. As a result, their scholarships were immediately revoked. Two days later, the school's Black Athletes Federation, along with all Black varsity athletes, announced their own intention to sit out the upcoming game with Fresno in protest.[47]

---

42. "Now for the first time ... the Church plans a mission to proselytize actively among Negroes—in Nigeria," in "The Perspective," *Newsweek*, Jan. 21, 1963, 14. Ambrose Chukwu, "They're Importing Ungodliness," *Nigerian Outlook*, Mar. 5, 1963, 3, rpt. Tanners, *Curse of Cain?* 56–57.

43. Anonymous [Gab Idigo?], "Evil Saints," *Nigerian Outlook*, Mar. 5, 1963, 3.

44. Glen W. Davidson, "Mormon Missionaries and the Race Question," *The Christian Century*, Sep. 29, 1965, 1184.

45. Davidson, 1184.

46. Davidson, 1183

47. "Negroes Quit All Sports at San Jose," Dec. 3, 1968 (clipping in Tanner and Tanner, Papers).

On October 17, 1969, fourteen Black athletes who played football for the University of Wyoming at Laramie were dismissed by their coach for wearing black arm bands to show solidarity with student demonstrations organized on campus by the Black Student Alliance. The players became known as "The Black 14," and today a monument celebrating their action stands in the University of Wyoming's Student Union building. In response to Wyoming's action against its own players, the student senate at the University of Arizona passed a resolution that called on the University of Wyoming to reinstate the Black 14 as well as on the WAC and their own University of Arizona to sever ties with Brigham Young University.[48] Similar actions were occurring elsewhere.[49]

BYU President Ernest L Wilkinson subsequently protested in a full-page newspaper ad.[50] In it Wilkinson stated that the Black 14 who had been thrown off the team for wearing black arm bands had lost their suit against the University of Wyoming on the grounds that their actions (the armbands) "violated the First Amendment of the Constitution which prohibits any state from interfering with freedom of religion." In the bizarre logic of the judge who had decided the case, at least according to Wilkinson, the Black 14 were equated with the State interfering with Mormons' freedom of religion because they played for a state university. Wilkinson insisted further that people like the Black 14 had been out of line anyway, since they weren't members of the church, claiming that Black "Members of the Church do not object to it [i.e., to being denied the priesthood]. The objection is raised by blacks who are not members of the Church and who therefore would have no desire to hold the Mormon priesthood." A Black church member named Monroe Fleming, a friend of the Tanners who would later become one of the first Black Mormons to receive the priesthood, responded that "the statement that the Negro is contented as a member in the church without the priesthood, is not true. I know most of the members of the Negro race in the

---

48. "NAACP Asks Injunction in Wyoming Grid Case," *Salt Lake Tribune*, Oct. 25, 1969 (clipping in Tanner and Tanner, Papers).

49. Haws, *Mormon Image*, 307n35.

50. Ernest L. Wilkinson, "Minorities, Civil Rights, and BYU," *Salt Lake Tribune*, Apr. 5, 1970, 18-A.

Church and know that they feel that they should have the priesthood if they live a life based on the principles of the Gospel."[51]

Wilkinson's ad carefully sidestepped all reference to the real seriousness of the problem, making it sound as if it primarily had to do with the actions of unruly students. He did not mention, for example, that both Stanford University and the University of Washington had already announced plans to cease participation in future competition with BYU.[52] A number of other WAC schools were similarly debating the possibility of cutting ties with BYU until such a time as the LDS Church changed its race policy.[53] In a more private setting Wilkinson described the media firestorm that followed the Wyoming dismissal of the Black 14 as "the worst publicity campaign against the BYU we have ever experienced."[54] No matter what the sport, game after game was accompanied by protests—some of which turned violent.[55] Student governments protested that they wanted nothing to do with BYU or, at the very least, that student athletes who refused to play against BYU should not be penalized.[56]

On January 18, 1970, the moderate David O. MacKay died and, before the week was out, Joseph Fielding Smith became president of the LDS Church. The *New York Times* ran a piece by Wallace Turner entitled "Mormon Liberals Expect No Change, Smith, McKay's Successor, Backs Policy on Negro."[57] One of the issues for Smith was that he had been around a long time and had written and spoken enough on the subject of race to make his own advocacy of the traditional view perfectly clear. Indeed, some of the most offensive Mormon comments on race in the twentieth century had

---

51. Qtd. in Tanner and Tanner, *Mormons and Negroes*, 23. See "Monroe Fleming, One of First Black Mormon Priests, Dies," *The New York Times*, Aug. 5, 1982, B-14.

52. "Stanford Alleges Discrimination, Ends Competition with BYU," *Salt Lake Tribune*, Nov. 13, 1969, clipping in Tanner and Tanner, Papers; "Washington U. to Sever Y. Tie," *Deseret News*, Mar. 9, 1970, B-1.

53. "League Directors See Breakup, Report Says," *Salt Lake Tribune*, Oct. 29, 1969, (clipping in Tanner and Tanner, Papers).

54. "Memo to the Board of Trustees, Re: Charges of 'Racism' and 'Bigotry' Against BYU and the LDS Church," Oct. 29, 1969, 7, qtd. in Haws, *Mormon Image*, 56.

55. "Call Truce in Sports," *Deseret News*, Feb. 11, 1970, 20-A.

56. "WAC Student Chiefs Post Y. Policy," *Salt Lake Tribune*, June 9, 1970, 38; Bergera, "This Time of Crisis."

57. Wallace Turner, "Mormon Liberals Expect No Change, Smith, McKay's Successor, Backs Policy on Negro," *New York Times*, Jan. 25, 1970, 50.

come from his writings or verbal remarks. It was Joseph Fielding Smith who had infamously granted that blacks were also children of God, "notwithstanding their black covering emblematic of eternal darkness."[58] It was Smith again who had assured the readers of *Look* magazine in the 1960s that "'darkies' are wonderful people and they have their place in our church,"[59] a gaffe significant enough to warrant being reported in the following month in a one paragraph insert in *Jet* magazine, a publication targeted to African American readers, entitled "Mormon Has No Animosity Toward 'Darkies.'"[60]

A further problem for the new president was that what he'd said in the past could come back to contradict what he was saying now.[61] When Smith said in 1962 that "the Latter-day Saints ... have no animosity towards the Negro, neither have they described him as belonging to an 'inferior race,'"[62] he seems to have forgotten that he himself had once used "inferior race" to describe them.[63] The *New York Times* article announcing Smith's presidency also presented a range of examples of such quotations from Smith on the race issue, yet at the same time noting that there were "many Mormons who disagree with all the points made by Mr. Smith in the statements printed here."[64]

The tensions soon moved closer to home, however. As conflict mounted over BYU athletics, panic began to take hold on another front. Rumors circulated that a bus of Black Panthers were planning

---

58. Smith, *Way to Perfection*, 102.

59. The comment appeared in an Editor's Note added to the end of Jeff Nye, "Memo from a Mormon: In which a Troubled Young Man Raises the Question of His Church's Attitude Toward Negroes," *Look*, Oct 22, 1963, 79. Describing blacks as "darkies" was viewed as inappropriate and offensive at that time. The *Merriam Webster's Third New International Dictionary* (1961) defines the word as "NEGRO - Often taken to be offensive". The *Merriam Webster's Second New International Dictionary* (1936 [orig. 1934]) marked it as colloquial but not as offensive. In 1944 the NAACP was queried as to the appropriateness of the term(s) on behalf of Walt Disney and was told it was not appropriate (Scott, *Cinema Civil Rights*, 52). Yet already by 1918 certain American newspapers were banning the term "darkies" from their pages, see "The Horizon," under the heading "Social Progress" in *The Crisis*, Sep. 1918, 242.

60. "Mormon Has No Animosity Toward 'Darkies'" *Jet*, Oct. 24, 1936, 52.

61. Smith had published on the topic as early as 1924. See his "The Negro and the Priesthood," *Improvement Era*, Apr. 1924, 564–65.

62. "President Smith Discusses Vital Issue," *Church News*, Jul. 14, 1962, 3.

63. Smith, *Way to Perfection*, 101.

64. Wallace Turner, "Mormon Liberals Expect No Change," 50.

to travel to Salt Lake to take over Temple Square and/or blow up Mountain Dell Reservoir.[65] A purported revelation circulated that had supposedly been given by LDS Church President John Taylor in 1885 to the mother of a certain Edward Lunt, which predicted the events that seemed to be unfolding all around.[66] "The Negro," it said,

> will make many demands upon the white people of America and gain them all, concerning 'civil rights,' except that the Mormon Church will not allow them to hold the Priesthood. Since the church will be the last holdout to their wishes, they will descend upon Salt Lake City in droves to demonstrate and force their will upon the church. When they arrive, a militia will meet them west of the city to prevent their entrance, but it will be quickly overcome by the numbers of Negroes.
>
> Their marching intruders will enter the city and break through the Temple Square. They will knock down the doors to the temple (east), enter and desecrate the temple, even to ravishing the women therein.
>
> When the people of the city shall hear of this, they shall gather themselves together and in their anger wipe out the intruders to the degree that blood will flow freely down the gutters of Salt Lake City.

This passage, however, seems to have been added to the Lunt prophesy sometime after it was originally written down. A March 30, 1970, First Presidency statement was issued explaining that of the five copies in their possession only "one contains a statement about the Negro that purportedly is not in any of the others and particularly the one 'version' which was signed by Edward Lunt."[67] At the same time there sprung up suddenly in the Salt Lake City area a large number of vigilante-type groups, such as the Neighborhood Emergency Teams (NET).[68] Part of the catalyst for the rise of such groups was a two hour tape derived from various speeches that included calls for violent action made at a gathering of radical movements in Oakland, California, in July 1969, which was widely distributed throughout the Salt Lake area for free by right wing organizations. By early January 1970, as many as fifty civilian vigilante

---

65. Wilson, "Paradox of Mormon Folklore," 4.

66. Lunt claimed he had heard it from his mother in the early years of the twentieth century but wrote it down in 1951.

67. "First Presidency Explains So-Called Prophesy," *Church News,* Apr. 4, 1970, 3.

68. Roger O. Porter, "NET [Neighborhood Emergency Teams] Critics Misinformed, Leader Says," clipping from Utah newspaper, c. Mar. 1970.

groups had been organized, causing Public Safety Commissioner James L. Barker Jr. to call a meeting on January 9, offering assurance that the "Salt Lake Police are fully informed and capable of dealing with any organized violent disruption of civil authority by extremist groups, should such action occur."[69] But these assurances did not quell the growing hysteria. Talk show pundits on conservative 630 AM K-Talk Radio fanned the flames of anxiety. On February 20, 1970, the verdict came down in the Chicago 7 Conspiracy Trial, with five of the seven being sentenced to five years imprisonment each, leading to violent demonstrations numbering in the thousands across the country.[70] In Fillmore, Utah, riot sticks were lathed in shop class for use by the Jeep Posse just in case "a bunch of those Black Panthers came down here to take over the town."[71] Even the Salt Lake City Police believed there was a real potential threat. In late February, Chief Deputy Andrus announced that "communications have been intercepted which indicate that at least two militant minority groups are planning violence in the Salt Lake area."[72] At the time Sandra worried, given the state of hysteria, that if a bus full of Black tourists were to innocently stop for a visit of Temple Square, it might easily result in a disaster.

On March 3, 1970, the LDS leadership announced that "the Church has no connection with the Neighborhood Emergency Teams (NET), nor does it approve of its members being active in such vigilante groups."[73] They also forbade the use of church facilities for NET meetings.[74] Even so threats of violence continued to be made, as when

---

69. "City Is Ready to Combat Civil Disorder," *Deseret News*, Jan. 10, 1970, B-3. The words aren't a direct quotation from Barker, but a summary of the meeting.

70. "Protest Chicago 7 Verdict," *Deseret News*, Feb. 20, 1970, 1. When the church expressed its disapproval of the Neighborhood Emergency Teams, William Koerner, a spokesperson for the group, said he felt that "if the church was going to make a statement against what we were doing they would also have made a statement against what Jerry Rubin was doing." Roger O. Porter, "NET Critics Misinformed. Rubin was one of the Chicago 7 defendants, and author of *DO IT! Scenarios of the Revolution*, 1970.

71. "Fillmore's Posse Preparing for Riot Control—Just in Case," *Salt Lake Tribune*, Feb. 22, 1970, B-5, qtd. in Tanners, *Mormons and Negroes*, 75.

72. "S.L. Area Officers Map Anti-Violence Strategy," *Salt Lake Tribune*, Feb. 22, 1970, B-13.

73. "Support Police, Shun Vigilantes, Church Advises," *Deseret News*, Mar. 3, 1970, B-1.

74. Roger O. Porter, "NET Critics Misinformed, Leader Asserts," *Salt Lake Tribune*, Mar. 15, 1970, B-1.

Harry Edwards, Assistant Professor of Sociology at Berkeley, warned in April: "If Mormon dogma isn't changed by next year, anybody who goes with the BYU football team had better wear a hard hat and an asbestos suit."[75] But happily such extreme measures were not needed and the predicted busload of Black Panthers never arrived.

As time progressed in America and the radical 1960s gradually gave way to the "Me Decade" of '70s disco and therapy, the fires over LDS racism subsided, but did not die out completely.[76] Joseph Fielding Smith died in 1972 and his successor, Harold B. Lee, followed him in death after only eighteen months as prophet. The new LDS president, Spencer W. Kimball, was more likely than any of his predecessors to make strides in matters of race.

Attention turned to South America, where slavery had been legal until 1888.[77] The same church that required a young teen in young Sandra McGee's stake to have his priesthood revoked for having a Black ancestor now began to turn a blind eye to priesthood ordinations in South America. *New York Times* reporter Wallace Turner wrote, "There is no question but that in Brazil they have been ordaining priests who are part Negro."[78] In March 1975, Kimball announced that a temple would be built at São Paulo, Brazil, and rumors abounded that changes would finally come to the priesthood and temple ban.[79]

It took three more years, but the announcement finally came. The headline on the front page of the June 9, 1978, *Deseret News* read, "The LDS Church extends Priesthood to all worthy male members," accompanied by a First Presidency statement issued the previous day announcing that a "revelation has confirmed that the long-promised day has come when every faithful, worthy man in the Church may receive the holy priesthood." Whether by coincidence or design, the unanimous vote in the Quorum of Twelve Apostles took place while

---

75. Steve Rudman, "Change Dogma, Edwards Says," *Salt Lake Tribune* Apr. 9, 1970, (clipping).

76. Wolfe, "The Me Decade and the Third Great Awakening."

77. Grover, "Mormon Priesthood Revelation," 40.

78. Turner, *Mormon Establishment*, 262–63.

79. Mark L. Grover, "The Church in Brazil, the Future Has Finally Arrived," *Ensign*, Mar. 2014, 45; Quinn, *Extensions of Power*, 16.

Mark E. Petersen, a longtime opponent of lifting the ban, was out of town on church business.[80]

In the meantime, Jerald and Sandra's attention turned in a new direction. The last book they wrote on the topic for the time being was *Mormons and Negroes* (1970), but they continued to report and revisit the issue in the *Salt Lake City Messenger*. In 2004, the Tanners' *Curse of Cain? Racism in the Mormon Church* summed up their earlier work with new discussion of more recent developments.

Kimball's revelation had come fifteen years after Dr. Martin Luther King Jr. led the March on Washington, and twenty-two years after Rosa Parks refused to give up her seat on a Montgomery bus. What had taken so long? Jerald and Sandra gave credit to the LDS Church for the change, noting it would "undoubtedly help blacks obtain equality in Utah."[81] But they also wrote that the 1978 announcement was an example of the church's bowing to social pressure. The decision also made them feel personally vindicated for their own part in applying that pressure:

> Since we have probably printed more material critical of the Mormon anti-black doctrine than any other publisher, the new revelation comes as a great victory and a vindication of our work. We printed our first criticism of this doctrine in 1959. This was certainly not a popular cause to espouse in those days. (In fact, at one time a Mormon threatened to punch Sandra in the nose over the issue).[82]

---

80. Kimball, "Spencer W. Kimball and the Revelation on Priesthood," 55.

81. "Blacks Receive LDS Priesthood: Pressure Forces Mormon President to Issue New "Revelation," *Salt Lake City Messenger* 39, July 1978, 2.

82. Tanner and Tanner, *Mormonism: Shadow or Reality?*, 293-A.

15

DOCUMENTS AND FORGERIES

In the July 1982 issue of the *Messenger* the Tanners offered a new publication entitled *Clayton's Secret Writings Uncovered*, which contained the extracts from the diaries of Joseph Smith's secretary William Clayton. The entries extended from January 22, 1843, to January 28, 1846, and detailed the events surrounding the emergence of the polygamy revelation that became Doctrine and Covenants 132, difficulties that arose between Joseph and Emma regarding it, Smith's death, and the events that followed in the aftermath.

By the time the Tanners went to press with the excerpts, copies of the extracts had been circulating for at least ten months in a sort of black market for suppressed documents commonly called the Mormon Underground. The Tanners got their copy of the extracts from Kent Walgren, an administrative law judge and owner of a bookstore in Salt Lake City, who in turn got his copy from Mormon historian Richard Van Wagoner.[1] Where Van Wagoner got his copy is unknown. By the time the Tanners got it, there were probably hundreds of copies in circulation.[2]

The story of the original leak of the document to the public is known. It broke in the January 18, 1982, issue of the *Seventh East Press*, an alternative independent newspaper for BYU students. The article opened with the line: "A BYU graduate student has accused a member of a bishopric of stealing copies of materials which the student obtained from the vault of the First Presidency."[3] The graduate student in question was Andrew F. Ehat, and the material he'd purportedly obtained from the First Presidency vault was the Clayton

---

1. Tanner and Tanner, *Tanners on Trial,* 99.
2. Celia Warner, "The Tanners on Trial," *Sunstone Review,* Apr. 1984, 7.
3. "Restricted Church Document Stolen: Bishopric Member Circulates Unauthorized Documents," *Seventh East Press,* Jan. 18, 1982, 1.

diaries.[4] Ehat had apparently given a copy to Lyndon Cook.[5] Cook had left a copy in his office, where Kelly Johnson,[6] a member of the LDS bishopric who used the office on Sundays and Tuesdays to do interviews, saw the document and made copies.[7] On September 18, 1981, Johnson gave one of the copies to John Stoker, a religion instructor at BYU,[8] who let Scott Faulring borrow a copy, from which he made five more. Ehat became aware of what had happened and managed to recover the five copies Faulring had distributed within twelve hours of his making them.[9] But it was too late.

Copies had already been made from Faulring's copies, and, even apart from those, others had apparently found their way into circulation. A former BYU student named Hal Palmer had a copy he insisted had not come from Faulring.[10] In an interview Ehat had implied "that he had made copies for others [besides the one that was borrowed from Cook's office] as well, but declined to mention any names."[11] Still another copy had been given by a stranger to the polygamist Ernest "Grandpa" Strack,[12] "so that the copies would get out; they didn't want them to disappear."[13] Strack was the owner of Grandpa's Used Books on 700 East in Provo, which had become a hub for the Mormon Underground. You could photocopy anything he had for the price of the copy. Ehat eventually managed to recover Strack's copy, but again it was too late since Mormon Fundamentalist Robert Black claimed he got his copy of the document from Strack.[14] Black himself played a big part in the circulation of

---

4. "Restricted Church Document," 1.

5. "Restricted Church Document" and "Deposition upon Oral Examination of Andrew Ehat," Nov. 23, 1983, 59–60.

6. Johnson was given the cover name David Brown in "Restricted Document Stolen," 1. On his actual identity, see "Ehat Deposition," 57.

7. "Ehat Deposition," 57–59.

8. "Ehat Deposition," 62. Stoker was given the cover name "Tom Wilson" in "Restricted Document Stolen," 1.

9. "Restricted Church Document ," 11.

10. "Restricted Church Document ," 11.

11. "Restricted Church Document ," 1.

12. Despite the nickname "Grandpa" Strack, (b. Apr. 18, 1952) was only in his late twenties at the time.

13. "Restricted Church Document ," 11.

14. "Black Deposition," Dec. 28, 1983, 5.

documents in the Mormon Underground and even ran a little printing outfit called "The Mormon Underground Press."[15]

Later, somewhere way down the line, Kent Walgren got a copy from Van Wagoner, which he traded to Jerald in exchange for a shorter, sixty-plus page version of the Clayton diaries that Jerald already had.[16] Walgren in turn provided Ehat, who was also apparently an active trader in documents in the Mormon Underground,[17] a copy of the summary he'd gotten from Jerald.[18]

Given that the originals of the Clayton diaries were in the public domain, the Tanners felt it within their legal rights to publish them. They were therefore taken by surprise after receiving notification on May 7, 1983, that a Mormon graduate student named Andrew Ehat, with whom they'd had no dealings, was claiming that he held the copyright to Clayton's journal and was suing the Tanners for up to $50,000 plus costs. The lawsuit, the Tanners argued in the June 1983 *Messenger*, was baseless due to Section 103(b) of Title 17, United States Code, which reads, "The copyright in a compilation or derivative work extends only to the material contributed by the author of such work, as distinguished from the preexisting material employed in the work, and does not imply any exclusive right in the preexisting material."[19] In other words, Ehat could only copyright his own work—annotations or marginalia—added to the diaries and not the original diaries themselves.

Ehat's lawyer, however, came back claiming the extracts the Tanners published did include some small contribution from Ehat's own hand, including certain dates and short annotations, ellipses, and so on. The Tanners responded by summoning the president of the LDS Church to appear in court with the original Clayton diaries so that the published version could be checked against the original in order to see whether Ehat's claim of adding text was true. The

---

15. "Black Deposition," 12.

16. Jerald Tanner Deposition, Nov. 22, 1983, 114.

17. "Tanners Found Guilty! Judge Threatens Damages 'Many Times' $16,000," *Salt Lake City Messenger* 54, Sep. 1984, 5.

18. Testimony of Kent Walgren in *Andrew F. Ehat vs Jerald Tanner and Sandra Tanner dba Modern Microfilm Company* (Civil Action File No: C83-0593C), Trial Transcript, 408–10.

19. "Suing the Tanners: Legal Action to Suppress Diaries about Joseph Smith," *Salt Lake City Messenger* 51, Jun. 1983, 1.

church's lawyer resisted the summons, stressing that he represented "an organization that is very concerned about parties attempting to frame issues through which its own private materials may be discoverable. It has no desire to submit to the scrutiny of the parties."[20] In deference to the church's wishes the subpoena was quashed and Judge Sherman Christensen got Ehat's lawyer instead to drop the copyright claim altogether. But the judge still awarded Ehat $16,000 for "unfair" competition and ordered the Tanners to stop selling copies of the diaries, but later retracted that order.

The Tanners may not have pursued the matter further if Wesley Walters had not given them a crash course on federal appeals. It would add another $10,000 to the $22,000 they had already spent defending themselves, but with Walters's encouragement, they decided to move forward. By a stroke of good fortune, Jerald was able to get the *Deseret News* to help due to the fact that their report concerning the outcome of the trial had been careless and as a result had contained statements about the Tanners that were clearly libelous. The paper claimed that it had been the Tanners themselves who had snuck into Lyndon Cook's BYU office and taken the document on that fateful day back in September 1981, claiming "Court documents" as the source of their information.[21] Normally the Tanners had no interest in suing people for liable even when they had a clear case for doing so.[22] In this case, however, they were able to leverage the situation to coax the newspaper into giving them "a nice apology and a chance to respond to the [libelous] statements."[23] But they used the opportunity not only to refute the paper's particular libelous statement, but also to set out their entire case, which had by this time been honed and sharpened by the court process. Anyone who read and believed the presentation there (which was an accurate and concise presentation of the evidence) could see that the Tanners

---

20. Qtd. in Tanner, *Jerald Tanner's Testimony*, 17; Tanner and Tanner, *Mormon Church Fights Subpoena*.

21. "Damages Awarded in Notes Suit," *Deseret News* Mar. 30, 1984, B-11.

22. The Tanners at the time used the example of an unnamed reporter who, on June 29, 1982, accused the Tanners of stealing documents from the LDS archives before a University of Utah audience where the Tanners were present. See, Tanner and Tanner, *Tanners on Trial*, 102. Sandra identified the reporter as Peggy Fletcher Stack, whom she recalls confronting immediately after the event.

23. "Are the Tanners Guilty?" *Deseret News*, Apr. 29, 1984, A-7.

had a good case for an appeal. They concluded the article by asking friends for financial help, offering free literature about the case and reminding their readers that Clayton's diary was still available for $3 or $4 including shipping and handling.

Even though Judge Christensen had retracted the ban on selling the diaries, the Tanners were hauled back into court for continuing to offer the diaries for sale, and Christensen threatened that he would increase what they had already been ordered to pay by "many times."[24] The Tanners viewed the action as an attempt "to intimidate us through threats of awarding vast sums of money to Mr. Ehat just so we will not publicly question his decision."[25] Christensen's statement, which seemed rash and vindictive, may have actually improved the Tanners' prospects during the appeal.

On April 8, 1986, Christensen's decision was overturned.[26] Not only was Ehat denied the $16,000 Christensen had awarded him, but he was now ordered to pay the Tanners' court costs as well.[27] The Tanners, believing that the order would financially cripple Ehat for years, and blaming Ehat's attorney, Gordon Madsen,[28] for advising Ehat to pursue a case that had no merit, asked instead for only $1 in court costs. Madsen took out his wallet, pulled out a dollar, and handed it to them. Jerald and Sandra were able to do this in part because of friends who had rallied around them providing financial support. Madsen, for his part, moved forward and tried to get the decision of the appeals court overturned by the US Supreme Court, which let the appeals court ruling stand.[29]

In writing up his account of the trial, Jerald questioned whether Christensen had been "soft on perjury."[30] And indeed it must be

---

24. "Tanners Found Guilty! Judge Threatens Damages 'Many Times' $16,000," *Salt Lake City Messenger* 54, Sep. 1984, 3.

25. "Tanners Found Guilty!"

26. "U.S. Judge Dismisses Suit Against Two Historians," *Salt Lake Tribune*, Apr. 9, 1986, C-1. The court of appeals's decision is reproduced in full as an appendix to Tanner and Tanner, *Tanners on Trial*.

27. "It is hereby ordered that the defendants should be and hereby are awarded their costs of court incurred in this matter." Judge David Sam's Order on Ehat v. Tanners and Modern Microfilm, sent to the Tanners by their attorney, Brian M. Barnard, Apr. 22, 1986.

28. Brother to Mormon Historian Truman Madsen.

29. "Justices Refuse to Enter Dispute over Research Taken from Church Scholar," *Deseret News*, Oct. 6, 1986, 4-B.

30. *Tanners on Trial*, 46.

said that there was a good bit of conflicting testimony being given throughout the entire process—from the taking of depositions to the evidence given in the courtroom itself. At the beginning, it had been claimed (or at least implied) that Ehat had been granted access to the original diaries held by the First Presidency. But his probable source, as was revealed during the trial, was a typescript that James Allen and Dean Jessee had jointly produced with the agreement that neither would share it with anyone else.[31] Allen testified to providing Ehat with only twelve double-spaced pages of text, which raises the question of where Ehat got the other seventy-some pages that made up the rest of the document the Tanners had published.[32] Ehat claimed that he had been granted access to a typescript by Church Archivist Don Schmidt in 1979.[33] Schmidt, however, testified that he had not known of the existence of any typescript of the Clayton diaries until he was deposed for the case in January 1984.[34] Allen was given permission to see the diaries while he worked on a biography of Clayton at the time, and testified he was "miffed" when he discovered that Ehat had gotten ahold of a substantial portion of his and Jessee's typescript without his specific permission.[35] In other words, according to Allen, Ehat had done to Allen precisely what he would sue the Tanners for allegedly doing to him,[36] except that Allen had been granted access to the diaries,[37] which was never clear in Ehat's case. Ultimately Ehat would claim he got his typescript from Dean Jessee, something he had initially denied.[38] Jessee, however, denied making the document available to Ehat for copying, although he did admit he agreed to let Ehat check some dates against his transcript.[39] In the end we only have Ehat's word for where he obtained the document.

---

31. Trial Transcript, 223–224.

32. Trial Transcript, 226.

33. *Tanners on Trial*, 32, and Ehat Deposition, Nov. 23, 1983, 32, 40, 43.

34. Schmidt Deposition, Jan. 24, 1984, in Trial Transcript, 21–22.

35. Trial Transcript, 222, 239.

36. "Dr. Allen had specifically made his typescript for a biography he is going to publish on William Clayton. How Mr. Ehat could sue us for 'unfair competition' after what he did with the Allen typescript is almost beyond our comprehension." In "Are the Tanners Guilty?" *Deseret News*, Apr. 29, 1984, A-7.

37. Francis M. Gibbons on behalf of the First Presidency to G. Homer Durham, Jan. 3, 1979.

38. Ehat, "Answers to Interrogatories," 5.

39. Trial Transcript, see 130–31 for Schmidt, and 304 and 308 for Jessee.

Robert Black, who was deposed for the trial, described Ehat as a significant player in the Mormon Underground, being considered "one of the places to get information in the area of Mormon documents."[40] According to Black, before the Tanners published the diaries, he had wanted to publish his own copy of the diary. "Ehat owed me some favors," Black said, "on some trading deals that we had done before that he hadn't followed through on his end yet."[41] So, when Black got his hands on Clayton's diary, he was eager to call in the debt by publishing it.[42] But before he could, Ehat's lawyer, Gordon Madsen, contacted him, threatening him with a lawsuit if he did.[43]

Ehat also admitted taking part in the Mormon Underground by noting that he had obtained a microfilm copy of the Wilford Woodruff diaries from Fred Collier. The fundamentalist Collier, who was another major player in the Mormon Underground document trade, had been banned from the LDS Historical Department for obtaining documents and disseminating them. Sandra recalls Collier telling her of requesting a microfilm he'd wanted, swapping it out with a dummy reel he'd brought with him, making a copy of the microfilm, then going back and re-swapping the original with the dummy he had temporarily put in its place.[44]

It could not even be proved if the book the Tanners published was a direct descendant of the copy from Cook's BYU office. Ehat had also given copies of the diaries to Richard Lloyd Anderson and Truman Madsen—might they have made copies that got out as well?[45] These issues were never satisfactorily resolved, but they became moot when the Tanners' appeal was granted and the case dismissed.

The Mormon Underground was trading copies of documents that could not otherwise be seen or were hard to view at church archives. Most were third- or fourth-generation photocopies or microfilms that were hard to read, but that nonetheless were valuable to

---

40. Black Deposition, 12. For examples of other documents Ehat allegedly traded with Black, see 11.

41. Black, 7.

42. Black, 9–11.

43. Black, 5.

44. Scott Faulring also testified that Collier told him his formula for stealing microfilms. Faulring, Deposition, Dec. 22, 1983, 67.

45. Ehat's "Answers of Interrogatories," 6.

researchers. But the members of the loose-knit group started to pay attention when a young documents dealer named Mark Hofmann began turning up remarkable finds; not photocopies or transcripts, but original holograph documents from the nineteenth century.

Hofmann probably visited the Tanners' bookstore a number of times before they knew who he was. On June 16, 1978, while Sandra was minding the store, Hofmann brought along one of his earliest handwritten forgeries, a second anointing document with the words "Salt Lake Temple" rubber stamped across the top.[46] At the time Hofmann refused to say who he was, except to claim that he was from a prominent Mormon family. He claimed he'd found the document in his grandfather's papers. Because "Destroy this copy," had been penciled in at the top and then erased, he claimed he'd spirited it away to keep it from perishing. He let Sandra take a copy and left.

If it had been Hofmann's hope that the Tanners would jump at the chance of publishing the document, he was disappointed. Sandra simply stuck it in a file because it lacked any credible provenance. From time to time people, who had somehow learned of its existence, would come by to ask for a copy. A year later, in October 1979, Hofmann sold the original to Utah State University head of Special Collections A. J. (Jeff) Simmonds for $60.[47] He asked Simmonds not to reveal where he got it. When Simmonds asked if he could send a copy to the Tanners, Hofmann said, "Oh, don't bother. They have one."[48]

In the spring of 1980, Hofmann burst upon the scene as a true celebrity when he made public his discovery—later learned to be a forgery—of the transcription of characters Joseph Smith had supposedly copied from the gold plates and sent with Martin Harris to Professor Charles Anthon in New York City to see if he could decipher them. This related to a famous incident reported in the Pearl of Great Price.[49] Hofmann had provided a seeming provenance for the document by purchasing a Cambridge Bible published in 1668, into which he inscribed "Samuel Smith," the name of both Joseph

---

46. The second anointing, an ordinance the LDS Church rarely acknowledges even exists, is the most sacred ordinance performed in temples.

47. "Forged LDS Documents and Cracked Ink," *Salt Lake City Messenger* 61, Oct. 1986, 3–4.

48. Sillitoe and Roberts, *Salamander*, 233.

49. *Pearl of Great Price* Joseph Smith—History 64–65.

Smith's grandfather and great-grandfather. As would become usual, Hofmann would not divulge the seller beyond saying that it was a Salt Lake collector who had purchased the Bible from the grand-daughter of Joseph Smith's sister Katherine.[50] On April 17, 1980, Hofmann took the Bible to A. J. Simmonds at Utah State, asking his help to separate two of the pages, stuck together where Psalms ended and Proverbs began, in order to get at a folded piece of paper held in between.[51] The two of them carefully separated the pages, and thus was the Anthon Transcript "discovered."[52] Hofmann had made his version of the Anthon Transcript look even more authentic than the well-known version that had come down through the David Whitmer family.

Hofmann did this by picking up on a comment in Anthon's own descriptions of the document that Harris had brought to him in 1834 as having been "arranged in perpendicular columns"[53] and, in 1841, as "arranged in columns, like the Chinese mode of writing."[54] In contrast the characters in the Whitmer transcript were presented in horizontal lines, Hofmann placed his characters, in essentially the same order as in the Whitmer transcript, but in vertical columns, seemingly "confirming" Anthon's memory.[55] Hofmann was also obviously aware of how Anthon's 1834 letter had said that "the whole ended in a rude delineation of a circle divided into various compartments, decked with various strange marks, and evidently copied after the Mexican Calendar given by Humboldt, but copied in such a way as not to

---

50. Turley, *Victims*, 25–26.

51. Turley, 24. Turley gives the location of the stuck pages.

52. The document is named for Charles Anthon. As the well-known story goes, Smith copied some of the Reformed Egyptian characters from the gold plates and asked Martin Harris to have their authenticity verified. Harris approached Anthon, a classics professor at Columbia University in New York City. From there, the story diverges; Harris insisted that Anthon verified the characters but became embarrassed after learning where they came from. Anthon, for his part, denied ever authenticating the Reformed Egyptian. Van Wagoner, *Natural Born Seer*, 300–03

53. Charles Anthon to E. D. Howe, Feb. 17, 1834, in Howe, *Mormonism Unvailed*, 271–72.

54. Charles Anthon to Thomas Winthrop Coit, Apr. 3, 1841, in Clark, *Gleanings*, 233.

55. See the comparative chart showing the order relation between the horizontal lines of characters in the Whitmer transcript and the vertical lines in Hofmann's forgery in Tanner and Tanner, *Book of Mormon "Caractors" Found*, 7.

betray the source whence it was derived.[56] This too, Hofmann "con-firmed" by recreating a circular item to match Anthon's description in the lower right-hand corner. On the back of the document Hofmann wrote the following statement in Joseph's hand:

> These C<h>aractors were dilligently coppied by my own hand from the plates of gold and given to Martin Harris <who took them> to new york Citty, but the learned could not translate it because the Lord would not open it to them in fulfilment of the prop<h>esy of Isa<i>h written in the 29th Chapter and 11 verse.
> Joseph Smith Jr.[57]

Hofmann's "new discovery" was first shown to the First Presidency on April 22, and on April 28 it was made public in a news conference.[58] A few days before, on April 18, when Dean C. Jessee was first shown the document, he said "that he felt pretty confident that it was Joseph Smith's handwriting," that it was "like looking a friend in the face."[59] This document would be one of six Hofmann forgeries that Jessee would later include in the 1984 first edition of his *The Personal Writings of Joseph Smith*.[60]

Hugh Nibley, who had gotten his first look at the document on Friday, April 25, 1980, was ready to declare it authentic to the author of an article published in a Provo, Utah, paper the following Thursday (May 1). "Nobody could have faked those characters,"

---

56. Charles Anthon to E. D. Howe (Feb. 17, 1834), in Howe, *Mormonism Unvailed*, 272. The reference is to the famous Aztec Calendar which appeared as Plate XXIII, in Humboldt, *Researches*, 1:276–77.

57. Jessee, *Personal Writings of Joseph Smith*, 224 and 226.

58. Janet Brigham, "Original Copy of Gold Plate Characters Discovered," *Ensign*, June 1980, 75. This article has been silently expunged without acknowledgment or explanation from the digital version of issue on the LDS Church website.

59. "LDS Scholars Study Joseph Smith Transcript," *Deseret News* Apr. 28, 1980, 2-A. Danel W. Bachman Journal, Apr. 18, 1980, qtd. in Turley, *Victims*, 28. See, also, a version of the quote in Danel W. Bachman. "A Look at the Newly Discovered Joseph Smith Manuscript," *Ensign*, July 1980, 71. Hofmann himself also contributed an article to this issue (p. 32). Both articles have been expunged without acknowledgment or explanation from the digital version of the issue on the LDS Church website.

60. Jensen, "Joseph Smith's Chronicler," 123. The six, according to the errata slip produced by Deseret Book and later tucked into the book were (1) Note to Anthon Transcript, Feb. 1828, (2) Letter to Emma Smith, May 25, 1838, (3) Letter to Hyrum Smith, May 25, 1838, (4) Joseph Smith III Blessing, Jan. 17, 1844, (5) Letter to Maria and Sarah Lawrence, June 23, 1844, and (6) Letter to Jonathan Dunham, June 27, 1844. Thanks to Rick Bennett for providing me with a copy of the slip.

Nibley told the reporter, "It would take 10 minutes to see that this is fake."[61] He was sure that the document wasn't only authentic, but also readily translatable. Nibley knew this, he said, because he had already "counted at least two dozen out of 47 characters of the Demotic alphabet that could be given a phonetic value," and he knew that the document was meant to be read "from right to left." Klaus Baer of the Oriental Institute of the University of Chicago, who had worked with the Joseph Smith Papyri, disagreed with Nibley. "What is it?" wrote Baer, referring to the characters on Hofmann's Anthon Transcript. "Probably not Egyptian, even if here and there signs appear that could be interpreted as more or less awkwardly copied hieroglyphs of hieratic signs ... I suspect that one could have the same batting average in comparing this with Chinese or Japanese."[62] Although Baer doesn't mention it, the same could be said when comparing the characters with the English alphabet.[63]

The Anthon Transcript was only the first of Hofmann's sensational "finds." On February 16, 1981, Hofmann walked into LDS Church Archivist Don Schmidt's office with a photocopy of a blessing dated January 17, 1844, by Joseph Smith Jr. to his son Joseph Smith III. The blessing announced that "he shall be my successor to the Presidency of the High Priesthood[,] a seer, and a Revelator, and a Prophet, unto the Church; which appointment belongeth to him by blessing, and also by right." The document appeared to have been written by Joseph's scribe Thomas Bullock. It was a major discovery, which, if authentic, would vindicate the claims of the Reorganized Church of Jesus Christ of Latter Day Saints (today Community of Christ) which had followed Joseph Smith III rather than Brigham Young. The document was purchased by the LDS Church, which then traded it to the RLDS Church for its only copy of the 1833 Book of Commandments. The story broke in mid-March and received national attention.[64]

---

61. John C. Speer, "Transcript of Characters May Support LDS Claims," *The Herald*, May 1, 1980, 48.

62. Klaus Baer to Dr. Fitzgerald, May 10, 1980, 1–2.

63. See "Reformed Egyptian or Deformed English?" *Salt Lake City Messenger* 43, Jul. 1980, 4–5.

64. See, e.g., John M. Crewdson, "Mormons of Missouri, Humble, Happy, Documented" *New York Times*, Mar. 23, 1981, A-12; "Founder Settles 137-Year-Old Latter Day Saint Dispute: Old Document Confirms Missouri Faction's Position," *Christianity Today*, Apr. 24, 1981, 42 [607].

But it didn't get front page coverage in the October 1981 issue of the Tanners' *Messenger*. There was another story that knocked the Joseph Smith III blessing story into the back pages,[65] namely the publication by the church of a new edition of the Book of Mormon in which the reference to Native Americans becoming in the last days as "a white and delightsome people" at 2 Nephi 30:6 had been changed to "a pure and delightsome people." The justification given was that the "white and delightsome" reading had been a typographical error that appeared in the 1830 and 1837 editions of the Book of Mormon. It had been corrected in the 1840 edition, but was somehow erroneously restored in subsequent editions.[66] In their lead article the Tanners pointed out that the church could not prove that "white" had actually been a typographical error because, even though the original Book of Mormon manuscript was not extant for that section, the handwritten printer's manuscript was and had the word "white" in the passage not "pure."[67] The Tanners compensated in that issue, however, by announcing a thirty-one-page booklet for sale on the new Hofmann document entitled *Joseph Smith's Successor: An Important New Document Comes to Light*.

In creating this document about Joseph Smith III being Joseph's real successor, Hofmann was cleverly confirming what people had long suspected.[68] In the document we already see Hofmann's tendency to borrow words and phrases from known sources, which would later cause Jerald to doubt their authenticity. Jerald already noted, for example, how the phrase in the newly discovered blessing, "the anointing of the progenitor shall be upon the head of my son, and his seed after him, from generation to generation," paralleled the similar wording in the January 19, 1841, D&C 124:57–59.[69]

---

65. "Joseph as a Prophet: An Important New Document Comes to Light," *Salt Lake City Messenger* 46, Oct. 1981, 9–12.

66. Bruce T. Harper, "The Church Publishes a New Triple Combination," *Ensign*, Oct. 1981, 17–18.

67. "A ~~White~~ Pure and Delightsome People," *Salt Lake City Messenger* 46, Oct. 1981, 1–2.

68. See, for example, Lee, *Mormonism Unveiled*, 161: "I heard Mother Smith, the mother of Joseph the Prophet, plead with Brigham Young, with tears, not to rob young Joseph of his birthright, which his father, the Prophet, bestowed upon him previous to his death."

69. Tanner and Tanner, *Joseph Smith's Successor*, 6–7.

In August 1982, Hofmann managed to "find" yet another remarkable document, a January 23, 1829, letter written by Joseph Smith's mother, Lucy Mack Smith.[70] Lucy indicated that she was writing between the time when the 116 pages of the Book of Mormon manuscript were lost by Martin Harris (June 1828) and the resumption of the translation.[71] Just as he had with the Anthon Transcript and the Joseph Smith III blessing, Dean Jessee pronounced Lucy's letter authentic; the handwriting was "definitely that of Lucy Mack Smith."[72] Jerald noticed more problems in the Lucy Mack Smith document. Lucy seemed to know the end of the Book of Mormon story well before her son had actually translated it.[73] While this could have represented an anachronism on the part of Hofmann, a tell-tale sign of forgery, the Tanners were still looking at things the wrong way round, taking it rather as an indication of Joseph's knowing beforehand how he was going to end the Book of Mormon story.[74]

Hofmann's most sensational forgery, and the one he is most often remembered for, was the so-called White Salamander Letter, which was supposedly written on October 23, 1830, by Book of Mormon witness Martin Harris to early Mormon leader W. W. Phelps. This was before Phelps had joined the Mormons, but after he'd become a serious inquirer. Instead of an angel appearing to Joseph Smith, Harris's newly "discovered" letter quotes Joseph Smith describing the scene of the discovery of the Book of Mormon plates in much more occultic terms:

> I [Joseph Smith] found it [the plates] 4 years ago with my stone but only just got it because of the enchantment the old spirit come to me 3 times in the same dream & says dig up the gold but when I take it up the next morning the spirit transfigured himself from a white salamander in the bottom of the hole & struck me 3 times & held the treasure & would not let me have it.[75]

---

70. Tim Slover, "Lucy Mack Smith Letter: Church Document Discovered," *Seventh East Press*, Aug. 24, 1982, 1, 6.

71. For more on the 116 pages, see Bradley, *Lost 116 Pages*.

72. Slover, "Lucy Mack Smith Letter," 1

73. Tanner and Tanner, *Lucy Smith's 1829 Letter*, 1. Page two of the document reads: "after many years they [the Nephites] become the more wicked than their accursed brethren and God seeing that they would not repent of the evil he visited them with extinction."

74. Tanners and Tanner, 1.

75. Transcribed from photos of the letter.

On November 29, 1983, Hofmann called researcher and historian H. Michael Marquardt to tell him about the letter and read it to him over the phone. On December 11 Marquardt spent five hours at Hofmann's home examining the letter and discussing its contents with Hofmann.[76] On each of these occasions Marquardt took notes, which he afterward summed up on one typewritten sheet and gave to Jerald. Jerald began preparing his report on the document for the upcoming March 1984 issue of the *Messenger*.[77] One of the pieces of evidence that seemed to support the authenticity of the document was a January 15, 1831, letter by W. W. Phelps, published in E. D. Howe's *Mormonism Unvailed*. Phelps described Harris's participation in the coming forth of the Book of Mormon in words strikingly similar to Harris's own language in the Salamander Letter, which had supposedly been written less than three months before. According to Phelps, Harris had declared that the golden plates had been "interpreted by Joseph Smith, through a pair of silver spectacles, found with the plates." In the Salamander Letter, Harris similarly spoke of Joseph's using "giant silver spectacles," Phelps reported how Harris had taken a copy of the Book of Mormon characters "to Utica, Albany, and New York; at New York, they were shown to Dr. Mitchell, and he referred to professor Anthon who translated and declared them to be the ancient shorthand Egyptian."[78] The phrases "Utica, Albany, and New York," and "shorthand Egyptian," both appeared in the Salamander

---

76. Author's conversations with H. Michael Marquardt (Oct. 19–21, 2017), and Marquardt's notes for calls from Mark Hofmann (Nov. 29, Dec. 10, 1983), and visit to Hofmann's home (Dec. 11) in Marquardt Papers, box 97, fd. 3. Sillitoe and Roberts incorrectly give December 1 as the date of Marquardt's visit to Hofmann's home (*Salamander*, 274).

77. Everything relating to the Salamander letter in the March 1984 *Messenger* comes from this single typed sheet, and everything on the typed sheet comes from H. Michael Marquardt's Nov. 29 and Dec. 10 and 11 conversations with Hofmann. Marquardt's typed notes inadvertently skipped over a word in a quotation that had been included in his notes. The version of the quote used by Jerald in the March *Messenger* lacks the same word. The typed sheet of excerpts was found in the Tanner papers and Marquardt confirmed that he was the one who typed it. The notes with quotation marks included what was copied from the letter. In addition to these notes, Marquardt also provided a notarized copy later, and writes: "I received Issue No. 53, March 1984, of the *Salt Lake City Messenger* on March 3, 1984. Later that month I gave Jerald a notarized copy of my typed notes. The date of the notarization was March 19, 1984." Personal communication, Oct. 26, 2017. Thanks to H. Michael Marquardt for reviewing and correcting this footnote.

78. Howe, *Mormonism Unvailed*, 276.

Letter as well. From this it seemed, as Jerald wrote at the time, "safe to conclude that Phelps used the Harris letter in preparing his own."[79]

"Safe" until Jerald turned over the page of Howe's book, and found yet another significant verbal parallel to the Salamander Letter past the point where Phelps's letter ended and Howe's own account resumed. Howe described how Joseph "looked into the hole, where he saw a *toad*, which immediately transformed itself into a spirit."[80] This seemed very close, perhaps too close, to the Salamander Letter's parallel line: "the spirit transfigured himself from a white salamander in the bottom of the hole."

For Jerald the fact that this parallel stood in such close proximity to those in the Phelps letter undermined what had previously seemed to indicate that Phelps wrote in reliance on Martin Harris's Salamander Letter. It opened up the possibility that literary dependence might actually be moving in the opposite direction, namely in the direction of the Salamander Letter being composed in part by someone copying lines out of both W.W. Phelps and E. D. Howe. Harris could not have been writing in light of Howe because Howe came latter, and in the section where the reference to the toad comes up, Howe seems to be using his own language to summarize the 1833 account of Willard Chase that he had reproduced earlier, which had said that Joseph "saw in the box something that looked like a toad, which soon assumed the appearance of a man."[81]

In addition Jerald also noticed a second short parallel that he actually circled at the time in his copy of Marquardt's typescript. When Joseph Smith asked the spirit, "when can I have it," referring to the Golden Plates, the question was identical to an account given by early Mormon Joseph Knight Sr. That account had been published for the first time in *BYU Studies* in 1976.[82]

Up to that point Jerald, along with everyone else, had been looking at early Mormon parallels as supportive evidence for the authenticity

---

79. "Moroni or Salamander: Reported Find of Letter by Book of Mormon Witness," *Salt Lake City Messenger* 53, Mar. 1984, 4.

80. Howe, *Mormonism Unvailed*, 276. Howe appears to include the full text of W.W. Phelps's letter, which would rule out the reference to a toad coming from an unquoted portion of the letter.

81. Howe, 242.

82. Jessee, "Joseph Knight's Recollection," 31.

of the forgeries. Hofmann, like any other truly accomplished forger, had been playing to the expectations of the experts, filling in gaps the experts knew were there, confirming pet theories, and providing smoking guns where the experts felt the need for smoking guns. In other words, paving the way for his forgeries to be welcomed with open arms. As Orson Welles once said, experts are "God's own gift to the faker."[83] Jerald himself had, until now, been perhaps too ready to listen to the judgment of experts, of whom the most prominent was Dean Jessee. But now that Jerald realized he might be dealing with a faker, he knew he would need to be looking at the evidence in a different way; he would need to be thinking of material found in early Mormon texts not only as possible contemporary parallels to the documents Hofmann was finding, but as possible sources drawn upon as a basis for forging them. Jerald recalled:

> Since I knew that it was very unlikely that anyone else would spot these parallels and realize their significance, there was some temptation to keep the matter to myself. I knew, however, that God knew what I had seen, and I began to feel that He had shown me these unpleasant facts to warn me against endorsing the letter. Furthermore, I knew that I would never be satisfied if my case against Mormonism was based on fraudulent material.[84]

In his initial report, Jerald neither endorses not disputes the Salamander Letter. Rather he warned that "we have some reservations concerning the authenticity of the letter, and at the present time we are not prepared to say that it was actually penned by Martin Harris."[85] But, Jerald continued, "if the letter is authentic, it is one of the greatest evidences against the divine origin of the Book of Mormon. If, on the other hand, it is a forgery, it needs to be exposed as such so that millions of people will not be misled." Jerald's use of "we" in the newsletter was premature: Sandra remained convinced the Salamander Letter and other documents were authentic. Jerald's initial experience with Marquardt's excerpts of the Salamander Letter prepared him with a better view for approaching its complete text when it became available,

---

83. *F for Fake* (1973), qtd. in Keats, *Forged*, 126n9. The quote is at minute twenty-two in the film.

84. Tanner, *Jerald Tanner's Testimony*, 28.

85. "Moroni or Salamander?" 1.

which happened not long after. The more he scrutinized the parallels the more he became convinced the letter was a forgery.

The Salamander Letter bristled with parallels in vocabulary and shared phraseology with other early accounts. But it was the Joseph Knight Sr. account that sealed the deal for Jerald. Given that it had only been available to the public since 1976, Jerald became convinced that the Salamander Letter had to have been produced since that time. Jerald produced an edition of the Salamander Letter that marked out seven different sources its forger seemed to depend on.[86]

Once Jerald became convinced that, despite its apparent age, the Salamander Letter had been forged *after* 1976, it also became clear to him that the rest of Hofmann's remarkable discoveries might turn out to be recent forgeries as well. In August 1984 he went public with his doubts.

The Salt Lake Sunstone Symposium that year took place on Thursday through Saturday, August 23–25, at the Hotel Utah just east of Temple Square (now the Joseph Smith Memorial Building). The day before the symposium began, Wednesday, August 22, Jerald published a nine-page tract entitled *The Money-Digging Letters: A Preliminary Study.* That evening he sent Sandra to stand in the lobby and pass out the tract to people arriving for registration and other preconference activities.[87] Sandra, fearing that distributing the pamphlets might lead to their being sued for libel, said to Jerald, "If we lose our house over this, we're going to have a problem!" The concern was real, because at the time they were still embroiled in the suit involving Andrew Ehat, which would not finally be over until April 8, 1986. Nevertheless, Jerald replied confidently: "They're not going to sue us. They can't prove anything. The documents are forgeries!"

In *The Money-Digging Letters* Jerald not only laid out reasons for rejecting the authenticity of the Salamander Letter, he also alluded to the more troubling implication that if the Salamander Letter were a forgery, it would cast a shadow of doubt over the "other important documents that have come to light during the 1980s," noting as well that the "questions raised by the Salamander Letter have forced us to take

---

86. Jerald Tanner, "Parallels to the Salamander Letter," cf. "Dilemma of a Mormon Critic," *Salt Lake City Messenger,* Jan. 1985, 5–6.

87. Lindsey, *Gathering of the Saints,* 135.

a closer look at some of these documents."[88] Still, Jerald's wording in the document was more restrained than his actual level of conviction.

In addition to his argument for the Salamander Letter's secondary dependence on early Mormon sources, Jerald also argued in *The Money-Digging Letters* that the letter didn't match the kind of letter historians would expect Martin Harris to write to an enquirer like W. W. Phelps. Phelps had purchased a Book of Mormon in 1830 and was baptized in June 1831. "It seems very hard to believe," Jerald wrote, "that he [Harris] would write a perspective convert like Phelps and leave out all the divine elements."[89]

Even though it would be many months before the text of the Salamander Letter itself was made public, the Tanners' counter-intuitive voice-crying-in-the-wilderness opposition to it represented enough of a "man bites dog" story to attract the attention of the press. Five days after Sandra distributed the tract at the Hotel Utah, *L.A. Times* writer John Dart published an article noting that "unusual caution about the letter's genuineness has been expressed by Jerald and Sandra Tanner, longtime evangelical critics of the Mormon Church," noting that "the purported Harris letter contains too many similarities to statements in the 1834 book by E. D. Howe."[90] But again it was actually Jerald who had made the argument; Sandra at that point was still far from sure that Jerald was right. Yet she did distribute the tract.

Perhaps that's why Hofmann came in to the Tanners' bookstore on August 23, 1984, the day after Sandra had distributed the tract,[91] to express his dismay that "of all people" the Tanners should be the ones to cast doubt on the authenticity of his documents. At the time Sandra was alone in the shop. Hofmann did not come across as angry but pleading. Sandra felt he was almost on the verge of tears. Didn't the Tanners realize, he implored, that calling the Salamander Letter's authenticity into question might well jeopardize some very important negotiations he had going on at the moment. Even as they

---

88. Tanner, "The Money-Digging Letters," [9].

89. Tanner, [7–8].

90. John Dart, "Joseph Smith: His Image Is Threatened: Letter Attacks Origin of Book of Mormon," *Salt Lake Tribune*, Aug. 27, 1984, B-3.

91. Tanner, "Salamander Murders," in Tanner and Tanner, *Tracking the White Salamander*, 9.

spoke, Hofmann assured Sandra, he was engaged in a very delicate back and forth with the family of the early Mormon leader Thomas Bullock, who had important early documents which contained some very damaging information about Brigham Young's handling of church finances. Wouldn't it be a shame if their opposition scuttled that whole negotiation and those documents never came out? Sandra found Hofmann's story about the family and Young believable. When Jerald returned, she told him about her encounter with Hofmann and his negotiations for the Bullock documents, and so on. When she'd finished, Jerald looked at her almost pityingly and said, "Yeah, right. If you believe that story, I got a bridge in Brooklyn to sell you."[92]

Although Jerald remained cautious in his writings about the Hofmann forgeries, or when talking about who the forger behind the Hofmann document might be, he personally believed it was Hofmann, or someone in his circle, or both, who were creating the forgeries. The remarkable versatility of the forger in producing so many different types of forgeries—stamps, coins, printed money, documents in many different hands—some of which, in addition, were definitely better than others, caused the Tanners to wonder whether Hofmann had a helper. As time went on it became clear that Jerald had a point.

If it were so easy for Hofmann to forge other people's handwriting, why had he, for example, had a metal plate made to print Jack London's signature and inscription into a first edition *Call of the Wild*? Some of the forgeries seemed more amateurish than others. Certainly this was the case with Hofmann's supposed 1807 Betsy Ross letter, which was easily identifiable as a forgery by the fact that in 1807 Betsy would have given her last name as "Claypoole" not "Ross."[93] Furthermore, the postmaster whose name had appeared on the letter hadn't entered office until 1835.[94]

Which was more likely, the Tanners asked themselves, that this young man, over a period of only four or five years, managed to discover such unprecedented numbers of a variety of different kinds of

---

92. Tanner, *Reminiscences*.
93. By 1807, she was twice widowed and, since 1783, married to her third husband, John Claypoole.
94. According to George Throckmorton, in Sillitoe and Roberts, *Salamander*, 546.

artifacts relating to Mormon or US history, or that he forged them all? And for them the answer always came back: Neither. Neither was more plausible. Neither in fact was plausible at all.[95] Jerald suspected Hofmann was helped in the process by his gifted friend Lyn Jacobs, who died in 1995. Jacobs once described himself as one of Hofmann's best friends,[96] and he had also been involved in a number of Hofmann's transactions, including the sale of the Salamander Letter. For a time, Jacobs claimed that he himself had discovered the document and was its sole owner.[97]

Handwriting samples from Jacobs are in abundant supply in his papers, which are housed at the University of Utah's Marriott Library. But his handwriting does not obviously resemble those found on the forgeries. This is even the case of the faked Salt Lake Temple second anointing document that Hofmann showed to the Tanners in 1978, which is particularly important in this connection because it was not written with the intent of simulating any particular known hand.

Brent Metcalfe, who had originally been introduced to Hofmann by Jacobs, did not "think Lyn would have been involved not without telling someone, especially when he knew he was dying. I don't think Lyn would have left that question unanswered. I could be wrong, but I have no reason to believe otherwise."[98] And when one listens to Jacobs's testimony from the preliminary hearing, one does note in his emphatic denials of any suggestion of his participation in the forgeries themselves, a note that admittedly sounds very much like outraged innocence.[99]

No one can doubt Hofmann's ability to produce his more mechanical forgeries, coins, printed documents, and so on, but that requires a whole different skill set from actually mimicking other people's handwriting. Was Hofmann capable of the latter?

There is some evidence to suggest he was. In 1981 he and his wife, Doralee, took a calligraphy class from a woman in their ward

95. Tanner, Reminiscences.
96. "Stalking the Wild Document: An Interview with Lyn R. Jacobs," *Sunstone*, Aug. 1985, 11.
97. Turley, *Victims*, 279.
98. Brent Metcalfe, personal communication with Huggins, Sep. 2, 2017.
99. Tape # 86-848, Hofmann 24: Testimony of Curt Bench and Lyn Jacobs, Tanner Collection.

named Darlene Sanchez, who was greatly impressed when Hofmann "brought in a number of beautifully written alphabets."[100] They were so good that she thought they might have been done with press-on letters. Shannon Flynn, another close associate of Hofmann, remembers an occasion while he and Hofmann were in Boston at a book fair, when Hofmann took up a crayon and started making forgeries of signatures, including one of George Washington.[101]

The LDS Church finally published the Salamander Letter in an April 28, 1985, *LDS Church News* article that included a statement from the First Presidency accepting the judgment of experts "that there is no indication that the letter is a forgery." In the article the text of the letter appears under the heading in large type: "1830 Harris Letter Authenticated."[102] This was more than a year after Jerald had publicly argued against its authenticity.

From the beginning Sandra was not persuaded Jerald was right about the letter. Now that all the experts and the church itself had lined up behind its authenticity, she began to feel that Jerald, who was not a forensic expert, was probably wrong. This led them to issue their one and only split editorial in the June 1985 *Messenger*. In her editorial Sandra outlined the various expert evidence supporting the authenticity of the letter and concluded: "When I look at all the different items used in authenticating the letter I wonder if it would be possible for a forger to have faked all these points without detection? I don't think so." In his editorial, Jerald stressed the importance of examining the text over the tests of forensic experts. "While most people," he wrote, "seem to feel that physical tests are more important, everyone would concede that if the letter mentioned Joseph Smith watching television or using a flashlight, it could not possibly be valid. In that case the evidence from the text would overweigh anything obtained from physical testing."[103] Jerald reminded his readers about the Howard Hughes "Mormon Will" forgery, the authenticity of which document expert Henry Silver had staked his reputation. In contrast Jerald had taken a strong

---

100. Sillitoe and Roberts, *Salamander*, 418–19.
101. Shannon Flynn to Huggins, Sep. 18, 2017.
102. John L. Hart, "Letter Sheds Light on Religious Era," *Church News*, Apr. 28, 1985, 7.
103. Hart, 14–15.

stand against the authenticity of the so-called will, and it turned out (in his view at least) that he had been right. Jerald also pointed to the similar situation that had occurred in connection with Clifford Irving's claim that the reclusive Howard Hughes had chosen him to write his biography. Irving had presented a number of handwritten letters from Hughes, which document experts at Osborn Associates had authenticated, only to be proven wrong when Howard Hughes himself went public on the matter.

As in all his writings on the Salamander Letter to that point, Jerald expressed willingness to consider additional evidence for its authenticity. He noted, for example, that Hofmann himself had claimed to have discovered the 116 pages of the Book of Mormon manuscript that Harris, who'd served as Joseph's scribe in producing it, had borrowed and lost in June 1828. If that important document actually existed, which could provide the most extensive sample of Harris's handwriting ever, why wasn't it involved at all in the authentication process? Finally there was the issue that had troubled Jerald from the beginning, namely Hofmann's total unwillingness to provide any sort of satisfactory provenance for the Salamander Letter or for any of his other documents.

When the existence of the Salamander Letter first became a matter of public discussion, the LDS damage-control apparatus slipped smoothly into action. In no time at all the faithful were being reassured that not only was there nothing embarrassing in the Salamander Letter, but that indeed the document, when viewed in the right light, was actually faith promoting.

The *Salt Lake Tribune* printed the remarks of LDS Church spokesperson Jerry Cahill, assuring members that the find "poses no threat to what is already known about the prophet or beginning of the Church."[104] The September 1984 *LDS Church News*, in an article entitled, "Harris Letter Could Be Further Witness,"[105] quoted author Rhett S. James as asserting that "by the time of Martin Harris, the word salamander also meant angel."[106]

---

104. "LDS Spokesman Says Letter Is Not Threat," *Salt Lake Tribune*, Aug. 27, 1984, B-1.

105. "Harris Letter Could Be Further Witness," *Church News*, Sep. 9, 1984, 11, 13.

106. "Harris Letter," 13. Apostle Dallin Oaks made the same claim in a talk given on August 16, 1985, qtd. in Tanner and Tanner, *Tracking the White Salamander*, 22–23: "A being that is able to live in fire is a good approximation of the description Joseph

On June 23, 1985, Gordon B. Hinckley gave a Young Adult fireside broadcast from Temple Square in which he said that the Salamander Letter and one of the other Hofmann discoveries, supposedly written by Joseph Smith himself, "have no real relevancy to the question of the authenticity of the Church or of the divine origin of the Book of Mormon."[107] The talk was published in the September 1985 issue of *Ensign*. Before much more could be said, however, the saga took a devastating turn.

The peaceful morning air on October 15, 1985, was suddenly shattered at 8:10 a.m. by the concussion of a bomb going off in downtown Salt Lake City. Steven Christensen, a financial consultant and Mormon documents collector, was killed when he picked up a package addressed to him. Around 9:45 a.m., in a neighborhood in another part of the city, another bomb rattled windows in homes as it killed Kathleen Sheets, the wife of a former business partner of Christensen. It was only then that the real story began to unfold. The next day, with the city on edge, Hofmann himself was seriously injured when a bomb went off in his own car while he was trying to move it. Police would discover that Hofmann had made all the bombs and placed two of them for Christensen and Sheets.

Hofmann claimed the murders were committed because he was desperate for money. Hofmann had joined his production of forgeries with a classic Ponzi scheme, getting rich collectors to invest in allegedly valuable documents with the understanding that they would receive either the documents themselves or a share in the profits once Hofmann had turned them around. But he got in over his head.

When all was said and done, Hofmann himself confessed to having produced the Salamander Letter pretty much as Jerald had suggested

---

Smith gave of the Angel Moroni ... the use of the words white salamander and old spirit seem understandable." Rhett James, who was initially supportive of the Salamander Letter, decided against its authenticity after it was made public in April 1985. Now he claimed instead that it had likely been "forged by critics hoping to discredit the church." "Authenticity of Letter Linking Joseph Smith to Folk Magic Is Questioned," *Deseret News*, May 18, 1985, clipping.

107. Gordon B. Hinckley, "Keep the Faith" *Ensign*, Sep. 1985, 4, and Hinckley, "Excepts from 'Keep the Faith,'" *Ensign*, Sep. 1985, 4–6, in Church Educational System Memorandum, Oct. 2, 1985.

he had done.[108] He even mentioned that he'd used the Tanners' reprint edition of E.D. Howe's *Mormonism Unvailed* to produce it.[109]

Hofmann was smart. He reportedly had an IQ of 137, top 2 percent of Americans.[110] When it was over and Hofmann was in prison, he asked his night sergeant, Charles M. Larson, how he might join Mensa, an organization that declares as its purpose identifying and fostering human intelligence for the benefit of humanity.[111] Larson himself was a member.[112] Yes, Hofmann was smart. Smart enough to go down in history as one of the greatest forgers of the twentieth century, smart enough to fool the experts who persuaded the LDS Church leadership to affirm the Salamander Letter's authenticity eight months *after* the publication of *The Money-Digging Letters*, but not smart enough to fool a poorly educated ex-machinist named Jerald Tanner.[113]

---

108. Tanner and Tanner, *Hofmann's Confession*, 440–46; Tanner and Tanner, *Confessions of a White Salamander*, 12–13.

109. Tanner and Tanner, *Hofmann's Confession*, 444; Tanner and Tanner, *Confessions of a White Salamander*, 12.

110. Shupe, *Darker Side of Virtue*, 83.

111. See us.mensa.org.

112. Charles M. Larson, phone conversation with the author, Sep. 6, 2017.

113. The affair of Hofmann, of his forgeries and his murders, would continue to engage the Tanners' attention for at least another two years. The original August 1984 edition of *The Money-Digging Letters* would be expanded two months later by an updated edition that ran thirty-two pages. Jerald would then go on to write the first full-length account of the Hofmann affair in the book *Tracking the White Salamander*, published in October 1986, which went through three editions. Finally, *Shadow or Reality?* would be updated in 1987 in a fifth and final edition to include information on the Hofmann case. See pages 125 A-G and 195 A-H. In addition, the Tanners wrote a number of other smaller books along the way, including, e.g., Jerald Tanner, *Parallels to the Salamander Letter* (1985), *Mr. Boren and the White Salamander* (1985), *Confessions of a White Salamander: An Analysis of Mark Hofmann's Disclosures Concerning How He Forged Mormon Documents and Murdered Two People* (1987), and *The Mormon Church and the McLellin Collection* (1993). Most recently, Sandra was interviewed for the Netflix documentary, *Murder Among the Mormons* (2021), a three-part series on the Hofmann forgeries and murders.

16

A SECOND FRONT

In July 1986, former Satanist and former Mormon William J. Schnoebelen gave a talk at the Capstone Conference titled "Joseph Smith and the Temple of Doom"[1] in which he outlined what he said were Satanic and occultic parallels in the LDS temple ceremony. The talk, based on an earlier tract, was later developed into a longer booklet published in 1987 as *Mormonism's Temple of Doom*. "I don't think there's too many people," Schnoebelen told the audience that night, "that have gone from being a witch and a Satanist to being a Mormon to being a born-again believer."[2] Schnoebelen pointed to a number of places where the temple was supposedly identical in its rites to those used in witchcraft and Satanism, including the priesthood tokens and the language of the endowment ceremony.[3]

Given such allegations, one would imagine Schnoebelen would have been eager to provide substantive proof of his claims. But when Jerald asked to see the evidence, Schnoebelen said he had burned all the occult books containing the evidence when he became a Christian. All he was able to produce were a few typed and handwritten copies of the passages allegedly corroborating his speech.[4] Anyone who knew Jerald understood that this was hardly satisfactory evidence. Jerald's concerns with Schnoebelen were the same that he had with Mark Hofmann: If attacks on Mormonism were based on

---

1. The Capstone Conference met annually and was sponsored by the ex-Mormon Christian organization Saints Alive in Jesus. Schnoebelen's talk was based on a 1985 tract, which took its title from the 1984 film *Indiana Jones and the Temple of Doom*.

2. "Covering Up Syn: Ex-Satanist Brings Confusion to Mormons and their Critics," *Salt Lake City Messenger* 67, Apr. 1988, 13. Schnoebelen had his name legally changed to Christopher Syn and then back again. Dr. Christopher Syn of Romney Marsh is a character in a series of historical novels by Russell Thorndike (1885–1972).

3. Schnoebelen and Spencer, *Mormonism's Temple of Doom*, 40–41.

4. "Magic in Mormonism," *Salt Lake City Messenger* 65, Nov. 1987, 10.

forgeries, misinterpretations, or made-up stories about the occult, then it allowed LDS apologists to dismiss all criticisms as false. At the very least, it allowed LDS defenders to spend their time ridiculing sensationalized and false accusations against the church while ignoring more substantive criticisms.

Jerald, who'd single-handedly spotted Hofmann's forgeries through textual analysis, dug in. The documents Schnoebelen gave Jerald provided enough evidence to show that they had, at the very least, been modified in modern times. Jerald noticed that the document containing the passage that paralleled language in the temple, which Schnoebelen claimed came from the eighteenth-century magical *Grimorium Verum*, spoke of "radioactive spheres of pure cosmic energy."[5] The word "radioactive" had to represent a modern addition to the text, since the term was first coined by Pierre and Marie Curie in 1898.[6]

Jerald found other problems. Schnoebelen seemed to rely heavily on the works of the notorious British occultist Aleister Crowley, taking over such trademark phrases of his as "do what thou wilt shall be the whole law" and "love is the law, love under will," as well as cribbing lines from a play and an esoteric liturgy written by Crowley.[7]

These works were published in the early twentieth century, long after they could have influenced Joseph Smith. The Tanners were confident they had proven the document could not have been as old as Schnoebelen was claiming, and that Joseph Smith could not have had access to it, at least not in its present form.

Schnoebelen had given Jerald another typescript that contained a striking parallel to Mormon rites in a marriage ritual called "Ye Rite of Hand Fasting" that sealed the couple "for time and all eternity."[8] Schnoebelen claimed it came from another book entitled *The Second Book of Wisdom*, written by a teacher of his whom he called "the highest-ranking Witch in the USA"[9] and "the head of all Druidic witches in North America."[10] But, again, Schnoebelen claimed

5. Tanner and Tanner, *Lucifer–God Doctrine*, 56.

6. Dry, *Curie*, 35.

7. See Crowley, *Book of the Law*, 1:40 and 57; *O.T.O. Ecclesiae Gnosticae Catholicae Canon Missae*, 251; and "The Ship," 78.

8. "Handfasting" is a neo-pagan way of referring to getting married.

9. Schnoebelen, "Joseph Smith and the Temple of Doom," 1.

10. William Schnoebelen to Jerald Tanner, Apr. 13, 1987, Tanner and Tanner, Papers.

that he had burned the book, and only had a two-page typescript with relevant passages.

Schnoebelen had also provided Jerald a certificate of his July 22, 1973, Satanic ordination to the High Priesthood of Melchizedek, from an organization called the "Mental Science Institute," signed by the "head of all Druids," B. C. Eli Taylor. Taylor's full name was Barney Calvin Taylor, and he had dubbed himself "Eli, the Teacher." If it were true that an occult organization had used the title "High Priesthood of Melchizedek" before Joseph Smith, it would be a significant parallel, and one that might be difficult to pass off as coincidence. Jerald wrote to the Mental Science Institute at the address on Schnoebelen's certificate, but the letter was returned as undeliverable.

The Tanners discovered that religious scholar J. Gordon Melton had included an entry on Barney "Eli" Taylor's Mental Science Institute in his *Encyclopedia of American Religions*. Melton had noted further parallels to Mormon theology, including a universe with three levels, celestial, terrestrial, and telestial, and the idea that God had once been a man.[11] The mention of the word "telestial" was a giveaway that Taylor had borrowed his beliefs from Mormonism, not the other way around.

By that time, however, Schnoebelen's speeches and pamphlet had convinced other ex-Mormon Christian leaders. James R. Spencer, who published the *Thru the Maze* newsletter, and Ed Decker of Saints Alive in Jesus were persuaded that Joseph Smith borrowed the precise terminology of the three degrees of glory from the occult. In a joint response, Decker and Schnoebelen dismissed the Tanners' views and accused them of misreading Melton. It did not have to be Taylor who had borrowed from Smith; Smith could have taken these terms from the occult. "Anyone with a knowledge of Wicca knows that it is FULL of made up words," Schnoebelen and Decker wrote.[12]

On January 4, 1988, Jerald wrote to Melton. He explained the disagreement between himself and Schnoebelen and Decker, and enclosed twenty dollars and a request for a couple of items he

---

The description of the importance of his teacher comes from Schnoebelen and Spencer, *Mormonism's Temple of Doom*, 11.

11. Melton, "Mental Science Institute," in *Encyclopedia of American Religions*, 2:285.

12. Decker and Schnoebelen, "Lucifer–God Doctrine," 21 (emphasis in original).

thought might help him get to the bottom of Schnoebelen's claims. Melton responded quickly, writing that he had a large collection of material from Taylor's Mental Science Institute that he would forward to the Tanners. He also included a prepared statement clearing up any doubts concerning his own view of the direction of influence: "All of the evidence suggests that Taylor created MSI himself using as content some books on Rosicrucianism, herbology, Mormonism, and the occult. ... I can say that beyond any reasonable doubt that any similarity between MSI and Mormonism on matters of teaching is due to Taylor's having taken Mormon ideas and incorporating them in MSI."[13] When the promised package of materials arrived, the Tanners were delighted to discover that Melton had sent a copy of *The Second Book of Wisdom*, the book that Schnoebelen said some of the parallels had come from. They quickly found that, contrary to Schnoebelen's claim, "Ye Rite of Hand Fasting" was not in it.

As the Tanners continued to dig deeper, it became increasingly clear that Taylor was at the center of many of Schnoebelen's claims about Mormonism's relationship to the occult. A significant portion of Schnoebelen's materials seemed to come from Taylor, and Taylor's teachings stood apart from other occult or Wiccan communities. The Tanners wondered how Taylor might have learned about Mormonism to borrow from its teachings. They asked Schnoebelen whether Taylor had ever owned Mormon books or perhaps had even been a Mormon. To their shock, he replied that Taylor was a former LDS bishop.[14] It was remarkable to Jerald and Sandra that Schnoebelen considered it irrelevant that Taylor had been a Mormon, and even a bishop, and that he did not think Taylor might be drawing on Mormon theology for his ideas.

In the meantime, Schnoebelen was becoming something of a rising star in the "counter-cult" community. He was invited to speak to different groups, and was even recommended as a possible speaker at Trinity Evangelical Divinity School's Tanner Annual Lectureship

---

13. J. Gordon Melton to Jerald Tanner, Jan. 13, 1989, 1, Tanner and Tanner, Papers.

14. Tanner and Tanner, *Lucifer-God Doctrine*, 52. A search of church records revealed a Barney Calvin Taylor being baptized into the church on August 7, 1938, endowed on February 28, 1949, and sealed to his wife, Alice Irene Gay, on the same day.

on Cults, named in honor of Jerald and Sandra.[15] But as with Dee Jay Nelson, the more the Tanners and others looked into Schnoebelen's career, the more questions piled up. At one point Schnoebelen claimed that he had a conversation with LDS Apostle James E. Faust in 1981, and that Faust admitted that Lucifer was the God Mormons worshipped in the temple.[16] It was not until the Tanners published the claim that Schnoebelen back peddled.

New questions emerged when Wesley Walters informed the Tanners of a contribution Schnoebelen had made during his time in the LDS Church to a book published by the respected LDS publishing firm Bookcraft in 1983 entitled *From Clergy to Convert*. In it Schnoebelen made no mention of having been involved in the occult but instead claimed he was a former Catholic priest who had married a former Catholic nun.[17] But that claim was impossible to reconcile with the timing of his school records, as was the chronology he later included in *Mormonism's Temple of Doom*.[18] Jerald and Sandra were able to learn that Schnoebelen was ordained in "Old Catholic" groups. The real Old Catholics are churches that broke away from the Roman Catholic Church in the past. These groups are broadly Catholic in doctrine but they are not in unity with Rome. In addition to these, however, there are also certain occult organizations that call themselves Old Catholic by virtue of someone in their history allegedly wangling an ordination from an Old Catholic bishop. It was on this basis, for example, that the occult group Aleister Crowley belonged to considered itself Old Catholic. Such groups are Old Catholic in name only.

Although at times Schoebelen very clearly sought to give the impression that he had been not an Old Catholic priest, but a Roman

---

15. Jerry Urban to Ruth [Tucker], Dave [Larson], and Barry [Beitzel], Oct. 8, 1986, Tanner and Tanner, Papers.

16. Tanner and Tanner, *Lucifer–God Doctrine*, 35; Ed Decker to Wes Walters, Feb. 9, 1988, [1], Tanner and Tanner, Papers; Spencer, *Attack on* Mormonism's Temple of Doom, 14–15.

17. Schnoebelen, "We Waited for Six Years," 67.

18. Schnoebelen and Spencer, *Mormonism's Temple of Doom*, 63. Msgr. James Barta to Jerald Tanner, Feb. 9, 1988, 1, Tanner and Tanner, Papers. One of the mysteries of Schnoebelen's career is how he used to be William *Robert* Schnoebelen but later William *James* Schnoebelen

Catholic one, it wasn't true.[19] Schnoebelen had applied to study for the Roman Catholic Priesthood but had been turned down.[20] He would eventually get himself ordained to three different offices—deacon, priest, and bishop—in three different "Old Catholic" organizations, only the first of which could claim any true and abiding connection to Old Catholicism as traditionally understood, and none of which added up to his ever being a Roman Catholic priest.

On February 19, 1988, the Tanners met with Schnoebelen to discuss his false claims. His coauthor of *Mormonism's Temple of Doom*, James Spencer, was there as well. Jerald had compiled a significant amount of evidence relating to Schnoebelen's statements about his background, and apparently came across as intense. "Jerald had his sitting room arranged like a courtroom," Spencer recalls. "He had a box full of file folders on his desk and a microphone in a stand."[21] Most of the meeting revolved around Schnoebelen saying he had been a Catholic priest. Spencer felt that it did not matter that Schnoebelen had been ordained in a splinter group, that Jerald was splitting hairs. The Tanners' continued attack on Schnoebelen resulted in the end of their relationship not only with Spencer, but even more dramatically with Saint's Alive founder Ed Decker.

The ex-Mormon Decker had promoted a story about LDS temples even more outlandish than Schnoebelen's. Decker circulated a tape of an interview with a man named Thomas Kellie who said he had befriended LDS president Spencer W. Kimball and participated in an extremely secret temple ordination that even N. Eldon Tanner, then first counselor in the First Presidency, knew nothing about. According to Kellie, the rite involved blood from diamondback rattlesnakes, the slitting of the wrists of the initiates, and the writing of 666 in Roman numerals on their foreheads.[22] Decker eventually disbelieved Kellie's stories.

Decker's career as a go-to-guy for evangelicals wanting to learn

---

19. Some of the stories he tells in "We Waited for Six Years," 68–69 and 71, could only relate to the experience of a Roman Catholic priest. This despite his avoidance of the actual words "*Roman* Catholic priest" in the piece, a fact he later appeals to as proof that he'd never claimed to be a Roman Catholic priest!

20. Msgr. Robert L. Ferring to Jerald Tanner, Feb. 23, 1988, 1, Tanner and Tanner, Papers.

21. Spencer, *Attack on* Mormonism's Temple of Doom, 10.

22. Tanner and Tanner, *Lucifer–God Doctrine*, 8–9.

about Mormonism had ballooned only a few years earlier with the release of his film *The God Makers*, which debuted on December 31, 1982, at John MacArthur's Grace Community Church in Sun Valley, California, with some four thousand people in attendance.[23] For Mormons, the film quickly became infamous for its re-enactments of LDS temple ceremonies, including portions believers promise never to discuss outside of the temple. Sandra had appeared in the movie, but when it opened in Salt Lake City, she still hadn't seen it. She and Jerald attended the premiere and were quickly ushered to the front row. Jerald was uncomfortable because he felt such "red-carpet treatment" might imply endorsement of the film before he saw it. Far from making him inclined to be less critical, seating him and Sandra front and center caused him to feel a sense of responsibility to point out weaknesses and errors in the movie.

When the film ended and the lights went up, a discussion ensued. Jerald was handed a microphone and asked for his reaction. Sandra was mortified as Jerald outlined the problems and errors in the film, especially the falsification of the credentials of those being interviewed. Why, Jerald asked, was John L. Smith, publisher of the *Utah Evangel* newspaper, called "Dr. John L. Smith" in the movie? Why were Dr. Charles Crane's credentials puffed to make him an "expert on Mormon archaeology?" If Ed Decker had hoped for the occasion to build good relations with the Tanners, it did not work.

Another confrontation with Decker came after ex-Mormons Dolly and Chuck Sackett published their temple exposé booklet, *What's Going On in There?* The Sacketts said that a phrase repeated three times in the ceremony was Hebrew for "wonderful Lucifer."[24] Decker picked up the Sacketts' claim and ran with it. Decker approached Wesley Walters for further confirmation of the claim, but when Walters told him that was *not* what the phrase meant, Decker reportedly replied that "he thought he would use it anyway."[25] Decker passed out his tract, *Questions for Your Temple Tour*, to visitors at LDS

---

23. Decker and Hunt, *God Makers*, 16; Introvigne, "Devil Makers," 153. The number four thousand comes from Decker.

24. This phrase was removed in 1990 when portions of the temple ceremony were changed. Participants in the endowment were taught that it was part of the pure Adamic language and the true order of prayer.

25. Wesley P. Waters to James R. Spencer, Feb. 5, 1988, 2.

temples. Jerald responded with his own tract explaining why Decker misunderstood the phrase and how it had likely originated from early Mormon leaders trying to patch together a few basic Hebrew words to make them say, not "wonderful Lucifer," but something else.[26]

Although Jerald did not mention anyone by name in his booklet, Sackett took it as a personal attack and lashed out in a five-page denunciation. The list of accusations against Jerald was long: an unprovoked personal attack; promoting strife and discord among brethren without cause; gross hypocrisy; pious, arrogant, self-righteous prideful conduct; jealousy of new ministry successes; deliberate misrepresentation; gross incompetency; and more.[27] Despite Jerald's and Wesley Walter's corrections, Decker continued to publish the erroneous charge that Mormons chanted "wonderful Lucifer" in their temples.[28]

It became clear to Decker and Schnoebelen that the Tanners were not going to back down in their criticism, so they declared that they were submitting themselves to outside judgment. They turned to Walter Martin and his Christian Research Institute (CRI) for arbitration. They submitted all of their materials to Martin and made it clear to Jerald and Sandra that they were "not asking your permission in this matter,"[29] and that the Tanners should submit themselves to the arrangement as well. "I'm sure they [CRI] will be contacting you soon after that for the full documentation behind your statements." This arrangement was not binding on Jerald and Sandra in any legal or ecclesiastical sense—the CRI was not their church, and Decker had no authority over them. But in the broader world of evangelical Christianity, a refusal might have been interpreted as divisive, even unbiblical.

Martin was well respected in the Christian community but lacked the expertise to fill the role Decker had assigned him. He was host of the *Bible Answer Man* radio program, a regular writer and speaker on many groups, including Mormonism, Christian Science, Seventh

---

26. Tanner, *Pay Lay, Ale*. See Ps. 54:2.

27. Spelling and punctuation in Sackett's list of accusations has been corrected. Sackett, "J. Tanner's Pay Lay Ale—Charges," July 22, 1982, unpublished paper. Sackett also lashed out in a phone call with Jerald. Chuck Sackett to Jerald Tanner, July 22, 1982, 1.

28. Decker, *My Kingdom Come*, 128.

29. Ed Decker to Jerald Tanner, Dec. 7, 1987, [4], Tanner and Tanner, Papers.

Day Adventism, and other "cults." But he was a generalist, not an expert on Mormonism. There were other issues with choosing Martin as well. Specifically, the validity of his doctorate, his right to call himself Dr. Walter Martin, and his alleged descent from Brigham Young.[30] Martin's doctorate was from a nonaccredited institution; however, it was not from a degree mill on the order of the one Dee Jay Nelson had purchased. Getting the degree involved some study, but nothing like the level expected for an earned doctorate in an accredited institution.[31] Jerald and Sandra had their own reservations about Martin, whom they considered incautious, at least when it came to Mormonism. But they had a good relationship with CRI, particularly with Marian and Jerry Bodine, who did much of Martin's research.

When CRI issued its statement in the fall of 1988, every effort was made to affirm the value, contribution, sincerity, and integrity of both Saints Alive in Jesus and the Utah Lighthouse Ministry; but the statement sided with the Tanners: "Utah Lighthouse Ministry and others have correctly pointed out, what similarities there are [between Mormonism and witchcraft] stem *not* from Mormonism borrowing directly from Witchcraft or Satanism, but the commonality that all three have in being heavily influenced by Freemasonry."[32] And then more specifically, "We ... cannot endorse his [Schnoebelen's] premises, nor his overall conclusions as represented in *Mormonism's Temple of Doom*."

CRI trod lightly. When Decker first came up with the idea of appealing the matter to CRI's arbitration, he averred himself ready to submit to the scrutiny of "Martin's and CRI's review," to whom he and his ministry had "given our word to take every correction given."[33] After CRI issued its statement, Decker wrote to the Tanners and said that Schnoebelen and Spencer agreed to make the changes indicated by CRI to the *Temple of Doom* booklet. The changes were never made.

---

30. There was a rumor in Martin's family that his mother was a descendant of Brigham Young. Brown and Brown, *They Lie in Wait to Deceive*, 2:99–115.

31. Brown and Brown, *They Lie in Wait to Deceive*, 3:58–59.

32. CRI (Christian Research Institute), "To Whom It May Concern," [2], undated, but fall 1988; "CRI Statement Ends Witchcraft Dispute," *Salt Lake City Messenger* 69, Sep. 1988, 10–12.

33. Ed Decker to Jerald Tanner, Jan. 9, 1987, 1, Tanner and Tanner, Papers.

Instead, shortly before Martin died on June 26, 1989, Spencer somehow managed to secure an endorsement from Martin for *Mormonism's Temple of Doom*. Baffled by the reversal, Jerald and Sandra wondered if the endorsement were a forgery. It was not; Spencer, unhappy with CRI's decision, appealed directly to Martin. The two of them agreed that Spencer would draw up a statement of endorsement, which Martin then tweaked and signed.[34] Wesley Walters inquired on behalf of the Tanners with CRI into what happened. He was told, "The discrepancy over the booklet *Mormonism's Temple of Doom* was due to a difference of opinion between Dr. Martin and the rest of the research staff at CRI. Dr. Martin chose to endorse the booklet while the rest of the staff upon further analysis ... decided not to endorse it."[35] In fact, as the sequence of developments clearly shows, the order of events had been just the reverse.

That should have ended it. The Tanners had a statement from CRI backing up their claims, and Spencer and Schnoebelen (and, by extension, Decker) had an endorsement from Martin. But then the rumors started. First, Craig Hawkins of CRI, who had drafted the initial statement, was accused of going "behind Dr. Martin's back" and of having his "judgment ... clouded by his own involvement in the occult."[36] Accusations also began circulating about the Tanners being either demonized or double agents working for the LDS Church.[37] The "proof" of Jerald's demonic possession was testimony from a follower of Decker who was present when Jerald had interviewed Schnoebelen on February 19, 1988:[38]

> Bill [Schnoebelen] answered all the charges and questions to everyone's satisfaction except Jerald's. We could not understand why Jerald would not accept Bill's thorough answers—then we saw why. He raised up, his body shaking, and in a different sounding voice, and with his finger pointed at Bill, he shouted, "Take all that occult material and burn it!" Jerald's eyes were fixed and piercing. We looked at one another,

---

34. Jim Spencer to Walter Martin, Nov. 3, 1988, 1–2, Tanner and Tanner, Papers.

35. Dan Kistler to Wesley P. Walters, Dec. 13, 1989, 1, Tanner and Tanner, Papers.

36. Hunsaker et al., "Tanner Problem," 3.

37. Hunsaker, 2; and Loftes Tryk, "Opposition in all Things," *Jacob's Well Report*, Spring 1989, 8.

38. Undated cover letter attached to Hunsaker et al., "Tanner Problem"; Douglas A. Wallace to Jerold [*sic*] and Sandra Tanner, Apr. 10, 1993, 2, Tanner and Tanner, Papers.

recognizing what this was—a demonic manifestation. We offered min-istry to the Tanners to break this spiritual bondage, but they refused.[39]

Two others were present, Sandra and their son, Dennis. Sandra also recalled Jerald's strong rebuke; his passion could morph into intensity. He did stand, he did point, and he did speak in a very firm voice, but Sandra also recalls Schnoebelen's answers being neither thorough nor satisfactory. To whatever extent Jerald and Sandra might have pre-ferred to leave the matter there, it seemed fated that, whether they liked it or not, they would keep being drawn into conflict with Ed Decker over the accuracy of his claims about Mormonism.

On the evening of Monday July 25, 1988, in Ogden, Utah,[40] Decker gave his testimony on how he had come to Jesus. This was in connection with the annual Capstone Conference, which was held that year at the Tri-Arc Hotel on 161 West 600 South in Salt Lake City. Decker was funny, he was engaging, he was downright inspira-tional. He spoke for a long time but easily held the attention of his listeners, who regularly burst into spontaneous laughter, or punctu-ated Ed's dramatic pauses with heartfelt "Amens!" and "Hallelujahs!" Decker was good and his stories were extraordinarily dramatic. So much so that one might even describe him that evening as the Paul H. Dunn of the Evangelical anti-Mormon set.[41] His talk was on Ne-hemiah, or rather on himself as a modern-day Nehemiah. And just as Nehemiah never turned aside from his mission, even in the face of threats on his life, neither had Ed. Indeed, Ed revealed that in 1985 God had told him that he was going to face opposition, and sure enough in the year that followed he'd suffered three coronaries, been poisoned twice, and "at least one gunman was caught dressed in battle fatigues" apparently intent on doing him harm.[42] Ed spent most of his time on the story of how he had been poisoned during a pastors' luncheon while lecturing in Scotland. One of the attendees, he said,

39. Hunsaker et al., "Tanner Problem," 2.

40. Tope, *"Poisoned" at Pizzaland,* 17.

41. Paul H. Dunn was a general authority who similarly exaggerated his World War II experiences and his baseball career in faith inspiring talks. Jerald and Sandra Tanner, *What Hast Thou Dunn?*; "Dunn in the Name of God," *Salt Lake City Messenger* 78, Jun. 1991, 1–10.

42. Ed Decker, "Turmoil in the Church," Capstone Conference, July 25, 1988 (cas-sette tape), copy in Tanner and Tanner, Papers.

had spiked his Diet Coke with arsenic. Once he'd realized what had happened, he decided not to go to the hospital but to try and get on a plane back to the U.S. in order to save them having to ship his body back. But that was very difficult, he said, because "by the time that the arsenic had gotten into my system ... it destroyed a lot of the muscle control system so that you you [sic] become spastic and that you have trouble it's like you you [sic] have cerebral palsy, and I couldn't, I'm trying to get my body out of that chair to get in that plane."

Fearing they would see how sick he was and refuse him on the plane, Ed nevertheless somehow managed to board a DC-10 from London. And while the rest of the passengers watched *Rocky IV*, he sat strapped in his seat thinking how good it was to die for Jesus. In this lecture he featured the story as an example of opposition from Christians. Later in 1991, when he repeated it on the *Phil Donohue Show* the blame shifted to the Mormons, and then in 1992 on the Martin Tanner show, to the Masons.[43]

Decker's recitation of the dramatic story of his poisoning by arsenic on that evening in Ogden was not the first time he'd told it. He spoke of it before in the April/May 1986 *Saints Alive Newsletter*.[44] But it was something that occurred earlier that same day in the Salt Lake Tri-Arc Hotel that would lead to a thorough investigation and exposé refuting Decker's poisoning story. Decker, earlier that afternoon, had broken the right index finger of engineer-turned-street-evangelist Wally Tope.

Tope had purchased and resold some Christian videos from Pat Matrisciana, founder of Jeremiah Films, which had produced the *God Makers* films. Tope was dismayed to find upon actually watching one of the films that it broke off prematurely and gave way to pornography. In trying to get to the bottom of what was going on, Tope began investigating Matrisciana.

The breaking of Tope's finger occurred in Decker's hotel room, probably in connection with his trying to get answers from Decker on Matrisciana. According to Tope, Decker became angry and began to swear at him while shoving him out of his room. Decker then grabbed a folder that was on Wally's clipboard:

---

43. See Tanner and Tanner, *Problems in* God Makers II, 78.
44. Tope, *"Poisoned,"* 1.

In absolute fury your [sic] tried to tear it in half. Failing to accomplish that ... you came after me. I remember the full-blown physical assault with fists. Instinctively perhaps, I apparently hit back one or more times. At some point in your outrage I said something like, "Have you gone nuts, Ed?" Jason [Decker's son] even appealed to you. You finally stopped and I pointed my right index finger at you and said something like, "I rebuke you in the name of Jesus Christ." With that you grabbed the finger and bent it backwards until I heard it snap.[45]

Decker told a different story. He said he'd grabbed the clipboard and file in self-defense, thinking Wally was intent on hitting him with it:

Wally responded by running at me and punching me several times about the head and shoulders. ... I hadn't really hit another person, even in self defense, since I was a teenager. I began to crank my right fist back, getting prepared to really plant one on him, but my son Jason, was standing next to me trying to intervene, said strongly, "Dad, keep control of yourself!" I let go my fist and instead brought out my left arm full length to keep him off me. That caught Wally in about the last inch of extension and he backed away. After which Wally came back again, jabbing his finger into my chest, yelling, "I rebuke you in the name of Jesus Christ." I was so offended by this long poking finger and his spiritual curse that I grabbed the finger and held it, I spoke to Wally as though I were speaking to a child, "Stop it, Wally." It was at that moment that, Wally let out a throaty scream and yanked back. I felt and heard the finger snap.[46]

Whether it was the broken finger or Decker's evasiveness when being questioned, the result was that Tope began investigating Decker, and in particular his claim about being poisoned in Scotland. Tope was eccentric but truthful, and the Tanners trusted him.[47] Sandra even likened his truthfulness to Jerald's, so they ended up helping him in his research, addressing the arsenic story for the first time in the July 1990 issue of the *Messenger*.[48] They later reported that a "man who was with Ed Decker at the time of the alleged poisoning

---

45. Wally Tope to Ed Decker, Aug 15, 1988, 1.

46. Saints Alive Board of Directors, "To whom it may concern," Sep. 20, 1988, 4.

47. Tope would die after being beaten into a coma by two looters in the Rodney King riots. When he learned the riots were happening he rushed down into the midst of the chaos to preach Christ and distribute Christian tracts.

48. "Witchcraft Controversy Rekindled," *Salt Lake City Messenger* 75, July 1990, 16–19.

has called us from Scotland and expressed his disbelief in Decker's story."[49] In response, Decker provided the Tanners with testimonials. Two friends of Decker, both pediatricians, wrote letters defending him, one said he had treated Decker upon his return. A third letter came from a man who had been with him on the 1986 Scotland trip when the poisoning supposedly occurred.

Even if the letters were well-meaning attempts to bolster Decker's story, they ended up providing Tope and the Tanners with important evidence that contributed to its debunking. When Decker told the story, he always left names, places, and other details vague. Once the specifics of the story began to emerge, Tope and the Tanners were able to learn Decker's itinerary, whom he was with on which particular day, what those people saw, and so forth. Not one associate of Decker's in Scotland remembers him suffering from the symptoms he later claimed were due to arsenic poisoning—severe convulsions, vomiting, and diarrhea.

Those who recalled the lunch stated that it began about noon. Afterward Decker did apparently feel ill, so he went back to the home he was staying at in Eglington to rest. A few hours later he rose to prepare for his videotaped sessions on Mormonism and Masonry, which was scheduled to start at 7:00 p.m.[50] According to Decker's story, it was about a half an hour after drinking the alleged arsenic-spiked Diet Coke that he became deathly ill—so ill that for the next six hours he suffered terrible convulsions, vomiting, and diarrhea.[51] But in his recorded presentation, nothing apparently gives the impression that he had spent the previous six hours suffering nor that he was losing muscle control and becoming, as he put it, "spastic."[52] Decker also gave the impression that once he had been poisoned, he refused to go to the hospital because he urgently wanted to get home to the U.S. From this, one might get the impression that he left soon after his six hours of convulsions and vomiting.

49. "The Tanners: Demonized Agents of the Mormon Church?" *Salt Lake City Messenger* 76, Nov. 1990, 12.

50. Tope, *"Poisoned,"* 4

51. Tanner and Tanner, *Problems in* God Makers II, 78; Keith A. Rodaway, "To Whom It May Concern," July, 19, 1990, 1, in Tope, *"Poisoned,"* Appendix D.

52. Tope, *"Poisoned,"* 9 and Appendix D; Decker, "Turmoil in the Church." The author does not have direct access to the video tape.

Except Decker did not leave Scotland for five days after the alleged poisoning. The day after he claimed he drank arsenic, Decker spoke at a meeting at Aberdeen. Three days later, he flew from Edinburg to Belfast where he took part in another meeting.[53] While later testimony did reveal that Decker probably was ill, he was told it had nothing to do with arsenic, despite Decker's later claim that doctors "found many times the lethal amount of arsenic" in his system.[54]

One of the problems was Decker's telling of the tale went national. He told it on both the *Phil Donohue Show* and *Geraldo*.[55] Decker had alleged that the poisoning took place during lunch on March 24, 1986, in a chain restaurant in Inverness, Scotland, called Pizzaland, with only four or five people present (including Decker). The tall tale could have had devastating, even life-destroying, consequences for whichever of his fellow diners that day might come to be accused of being the poisoner. The poison had allegedly been administered by a "young man" in the group who'd offered to refresh Decker's Diet Coke.[56] The only "young man" present was Les Jappy, who worked on an oil rig off the northeast coast of Scotland. Jappy wouldn't have been present at all except that his pastor, Sam Burton, had asked him to tag along for the fifty or sixty mile ride to Inverness where Decker had agreed to let Burton buy him lunch. Burton had previously rented a hall to show *The God Makers* and had hoped Decker could address his congregation. "One of the odd things about the story," Burton recently told me, "is that poor Les was dragged into it. ... Ed Decker ... used my name and that of my friend, who only joined us for lunch at my request, to over dramatize his story."[57]

Decker sometimes blamed his poisoning on the Mormons and other times on the Masons.[58] Neither Burton nor Jappy had any con-

---

53. Tope, *"Poisoned,"* 9.

54. Tope, 1.

55. Tanners, *Problems in* God Makers II, 78; Tope, *"Poisoning,"* 17.

56. Eric H. Clarke, "To Whom It May Concern," July, 20, 1990, in Tope, *"Poisoning,"* Appendix B.

57. Sam Burton, email to Huggins, Jan. 9, 2018.

58. For Decker blaming the Mormons on the *Phil Donohue Show* and *Geraldo*, see Tope *"Poisoned,"* 17, and Tanner and Tanner, *Problems in* God Makers II, 78. For the Masons being blamed, see Ed Decker to Jeff Crane, Dec. 7, 1990, in Tope, *"Poisoned,"* Appendix I. On at least one occasion, Decker blamed fellow Christians. See Ed Decker, "Turmoil in the Church."

nection with either group.[59] In fact, the story was implausible from the beginning for other reasons. First of all, Pizzaland had waitress service, which meant diners didn't get their own refills, making implausible the claim that Jappy had refreshed it for him. Then second, when Decker finally was tested for arsenic poisoning, his levels were inconsistent with his assertion that only a few days before he had ingested "many times the lethal amount."[60]

After the Tanners first wrote on the poisoning story in the *Messenger*, Decker complained to friends that if Jerald and Sandra had only come to him first, he would have provided them all the information they needed to verify that he had indeed ingested a fatal dose of arsenic. He later promised he would send detailed medical records, *"including the results of both blood and urine tests to prove it."*[61] Instead of answers, the Tanners received a copy of a letter, purportedly from Linda Roberts on behalf of the board of Saints Alive in Jesus, instructing Ed to "refrain from any further discussion with the Tanners and their organization Utah Lighthouse Ministry and any affiliated persons [presumably Wally Tope] associated with that organization," since they "refuse to be satisfied with reasonable answers and continue to raise endless questions with questionable motives."[62] The Saints Alive board included Decker as president, his wife, and a few friends. The Tanners called it "a transparent attempt by Mr. Decker himself to get around answering the serious questions we have raised."[63] Tope suspected that Ed wrote the document himself, since two of the board members admitted to him that Ed had read the statement over the phone to them.[64] Decker had effectively pleaded the fifth.

If there were some who deluded themselves into believing the Tanners were secret LDS agents because of their clashes with Decker and others, their worst fears would have seemed to be confirmed

---

59. Tope, "*Poisoned,*" 17. Leslie Jappy to Wally Tope, Apr. 19, 1989, and Sam Burton, undated statement in Tope, "*Poisoned,*" Appendices E and F.

60. According to Christine Baxter, deputy manager of the Inversness, Scotland, Pizzaland, 1989, in Tope, "*Poisoned,*" 7, and e.g., Tope's interview with William Robertson, medical director of the Washington Poison Network, Apr. 5, 1990, qtd. in "Poisoning," 13.

61. Ed Decker to Tony Maneri, July 20, 1990, 2, emphasis original, Tanner and Tanner, Papers.

62. Linda Roberts to J. Edward Decker, Oct. 1, 1990, 1, Tanner and Tanner, Papers.

63. Tanner and Tanner, *Serious Charges*, 39. See also Tope, "*Poisoning,*" 21.

64. Tope, "*Poisoning,*" 21.

Pastor Sam Burton and Les Jappy (2018)

when Jerald and Sandra defended LDS Apostle Gordon B. Hinckley. It began with a tract titled *A Statement Concerning Some Charges of Immorality Made Against a Mormon Leader*. It was not advertised in the *Messenger* but answered widely circulated rumors being pushed to the media about Hinckley. A group calling itself the Committee for Morality in Church Government (CFM) was pushing journalists and others to run a story accusing Hinckley of sexual misconduct. The group had been formed to promote the story that had originally been researched by a couple from Provo, Utah, named Bill and Diane Claudin. Diane's father, Garn Baum, had lost the family farm to the LDS Church through what he believed was an abuse of power to put him out of business. There was even a *60 Minutes* piece playing the angle of the big corporate empire using its millions to squash the little guy. The program later backed off on its story. In Baum's view Gordon B. Hinkley had been directly involved in the "predatory anti-competitive conduct" that led to his farm becoming the property of the LDS Church.[65] So when someone approached Baum with the story of Hinckley's alleged sexual misbehavior, Baum was interested. At the center of the "evidence" was the testimony of a man dying of AIDS and suffering from dementia named Charles Van Dam. Van

---

65. Heinerman and Shupe, *Mormon Corporate Empire*, 6668 (esp. 67); Tanner and Tanner, *Problems in* God Makers II, 12–13; Wallace, *Under the Mormon Tree*, 233–41.

Dam claimed first-hand knowledge of (and participation in) Gordon B. Hinckley's illicit, bisexual, cross-racial promiscuous affairs, which supposedly had occurred decades before.[66]

After being approached by the Associated Press and a local television station to comment, the Tanners wrote the tract to explain their reasons why the story should not be accepted without additional evidence. The Tanners had themselves been accused of too many false things to remember—of being secret spies working for the LDS Church, of stealing documents from church archives, of having been excommunicated for polygamy, or adultery, of having sex orgies in their house, of being Communist agitators, and of Jerald's having spent time in prison for forgery.[67]

Jerald and Sandra's rebuttal of the story only spurred more rumors about them. Now they were blamed for being afraid of the church. In the tract, the Tanners did not name Hinckley but referred to him only as "Elder Accused." They argued that the evidence was weak and, even in the off chance the charges were true, dealt with issues long past. "We can see no reason," they wrote, "why we should labor to cause the humiliation of members of the Mormon hierarchy and their families."[68] The Tanners were not alone in finding the story implausible. Steven Naifeh, who had co-written a book on the Mark Hofmann case that was hardly friendly towards the LDS Church, had apparently been approached but declined to run the story.[69]

A common conspiracy-theory technique is to interpret media disinterest as media suppression. The person who finally did swallow the Hinckley story was, again, Ed Decker, who described it as "an extraordinary media blackout [that] stopped the hottest story of the '80s."[70] Decker featured the accusations against Hinckley in his 1992 film *The God Makers II*.

The God Makers had turned Decker into something of a star on the evangelical circuit. But now *The God Makers II* burned bridges and alienated colleagues. Dick Bear, an ex-Mormon who played a

66. Dew, *Go Forward with Faith*, 445–47.

67. Tanner and Tanner, *Statement Concerning Some Charges*, 1–2, and Tanner, Reminiscences.

68. Tanner and Tanner, *Statement Concerning Some Charges*, 1.

69. Tanner, Reminiscences. See Naifeh and Smith, *Mormon Murders*.

70. Ed Decker, *The God Makers II*, Jeremiah Films, 1992, VHS.

prominent part in the first movie, said of the sequel, "Ed has penchant to sensationalize, embellish on facts and center on bizarre issues to try to shock people. ... This film will so turn Mormons off that it will be difficult to even talk to them."[71] Believing Latter-day Saints may have found Jerald and Sandra Tanner's publications distasteful, even offensive, but they were centered in trying to be careful and accurate, a quality Decker more and more seemed to lack.

So now too Decker abandoned his pledge to adhere to the judgment of Walter Martin's CRI's review of his and William Schnoebelen's assertion that the LDS temple had Satanic and occult influences. And so we find Schnoebelen in *The God Makers II* once again stating that the temple ceremonies, "are straight out of the occult. How do I know that, because I was a Mormon who went to the Temple ... but more importantly I was also a High Priest of Satan."[72]

The LDS Church, savvy enough to know that responding to the allegations against Hinckley would only amplify them, said nothing. So ironically it fell to the Tanners to be the Mormon leader's most vigorous advocates. They did this first in their review of the film in the April 1993 *Messenger*,[73] by which time they were also offering a new 94-page book, *Problems in* The God Makers II. In September of the same year, Sandra prepared an additional one-sheet response to the movie, highlighting eight major problems with its content.

Jerald and Sandra were wearied by these ongoing battles with fellow Christians they felt should be held to a higher standard. As Christians, a lie was a lie, whether it came from Mormons who tried to hide problems in the LDS Church or from fellow evangelical Christians inventing nonsense about what happens inside LDS temples. They also understood that making absurd accusations of sexual immorality against LDS leaders or lying about temple ceremonies made it easier for LDS apologists to dismiss all critics as laughable fools who knew nothing about the church they deigned to rebut. As recently as April 17, 2018, Ed Decker was trying to revive the accusation against Hinckley and other claims he made in *God*

---

71. "*The God Makers II*: Under Fire from Within and Without," *Salt Lake City Messenger* 84, Apr. 1993, 1.

72. *The God Makers II*, 28:52–29:08 and 29:19–31.

73. "*The God Makers II*: Under Attack Within and Without," 1–4.

Makers II by asserting that the reason its arguments failed to persuade the first time round was that "one ministry in Salt Lake City went to the extreme measure of mailing an extremely derogatory letter to every Christian book store in America, we were told."[74] If, as Sandra suspects, Decker is referring to her and Jerald, then what he suggests about letters being sent simply never happened.

---

74. Group email entitled "Men of God or Sexual Deviants?" Apr. 17, 2018, copy in author's possession.

17

"I JUST NEED SOME REST"

The coming of the new decade of the 1990s was accompanied by one of the most painful events for Jerald and Sandra, the news of the sudden death of Wesley P. Walters in November 1990. Besides being a partner in research with the Tanners, Wes was also one of the most important people in their lives. Wes suffered from a hereditary heart condition involving an elongated heart valve that tends to collapse inward and cut off the blood flow. Not only did Wes die from it, but three of his children did as well.

The dawn of the 1990s saw the appearance of a book that Jerald considered one of his most important works: *Covering Up the Black Hole in the Book of Mormon* (1990). The book delved into early Mormon history and textual analysis to reveal what Jerald believed to be the extraordinary measures Joseph Smith took to rescue and preserve the Book of Mormon project after Martin Harris lost the first 116 pages of the manuscript.

Smith, as he dictated the text for the Book of Mormon, used a number of scribes. One of them was Martin Harris, a Palmyra, New York, farmer who mortgaged his land to help fund the first edition of the book with a print run of 5,000 copies. Harris served as Book of Mormon scribe from April to June 1828. Harris's wife, Lucy, was skeptical of the project and saw Smith as little more than a charlatan. Harris asked Smith to borrow the first 116 or so pages of the Book of Mormon dictation manuscript, called the Book of Lehi, to show Lucy and some friends, so that he could convince her that the project was genuine. After some reluctance, Smith loaned Harris the pages and they were promptly lost. Over 190 years later, what happened to those now-famous pages remains a mystery; the most likely scenario may involve Lucy destroying them.[1]

---

1. Bradley, *Lost 116 Pages*.

While the loss of the pages devastated Smith and represented a setback, it need not have been a major obstacle if Smith had been telling the truth about what he had been doing. If Smith really had been engaged in a miraculous translation process, he should have been able to go back and start over again from the beginning.[2] Tedious, but doable. Describing the translation process, Harris said that "sentences would appear and were read by the Prophet ... and when finished he would say, 'Written,' and if correctly written, that sentence would disappear and another appear in its place, but if not written correctly it remained until corrected."[3] So if Smith had fabricated the story as he went along, the situation was a disaster. How could he replicate word for word, sentence by sentence, what he was just making up as he went along? How could he ensure that names, dates, and places matched what he had in the original 116 pages?

Even before *Covering Up the Black Hole in the Book of Mormon* appeared, its main argument had been rolled out in the July 1989 *Salt Lake City Messenger.*[4] How would Smith proceed with the Book of Mormon project when the potential reappearance of the 116 pages might show differences between that text and his new "retranslated" text? Smith claimed a revelation that said the 116 pages still existed and had fallen into the hands of wicked persons who "have altered the words," so that they "read contrary from that which you translated and caused to be written" (D&C 10:11). God therefore told Smith in the same revelation, "You shall not translate again those words which have gone forth out of your hands.... For, behold, if you should bring forth the same words they will say that you have lied and that you have pretended to translate, but that you have contradicted yourself" (30–31).

Fortunately, according to the revelation, the gold plates were now discovered to have included a second account covering the exact

---

2. Smith later said the Angel Moroni confiscated the plates and the Urim and Thummim as punishment, but they were eventually returned to him, and he was rebuked for his foolishness in loaning the pages to Harris. MacKay and Dirkmaat, *From Darkness unto Light*, 93–97; Morris, *Documentary History of the Book of Mormon*, 273–75; Anderson, *Lucy's Book*, 417–18.

3. Edward Stevenson, "One of the Three Witnesses: Incidents in the Life of Martin Harris," letter to the editor, *Deseret Evening News*, Dec. 13, 1881, [4].

4. "A Black Hole in the Book of Mormon: Computer Reveals Astounding Evidence on Origin of Mormon Book," *Salt Lake City Messenger* 72, July 1989, 1–15.

period of time as the lost 116 pages, which came to be called the small plates of Nephi.[5] God commanded Smith to translate those smaller plates instead, thus thwarting the schemes of those who had stolen the original manuscript. Smith was to translate the lost part from the *small plates* of Nephi and the remainder of the Book of Mormon from the *large plates* of Nephi. With this solution in place, it appears that Smith continued to translate beginning with Mosiah 1:1 to the end of Moroni from the large plates, and then started over at the beginning of the story from the small plates.[6] The current edition of the Book of Mormon explains that "the first portion (the first six books, ending with Omni) is a translation from the small plates of Nephi. Between the books of Omni and Mosiah is an insert called the Words of Mormon. This insert connects the record engraved on the small plates with Mormon's abridgment of the large plates."[7]

Jerald believed that textual clues within the Book of Mormon could provide a window into the contents of the lost 116 pages. The large and small plates of Nephi are distinguished in 1 Nephi 9,[8] by telling readers that the large plates contained "a full account of my people ... of the reign of the kings, and the wars and contentions of my people" (1 Ne. 9:2, 4). 1 Nephi 19 says that the Book of Lehi also included "the record of my father, and the genealogy of his fathers, and the more part of all our proceedings in the wilderness," and again, "the wars and contentions and destructions of my people" (1 Ne. 19:2, 4).

Jerald reasoned therefore that the lost 116 pages must have "contained many names of people, cities and lands ... the names of many kings and the years in which they reigned ... of the prominent leaders who took part in important battles and when they occurred," as well as the "location of where these battles took place." Consequently, if Smith had been creating the names of places and things and people—mothers, sisters, fathers, brothers and children, friends

---

5. The simple division between the small and large plates of Nephi only seems to become clear in the process of actually attempting to reproduce the earlier part of the Book of Mormon. This is seen in God's claim in D&C 10:44 that those who had secreted the 116 pages "have only got a part, or an abridgment of the account of Nephi."

6. Brent Lee Metcalfe, "The Priority of Mosiah: A Prelude to Book of Mormon Exegesis," in Metcalfe, *New Approaches*, 395–444.

7. See "A Brief Explanation about the Book of Mormon" in the most current edition.

8. The words "large" and "small" are not specifically used (see 1 Ne. 9:2).

and enemies—as he dictated the original 116 pages, it would have been impossible to recollect them all accurately as he rewrote the history of the same period afterward. "While the idea of having a second set of plates from which to translate released him from having to come up with the exact wording he had previously used," Jerald argued, "it did not free him from the possibility of making mistakes with regard to names, dates, locations and other matters." Hence Smith's small plates of Nephi would need "to be as vague as possible," and "very indefinite with regard to details."[9] This was the "black hole" that Jerald spoke of, a dearth of proper nouns and specific details in the replacement text for the original 116 lost pages.

According to Jerald's thesis, Smith even had the ancient Book of Mormon prophet provide an excuse for the lack of detail in the small plates when Nephi commanded Jacob that he "should not touch, save it were lightly, concerning the history of this people which are called the people of Nephi. For he said that the history of his people should be engraven upon his other plates" (Jacob 1:2–3). Smith seems to have remembered the details of the story of Lehi and his family up to where they arrive in the Americas in 1 Nephi 18:23. From there until Omni 12, the last book of the small plates, Smith avoided referring to characters mentioned in the lost 116 pages whose names and details he could no longer remember. The result was that the description of a period of over 400 years was kept nebulous. Jerald argued that Smith remembered eleven names, not a difficult task. Lehi and his wife Sariah, his sons, Laman, Lemuel, Sam, Nephi, Jacob, Joseph, and a servant named Ishmael and his family who are not individually named. He also remembered Laban and his servant Zoram.

Women are seldom named in the Book of Mormon, so the lack of female names in the smaller plates of Nephi is unsurprising. What is surprising is the lack of almost any other names. Nephi handed the plates not to his sons, but to his younger brother Jacob. The next book is written by Jacob's son Enos, the next by his son Jarom, and the next is started by his son Omni, and in the space of twelve verses, the plates are passed down to four people.[10] Between the mention

---

9. "A Black Hole in the Book of Mormon," 3.

10. The plates go to Omni's son Amaron, then to Amaron's brother Chemish, Chemish's son Abinadom, and Abinadom's son Amaleki.

of the first eleven named people in the Book of Mormon, only one person is introduced apart from those actually said to be writing on the small plates: Sherem at Jacob 7:1. Hence, nine names in all, added to the original eleven. Jerald noted that once the reader reaches Amaleki, just at the point beyond where the lost 116 pages ended, new names begin to flow freely again. Mosiah, Coriantumr, Benjamin. Amaleki, Jerald wrote, must have emerged unscathed from the other side of the "black hole" of names and places.[11]

Despite this dearth of Nephite and Lamanite names in the black hole section, the same cannot be said about Bible names, of which a number appear, including Abraham, Isaac, Jacob, Moses, Adam, Eve, Zedekiah, Jeremiah, Isaiah, and Joseph.[12]

Jerald also realized that the replacement pages for the lost 116 pages lack the names of any kings. Nephi essentially served as the first king of the Nephites. When it came to anoint a man as king in his place, the man is mysteriously left unnamed: "Now Nephi began to be old, and he ... anointed a man to be a king and a ruler over his people now, according to the reigns of the kings" (Jacob 1:9). If Smith in the lost 116 pages had made up names for the four hundred years of Nephite kings, it might well have been extremely difficult for him to get all the names correct. In what looks suspiciously like a solution to that problem, Joseph has Jacob report that "the people were desirous to retain in remembrance his [Nephi's] name," so whoever "should reign in his stead were called by the people, second Nephi, third Nephi, and so forth, according to the reigns of the kings" (Jacob 1:11). But after the time period that mirrors the lost 116 pages section, the practice of calling each king "Nephi" is mysteriously abandoned, starting with Mosiah (Omni 19) and his son King Benjamin (Omni 25). The vague replacement text for the 116 pages (after Lehi's family arrives in the Americas) relates not only to names of people, but to specifics about battles, dates, geography, topography, and cities.

The Tanners also noted the large amount of what they called "filler" in the replacement text for the lost 116 pages. Included, for

---

11. "A Black Hole in the Book of Mormon," 11.
12. See, "A Black Hole in the Book of Mormon," 4. There is reference made to a prophet named Zenos (Jacob 5:1).

example, was the extensive material taken virtually verbatim from the King James version of the Book of Isaiah in 1 Nephi 20–21 (Isa. 48–49), 2 Nephi 7–8 (Isa. 50–52:2), and 2 Nephi 11–24 (Isa. 2–14), Lehi's dream in 1 Nephi 8, which paralleled a dream of Joseph Smith Sr.,[13] Lehi's recitation of future Bible history up to and including precise details concerning the coming of Jesus and his baptism at Bethabara (1 Ne. 10), and the prophet Zenos's long and ponderous allegory of the wild and tame olive trees that takes up several pages in Jacob 5.[14]

If the Tanners' black hole theory is correct, then Smith wrote the Words of Mormon immediately following the black hole replacement text to give credence to the convenient story that the gold plates included both the small plates and the large plates of Nephi: "For after I had made an abridgment from the [large] plates of Nephi, down to the reign of this king Benjamin, of whom Amaleki spake," wrote Mormon, "I searched among the records which had been delivered into my hands, and I found these [small] plates, which contained this small account of the prophets, from Jacob down to the reign of this king Benjamin, and also many of the words of Nephi" (Morm. 3).

Smith's actions to cover the "black hole" left by the loss of the 116 pages also had significant implications in further discrediting the Spalding Theory, the long-standing claim that Sidney Rigdon had borrowed or stolen a manuscript written by Solomon Spalding and given it to Joseph Smith, who used it as the basis of the Book of Mormon.[15] The theory was first publicly proposed in the 1830s based on the memory of people who had heard Spalding read from his manuscript some twenty years earlier and felt certain it was the same story with the same named characters that now appeared in the Book of Mormon.[16] But if Smith had dictated the 116 pages

---

13. Anderson, *Lucy's Book*, 278–98.

14. "A Black Hole in the Book of Mormon," 11. The Tanners regarded it as being conspicuously based on Romans 11:17–20 along with certain words of Jesus.

15. Spalding's (also spelled Spaulding) manuscript was a novel, and, while it contained some parallels of sort to the Book of Mormon, most scholars today reject the so-called Spalding Theory. For more, see Bush, "Spalding Theory," and Rex C. Reeve Jr., "What is 'Manuscript Found'?" in Spaulding, *Manuscript Found*, vii–xxviii.

16. Howe, *Mormonism Unvailed*, 278–90 (Vogel ed., 391–412).

from Spalding's Manuscript directly, he would have been able to reproduce the material in those pages verbatim to what he had before. Even if he had used only its basic story line as a launching pad for his elaborations, including the names of people, battles, locations, and so on, then he would not have needed to go to the lengths that he did to avoid all points of detail and to introduce filler in the material he wrote to replace the 116 pages.

The Spalding Theory of the Book of Mormon was believed by many non-Mormons during most of the nineteenth century and into the twentieth century. The Tanners, however, had never taken it seriously. David Whitmer, who was present during portions of the translation process, had rejected the theory out of hand.[17] But in late June 1977, newspapers reported that researchers Wayne L. Cowdrey,[18] Donald R. Scales, and Howard A. Davis announced that three handwriting experts had independently confirmed that the unknown scribe responsible for 1 Nephi 4:20–12:8 in the original handwritten manuscript of the Book of Mormon was Spalding.[19] The story was featured both in the July 8 *Christianity Today* magazine and the July 11 *Time* magazine.[20]

The Tanners learned of the forthcoming announcement some months before, which led Jerald to set about comparing the handwriting of the unknown Book of Mormon scribe to extant samples of Spalding's handwriting. He became convinced quickly that the two hands were not the same. Sandra compared the handwriting as well and noticed that some of the similarities could as easily be attributed to features common to the era. Jerald was also disturbed to learn that one of the handwriting experts was Henry Silver, who had confirmed the authenticity of the forged Howard Hughes will.[21] But in this case Silver backed off from his endorsement almost as soon

---

17. Whitmer, *An Address to All Believers in Christ*, 10–11.

18. Cowdrey is distantly related to Oliver Cowdery; at some point an ancestor changed the spelling of the last name. "Author's Bios," Spalding Research Associates, www.solomonspalding.info.

19. "Book of Mormon Challenged Anew: Researchers Claim Evidence Questions Authenticity," *Los Angeles Times*, June 25, 1977, clipping.

20. Edward J Plowman, "Who Really Wrote the Book of Mormon," *Christianity Today*, July 8, 1977, 32–34 [1088–90], and "Mormon Mystery," *Time*, July 11, 1977, 69.

21. For more, see chapter 11, herein.

as the story went public.[22] The second expert, Howard C. Doulder, walked back his endorsement as well, citing the same reason Sandra had proposed: "At first in the photocopies, I noted some writing similarities and letter characteristics that appeared in both.... I now attribute these similarities to the writing style of the century."[23]

The third handwriting expert, William Kaye, came to Salt Lake City on July 6, 1977, to examine the portion of the original Book of Mormon manuscript containing the unknown scribe's hand. The original manuscript was held at the LDS Church archives. Unexpectedly, a friend of the three researchers who had instigated the new look at the Spalding Theory called Jerald to ask him to accompany Kaye. Jerald, thrown by the request, doubted that he would be welcome at the church, but he agreed to attend. He and Kaye went to the archives together and were eventually ushered into a conference room.[24] A few minutes later, Church Archivist Donald Schmidt came in wheeling a cart full of documents. Kaye introduced himself and then introduced Jerald as "Mr. Tanner." Schmidt shook his hand, and asked his first name. "Jerald," answered Jerald.

An awkward silence followed while Schmidt decided what to do about Jerald before allowing him to stay. Historian Dean Jessee and church spokesperson Don LeFevre also appeared, and the meeting began. First, they examined the twelve pages in the Book of Mormon manuscript, but then another document was produced that Jerald felt clearly represented "the final blow ... to the ... theory." It was a handwritten copy of Joseph Smith's revelation dated June 15, 1831 (D&C 56), which Jerald became convinced was written by the same person who had written the Book of Mormon passages Cowdrey, Davis, and Scales said had been written by Spalding.[25] It

---

22. "Handwriting Expert Unsure About Book," *Salt Lake Tribune*, June 29, 1977, 8-B and "Expert in Writing Quits Mormon Book Charge," *Provo Daily Herald*, July 10, 1977, 20.

23. "Expert's Report Quells Attack on Authenticity of the Book of Mormon," *LDS Church News*, Oct. 15, 1977, 14.

24. Tanner and Tanner, *Did Spalding Write the Book of Mormon?*, 4–5.

25. The scribe of this revelation remains unidentified by the Joseph Smith Papers project. See June 15, 1831, Revelation, Kirtland Township, Geauga Co., Ohio [D&C 56], in "Calendar of Documents," Joseph Smith Papers, josephsmithpapers.org. Historians Brent and Erin Metcalfe believe the author may have been Christian Whitmer. Metcalfe and Metcalfe to Huggins, Apr. 27, 2018.

was already a stretch to say Spalding, who died in 1816, had written a portion of the Book of Mormon, but it was impossible that he could have written a June 1831 revelation. Jerald "felt the evidence furnished by the revelation was so devastating that [he] immediately went to the press with a statement hoping that the whole matter could be resolved before more damage was done."[26] But, like other times when the Tanners debunked a theory, those pushing the theory stuck to their story. Kaye stood by his identification of Spalding as the unknown Book of Mormon scribe, and Cowdrey, Davis, and Scales published their book, *Who Really Wrote the Book of Mormon?* Jerald followed up with a letter to Kaye, who only reiterated that the Book of Mormon manuscript pages and the Spalding pages "undoubtedly have all been executed by the same person."[27] With Kaye's help, Cowdrey, Davis, and Scales reignited the Spalding Theory, at least among some critics of the LDS Church.

Counter-cultist Walter Martin embraced the Spalding Theory, though he did not understand the issues. He wrote the foreword to *Who Really Wrote the Book of Mormon?* and included a discussion of it in the second edition of his book *The Maze of Mormonism*. But in doing so, he mangled the basic details of the theory:

> Almost thirty years ago, when I was first researching Mormonism, I examined a copy of Spalding's *first* novel, *Manuscript Story*, which is still in existence and in the possession of Oberlin College in Ohio ... As the crowning touch to their work, part of Spalding's original manuscript of his *second* novel, which had been lost since around 1828, and which was in Spalding's own handwriting, has evidently resurfaced! Twelve pages of manuscript writing has been examined by careful handwriting analysis and attested to be in the handwriting of Solomon Spalding himself, *and is a word-for-word portion of the Book of Mormon!*[28]

In fact, no pages from any second novel of Spalding's had resurfaced. The material the handwriting experts examined were the materials that had been housed at Oberlin College since 1884. And there

---

26. Tanner and Tanner, 5; David Briscoe, "Mormon Critic Sides with Church on Book," Ogden *Standard–Examiner*, July 8, 1977, 20-A.

27. William Kaye to Wayne Cowdrey, Sep. 8, 1977, 1, in Tanner and Tanner, Papers.

28. Martin, *Maze of Mormonism*, 61.

Cowdrey, Davis, and Scales mock the Tanners' opposition to the Spalding theory.

certainly was also no Spalding writing found to be "a word-for-word portion of the Book of Mormon!"

Jerald and Sandra had published their book, *Did Spalding Write the Book of Mormon?*, and tried to warn off Martin's organization, the Christian Research Institute (CRI), from endorsing *Who Really Wrote the Book of Mormon?* But to no avail. That the Tanners had come out with their results before Cowdrey, Scales, and Davis's book appeared was a sore spot: "The three researchers were a bit dismayed at the publishing of your book, before theirs was out," wrote Marian Bodine on September 13, 1977.[29] Marian and Jerry Bodine were among the most careful people at CRI, but in this case they felt sure the Tanners were wrong. Marian wrote, "The handwriting is really but a small amount

29. Marian Bodine to Sandra Tanner, Sep. 13, 1977, 1, Tanner and Tanner, Papers.

of the alleged facts pointing to Spalding being at least an inspiration of the Book of Mormon." The Bodines, or Marian at least, had also been reinforced in their belief in the validity of Kaye's report by Kaye's own claims about the extent of his ability. According to Marian, Kaye believed that "Dean Jesse[e] and anyone else who is not an expert in the area of Handwriting Analysis [is] a fool for giving their opinion." When Kaye examines a document, she said, "he looks not just for similarity in form, but the electrical impulses and the heart beat are shown under magnification. So that you can make a decision as to who wrote something as you could check a fingerprint. ... No one can copy the electrical impulses of your brain and the beat of your heart, etc." But by the time the scribe who took down D&C 56 on June 15, 1831, and the translation of the twelve pages of the Book of Mormon covering 1 Nephi 4:20–12:8 sometime after the spring of 1829 (see D&C 10),[30] Solomon Spalding's brain hadn't produced any electrical impulses nor his heart any beats for about a decade and a half.

In 1992, two of the original authors, Wayne L. Cowdrey and Howard A. Davis, together with a new author, Art Vanick, started pursuing the idea of coming out with a new edition of the Spalding book, which ultimately came out in 2005 as *Who Really Wrote the Book of Mormon? The Spalding Enigma*.[31] It was Vanick who initially approached the new publisher, Concordia (a Lutheran firm), and Concordia in turn wrote to the Tanners asking for advice on whether to publish it.[32] One cannot help but wonder whether their

---

30. If Joseph Smith were dictating the replacement pages for the lost 116 pages and wanted to inset twelve actual pages from Spalding, one would expect that some sign of assimilation of the material would show in relation to what came before and after, rather than the story flowing smoothly from a known Book of Mormon scribe to the Spalding material and on to another scribe. There are also other reasons for definitively rejecting the idea. See Wes Walters's comments in "Honesty with Mormons on Spalding," *Salt Lake City Messenger* 39, July 1978, 12.

31. Cowdrey, Davis, and Vanick, *Who Really Wrote the Book of Mormon?*

32. Rev. David V. Koch to Mr. and Mrs. Gerald [*sic*] Tanner (Nov. 1, 1992), Tanner and Tanner, Papers. Vanick kindly informed me in more detail about his role in both books:

I started doing research with Howard Davis and Wayne Cowdrey in 1975, and was at one time listed as one of the authors of their 1977, controversial book, though just before publication, I was then moved to the acknowledgements. I helped write and produce our limited edition, data CD book in 1995, and I was the one who contacted CPH [Concordia Publishing House] and worked with their editor in chief to get the publishing contract, and was also one of the co-authors of the 2005 book.

input led to the new edition's leaving out the claims about the unknown Book of Mormon scribe being Solomon Spalding. In any case, the Spalding theory still has many followers on a more popular level, even though most scholars of Mormon history reject it.

Jerald turned fifty-five on June 1, 1993, and, although hounded by health issues much of his life, he wanted to see if he could climb to the summit of Mount Timpanogos in Utah Valley as his father, George, had boasted of doing at the same age. Jerald went alone, scrambling among the barren rocks and mountain goats making the final push to reach the windy summit at 11,749 feet. When he reached the top, he stood for some time gazing off into the distances, down at Utah Lake below, and then made his way back down.

George Tanner had lived to eighty-one, and Jerald had led a much healthier lifestyle than his father. So he might have expected two or three more decades of fruitful writing and research at least. But that wasn't to be. Within five years Jerald's research and writing would largely cease. By 1992, he and Sandra were renovating a house next door with the intent of moving the printing operations and bookstore out of their home and into its own building. To those who only knew them as "the Tanners," this move might seem insignificant. But Jerald and Sandra were people of deep Christian faith, and they saw God's hand in their life together as new challenges and new changes confronted them. They were helped tremendously by Mike Magnano, a man Jerald had prayed and counseled with at the mission, whose life had been turned around by Christ. Mike came and stayed in the house and did demolition work to get things ready for the planned renovation.

Sandra oversaw the renovation and expansion. As it progressed, she dealt with the city to make sure everything was up to code. It became clear that they were going to need more money to complete the project—a lot more. At one point, she was told that a brick wall needed to be moved two inches; at another, that a stairwell had to be dug on the side of the building to provide a second exit from the basement. Sandra turned to land in rural Utah she and Jerald had been gifted in the mid-1980s. A man named George Flora, who said he saw the land in a dream and was inspired to buy it, had given it to Jerald and Sandra who maintained the property for several years.

A few years before in 1986, Sandra had the vacant property appraised at about $65,000. Now, in the middle of the renovation, a realtor called unsolicited and said she had two buyers, one who was offering $195,000 and the second even more. When George Flora's children heard the Tanners were selling, they contacted the Tanners saying they wanted to buy the land themselves. Sandra offered to sell it to them at the 1990 appraisal price of $65,000, but said she had to know by a certain date, or she would sell the property to one of the other buyers. They did not call back until after the date had passed—the papers were signed, and the property was sold to the initial buyer for $198,450.

Jerald and Sandra moved their operations next door into the new facility in 1995. At the time, they did not realize the scope of Jerald's health problems. He had played a minimal role in the planning and execution of the new building, and had become less involved in writing and publishing the *Salt Lake City Messenger*. When the ministry moved to the new building, Jerald moved his library from upstairs into the basement of their home, hoping to be able to spend more time writing. Looking back, Sandra sees God's hand even then setting the stage to facilitate the ministry's change of focus from research to outreach, as Jerald's productivity slowed. His strong point had always been research. Even though Sandra represented the public face of the ministry, the Sisyphean task of trying to keep up with the production demands of Jerald's endless stream of books meant that much of her time was spent on editing, printing, advertising, and so on.

Little things began to happen, which Jerald and Sandra at first joked about as being the result of Jerald's being something of an "absent minded professor." On Sandra's fifty-fifth birthday, Jerald played on their inside joke when he gave her a stuffed bear with a card inscribed, "To: CASANDA From: I CAN'T REMEMBER." But soon he began to be unable to find things if they were not exactly in their usual spot. If a box of cereal was in one cupboard over, or if milk in the refrigerator was obscured by a bottle of cola, Jerald couldn't find it. He started to get nervous driving; he traded off driving with Sandra during the day and stopped driving altogether at night.

By 1998, as Jerald approached sixty, Sandra began noticing other problems. For years, Jerald had been the financial secretary at their

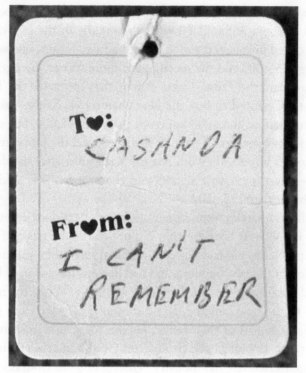

Jerald jokes about his forgetfulness on Sandra's 55th birthday.

church, responsible for counting the offerings. Although he didn't seem to have trouble tallying up the checks with the adding machine, it began to be difficult for him to count the change.

Between 1990 and 1996, Jerald wrote, updated, or reprinted over a dozen books; between 1997 and 1998, he wrote one. Reality hit Sandra all at once one day as they watched a Utah Jazz game on television:

> Jer asked about the score and how many points our team was down. He had always been a wiz at math so I was startled to realize he couldn't subtract a score of 28 from 32. My world fell apart that night as I realized what must be happening, [I] laid awake half the night silently crying and trying to process this. It made sense out of a number of odd behaviors of Jer.[33]

---

33. Sandra Tanner, "Annotated Timeline of Jerald Tanner's Life," 2018 update, 12. Tanner and Tanner, Papers.

A few days later, Sandra sat down with Jerald and voiced her suspicion: She thought he might have Alzheimer's disease. He didn't speak to her for the rest of the day. "I suspect he was rethinking his problems," Sandra recalls, "putting two and two together and scared of the answer."[34]

Sandra took Jerald to their usual doctor. He put a number of simple questions to Jerald of the "What year is it?" and "Who's the president?" variety, usually reserved for patients who are disoriented. Then he asked Jerald to subtract 7 from 100 and then 7 from that and 7 from that, and so on until you run out of numbers. Jerald gave one answer: 3. The doctor asked him to take it farther, but he couldn't. To Sandra's astonishment, the doctor told Jerald that he was just overtired, overworked, getting older, and that age comes to us all. Jerald's relief was tremendous and he clung to the doctor's diagnosis. "See?" he told Sandra. "You're just being a worry wart. I just need some rest."[35]

The memory lapses persisted and grew more pronounced. On August 15, 1998, Jerald and Sandra traveled to Boise, Idaho, for the wedding of their daughter Teresa to Chuck Vanderpool. Sandra had notified the wedding party of Jerald's increased difficulties with memory. He was still able to drive on open roads where the traffic was light and when no decisions were needed as to which way to go. When things became more complicated, he would pull over and Sandra would drive.

Jerald's symptoms emerged aggressively at the wedding rehearsal, exacerbated by the excitement of the event. When it came time for them to practice Jerald's part of giving away the bride, he could not follow the instructions. After Jerald walked Teresa to the front of the church, the pastor would ask, "Who gives this woman to be married to this man?" Jerald was supposed to say, "Her mother and I." Only he couldn't. An alternative was tried: Jerald would accompany Teresa to the front and then simply put her hand in Chuck's. He couldn't do that either. Eventually, the issue became how to get Jerald to go and sit down after leading Teresa to the front. A signal was arranged to tell Jerald to go sit down, but he had difficulty responding to it.

---

34. Tanner, Reminiscences.
35. Tanner.

Sandra and the pastor agreed that if Jerald didn't recognize the sign, Sandra would step forward, take him by the arm, and lead him to their seats. This final plan worked.

Jerald had talked for years about his final book, and he gave the impression that it would be a sort of magnum opus. Sandra knew the work was taking Jerald longer than usual, but his hopes for the work caused her to attribute his uncharacteristic delay to the size and scope of the project. But over time, she came to feel that the project was burning him out and deflating him. When *Joseph Smith's Plagiarism of the Bible* finally arrived in 1998, it was a significant work, with a substantial opening section arguing for Smith's literary reliance on the Bible and other sources. This was followed by a list of hundreds of phrases that appear both in the Book of Mormon and the New Testament. Jerald was aided in compiling this list by the computer software that was then becoming available. The typeface Jerald used was larger than usual because Jerald, not realizing that his vision was failing, insisted that the print should be "big enough to see."

As his memory problems worsened, Jerald was formally diagnosed with Alzheimer's. He was slow to accept it and still clung for a time to the earlier diagnosis of overwork and age-related issues. He sought various ways of rescuing his memory—diet and exercise, memory enhancing pills, and vitamins. His ability to read for any sustained period of time slipped away. He had Sandra read a couple of books to him recommending solutions. A specialist put him on a cognition-enhancing medication.

In March 1999, Jerald and Sandra flew to Chicago to be with her oldest daughter, April, for the birth of their granddaughter. While there, Sandra became ill with severe bronchitis and was hospitalized for five days. Her daughter and son-in-law had their hands full with a new baby and two other children, so Jerald tried to drive to the hospital on his own to visit Sandra. He got lost and was too confused to call a cab. Going forward he needed April and her husband, Brian, to drive him to visit Sandra.[36] After that Jerald gave up driving for good.

---

36. Tanner, "Annotated Timeline," 12.

Jerald tried to keep writing for as long as he could. After he finished *Joseph Smith's Plagiarism of the Bible*, he returned to the subject of the first tract he ever published: racial prejudice. Jerald attempted a new edition of the book whose original title had been *The Negro in Mormon Theology*. But as he progressed, using a computer became increasingly difficult, and he kept complaining that standard functions, such as italics, were broken. He wrote notes for himself on how to use keyboard shortcuts and edit functions, but to no avail. He was unable to finish the project. And so it happened that Jerald came full circle, as the subject of the final project he worked on was the same as the first.

The first time Jerald was able to use the word Alzheimer's to describe his condition was during a 2002 trip to Bellingham, Washington, where April and Brian had moved from Chicago. Near April and Brian's home was a large wooded area with parks and trails that ran along Whatcom Creek. Jerald had gone for walks there on a previous visit, so no one thought much of it when he went for another walk. But he didn't come back. They went looking for him and eventually called the police. Jerald had walked in the opposite direction, a long way down into the city of Bellingham itself where he had become lost. Eventually, he went into a café and sat down. The waitress asked him what he wanted to eat, and he told her he had Alzheimer's and that he was lost. She called the police, and an officer and April picked him up.

The mechanics of life became more difficult for Jerald. He lost the ability to read the hands on the clock, though he could still understand a digital display for a time. When that simple ability left him, he could still sense when it was near closing time, and he would make his way next door to the bookstore to collect Sandra.

It became difficult for Jerald to sit for very long, making it hard for them to sit through an entire service at church or wait in a restaurant. Still, Jerald continued to walk to the mission every morning to meet and pray with the men. Sandra was unable to stop him from going even when she feared he would get lost or misread the stop light and walk into traffic. When he couldn't walk anymore, Sandra drove him. Steve Trost, the director for the mission at the time, remembers how "Jerry would come in every day, and go down to the prayer room and pray even after it became impossible for most of the men to understand what he was saying."[37]

In 2003, Jerald formally retired from the ministry and began collecting Social Security. Sandra declined invitations to speak in order to care for Jerald. Her last public appearance was at a conference on Mormonism in a church in Keokuk, Iowa, arranged by Collene Ralson of the Nauvoo Christian Center. During her presentation, Jerald wandered in the back of the church. Afterward, a woman came up and asked her if Jerald had Alzheimer's; the woman had recognized the look and the actions in his behavior, which mirrored her late husband's.

---

37. Huggins, Interview with Steve Trost, Dec. 27, 2019, paraphrased. Almost no one who knew Jerald ever called him Jerry, but that was apparently what the men called him at the mission during his final years.

18

LAWSUITS AND DEPARTURES

At just around 11:00 a.m. on October 13, 1999, a black limousine slid into the driveway at the Utah Lighthouse bookstore. Two men in long black coats emerged and walked into the store where Sandra was working. One of them said, "I assume you know why we're here," and handed her a letter from the law offices of Kirton & McConkie on behalf of Intellectual Reserve, Inc., the LDS Church's copyrights management company. Sandra had no idea why they were there.

"You've been put on notice." one of them said to Sandra.

"What's this all about?" Sandra asked.

"It's all in there," said one of the men. And then they left.[1]

When Sandra looked at what they had handed her, it was not a summons, but a letter. It had to do with the several pages from the *Church Handbook of Instructions* that the Tanners had posted on their website.[2] The letter demanded that the Tanners "remove all portions of the *Handbook* from your website" by 2:00 p.m. that same day, and that they "post verbatim on your website the following acknowledgement in place of, and with the same prominence as, the removed texts of the *Handbook*":

> The *Church Handbook of Instructions* is copyrighted by Intellectual Reserve, Inc. Our prior posting of portions of the *Church Handbook of Instructions* at this website was neither authorized nor lawful, and such posting has been discontinued. We request that all copies of any portion of the *Church Handbook of Instructions* downloaded from this website be destroyed.

---

1. This statement as well as the general description of unfolding events that day are based on the recollections of Sandra, Marlene and Mark Reeves, and "LDS Church Sues Ministry," *Salt Lake City Messenger* 96, Feb. 2001, 1.

2. The full title is *Church Handbook of Instructions, Book 1: Stake Presidencies and Bishoprics*. In 2010 the title was shorted to *Handbook 1: Stake Presidents and Bishops*.

The pages the Tanners had posted explained how to get one's name removed as a member of the church. Bishops in the LDS Church sometimes refused to honor people's requests to have their membership canceled because they had neglected to follow precisely the procedure outlined in the *Handbook of Instructions*, which was available to church leaders but not to rank-and-file members. The Tanners felt that the LDS Church had the right to expect its members to adhere to certain standards of conduct and belief so long as those people wished to remain members. But they felt strongly that once the members wished to sever their relationship with the church, it was improper for leaders to refuse to honor their request based on technicalities in procedure that those members could not be aware of. To help people wanting to leave, the Tanners posted chapter 10 of the *Handbook* and a few quotes from other places that had to do with the topic. It amounted to seventeen pages out the 160-odd page 1998 edition of the *Handbook*.

Jerald was still at the rescue mission when the cease-and-desist letter was delivered, as he was most mornings. Sandra made the decision to comply and take down the *Handbook*. The intimidating way the letter had been delivered and the narrow window of time to comply to its demands appeared to be an attempt on the part of the church's attorneys to create an atmosphere of panicked urgency intended to scare the Tanner into acting without thinking. The statement that the letter demanded be posted "verbatim" had been crafted to make it impossible for the Tanners to comply without admitting wrongdoing: "Our prior posting ... was neither authorized nor lawful."

Sandra did not accept that description of their posting of the *Handbook* material. By the time the Tanners had originally uploaded the pages, they had been carefully negotiating copyright issues for many years. In this case, they had carefully thought through the matter, informed by guidelines set forward in authoritative sources.[3] They were aware of the church's ongoing hostility toward them and believed they were careful to attend to questions of copyright and maintaining the bounds of fair use when posting the *Handbook* materials.

---

3. "LDS Church Sues Ministry," *Salt Lake City Messenger* 96, Feb. 2001, 2.

The LDS Church had every right to challenge the Tanners' understanding of fair use, but to demand that they incriminate themselves on their own website was another matter.[4] Sandra was willing to comply, but without admitting guilt. In doing so, she hoped to avoid being sued. But she couldn't have known that Kirton & McConkie apparently intended to file a lawsuit against them that very afternoon, whether they complied with the demands of the letter or not.

Mark Reeves, who worked for the Tanners' Utah Lighthouse Ministry, played an increasingly important role as Jerald's capacities declined. He removed all the material from the Tanners' website and brought everything into compliance by 1:00 p.m. They complied with the demand of the letter by posting the letter itself, which contained the verbatim paragraph the church's lawyers demanded they post.

Whether the seventeen pages actually exceeded fair use laws or not, the extent of the church's copyright over those pages was not clear. It was true that the church had secured a copyright for the 1998 edition of the *Handbook*, but much of the material had been copied verbatim from the 1989 edition, which the Tanners argued the church had not secured a copyright for. Approximately 73 percent of what the Tanners posted had been carried from the uncopyrighted 1989 edition into the 1998 edition. The Tanners' attorney, Brian M. Barnard, argued that "if there has been a copyright infringement, it is of a work that was created in 1989 ... and because of the requirements of copyright law, we have to have a registration of the '89 version."[5]

Since the 1989 edition had not been copyrighted, Barnard went on to argue, there was no basis for the lawsuit. At issue was the status of the 1998 book as a derivative work. If it was considered derivative, copyright law only extended to the changes and additions to the 1989 *Handbook*. Copyright "protection does not extend to any

---

4. As the Tanners' Lawyer Brian M. Barnard pointed out, an "order requiring a party to publicly confess wrongdoing prior to a final ruling by the Court is inappropriate under and not contemplated by Fed. R. iv. Pro. 65" "Consent to Extension of Restraining Order and Response," Oct. 28, 1999, 3 Intellectual Reserve v. Utah Lighthouse Ministry, US District Court Central Division, Civil No. 2:99-CV-808C; hereafter *Church v. Tanners*.

5. "Defendants' Motion to Dismiss," Jan. 4, 2000, *Church v. Tanners*.

preexisting material."[6] In addition, there could be no question of the church losing money (or the Tanners making money) from the posting; the *Handbook* was provided to bishops free of charge by the church, and the Tanners were not selling it. Sandra felt their posting of the material fell within appropriate standards.

Getting the Tanners to take down the pages was apparently not the main goal of Kirton & McConkie. Church lawyers Berne Broadbent and Todd Zengler ignored the Tanners' compliance by the deadline and filed a lawsuit against them later that same afternoon without consulting Jerald and Sandra or their attorney. As in the Ehat case so now it didn't matter how many others were circulating the material before the Tanners, the church did not seem interested in going after anyone but them, even though others had been much more flagrant in distributing the material. This suggested to the Tanners that the church hoped to match their vast financial reserves against their comparatively modest means to string things along until they had managed to drive them into bankruptcy.[7]

Had Sandra left the posts up, Broadbent and Zengler might have had an easier time pursuing the lawsuit, since the posts were something that could conceivably be argued as a violation of the church's copyright. But after the Tanners complied with their demands, Broadbent and Zengler greatly expanded the definition of copyright violation. The church's lawyers argued to the judge that the Tanners had done an "end run" around their intentions by reproducing their letter rather than admitting guilt. Zengler said, "The letter is our demand. And they post our demand rather than an acknowledgment by them." He further complained that the Tanners undermined the presentation of the letter on their website by asserting their innocence in the press.

From the time the Tanners complied with the church's demand to remove the material they had posted from the *Handbook*, the case ceased to be about copyright and became about the ongoing validity of the First Amendment in the age of the internet. In response to the church, Judge Tena Campbell expressed her unwillingness to keep

---

6. United States Copyright Office, "Copyright in Derivative Works and Compilations," Circular 14, online at www.copyright.gov.

7. "LDS Church Sues Ministry," 2.

the Tanners from publicly stating their opinion or innocence on the grounds that "we're running into First Amendment implications."[8] The church quickly turned its attention to accusing the Tanners of other alleged infringements. They succeeded in having the Tanners remove the words *Handbook of Instructions* from the index of their website. Attorney Zengler said the Tanners might be "inviting inquiries about it; that they might make copies available in another form, be it in print media or on a disk, or in some other fashion." Jerald and Sandra were not doing any of these things, and the church had not initially asked them to take the name of the *Handbook of Instruction* down from their website, only its contents. Campbell may not have fully grasped the arguments, pronouncing them, "a little too complex for me,"[9] due to Zenger's use of even the most basic computer and internet jargon. She had to ask, for example, for an "idea on a screen how big a thumbnail is," and did not know that at the time word processors automatically printed web addresses in bold.[10]

Zengler's remarks were forming one of the pillars of the church's argument: even writing the name of the *Handbook of Instruction* was a copyright violation as a "contributory infringement." This means that even using the title amounts to an advertisement enticing others to obtain illegal copies. In other words, the church's lawyers attempted to stretch the pre-existing concept of "contributory infringement" to include such things as the mention of a title of a book. Incomprehensibly, Campbell agreed with the argument for the time being and issued a temporary restraining order, asking the Tanners to remove the reference to the *Handbook* from the website index.

The church's lawyers complained anew when the Tanners created a new page on their website tracing the chronology of the case, including screenshots and copies of documents. It turned out to be a wise move since the church later presented an inaccurate chronology to the judge. Doing this also protected the Tanners against later misrepresentations about how much they had published on their website.

By the end of October, the *Salt Lake Tribune* was asking why

---

8. "Plaintiff's Motion for Temporary Restraining Order," Oct. 18, 1999, *Church v. Tanners.*

9. "Plaintiff's Motion."

10. "Plaintiff's Motion."

the lawsuit existed at all; the entirety of the *Handbook of Instructions* was elsewhere on the web, with no possible way to take all copies down.[11] The *Tribune* article even provided web addresses of two sites where part or all of the *Handbook* could be accessed. But less than a week later the church filed a document that blindsided the Tanners. The church insisted Jerald and Sandra had "openly flouted and disregarded the court's restraining order by not merely continuing to publish portions of the *Handbook* without authorization but by now publishing and inducing publications of the entire *Handbook*."[12] "This slanderous charge," the Tanners insisted, "is totally false."[13]

Adding to the Tanners' struggles, Jerald's Alzheimer's was increasingly debilitating. He could no longer coherently write or perform basic math, but he could still read some documents and make suggestions. The decision-making at the ministry began to shift to the full-time employees and Sandra, who would meet and discuss what should be done. Marlene Reeves had worked for the ministry for twenty years, and her son Mark was employed to help with the computers and other machines. It was Mark who noticed that the church's lawyers conspicuously flipped the chronology at certain crucial points to represent the Tanners as the fountainhead from which others learned how to find material from the *Handbook* on the internet.

In reality, the full *Handbook of Instructions* had been put online by an Australian named David Gerard. After the *Salt Lake Tribune* article printed his web address, there was a significant uptick of hits on his website. The church argued to the court correctly that the uptick in web traffic was due to the article in the *Tribune*, but incorrectly insinuated that the Tanners were the source of the *Tribune's* information as a way of making it seem they had "advertised the website."[14] But neither Jerald nor Sandra, nor anyone else from the Utah Lighthouse Ministry, made any such statement in the *Tribune*. There was no evidence that the Tanners were even interviewed for the article.

11. "Sheila R. McCann, "With LDS Book on Net, Lawsuit Might Be Moot," *Salt Lake Tribune*, Oct. 30, 1999, D-2.

12. "Plaintiff's Reply in Support of Its Motion for Preliminary Injunction," Nov. 5, 1999, 4, *Church v. Tanners*.

13. "LDS Church Sues Ministry," 4.

14. "Plaintiff's Reply."

The church's attorneys also heavily redacted the language of third-party emails that were posted on the Tanners' website, giving the impression that what was written in them represented the Tanners' own words. One email was so heavily redacted that Judge Campbell complained, "I have to tell you, it was so whited out, I had a little bit of trouble figuring out what was what."[15] Consistent with their earlier arguments, the church's lawyers represented the contents of these letters posted from others as further examples of advertising infringement.[16]

The church's argument that the Tanners were guilty of copyright infringement even after they had complied with the attorneys' demands hinged on a technical understanding of how computers work. When anyone looks at a website, a copy of the page is stored in the computer's random access memory (RAM).[17] The church argued that, since the Tanners knew the entire *Handbook* was online and since they had read it, they had "copied" it—knowingly or not—onto their computer's RAM, thereby violating copyright laws. Campbell, astonishingly, agreed.[18]

For precedent, Judge Campbell cited the 1993 *MAI Systems Corp. v. Peak Computer, Inc.*, which dealt with infringing copyright by downloading software on a computer for which one does not have a license. Campbell universalized the principle by making it cover potentially anything one might happen to run across while browsing the internet.

On another point at least, the church lost. Zenger and Broadbent argued that the mere mention of a word or title was paramount to advertising websites where the full *Handbook* was published, and therefore was also copyright infringement. Campbell rejected this: "The court concludes that plaintiff [the LDS Church] has not shown

15. "Plaintiff's Continued Motion for Injunctive Relief," Nov. 10, 1999, *Church v. Tanners.*

16. Compare "Plaintiff's Reply" with Barnard's response in "Plaintiff's Continued Motion."

17. Every computer has a certain amount of space dedicated to RAM, which allows the machines to work faster by retrieving recently accessed data from the RAM instead of a hard drive.

18. "Preliminary Injunction," Dec. 6, 1999, 6–7.

that defendants [Utah Lighthouse Ministry] contributed to the infringing action of those who operate the infringing websites."[19]

But the other part of Campbell's December 6, 1999, preliminary injunction sent shockwaves through the national media. It is not hard to understand why. Her reasoning that reading any document linked to another website could constitute copyright infringement because a computer automatically stored the document temporarily in its RAM meant that, at one time or another, everyone who browsed the internet was likely guilty of copyright infringement. Carl Kaplan reported in the *New York Times Cyber Law Journal* that some in the legal profession "found the court's decision disturbing and, if it stands, a possibly dangerous precedent that could inhibit one of the most fundamental features of the Web—the ability to direct viewers from one Web site to another."[20] Steven L. Lawson for CNN said the decision "could represent a body blow to a key feature of the Web."[21] Jessica Litman, a law professor at Wayne State University with expertise in intellectual property, concurred: "If I give a footnote in a law review article for a plagiarized book, that seems to be just telling people where the book is, not materially facilitating their infringement. ... This decision is like saying that providing footnotes to illegal material is illegal."[22]

The Tanners filed an appeal to the US 10th Circuit Court of Appeals in Denver on December 24, 1999. The Court of Appeals directed the two sides to work with a 10th Circuit appointed mediator, which they began to do in February 2000. The process dragged on for nearly a year until an agreement was reached on November 30, 2000. Sandra agreed to work with the mediator despite her strong belief that had they pursued the matter with the 10th District Court directly, they would have prevailed. But, she asked herself, at what cost? She had taken Jerald to Hawaii the month before the church brought its suit because she wanted to cherish the time she had left with him. The effects of his Alzheimer's were exacerbated by anxiety.

---

19. "Preliminary Injunction."

20. Charles S. Kaplan, "Copyright Decision Threatens Freedom to Link," *New York Times Cyber Law Journal*, Dec. 10, 1999.

21. "Copyright Ruling Targets Web Links," Dec. 14, 1999, quoted in "LDS Church Sues Ministry," 5.

22. Kaplan, "Copyright Decision Threatens Freedom."

The case was not only robbing them of time, but also assuring Jerald's premature demise.

Sandra decided that if she could accomplish three things in the mediation, she would agree to let the matter go: (1) That Campbell's preliminary injunction, along with the earlier restraining orders, be dissolved and vacated, with the intent that the legal reasoning underpinning them be essentially taken back; (2) that she and Jerald give no money to the church; and (3) that she and Jerald admit no guilt. The church accepted these in exchange for three demands of its own: (1) the Tanners would in future use no more than fifty words from the *Handbook* in any given work; (2) that they would not post any links or web addresses to the *Handbook of Instructions* elsewhere on the web; and (3) they would destroy any physical copies of the *Handbook* on the premises and remove any digital copies from their computers.

Intellectual Reserve Inc. v. Utah Lighthouse Ministry became a famous case because of the dangerous logic deployed by Kirton & McConkie.[23] Judge Campbell's reasoning in the case was vacated as part of the mediation agreement, but that is often forgotten. The church relied on increasingly dangerous, freedom-curtailing definitions of copyright infringement, to the point that anyone who clicks on any copyrighted material on the web, knowingly or unknowingly, is guilty of "copying" it to their computer's RAM. Twenty years after the court's arbitration decision, copies of the *Handbook* are still ubiquitous across the internet, and at the beginning of 2020 the LDS Church announced its intention to make the *Handbook of Instructions* available to all online.[24]

Three years after the trial, as Sandra continued to act as Jerald's caregiver, more bad news came. Sandra's mother, Georgia, then living in a mobile home park in Sylmar, California, had been diagnosed with terminal pancreatic cancer. Sandra and her daughter Teresa arranged to visit her. While there, Teresa asked her grandmother whether she was ready to meet God.

"Why do you think I'm *not* ready?" Georgia had replied defensively.

---

23. Intellectual Reserve v. Utah Lighthouse Ministry, 75 F. Supp. 2d 1290 (D. Utah 1999).

24. Stacy Johnson and Genelle Pugmire, "LDS Church Announces Update to Now Fully-Public Handbooks," *Daily Herald*, Jan. 30, 2020.

"Well, Mom," Sandra said, "I'm not sure you have forgiven your mother, or dad (Ivan), for the wrong they did you, that raises the question whether you really understand grace and forgiveness." Even though Georgia had taken Sandra's father back, and taken care of him until he died, she still nursed a great deal of bitterness over how much trouble and pain he had brought into her life. Throughout her life she also harbored resentment toward her mother, Sylvia Pearce Young, over incidents in her childhood as well. Georgia said she would think about it.

A number of people had spoken to Georgia through the years about Jesus, but, typical of her background, she was very skeptical of the Bible as history, and also generally a very self-reliant woman. When Sandra's sister Carolyn had become a Christian some years before, Georgia had actually said it was probably good for her, while insisting that she herself didn't need it. She eventually got to the point where she believed in prayer and in a Supreme Being, but she balked at the idea of Christ's atoning for her sins.

But a few days after Sandra and Teresa spoke to her, Georgia called Carolyn to come and pray with her so that she could receive Jesus. Carolyn initially felt unsure and offered to have her pastor visit, but Georgia insisted. Carolyn and her husband, Howard, met with Georgia, and she received Jesus as her Lord and Savior, delighting her two daughters and grandchildlren.

On December 13, 2003, Georgia's children Sandra, Carolyn, and Jon, and other family and friends were visiting when Georgia's sister Julia dropped in to see her on the way to a nearby Christmas party. After she had visited and it was time to leave, Julia took her sister's hand and said, "Well, Georgia, I've got to go to my party now," then she turned, opened the door, and left. As she did everyone watched her go. When they turned back, Georgia was gone as well, leaving a strange sense that she had wanted to go to the party too, and that her spirit had just followed Julia out the door.

While in California for Georgia's funeral, Jerald caught the flu, and it looked for a time as though he would not recover. He quit eating, and finally it was decided to place him in hospice care. Being put on hospice meant discontinuing the mind-preserving medication he had been taking, which made little difference. In its place, he was put on tranquilizers, to help with his agitation, and sleeping medicine, but both were ineffective. Jerald's condition also meant that Sandra would have to spend more time caring for him at home. She kept herself distracted by using the notes Jerald prepared for an updated edition of his work on race that he had been unable to finish. She published the book as the *Curse of Cain?: Racism in the Mormon Church.*

The hospice doctor came to check on Jerald and, seeing he was still not eating, addressed him firmly. "Mr. Tanner," she said, "if you do not start eating, you *will* die." Somehow, this was the shock Jerald needed, and he began eating again. He soon recovered enough for Sandra to be able to take him on one last trip to Hawaii, where they celebrated their forty-fifth wedding anniversary.

It was after he seemed to recover that Jerald admitted to himself that the time had come to give up his daily walk to the rescue mission and back. Sandra tried driving Jerald to the mission, but he would get nervous or confused and start walking home before she arrived to pick him up. When Jerald was no longer able to form sentences at prayer time, he eventually exchanged prayer with having coffee with the men. The mission director, Steve Trost, remembers that even after Jerald was unable to communicate, the men continued to be completely accepting of him.[25] But eventually he had to abandon even that simple contact.

A few family and friends suggested that Sandra close the ministry, sell her house, and move nearer to one of her daughters. That way she could put Jerald in an assisted-living facility and have the time to be with him during the days, as well as the support of her children. Sandra considered this to the point of investigating the housing market near one of her daughters. But all the logistics of the plan—closing her business, selling not just her own home but the building that held the bookstore, relocating, finding new doctors for Jerald—were too much for her to handle while caring for Jerald, and too much upheaval for Jerald in his confused state.

One of the many cruelties of Alzheimer's is the slowness of the disease. Death can take years while loved ones watch the disease

---

25. Trost, conversation with Huggins, Dec. 27, 2019.

rob their family member of their memory and cognitive functions. Jerald began showing symptoms in the mid-1990s. A decade later, in March 2004, Sandra wrote her daughter April about his condition, and her words provide a window into the snail-like pace of his decline. "Dad," Sandra wrote, "struggles with communication. He understands most conversations and remembers past events and people." But it was the day-to-day existence that had grown most challenging. "The mechanics of life give him the most trouble—like putting cream in his coffee, dressing himself, taking a shower, putting on his seatbelt, etc." Sandra explained that Jerald was "generally happy," but "very depressed about giving up his time at the mission." They would go out to eat once or twice a day to give him something to do, and his sister Evelyn would take him to lunch and for a walk once a week. Also an unexpected solution to Jerald's need for walking was not long in coming, and arrived unexpectedly, or as Sandra puts it, as "a real Godsend": Tony Higgins, who had begun working at the ministry in the spring of 2005. One of the issues with Jerald's sickness was his general agitation and hypersensitivity to other people's heightened emotions. Tony's calm, placid, almost buddha-like manner made Jerald feel especially at ease in his presence. "Since he [Jerald] was becoming more prone to wandering," Tony recalls, "I specifically took on the 'duty' of walking the dogs with him, which greatly helped him to maintain some semblance of daily routine and stability ... he was an avid walker all of his adult life. ... So the daily walk was something that helped keep him a little more focused... Even though he could no longer articulate himself in a conversation, he enjoyed our silent walks together, sometimes with me just monologing, which he seemed to be able to track but not respond to."[26]

After Jerald and Sandra's last trip to Hawaii in April 2004, their time was spent with Sandra managing the ministry with the help of the staff and caring for Jerald. Jerald was able to attend a handful of events, including the funeral of their longtime friend and mentor, LaMar Petersen. Petersen had died a few months shy of his ninety-fifth birthday in September 2005. He had been one of three mentors who had influenced the Tanners the most. There was

---

26. Higgins, email to Huggins, Feb. 9, 2018.

the people-loving Pauline Hancock, who never lost her faith in the Book of Mormon; James D. Wardle, that curious blend of barber, historian, and comic; and the patient and fair-minded skeptic La-Mar Petersen.[27]

After being on the receiving end of lawsuits, the Tanners found themselves back in court in 2005, this time as the plaintiff. The Mormon-themed Foundation for Apologetic Information & Research (FAIR), aided by Allen Wyatt, had registered thirteen internet domain names that led to sites that mimicked the appearance of the Utah Lighthouse Ministry site, but with links that directed people to FAIR articles instead of the Tanners' work. The choice of the domain names made it appear that they were intentionally trying to create confusion on the web to draw traffic away from the Tanners' website. For example, the Tanners' website was www.utlm.org, but if someone typed in utahlighthouseministry.com, or even sandratanner.com and jeraldtanner.org, they were directed to FAIR's websites. They even exploited the frequent misspelling of Jerald's name with a G instead

---

27. LaMar's granddaughter Michelle Petersen, a missionary Bible translator in Africa remembers warmly her interactions as a Christian with her skeptical grandfather:

He loved me very much. He respected my work in Africa, or came to respect it in time. Then he started bragging on me to people saying I spoke nine African languages, which he inferred wrongly when I said I'd been part of training literacy supervisors from nine language groups. I explained to him that I only ever spoke English, French, Jula and Sango, and when I taught people to be literacy supervisors for classes in other ethnic groups, I taught bilinguals via French to work in their mother tongues. I think he was usually moderately to highly proud of me and came to respect the Bible as being more reliable than the Book of Mormon.

While working in the Central African Republic with Wycliffe Bible Translators in the 1990s, I wrote him my testimony and the Gospel in a letter which he read in its entirety to our family gathered at Christmas.

Then when I took breaks from working in various African countries over the years, we talked about the Gospel various times when I was visiting home.

As he aged, there came a time when he was no longer able to play his beloved piano, and he prayed and asked God to let him play piano again, and he was able to do that, which he told me with tears in his eyes was an answer to prayer that meant a great deal to him.

Shortly before he passed, I read him Romans 10:9–10 and asked him if he believed that. He said, "That's the way the Bible tells it, and we have no reason to doubt it." That was a huge change from the negative ways he had spoken about faith in Christ from an atheistic perspective earlier in his life. I cannot tell for sure if he was saying what I wanted to hear or if he truly believed it, but I am hopeful he may have truly believed in the real Lord Jesus Christ. (Emails from Michelle Petersen to the author slightly rearranged, Nov 2 and 4, 2016.).

of a J.[28] Sandra filed suit to prevent "the exploitation of the ministry trademark and our personal names, and to ensure that those seeking our information are not misled."[29]

The case dragged on for years, and was ultimately lost on the grounds that the websites had ostensibly been intended as "parodies." There is irony in the defeat given the shadow cast by the church's case against the Tanners with regard to the *Church Handbook of Instructions* where it was argued that the mere posting of a web address or even the title of a book represented full scale copyright infringement. But happily, although the Tanners didn't prevail in the suit, they were able to retrieve all but one of the domain names.

By the fall of 2005, Jerald's mental state was in serious decline. It became difficult for him to sleep, so he was up and around the house all night, keeping Sandra awake. In October, Sandra took Jerald to a twentieth-anniversary symposium on the Mark Hofmann murders, but it was difficult to keep him by her. During the talks, he would see someone in the audience he recognized—including people who had been his lifelong adversaries—and he would want to get up to greet them. Even during the breaks when he could have chatted with old friends and acquaintances, he was not able to say anything coherent.

Jerald never lost his sense of recognition, however. He always knew Sandra and the other people he encountered on a regular basis. Members of the family pressed Sandra to put him in a care facility, but she was determined not to do so as long as he recognized her. Part of the problem was Jerald's increasing discomfort around caregivers. He fought a hospice worker helping him shower when the worker got water in Jerald's eyes. A masseuse was sent to help Jerald relax, but he refused to let her touch him. Sandra was his lifeline, and as his health and memory worsened, she was the one person he did not fight or try to argue with when she did what she felt he needed. Over the next nine months things became exhausting for her. The social isolation imposed on her by the situation was difficult. On one occasion she confided how she "told jer sunday afternoon that 'i' needed church…i told him it was my only contact with friends…

---

28. The domains FAIR registered included variations on utahlighthouse, utahlighthouseministry, sandratanner, and jeraldtanner, including .com, .org, and .info.

29. "Ministry Files Lawsuit," *Salt Lake City Messenger* 104, June 2005, 8.

after our 'talk' he cried and said he was sorry, we both cried and hugged." Jerald grew "very sentimental, constantly rubbing my arm or hand or trying to hug me." He became confused using "forks, spoons, etc." Jerald "claimed there was a man in the front room the other night." Sandra struggled with her own emotions. "As I sit here I am fighting depression and tears. Jer is losing ground and it breaks my heart for him." Jerald would stop eating for long periods of time, but then tell her he was sorry. "Jerald is very sweet and keeps apologizing for being sick." Some of the most heartbreaking moments were his realizations of what was happening to him. One night Jerald told Sandra out of the blue, "I don't think I'm going to make it." It devastated her.[30]

Another evening, Jerald managed to get out of the house and became lost. Dennis and Sandra went looking for him. As Dennis was passing a construction site, he heard a noise in the dark that led him to Jerald. Sandra began bolting the door at night, but when Jerald still got the urge to go out he would start banging on the door.

Going to the grocery store or even church became difficult and, over time, almost impossible. Jerald became alarmed riding in the car. He felt as though it was going a lot faster than it was, and he would clutch the dashboard in fear. She couldn't leave him in the car for any amount of time because she knew he would wander off. She ingrained in him that if he got lost he should sit down and wait for her to find him. He seemed, to her immense relief, at least to understand that.

In September 2006, Teresa, who was coming down from Boise every few weekends to help Sandra with Jerald, was in town. Another family member offered to sit with Jerald to give Sandra and Teresa the opportunity to attend church. On the way, Teresa said to Sandra, "Mom, you've got to put Dad in a home. You just can't keep going on this way!"[31] Sandra pulled the car over to the curb, broke down, and wept. She knew Teresa was right; she could not go on anymore. They called Dennis at church to come so that the three of them could find a place for Jerald. Some places they checked

---

30. Taken from a series of emails Sandra sent to friends and family in 2005–06, copies in my possession.
31. Tanner, Reminiscences.

felt overcrowded or depressing; others were not lock-down facilities. Deflated, they called hospice for help. They could take Jerald, they said, but not until Thursday. In the meantime, they could provide someone to stay the nights so that Sandra could get some sleep. Sandra set up a sleeper bed in the living room for Jerald and instructed the girl who came to let Jerald walk around in hopes that he would lie down on the extra bed and sleep for a while. But Sandra begged her not to let Jerald into the basement where Sandra was getting some desperately needed rest.

Thursday came. They took Jerald in the morning to a hospice facility. Jerald was scared at being left, and the nurses had to have someone sit with Jerald during the night. The next morning when Sandra arrived, the nurses remarked that usually when Alzheimer's was this advanced, the patient was in bed.

On Saturday morning, Jerald was up. By lunchtime he was in bed; by dinner he was in a coma. On Sunday morning the nurse told Sandra that if there was anyone who should be present, she should call them since Jerald would be gone by that night.

"How do you know that," Sandra asked, amazed at the nurse's confidence.

"You can feel it in the legs," the nurse said, "all the forces of life are drawn up into the central core of the body, and you can feel weakening of the pulse in the legs."[32]

The nurse was right. On a clear and pleasant afternoon, Sunday, October 1, 2006, at around 5:00 p.m., Jerald Dee Tanner breathed his last. It was the moment he had looked forward to for almost half a century as the time he would finally see the face of his Savior and Lord.

Dennis, who was with his father when he died, walked out into the garden of the facility and sat down to pray. As he watched the sun set, he thought what a perfect day this was for the Lord to take his father—just the sort of day that would have inspired his dad to head out for the canyons with the dog for a hike. He remembered when Jerald's father had died, Jerald took the family to the Great Salt Lake, and he and Dennis walked together way out into the lake without saying a word. They positioned themselves to float in

---

32. Tanner.

the briny waters and watch the sunset turn the mountains to the east purple and gold.[33]

When the *Salt Lake Tribune* was writing an obituary, reporters approached the LDS Church for comment, but the article could only explain, "LDS Church spokesman Dale Bills declined comment on Tanner's death."[34] An even-handed obituary appeared on the LDS-themed *By Common Consent* blog:

> As much as he opposed the teachings of our church, he certainly didn't slander the church like other anti-Mormons. He opposed the church because he sought to lead its members to Christ. He was a missionary for the other side of Christianity—the side that we proselyte among. ... To be sure, Jerald Tanner always saw what was worst about Mormonism, but his vision was limited by an integrity sorely lacking in many other anti-Mormons. Jerald's career was replete with examples of his honesty.[35]

Sandra and her church thought the funeral might be well attended, so it was held at the Salt Lake Christian Center, a couple of miles from the Tanners' usual church. When it was realized that the building was being rented for Jerald Tanner's funeral, it was determined that there was no way they were going to charge to have it at their facility. It was, they said, an honor. And they graciously took care of everything, even, as Sandra recalls, providing a nursery.

The service was Saturday, October 7, 2006. Various Christian ministry leaders from different Christian denominations came from around the country, including Roger Hanson and Luke Wilson from Michigan, Latayne Scott from New Mexico, James Walker from Texas, Jim Valentine from Wisconsin, and Marshall Almarode from Washington. The service was also populated by local friends and family. Some Latter-day Saint friends and family were present as well.

Jerald and Sandra's son Dennis shared family recollections instead of focusing on Jerald's work. Dennis talked about the Jerald he knew growing up: the lover of hikes in the canyons, of dogs and

---

33. Dennis Tanner told the story at the funeral service. Obituaries appeared in the *Salt Lake Tribune*, Oct. 4–6, 2006.

34. Jeremiah Stettler, "Author-Historian Remembered for Honesty," *Salt Lake Tribune*, Oct. 6, 2006, B-4.

35. DKL [David King Landrith], "Obituary: Jerald Tanner," at www.bycommon-consent.com.

birds who had once trained a parakeet to say phrases like "birds don't talk, silly." He explained that his father never told a joke, but was instead a great practical joker. He hid stuffed gorillas in a closet so that when Sandra opened the door monkeys would swing out at her. Jerald had loved playing hide-and-seek with him and his sisters when they were small, and Jerald avoided detection by climbing on top of the refrigerator. Dennis had also shared with the *Salt Lake Tribune* some of Jerald's fastidiousness in matters so insignificant that they could be both simultaneously humorous and annoying. Jerald never jaywalked, never drove over the speed limit, and if a cashier at a store gave him so much as an extra quarter by mistake, he would drive back to return it.[36]

Other speakers focused more on Jerald's ministry, likening him to Martin Luther, a flawed human being but a bold one who loved the truth. Bill McKeever quoted from Jerald's own published testimony, where he wrote that he felt like the Gadarene demoniac: "Although I have not literally lived among the tombs or cut myself with rocks, I can really relate to this story. ... I feel that I must tell how much the Lord has done for me."[37] Then Pastor Melzer brought the service to a stirring close: "Jerald Tanner was on the side truth. He listened to the voice of Jesus. He loved the truth of God's Word. And now for Jerald God gets the last word: 'Well done, good and faithful servant, Enter into the joy of your Lord.'"

36. Stettler, "Author-Historian."
37. Tanner, *Jerald Tanner's Testimony*, 1.

19

A NEW WORLD

When Jerald Tanner passed away, it had been more than ten years since his Alzheimer's symptoms had begun to manifest and eight years since he was officially diagnosed. Sandra was there for it all. When the disease moved into its final stages, it was a lonely and devastating time for her. Jerald's care and nocturnal wanderings left Sandra with little sleep, and she slowly sunk into a deep depression. She had health problems of her own, starting with skin cancer on her leg in 2001. The lesions were successfully removed. Then in the late fall of 2005, she experienced such chest pain in the middle of the night that she felt sure she was having a heart attack. Since it would be too complicated to get Jerald up and ready, she decided to tough out the night taking aspirin in the hope of going to the hospital in the morning. Fortunately the problem was her gall bladder, not her heart. The gall bladder was removed a few days later, and their son, Dennis, and his wife, Sherri, stayed with Jerald, who was beside himself with worry. A few months later in February 2006, Sandra had a breast cancer scare. She had surgery to remove a lump, which happily was benign, and Dennis stepped in again to care for Jerald.

Sandra put on an upbeat, positive face, even as she slipped into depression. Jerald picked up on and mirrored her emotions, so she knew she had to smile and be cheerful on the outside, no matter how devastated she actually felt. After Jerald died, the weighty burden did not lift. Instead, guilt crept in. Had she done all she could for Jerald? Those close to the situation would say yes. Even in the final stage of Jerald's illness the hospice workers commented on how well Jerald had been cared for, and it gave Sandra some comfort but did not grant her relief from self-recriminations.

A few days after Jerald's death, Sandra had an experience that she

317

admits she would be disinclined to believe had it happened to someone else. While she willingly grants that it may have been a dream, it seemed so real when it occurred. In bed one night, she looked up and Jerald was standing there. Surprised, she got up, walked to him, put her right hand on his cheek and her left hand on his arm, both of which were warm, and said, "Jerald, I know you're dead, but it sure is good to see you." Jerald smiled at her reassuringly but said nothing. Still his smile communicated a clear message: Don't worry about these past few years, Sandy, about whether you cared for me enough, or about anything. I'm good. And you and me, we're just fine too. A sense of peace settled over her, and the anxious self-recrimination relaxed its grip on her soul. Then Jerald was gone, and Sandra was left standing alone in the room.

Sandra's sister Carolyn stayed to visit after the funeral. Then she and Sandra took a road trip together through Bryce Canyon, the Grand Canyon, Las Vegas, and finally to their brother Jon's in Huntington Beach. Sandra stood on an overlook, gazing out at Bryce Canyon's brown and red cliffs looming over the landscape dotted with bursts of green from the juniper trees. Her tears started gradually, then came in torrents. Carolyn put her arm around Sandra's shoulder and prayed for her. Both sisters had gone down separate spiritual roads. Carolyn became inactive in the LDS Church sometime after Sandra left. She rejected traditional Christianity and embraced New Age teaching for a time. But eventually she had found Christ, and now, as the two sisters stood together with Carolyn ministering healing and peace to her widowed sister, Sandra's heart was brimming over with comfort and gratitude for a treasured intimacy that for a long time during their lives would not have even seemed remotely possible.

The sisters stayed in motels along the way and took their time. They did not plot their route using Google Maps or scour reviews for restaurants. They meandered south through Utah, Arizona, Nevada, and finally California. After spending time at their brother's, they drove to Carolyn's home in Frazier Park. When it was time for Sandra to return to Utah, her family expressed concern that she would be driving alone. But she insisted she needed the solitude. She knew she had made the right decision as she basked in the silence.

Sandra and Carolyn

A growing desire was rising in Sandra to be done with it all. To get away. Change her name. Disappear. Move somewhere where nobody knew her. She was tired of being hated by Mormons and told she was doing it wrong by Christians. Let somebody else do it, if they know so much better, she thought. It was unnatural and strange being pigeonholed her entire adult life, people praising her and Jerald to the high heaven or damning them to hell. She had been married to Jerald for nearly half a century, and they knew each other's flaws and strengths better than anyone. She knew they weren't anything like as good or as bad as people wanted to portray them. It wasn't natural. Maybe it was time for this whole "The Tanners" thing to just stop. She was sixty-five years old when Jerald died, and that was when most people retired. Jerald's work was done, and just now it felt as if it had been more his work than hers. Why couldn't she just live out the rest of her life as an ordinary person?

But deciding how to move forward in the face of such challenges wasn't so easy. What about the ministry? Could she pass it on to someone else? Perhaps there was someone like her and Jerald who had left Mormonism to become Christian. But would that someone be as fastidious and careful as she and Jerald? As time passed, it became increasingly obvious that it was unlikely that she would ever find such a person. That meant if she wanted to get away, she would need to close things down herself. There was the staff, the building, the stock, her own house full of stuff and dark memories of Jerald's decline? What was she to do? It was all very daunting.

While Jerald was ill the world had been changing. It had been a long time since friends gathered in James Wardle's barbershop to chat Mormonism and swap documents. Many of the documents the Tanners worked so hard to find in the 1950s and 1960s were now a Google search away. Diaries and journals of the sort they had been refused access to were being published by the LDS Church or independent outlets. Conversations were moving to online forums, to blog posts, to discussion boards, to Facebook. Instead of sitting down in front of a computer plugged into a wall, anyone could pull a phone out of their pocket and tap away.

As days stretched into months, Sandra sat in the bookstore. People would come in and want to talk, and she would talk to them, of course. Then, the requests started to come in. Sandra was asked to speak at churches, for podcasts, and for television. The first invitation she accepted came three months after Jerald died when she appeared on Shawn McCraney's *Heart of the Matter* television show.[1] She spoke across the country. Some of these presentations were typical Christian responses to Mormon history and theology. But some of the interviewers asked her to talk about her life and her ministry. People were starting to take an interest in who the Tanners were, not just what they had done. In August 2007, just shy of a year since Jerald had passed away, a session dedicated to the Tanners' lives and research was held at the Sunstone Symposium in Salt Lake City. "Critical Vision: The Research and Writings of Jerald and Sandra Tanner" was moderated by Carolyn Campbell and featured authors Lawrence Foster, Allen Roberts, Ronald Huggins,

---

1. McCraney, an ex-Mormon, hosted an evangelical television show with guests and live callers from 2006 to 2013, then moved the show online. His older shows and newer podcasts are online at www.hotm.faith. McCraney has since moved on from evangelicalism to create his own version of Christianity.

and Will Bagley. Sandra was invited to sit in the audience and re-spond informally during the Q&A. The panel represented a range of perspectives, but even the more critical panelists had some positive things to say. The narrative of Jerald and Sandra Tanner was becom-ing more nuanced.

Lawrence Foster, a well-known non-LDS scholar of nineteenth-century American new religious movements and one-time president of the Mormon History Association, was the most critical presenter. Foster had previously written about Jerald and Sandra in a journal article for *Dialogue: A Journal of Mormon Thought*.[2] Nevertheless, he was willing to grant that "the Tanners have been far more than sim-ply gadflies, in curious and in often indirect ways I think their work has helped to stimulate serious Mormon historical scholarship." He also said that the Tanners had been "meticulous" and "scrupulous" with regard to factual accuracy, "even though they may have their interpretations." Foster spoke of how "Jerald in particular was a bril-liant analyst of detail, with an almost uncanny ability to spot textual inconsistencies that demand explanation."

Foster, like other critics of the Tanners, expressed impatience with their belief that any religion other than their own was inade-quate. He also repeated the common assertion that had Jerald and Sandra applied the same scrutiny to Christianity as they had to Mormonism, they would have seen that it was no more or less true than the LDS Church. Sandra took issue with this, arguing, "One can say we didn't look at [Christianity] hard enough, because we didn't end up with your conclusion, but that's not the same as saying we didn't look at it."

Allen Roberts, coauthor of the 1988 book *Salamander*, an ac-count of the Mark Hofmann forgeries and murders, told how his view of the Tanners changed as his own faith changed. As a believ-ing Mormon, Roberts had viewed the Tanners as the enemy. But as he became more of a secular humanist, he felt that "the Tanners and I were stuck with the same affliction, the need to pursue the truth, even with the small t that transcended our need to conform to the belief system of our youth." Roberts came to know the Tanners while

---

2. Foster, "Career Apostates."

researching the Hofmann case. His presentation was not entirely uncritical of the Tanners, but it was affirming of them as individuals, finding the Tanners to be "kind, friendly people, Christian in their behavior and demeanor, good Samaritans." He regretted the recent "loss of gentle Jerald Tanner."

Will Bagley, author and editor of over a dozen books on Mormonism and the West, spoke of his friendship with the Tanners over the years, and he rejected the oft-applied label of "anti-Mormon" to them. "The work is born out of love," he said, and although he and other historians had no love for rank-and-file anti-Mormons, they felt Jerald and Sandra were different.[3] Bagley especially praised Jerald for his integrity during the Hofmann years. "I believe," he said, "that the honesty and integrity that was reflected when he rejected a piece of evidence that could have been easily used as a cudgel or a support for many of the Tanners' basic arguments reflects a commitment to the truth that all of us as historians no matter what our faith or religious commitments must honor."

Bagley openly wondered if Foster, because of his criticisms, was trying to curry favor with the LDS Church for access or funding. Bagley's comments were taken in stride, and any tension in the room soon dissipated. Despite Bagley's conciliatory remarks, there was little doubt that Foster clearly saw himself as the representative on the panel of a critical scholar who assumed that all religious claims weren't true or untrue but matters of personal taste, like preferences in food or art, making it better not "to convert individuals from one faith to another. But ... to encourage individuals to explore the positives and the potential of their own faiths, and if you will to become better Catholics, Methodists, Mormons, Jews, Muslims, Buddhists, whatever." Foster branded the Tanners "career apostates," the same title he used in his *Dialogue* article, asking, "Why would individuals [devote] their entire lives, adult lives, to attacking a faith in which they had once deeply believed. This is actually quite an unusual phenomenon. It requires a certain dedication, or firmness, to barrel ahead where others wouldn't go." In this Foster seemed to miss the fact that many Mormons who cease to believe in the doctrines of

---

3. Bigler, "More Than a Beacon," 257.

the LDS Church or question its authority continue to engaged in research and writing and speaking on Mormonism, sometimes critically, sometimes even affectionately, for the rest of their lives.[4] It's not just about being part of the Mormon Church, it's about being part of the Mormon people. In her response Sandra pointed out that Foster's ivory-tower perspective didn't adequately deal with the realities of what it meant and means to be a Mormon:

> Mormonism asked so much more of people than preferences in art or food—give up your wife, your bank account, your daughter, kill in the name of God, march across a wild frontier for it. If Mormonism isn't true, setting aside the eternal question, just what it inflicted on my ancestors is enough to demand an accounting.[5]

But Foster's challenge did touch on a point Sandra herself had been thinking about. Now that Jerald was gone, must she continue? She saw herself as Jerald's lifelong supporter. Certainly she believed in the work, offered feedback, printed pamphlets and books, sold them, acted as the public face of the ministry. And yet, hadn't it been basically *his* work? Should she continue? As time passed, as more speaking and interview requests poured in, as more Mormons kept wanting to talk to her about their faith crises, Sandra began to feel that this was not only Jerald's life calling. Perhaps God still had a plan for her in it. Maybe she could continue to embrace the life she had lived over so many years as her own, even now that Jerald was gone.

Clarity came when she was invited to speak at the Kauai Christian Fellowship in Hawaii in September 2007. The organizers covered the expenses for Sandra and her sister Carolyn so that Sandra might have a traveling companion. After Sandra spoke, the sisters went to the Big Island at their own expense and checked into the Keauhou Beach Hotel, a favorite place filled with memories of her and Jerald together. "When I picture Jerald in my mind," Sandra recalled, "I see him standing alone on the rocks watching the waves come in on

---

4. Including, for example, David Bigler, Will Bagley, Ed Decker, D. Michael Quinn, Lavina Fielding Anderson, Dan Vogel, Brent Metcalfe, Dennis and Rauni Higley, Grant Palmer, H. Michael Marquardt, Sterling McMurrin, and Thelma "Granny" Geer, to name but a few.

5. Tanner, Reminiscences.

the Big Island."[6] Jerald had been cremated, and Sandra had brought some of his ashes along. Early one morning, she went out alone and scattered them on those same rocks.

When Sandra returned home, she was ready to start work again. But now it was her calling. She still ran the store and wrote the newsletters, although she asked guest authors to contribute on occasion.[7] There was never a lack of newsworthy items, and in the absence of Jerald's ongoing research there was finally time for Sandra to synthesize their work over the years into broader articles. This still required research, however, and Sandra struggled to find the time to keep everything going. She explained, "I have had to assume Jerald's role, it is very hard for me to do both jobs. Before Jerald and I were two halves of a whole. Jerald was the researcher and I was the public person and ran the bookstore and the business. And it took both of us to do all of that."[8]

While Sandra's life changed and evolved, Mormonism was also evolving. More LDS Church members than ever were finding their faith upended by information they found on the web. But instead of the internet and the availability of documents making the Tanners' work irrelevant, it brought more questioners to Sandra. One example highlighted the new challenges facing the LDS Church. Some of the Tanners' old work was found by a member of an LDS congregation in Bremen, Germany, who was disturbed by the various First Vision accounts, changes in the revelations in the Doctrine and Covenants, and problems with the Book of Mormon.

Another member translated portions of the Tanners' material into German and distributed it, which led to "a wave of apostasy." The local LDS mission president tried to address the problem at a meeting. But instead of diving into the history and reassuring his listeners, his answers did not address the specific concerns posed to him. When the mission president was pressed, he defined truth as "whatever the prophet says, if he is not mistaken."[9] Thirty members left the ward, including two former bishops and a former branch president.

---

6. Tanner, Reminiscences.
7. See, e.g., various issues of the *Salt Lake City Messenger*, 2011–present.
8. Comments delivered at "Critical Vision" session in the 2007 Sunstone Symposium.
9. Dittberner, "One Hundred Eighteen Years of Attitude," 68.

Most of those who left had been "long active in responsible church positions such as branch and district presidencies, district and stake high councils." The result was that "the Delmonhorst Branch was subsequently dissolved."

Another prominent example also involved Europe, but this one ensnared Hans Mattsson, an LDS area authority seventy, a calling higher than a bishop or a stake president. Mattsson, a Swedish Mormon, called the internet "the Crystal Ball," because "you can't hide anything, everything is there."[10] Mattsson began investigating the historical claims of the LDS Church when members who had been troubled by information they found on the internet came to him with questions. Eventually, Mattsson called on the church for help and a meeting was arranged with Apostle L. Tom Perry. At the meeting, Perry claimed he had a manuscript in his briefcase that "once it was published, would prove all the doubters wrong."[11] The promised text never appeared, and when Mattsson asked Perry about it later, "he was told it was impertinent to ask."[12] That kind of answer was no longer enough. Mattsson organized an internet group with around 600 members, mostly from Sweden like himself, where troubling issues could be discussed. In 2010 official LDS Church historians Marlin Jensen and Richard Turley were dispatched on what came to be called the Swedish Rescue Mission. It was not the catastrophe that the intervention in Bremen, Germany, had been, but it did not stem the tide of questions, doubts, and, in some cases, members leaving the faith.

The LDS Church's response to this upheaval has been a partial but significant reversal of past policies to sequester and restrict information. Instead, the church has embarked on an ambitious publishing campaign to reframe information that is potentially troubling to members. It has published thirteen Gospel Topics Essays online that navigate controversial issues like polygamy, the

---

10. Channon Hodge, "A Mormon Doubts," *New York Times*, July 21, 2013.

11. Laurie Goodstein, "Some Mormons Search the Web and Find Doubt," *New York Times*, July 20, 2013.

12. In response, the church said that Perry "recalled satisfying their questions with a letter written by the church's history department." Goodstein, "Some Mormons Search the Web."

Book of Abraham, women's roles, and racism.[13] It has whetted the appetites of historians and scholars by releasing documents housed in the First Presidency office for so long they gained their own mystique, such as the Nauvoo Council of Fifty Minutes and the journals of Apostle George Q. Cannon.[14] In 2001 the church announced the founding of the Joseph Smith Papers project and later the establishment of the Church Historian's Press in February 2008. The first volume of the Smith Papers project, released on December 1, 2008, was Joseph Smith's journals from 1832–39.[15] The journals included information that earlier apostles had excoriated the Tanners for seeking out and publishing.

The church's publications, especially those online or otherwise aimed at believing members, are not intended as neutral evaluations of its own history, anymore than the Tanners' writings on the church may be called neutral. Just as Jerald wrote to persuade Latter-day Saints to come to Christ, the church's recent publications are written to persuade members to stay in the Mormon fold. But the church has now started publicly acknowledging the basic facts of its past, of changes to revelations, of Joseph Smith's use of a seerstone to translate the plates, of polygamy, of racism, and of violence in early Utah. It is a shift in direction from when the Tanners first started publishing that is nothing short of remarkable.

As the internet has brought information into LDS homes in new and unprecedented ways, podcasts have emerged to tell stories, detached from the official church and uncorrelated. One podcast Hans Mattsson discovered was John Dehlin's popular *Mormon Stories*.[16] Dehlin has a controversial manner; he developed a large following and his reach today extends beyond his podcast to blogs, publishing, and retreats with popular speakers. His podcast initially began as an inquisitive but faithful endeavor. He spoke to believing LDS historians, and even apologists who were critical of Jerald and Sandra

---

13. "Gospel Topics Essays," Church of Jesus Christ of Latter-day Saints, www.churchofjesuschrist.org.

14. See Grow et al., *Council of Fifty*; Cannon, Journal.

15. Jessee, Ashurst-McGee, and Jensen, *Journals, Volume 1*.

16. "Hans Mattsson—Former LDS Area Authority Seventy (Sweden)," interview by John Dehlin, *Mormon Stories*, nos. 430–34, www.mormonstories.org; Goodstein, "Some Mormons Search the Web."

Tanner. But he also interviewed Latter-day Saints who were experiencing crises of faith, which proved a counterbalance to the way both the institutional church and rank-and-file Mormons sometimes demonize those who question LDS beliefs. Over time, Dehlin shifted to more and more critical interviews, and his own beliefs seemed unorthodox at best. On February 9, 2015, he was excommunicated. It made national news and his influence has not faded.

Dehlin interviewed Sandra in 2014 and posted the interview online between May 9 and June 4.[17] The appearance greatly increased Sandra's visibility, and she suddenly found herself in demand more than ever by Mormons anxious to talk about hard questions in their faith. It helped that Sandra came across as a reasonable, friendly person who was nevertheless very frank, but who was also an expert who had already decades ago worked her way through questions people are now facing. She long ago lost count of how many people have visited her bookstore to talk to her after they listened to her interview with Dehlin.

A generation of Mormons has grown up surrounded by information that the Tanners published long ago, information that earlier generations of Latter-day Saints were denied, at least by the institutional church. In 2016, Sandra was, for the first time, invited formally as a presenter at the Salt Lake Sunstone Symposium. She gave a paper on plagiarism in the Book of Mormon, and appeared on a panel on "Repairing and Preserving Relationships Damaged by Faith Crises." Some of the people who attended the digital version of the Sunstone Symposium during the Covid lockdown of 2020 were not even born yet when the Metropolitan Museum gave the LDS Church the Book of Abraham Papyri, when Mark Hofmann murdered two people, or when six prominent LDS scholars were excommunicated in 1993.[18] In 2021 Sandra appeared along with many of the original players in the drama surrounding the Hofmann forgeries and murders in the powerfully moving Netflix series "Murder among the Mormons." That same year

---

17. "Sandra (and Jerald) Tanner," interview by John Dehlin, *Mormon Stories*, nos. 472–75, www.mormonstories.org.

18. For more on the scholars who were excommunicated, see "Six Intellectuals Excommunicated for Apostasy," *Sunstone*, Nov. 1993, 65–73.

she participated on a panel at the Mormon History Association about Hofmann, alongside Richard Turley, the LDS Public Affairs spokesperson. In many ways, it's a new world.

EPILOGUE:
FRIDAY MARCH 9, 2018

It is near closing time and Sandra is exhausted. It has been eleven years since Jerald passed away and things have not slowed down, even though she is now seventy-seven. People still stop by to talk to her, to ask questions, to argue, to say thank you, or just to be able to say they met Sandra Tanner. She still works in the bookstore most weekdays, with help from her employees and volunteers Bill McKeever and Eric Johnson. When it comes time to print the latest edition of the *Messenger*, the very mild Wendell Crothers still drives over from Nebraska to help with the printing and update the bookkeeping.

She hoped, vainly as it turned out, that today would be quiet so that she could spend time working on an upcoming presentation, part of a six-part series of lectures she is giving at her and Jerald's church, Discovery Christian Community. Last Sunday an atheist attended her previous lecture and afterward put up a post entitled "Sandra Tanner: Our Rock Star...." "As an atheist," he said, "there are few things that ever tempt me to go within the walls of any church, but to listen to someone as iconic as Sandra is the exception I always make." Sandra still travels a fair bit and speaks to much larger audiences, but she put a lot of work into these lectures, which are being filmed and placed on the internet. But instead of working on the presentation, as she hoped, she spends the day entertaining visitors of every kind. In the morning, a film crew from French Television showed up unannounced wanting an interview. They were in Salt Lake City for a story on Mormonism and were told by Richard Packham, founder of the Ex-Mormon Foundation, that Sandra is someone they need to talk to. Like Wallace Turner more than half a century ago they are glad they came and find Sandra's answers seemed more straightforward and direct than those of the church representatives they talked to.

As she is interviewed, a group of students from Azusa Pacific University appear, again unannounced, wondering if Sandra could talk to them about Mormonism. She said she could, but that they would have to wait a few minutes. Sandra speaks to a lot of college groups and Christian mission teams that come to Utah, especially in the spring, though usually with advance notice. After hearing Sandra, one of the students from Azusa wrote to her telling how, when she told her mother she had heard Sandra speak, her mother said she had left Mormonism many years before as a twenty-year-old college student after reading *The Changing World of Mormonism*.[1]

In the afternoon, a Tongan couple stop by. The husband, who says he is the descendant of one of Mormonism's earliest Tongan converts, is leaving Mormonism in part after listening to Sandra's presentations on the internet. Now he wants his wife to meet Sandra and hear what she has to say. Near the end of the day, Sandra feels punchy and worn out. Maybe she could go home, have something to eat, and decompress watching a mystery show on television. The day had not gone as planned, but it had still been good.

And so things continued day in and day out for two more years until she finally was able to slow down a bit as a result of Covid lockdowns.

Now, at eighty, Sandra still hasn't retired, but she is starting to feel that perhaps the time to do so might not be too far off. For a time she had hoped that someone might take over and continue the work, but by now she has come to terms with the fact that that probably isn't going to happen. Still she has a real sense that her work, and Jerald's work, is complete.

The ministry still has its detractors from both the Mormon and evangelical communities, although fewer perhaps than in the past. Angry Mormons have swapped letters for emails. One told her not long ago that she will join Jerald in outer darkness because she has "accepted the antichrist as your savior, Satan."[2] Sandra has long come

---

1. Caroline Williams to Sandra Tanner, Mar. 10, 2018, 1, in Tanner and Tanner, Papers.
2. Email to Sandra Tanner, Feb. 7, 2018, Tanner and Tanner, Papers.

to recognize these for what they are: an excuse to lash out at her clothed in the language of righteousness and concern over her soul.

Toward the end of his *Mormon Stories* interview with Sandra, John Dehlin asked, "Have you seen people leave Mormonism and find joy?"[3]

"Yes," Sandra said, a smile spreading across her face.

"Is it rare?"

"No."

---

3. "Sandra (and Jerald) Tanner, interview by John Dehlin, *Mormon Stories*, no. 475, 1:06:26–28.

BIBLIOGRAPHY

Allen, James B. "The Significance of Joseph Smith's 'First Vision' in Mormon Thought." *Dialogue: A Journal of Mormon Thought* 1, no. 3 (Autumn 1966): 29–45.

Allen, Thomas George, ed. *The Egyptian Book of the Dead Documents in the Oriental Institute Museum at the University of Chicago*. University of Chicago Oriental Institute Publications no. 82. Chicago: University of Chicago Press, 1960.

Anderson, Lavina Fielding, ed. *Lucy's Book: A Critical Edition of Lucy Mack Smith's Family Memoir*. Salt Lake City: Signature Books, 2001.

Angell, Avery F. *Genealogy of the Descendants of Thomas Angell, Who Settled in Providence, 1636*. Providence: A. Crawford Greene, 1872.

Angell, Israel. *Diary of Colonel Israel Angell: Commanding the Second Rhode Island Continental Regiment during the American Revolution 1778–1781*. Edited by Edward Field. Providence: Preston and Rounds, 1899.

Angell, Thomas O. "Autobiography of Truman Osborn Angell."

Annis, J. Lee, Jr. *Howard Baker: Conciliator in an Age of Crisis*. 2nd ed. Knoxville: University of Tennessee Press, 2007.

Anonymous. *Jerald and Sandra Tanner's Distorted View of Mormonism: A Response to* Mormonism: Shadow or Reality? [Salt Lake City]: N.p., 1977.

Arrington, Leonard J. *Adventures of a Church Historian*. Urbana: University of Illinois Press, 1998.

———. *Confessions of a Mormon Historian: The Diaries of Leonard J. Arrington, 1971–1997*. Edited by Gary James Bergera. 3 vols. Salt Lake City: Signature Books, 2018.

Ashment, Edward H. "The Facsimiles of the Book of Abraham: A Reappraisal." *Sunstone* 4, nos. 5–6 (Dec. 1979): 33–48

Atiya, Aziz S. "The Discovery and Date of the Joseph Smith Papyri." In Tvedtnes, *Book of Abraham Symposium*.

Avigad, Nahum, and Yigael Yadin. *A Genesis Apocryphon: A Scroll from the Wilderness of Judaea*. Jerusalem: Magnes Press of the Hebrew University, 1956.

Ayton, Mel. *The Dark Soul of the South: The Life and Crimes of Racist Killer Joseph Paul Franklin*. Washington: Potomac Books, 2011.

Backman, Milton V. *Joseph Smith's First Vision: The First Vision in Its Historical Context*. Salt Lake City: Bookcraft, 1971.

Backus, Isaac. *Church History of New England from 1620–1804*. Philadelphia: American Baptist Publication and S. S. Society, 1844.

———. *A History of New England with Particular Reference to the Denomination of Christians Called Baptists, Vol. 1*. 2nd. ed., with notes by David Weston. Newton MA; Isaac Backus Historical Society, 1871.

Baer, Klaus. "The Breathing Permit of Hôr: A Translation of the Apparent Source of the Book of Abraham." *Dialogue: A Journal of Mormon Thought* 3, no. 3 (Autumn 1968): 109–34.

Bagley, Will. *Blood of the Prophets: Brigham Young and the Massacre at Mountain Meadows*. Norman, OK: University of Oklahoma Press, 2002.

Baptists in Early America III: Newport, Rhode Island, Seventh Day Baptists. Edited by Janet Thorngate; Macon, GA: Mercer University Press / Seventh Day Baptist Historical Society, 2017.

Barlett, Donald L., and James B. Steele. *Howard Hughes: His Life and Madness*. New York: W. W. Norton, 2011.

Bart, Peter. *Thy Kingdom Come*. New York: The Linden Press, 1981.

Belnap, Daniel L. "The King James Bible and the Book of Mormon." In *The King James Bible and the Restoration*, edited by Kent P. Jackson, 162–81. Provo: Religious Studies Center, 2011.

Bennett, Rick. *Gospel Tangents Interview: Anne Wilde, Expert on Modern Day Polygamy*. San Bernardino: Gospel Tangents, 2017.

Bergera, Gary James. "The 1966 BYU Student Spy Ring." *Utah Historical Quarterly* 79, no. 2 (2011): 164–88.

———. "Dissent in Zion: Jerald and Sandra Tanner." Unpublished manuscript, 1978.

———. "Tensions in David O. McKay's Presidencies." *Journal of Mormon History* 33, no. 1 (Spring 2007): 209–41.

———. "'This Time of Crisis': The Race-Based Anti-BYU Athletic Protests of 1968–1971." *Utah Historical Quarterly* 81, no. 3 (Summer 2013): 204–29.

Bernstein, Carl, and Bob Woodward. *All the President's Men*. 40th Anniversary Edition. New York: Simon & Schuster, 2014.

Berrett, LaMar C. *The Wilford C. Wood Collection: An Annotated Catalog of Documentary-Type Materials in the Wilford C. Wood Collection*. N.p.: Wilford C. Wood Foundation, 1972.

Berrett, William E. "The Church and the Negroid People." In John J. Stewart, *Mormonism and the Negro*. Bountiful: Horizons, 1978.

Bigler, David L. "More Than a Beacon: A Tribute to Jerald and Sandra Tanner." In *Confessions of a Revisionist Historian: David L. Bigler on the Mormons and the West*, edited by Will Bagley, 253–58. Salt Lake City: Tanner Trust and J. Willard Marriott Library, 2015.

Bitton, Davis. "Ten Years in Camelot: A Personal Memoir." *Dialogue: A Journal of Mormon Thought* 16, no. 3 (Autumn 1983): 9–33.

Black, Robert R. "Bibliography on Jerald and Sandra Tanner and the Modern Microfilm Co." Unpublished BYU library science paper, May 25, 1970.

Bradley, Don. *The Lost 116 Pages: Reconstructing the Book of Mormon's Missing Stories*. Salt Lake City: Greg Kofford Books, 2020.

Bringhurst, Newell G. "A Biography of a Biography: The Research and Writing of *No Man Knows My History*." In Newell G. Bringhurst, ed. Reconsidering No Man Knows My History: *Fawn M. Brodie and Joseph Smith in Retrospect*. Logan: Utah State University Press, 1996.

———. *Fawn McKay Brodie: A Biographer's Life*. Norman: University of Oklahoma Press, 1999.

———. *Saints, Slaves, and Blacks: The Changing Place of Black People within Mormonism*. 2nd ed. Salt Lake City: Greg Kofford Books, 2018.

Brinkley, Douglas, and Luke A. Nichter. *The Nixon Tapes: 1973*. New York: Houghton Mifflin Harcourt, 2015.

Brodie, Fawn M. *No Man Knows My History: The Life of Joseph Smith the Mormon Prophet*. New York: Alfred A Knopf, 1946.

Brooks, Juanita, *Mountain Meadows Massacre*. 2nd ed. Norman: University of Oklahoma Press, 1962.

Brown, Robert, and Rosemary Brown. *They Lie in Wait to Deceive*. 4 vols. Mesa: Brownsworth, 1981–95.

Brown, Samuel. "The Translator and the Ghostwriter: Joseph Smith and W. W. Phelps." *Journal of Mormon History* 34, no. 1 (Winter 2008): 26–62.

Brunsman, Frank. "From Lynchings to Legal Rights: Historian Traces Part of Utah Blacks." Unpublished paper, Sep. 20, 1976.

Budge, E. A. Wallace. *Easy Lessons in Egyptian Hieroglyphics: With Sign List*. London: Kegan Paul, Trench, Trübner, 1899.

———. *Egyptian Hieroglyphic Dictionary*. 2 vols. London: John Murray, 1920.

Bugliosi, Vincent. *Reclaiming History: The Assassination of President John F. Kennedy*. New York: W. W. Norton, 2007.

Burgess, Walter H. *John Smyth the Se-Baptist, Thomas Helwys and the First Baptist Church in England, With Fresh Light Upon the Pilgrim Fathers' Church*. London: James Clarke, 1911.

Bush, Lester E. "Ethical Issues in Reproductive Medicine: A Mormon Perspective." *Dialogue: A Journal of Mormon Thought* 18, no. 2 (Summer 1985): 41–66.

———. "The Spalding Theory: Then and Now." *Dialogue: A Journal of Mormon Thought* 10, no. 3 (Autumn 1977): 40–69.

———. "Writing 'Mormonism's Negro Doctrine: An Historical Overview': Context and Reflections, 1998." *Journal of Mormon History* 25, no. 1 (Spring 1999): 229–71.

Bushman, Richard Lyman. *Joseph Smith: Rough Stone Rolling*. With Jed Woodworth. New York: Alfred A. Knopf, 2005,

Callender, John. *An Historical Discourse, on the Civil and Religious Affairs of the Colony of Rhode Island*. Newport: S. Kneeland & T. Green, 1739.

335

Campbell, Douglas. "'White' and 'Pure': Five Vignettes." *Dialogue: A Journal of Mormon Thought* 29, no. 4 (Winter 1996): 119–35.

Cannon, George Q. The Journal of George Q. Cannon, 1849–1901. Online typescript. Salt Lake City: Church Historian's Press, churchhistorians-press.org/george-q-cannon.

Caranci, Paul F. "Mary Ann Angell Young." In *North Providence: A History and the People Who Shaped It*, 68–70. Charleston: The History Press, 2012.

Carter, Jared. Journal, 1831–1833. Typescript, MS 1441. CHL.

Carter, Kate B. *Denominations that Base Their Beliefs on the Teachings of Joseph Smith*. Salt Lake City: Daughters of Utah Pioneers, 1962.

———*Our Pioneer Heritage*. 20 vols. Salt Lake City: Daughters of Utah Pioneers, 1957–77.

Chaplin, Jeremiah. *Life of Henry Dunster: First President of Harvard College*. Boston: James R. Osgood, 1872.

Cheesman, Paul R. "An Analysis of the Accounts Relating Joseph Smith's Early Visions." Master's thesis, Brigham Young University, 1965.

———. *The Keystone of Mormonism: Early Visions of the Prophet Joseph Smith*. Provo: Eagle Systems International, 1988.

Christenson, Ross T. *Mummies, Scrolls, and the Book of Abraham*. Provo: Brigham Young University, n.d.

Church Historian's Office. History of the Church, 1839–ca. 1882. CR 100 102, CHL.

Clark, James R. "History and Translation of the Book of Abraham." In *Pearl of Great Price Conference*, conference held Dec. 10, 1961, 60–61. Provo: Brigham Young University Department of Extension Publications, 1964.

———. *The Story of the Pearl of Great Price*. Salt Lake City: Bookcraft, 1955.

———. *Study Guide of the "Story of the Pearl of Great Price."* Provo: Brigham Young University Department of Extension Publications, 1963.

Clark, John A. *Gleanings by the Way*. Philadelphia, PA: W. J. & J. K. Simon/ New York: Robert Carter, 1842.

Clarke, John. *Ill Newes from New-England: Or a Narrative of New-Englands Persecution ... Confirmed and Justified*. London: Henry Hills, 1652.

Colson, Charles W. *Born Again*. Grand Rapids, MI: Chosen Books, 2008, orig. 1976. 218.

Cook, Lyndon W., ed. *David Whitmer Interviews: A Restoration Witness*. Orem: Grandin Books, 1991.

Cowdery, Oliver [forgery]. *Defence in a Rehearsal of My Grounds for Separating Myself from the Latter Day Saints*. Norton, Ohio: Pressley's Job Office, 1839.

Cowdrey, Wayne L., Howard A. Davis, and Donald R. Scales. *Who Really Wrote the Book of Mormon?* Santa Ana, CA: Vision House Publishers, 1977. 2005 edition by Cowdrey, Davis, and Art Vanick, St. Louis: Concordia.

Crapo, Richley. "Emic and Etic Studies: The Proper Approach to the Book of Abraham." In Tvedtnes, *Book of Abraham Symposium*.

Crowley, Aleister. *The Book of the Law*. London: Ordo Templi Orientis, 1938.

————. *O.T.O. Ecclesiae Gnosticae Catholicae Canon Missae. The Equinox 3.1* (1919).

————. *The Confessions of Aleister Crowley: An Autobiography*. Edited by John Symonds and Kenneth Grant. London: Jonathan Cape, 1969. Originally published as 2 vols., 1929.

————. "The Ship." *The Equinox* 1, no. 10 (1913).

Davidson, Karen Lynn, David J. Whittaker, Mark Ashurst-McGee, and Richard L. Jensen, eds. *The Joseph Smith Papers: Histories, Volume 1: Joseph Smith Histories, 1832–1844*. Salt Lake City: Church Historian's Press, 2012.

Davis, Andrew McFarland. *Bibliographical Contributions, No. 50: An Analysis of the Early Records of Harvard College, 1636–1750*. Cambridge: Library of Harvard University, 1895.

Davis, France. *Light in the Midst of Zion: A History of Black Baptists in Utah: 1892–1996*. Salt Lake City: Empire Publishing, 1997.

Dean, John. *Blind Ambition: The Whitehouse Years*. New York: Simon and Schuster, 1976.

Deane, Charles, ed. *Some Notices of Samuel Gorton, One of the First Settlers of Warwick, R. I. … with a Brief Introductory Memoir*. Boston: Coolidge and Wiley, 1850.

Decker, Ed. *My Kingdom Come: The Mormon Quest for Godhood*. Maitland, FL: Xylon Press, 2007.

Decker, Ed, and Bill Schnoebelen. "The Lucifer–God Doctrine: Shadow or Reality?" Unpublished response to the Tanners, ca. Dec. 1987.

Decker, Ed, and Dave Hunt. *The God Makers: A Shocking Expose of What the Mormon Church Really Believes*. Eugene, OR: Harvest House, 1984.

Denison, Fredric. *Westerly (Rhode Island) and Its Witnesses, for Two Hundred and Fifty Years*. Providence: J. A. & R. A. Reid, 1878.

Deseret News. Salt Lake City, 1850–present. Also published as *Deseret Evening News, Deseret Weekly*, and *Deseret Semi-Weekly*.

Dew, Sheri L. *Go Forward with Faith: The Biography of Gordon B. Hinckley*. Salt Lake City: Deseret Book, 1996.

Dexter, Henry Martyn. *As to Roger Williams, and his 'Banishment' from the Massachusetts Plantation … a Monograph*. Boston: Congregational Publishing Society, 1876.

Dittberner, Jörg. "One Hundred Eighteen Years of Attitude: The History of The Church of Jesus Christ of Latter-Day Saints in the Free and Hanseatic City of Bremen." *Dialogue: A Journal of Mormon Thought* 36, no. 1 (Spring 2003): 51–70.

Document Containing the Correspondence, Orders, &c. in Relation to the Disturbances with the Mormons … and other Crimes Against the State. Fayette, MO: Boon's Lick Democrat, 1841.

Dry, Sarah. *Curie*. London: Haus Publishing, 2003.

Dunster, Samuel. *Henry Dunster and His Descendants*. Central Falls, RI: E. L. Freeman, 1876.

Durham, Reed, Jr. "Institute of Religion Faculty Forum." Paper of Mar. 7, 1972. Reed Durham Papers, 1828–1998. Accn0444, box 18, fd. 5, Marriott Library Special Collections, University of Utah.

Dyer, Alvin R. "For What Purpose." Unpublished typescript of a talk given at a missionary conference in Oslo, Norway, Mar. 18, 1962.

Dykman, Judy, and Coleen Whitley. "Settling in Salt Lake City." In *Brigham Young's Homes*, edited by Colleen Whitley, 82–123. Logan: Utah State University Press, 2002.

Early, Joe, Jr. ed. *The Life and Writings of Thomas Helwys*. Macon: Mercer University Press, 2009.

Edwards, Don. "Watergate Hearings, Book II, Vol. I: Events following the Watergate break-in, June 17, 1972 - February 9, 1973 (allegations involving Presidential interference with the official Department of Justice investigation)." Digital collection of Congressman Don Edwards Watergate papers, Mabie Law Library, Santa Clara University School of Law. Online at https://digitalcommons.law.scu.edu/watergate.

Elders' Journal of the Church of Jesus Christ of Latter-day Saints. Kirtland, 1837–38.

Encyclopedia of Genealogy and Biography of the State of Pennsylvania. 2 vols. New York & Chicago: Lewis Publishing, 1902–04.

Evening and Morning Star. Independence, 1832–34.

Everett, James A. *The Making and Breaking of an American Spy*. Durham, CT: Strategic Book Group, 2011.

Faulring, Scott Harry. "An Oral History of Modern Microfilm Company, 1959–1982." Senior thesis, Brigham Young University, Apr. 1983.

———, ed. *An American Prophet's Record: The Diaries and Journals of Joseph Smith*. Salt Lake City: Signature Books, 1989.

Felt, Mark, and John O'Conner. *A G-Man's Life: The FBI, Being 'Deep Throat,' and the Struggle for Honor in Washington*. Cambridge, MA: Perseus, 2006.

Final Report of the Senate Select Committee on Presidential Campaign Activities (June 1974), Washington: U. S. Government Printing Office, 1974.

Finney, Charles G. *The Memoirs of Charles G. Finney: The Complete Restored Text*. Annotated critical edition by Garth M. Rosell and Richard A.G. Dupuis. Grand Rapids, MI: Zondervan, 1989.

———. *Power from on High: Selections of Articles on the Spirit-Filled Life*. Eastbourne, Sussex: Victory, 1944.

Fisher, V. H. *The Godhead: A Discussion of the Godhead as Revealed in the Bible, Book of Mormon, and Doctrine and Covenants*. N.p.: n.p. 1953.

Fitch, Asa. *The Asa Fitch Papers*. 3 vols. Edited by Laura Penny Hulslander. Fort Campbell & Hopkinsville, KY: Sleeper Company, 1997–1998.

Flake, Chad. "Mormon Bibliography 1963." *BYU Studies* 5, nos. 3–4 (Spring/ Summer 1964): 241–45.

Foley, Janet Wethy. *Early Settlers of New York State: Their Ancestors and Descendants*. 6 vols. Akron, NY: by the author, 1934.

Foster, Lawrence. "Career Apostates: Reflections on the Works of Jerald and Sandra Tanner." *Dialogue: A Journal of Mormon Thought* 17, no. 2 (Summer 1984): 35–60.

Fox, George, and John Burnyeat. *A New-England Fire-Brand Quenched: Being Something in Answer … The Second Part*. [London], 1678.

Gardiner, Alan. *Egyptian Grammar: Being and Introduction to the Study of Hieroglyphics*. 3rd ed. Oxford: Griffiths Institute, Ashmolean Museum, 1957.

Gee, John. *Introduction to the Book of Abraham*. Provo: Religious Studies Center, Brigham Young University/Salt Lake City: Desert Books, 2017.

———. "A Tragedy of Errors." Review of *By His Own Hand upon Papyrus: A New Look at the Joseph Smith Papyri*, by Charles M. Larson. Review of Books on the Book of Mormon 4, no. 1 (1992): 93–119.

General Handbook of Instructions: Book 2: Administering to the Church 2010. Salt Lake City: The Church of Jesus Christ of Latter-day Saints, 2010.

Goldman, Shalom. "Joshua/James Seixas (1802–1874): Jewish Apostasy and Christian Hebraism in Early Nineteenth-Century America." *Jewish History* 7, no. 1 (Spring 1993): 65–88.

Graff, Garrett M. *Watergate: A New History*. New York: Simon & Schuster, 2022.

Grover, Mark L. "The Mormon Priesthood Revelation and the São Paulo, Brazil, Temple." *Dialogue: A Journal of Mormon Thought* 23, no. 1 (Spring 1990): 39–53.

Grow, Matthew J., Ronald K. Esplin, Mark Ashurst-McGee, Gerrit J. Dirkmaat, and Jeffrey D. Mahas, eds. *The Joseph Smith Papers: Administrative Records, Volume 1: Council of Fifty, Minutes, March 1844–January 1846*. Salt Lake City: Church Historian's Press, 2016.

Guers, Emilius. *Irvingism and Mormonism: Tested from Scripture*. London: James Nisbet, 1854.

Guignebert, Charles. *Jesus*. Translated by S. H. Hooke. New Hyde Park, NY: University Books, 1958.

Hamilton, Alexander. *Gentleman's Progress: The Itinerarium of Dr. Alexander Hamilton: 1744*. Edited by Carl Bridenbaugh. Chapel Hill: University of North Carolina Press, 1948.

Hardy, B. Carmon. *Solemn Covenant: The Mormon Polygamous Passage*. Urbana: University of Illinois Press, 1992.

Harris, Matthew L., and Newell G. Bringhurst. *The Mormon Church and Blacks: A Documentary History*. Urbana: University of Illinois Press, 2015.

Hawley, John Pierce. "Autobiography of John Pierce Hawley." In *Innocent Blood: Essential Narratives of the Mountain Meadows Massacre*. Edited by David L. Bigler & Will Bagley. Norman, OK: Arthur H. Clarke, 2008.

Haws, J. B. *The Mormon Image in the American Mind: Fifty Years of Public Perception*. New York: Oxford University Press, 2013.

Heinerman, John, and Anson Shupe. *The Mormon Corporate Empire*. Boston: Beacon, 1985.

Heward, Grant S. *What about Joseph Smith's Egyptian Grammar?* Salt Lake City: Modern Microfilm, 1967.

Heward, Grant S., and Jerald Tanner. "The Source of the Book of Abraham Identified." *Dialogue: A Journal of Mormon Thought* 3, no. 2 (Summer 1968): 92–98.

Hill, Marvin. "The 'New Mormon History' Reassessed in Light of Recent Books on Joseph Smith and Mormon Origins." *Dialogue: A Journal of Mormon Thought* 21, no. 3 (Autumn 1988): 115–27.

Hopkins, Charles Wyman. *The Home Lots of the Early Settlers of the Providence Plantations, with Notes and Plats.* Providence: Providence Press, 1886.

Howe, Eber D. *Mormonism Unvailed.* Painsville, OH: By the author, 1834. Critical edition by Dan Vogel. Salt Lake City: Signature Books, 2015.

Huggins, Ronald V. "Did the Author of 3 Nephi Know the Gospel of Matthew?" *Dialogue: A Journal of Mormon Thought* 30, no. 3 (Fall 1997): 137–48.

Humboldt, Wilhelm von. *Researches Concerning the Institutions and Monuments of the Ancient Inhabitants of America* (2 vols.; trans. Helen Maria Williams; London, UK: Longman, Hurst, Rees, Orme & Brown, J. Murray & H. Colburn, 1814).

Hunsaker, Blaine, Randi Hunsaker, Donald Meyer, and Gwenda Meyer. "The Tanner Problem." Unpublished paper, July 16, 1990.

Hunt, E. Howard. *Undercover: Memoirs of an American Secret Agent.* New York: Berkley, 1974.

Hunt, E. Howard, with Greg Aunapu. *American Spy: My Secret History in the CIA, Watergate & Beyond.* Hoboken: Wiley, 2007.

Hunt, Howard St. John. *Dorothy "An Amoral and Dangerous Woman": The Murder of E. Howard Hunt's Wife—Watergate's Darkest Secret.* Fwd. Roger Stone. Waterville, OR: Trine Day, 2014.

Hutchinson, Anthony A. "Prophetic Foreknowledge: Hope and Fulfillment in an Inspired Community." In *The Word of God: Essays on Mormon Scripture,* Edited by Dan Vogel, 29–42. Salt Lake City: Signature Books, 1990.

Inquiry into the Alleged Involvement of the Central Intelligence Agency in the Watergate and Ellsberg Matters, Washington: U.S. Government Printing Office, 1975.

"An Interview with Dr. Fischer." *Dialogue: A Journal of Mormon Thought* 2, no. 4 (Winter 1967): 55–64.

Introvigne, Massimo. "The Devil Makers: Contemporary Evangelical Fundamentalism Anti-Mormonism." *Dialogue: A Journal of Mormon Thought* 27, no. 1 (Spring 1994): 153–68.

Janssen, Jac. J., comp. *Annual Egyptological Bibliography/Bibliographie Égyptologique Annuelle 1968.* Leiden, Brill, 1973.

Jensen, Robin Scott. "Joseph Smith's Chronicler: An Interview with Dean Jessee." *Mormon Historical Studies* 13, nos. 1–2 (Spring/Fall 2012):

Jensen, Robin Scott, Robert J. Woodford, Steven C. Harper. *The Joseph Smith Papers: Revelations and Translations: Manuscript Revelation Books, Facsimile Edition.* Salt Lake City: The Church Historians Press, 2009.

Jensen, Robin Scott, and Brian M. Hauglid, eds. *The Joseph Smith Papers: Revelations and Translations, Volume 4: Book of Abraham and Related Manuscripts, Facsimile Edition*. Salt Lake City: Church Historian's Press, 2018.

Jenson, Andrew. *Latter-day Saint Biographical Encyclopedia*. 4 vols. Salt Lake City: Andrew Jenson History, 1901–36.

Jerald Tanner, aka Modern Microfilm Company, v. the United States Department of Justice, Civil Action # C-81-0670 J.

Jessee, Dean C. "The Early Accounts of Joseph Smith's First Vision," *BYU Studies* 9, no. 3 (Spring 1969): 275–94.

———. "How Lovely Was the Morning," review of *Joseph Smith's First Vision: The First Vision in Its Historical Context*, by Milton V. Backman. *Dialogue: A Journal of Mormon Thought* 6, no. 1 (Spring 1971): 85–88.

———. "Joseph Knight's Recollection of Early Mormon History." *BYU Studies* 17, no. 1 (1976): 29–39.

———. "The Writing of Joseph Smith's History." *BYU Studies* 11, no. 4 (Summer 1971): 439–73.

Jessee, Dean C., Mark Ashurst-McGee, and Richard L. Jensen, eds. *The Joseph Smith Papers: Journals, Volume 1: 1832–1839*. Salt Lake City: Church Historian's Press, 2008.

Johanson, W. F. Walker. *What Is Mormonism All About?: Answers to the 150 Most Commonly Asked Questions about the Church of Jesus Christ of Latter-day Saints*. New York: St. Martin's Griffin, 2002.

Johnson, Crisfield. *History of Washington Co., New York: With Illustrations and Biographical Sketches of Some of Its Prominent Men and Pioneers*. Philadelphia: Everts & Ensign, 1878.

Johnson, Jeffery Ogden. "Determining and Defining 'Wife': The Brigham Young Households." *Dialogue: A Journal of Mormon Thought* 20, no. 3 (Fall 1987): 57–70.

Journal of Discourses. 26 vols. London: Latter-day Saints' Book Depot, 1854–86.

Kamil, Jill. *Labib Habachi: The Life and Legacy of an Egyptologist*. New York, Cairo: American University of Cairo Press, 2007.

Keats, Jonathan. *Forged: Why Fakes are the Great Art of Our Age*. New York: Oxford University Press, 2013.

Kepler, James. *The Jordan Beachhead: A Novel of Biblical Times*. New York: Exposition Press, 1956.

Kimball, Edward L. "Spencer W. Kimball and the Revelation on Priesthood." *BYU Studies* 47, no. 2 (2008): 4–78.

King, Henry Melville. *A Summer Visit of Three Rhode Islanders to the Massachusetts Bay in 1651*. Providence: Preston and Rounds, 1896.

Kirkham, Francis W. *A New Witness to Christ in America*. 2 vols. Salt Lake City: Utah Printing, 1942, 1951.

Kraut, Ogden. *Complaint Against Ogden Kraut*. N.p.: by the author, 1972.

Kutler, Stanley I. *The Wars of Watergate: The Last Crisis of Richard Nixon*. New York: W. W. Norton & Co., 1990.

Lamb, M. T. *The Golden Bible, or, The Book of Mormon: Is It from God?* New York: Ward & Drummond, 1887.

Latter-day Saints Millennial Star. Liverpool, 1840–1970.

Lee, John D. *Mormonism Unveiled: Or the Life and Confessions of the Late Mormon Bishop, John D. Lee ... and Crimes of the Mormon Church.* St. Louis: Sun, 1882.

Lemons, J. Stanley, ed. *Baptists in Early North America, Vol. II: First Baptist, Providence.* Macon: Mercer University Press, 2013.

Liddy, G. Gordon. *Will: The Autobiography of G. Gordon Liddy.* New York: St. Martin's Press, 1996.

Lindsey, Robert. *Gathering of the Saints: A True Story of Money, Murder and Deceit.* New York: Simon and Schuster, 1988.

MacKay, Michael Hubbard, and Gerrit J. Dirkmaat. *From Darkness unto Light: Joseph Smith's Translation and Publication of the Book of Mormon.* Salt Lake City: BYU Religious Studies Center and Deseret Book, 2015.

MacKay, Michael Hubbard, Gerrit J. Dirkmaat, Grant Underwood, Robert J. Woodford, and William G. Hartley, eds. *The Joseph Smith Papers: Documents, Volume 1: July 1828–June 1831.* Salt Lake City: The Church Historian's Press, 2013.

Magnesen, Gary. *Investigation: A Former FBI Agent Uncovers the Truth Behind Howard Hughes, Melvin Dummar and the Most Contested Will in American History.* Fort Lee, NJ: Barricade Books, 2005.

Marquardt, H. Michael. *The Joseph Smith Egyptian Papers: Includes Joseph Smith's Egyptian Alphabet and Grammar.* Salt Lake City: Modern Microfilm, 1981.

———. Papers, 1800–2017. Accn0900, Marriott Library Special Collections, University of Utah.

———. "A Tanner Bibliography, 1959–2014." Salt Lake City: by the author, 2014. Online at http://www.utlm.org.

Marsh, Christopher W. *The Family of Love in English Society, 1550–1630.* Cambridge: Cambridge University Press, 1994.

Marshall, Richard Stephen. "The New Mormon History." Senior honors thesis. University of Utah, 1977.

Martin, Walter. *The Maze of Mormonism.* 2nd ed. Ventura: Regal Publishing, 1978.

Massey, Gerald. *The Historical Jesus and the Mythical Christ: What Christianity Owes to Ancient Egypt.* London: The Pioneer Press, n.d.

Mather, Cotton. *Magnalia Christi Americana.* 7 books in 2 vols. London: Thomas Parkhurst, 1702.

Mather, Increase. *A Further Account of the Tryals of the New-England Witches,* London: J. Dunton, 1693.

May, Dean L. *Utah: A People's History.* Salt Lake City: University of Utah Press, 2002.

Mayfield, Steven L. Papers. Ms 3088, L. Tom Perry Special Collections, Harold B. Lee Library, Brigham Young University.

McConkie, Bruce R. *Mormon Doctrine*. Salt Lake City: Bookcraft, 1958.

McGee, Georgia. "Response to the First Vision Controversy," unpublished 1982.

McGlothlin, W. J. *Baptist Confessions of Faith*. Philadelphia: American Baptist Publication Society, 1911.

McNeill, John T. *The History and Character of Calvinism*. Oxford: Oxford University Press, 1954.

McNiece, Robert G. "Mormonism: It's Origin, Characteristics, and Doctrines." In *The Fundamentals: A Testimony to the Truth*. Vol. 4, 131–48. Los Angeles: Bible Institute of Los Angeles, 1917.

McPheters, Mike. *Agent Bishop: True Stories from an FBI Agent Moonlighting as a Mormon Bishop*. Springville, UT: Cedar Fort, 2009.

Melton, J. Gordon, ed. *The Encyclopedia of American Religions*. 2 vols. Wilmington, NC: McGrath, 1978.

Metcalfe, Brent Lee, ed. *New Approaches to the Book of Mormon: Explorations in Critical Methodology*. Salt Lake City: Signature Books, 1995.

Metzger, Bruce M. *A Textual Commentary on the Greek New Testament*. Corr. ed. New York: United Bible Society, 1975.

Morgan, Dale. *Dale Morgan on Early Mormonism: Correspondence & A New History*. Edited by John Phillip Walker. Salt Lake City: Signature Books, 1986.

Morris, Larry E. *A Documentary History of the Book of Mormon*. New York: Oxford University Press, 2019.

Morton, Nathaniel. *New-England's Memoriall: Or, a Brief Relation. …* Cambridge: S. G. and M. J., 1669.

Mueller, Max Perry. *Race and the Making of the Mormon People*. Chapel Hill: University of North Carolina Press, 2017.

Mullen, Robert. *The Latter-day Saints: The Mormons Yesterday and Today*. Garden City, NY: Doubleday, 1966.

Naifeh, Steven, and Gregory White Smith. *The Mormon Murders: A True Story of Greed, Forgery, Deceit, and Death*. New York: Weidenfeld and Nicholson, 1988.

Neibaur, Alexander. Journal, 1841–1862. MS 1674, CHL.

Nelson, Dee Jay. "The Book of Abraham Papyri." Transcript, 1975.

———. *The Joseph Smith Papyri Part 2: Additional Translations and a Supplemental Survey of the ta-shert-Min, Hor and Amen-Terp Papyri*. Salt Lake City: Modern Microfilm, 1968.

———. *A Translation & Study of Facsimile No. 3 in the Book of Abraham*. Salt Lake City: Modern Microfilm, 1969.

Nelson, Dee Jay, and David H. Coville. *Life Force of the Great Pyramids*. Marina del Rey: DeVorss, 1977.

Newell, Quincy D. *Your Sister in the Gospel: The Life of Jane Manning James, a Nineteenth-Century Black Mormon*. New York: Oxford University Press, 2019.

Nibley, Hugh. "Getting Ready to Begin: An Editorial." *BYU Studies* 8, no. 3 (1968): 245–54.

———. "The Meaning of the Kirtland Egyptian Papers." *BYU Studies* 11, no. 4 (Summer 1971): 350–99.

———. *The World and the Prophets*. Salt Lake City: Deseret Book, 1954.

Noll, Mark A. *The Civil War as a Theological Crisis*. Chapel Hill: The University of North Carolina Press, 2006.

Oberlin Evangelist. Oberlin, Ohio, 1838–62.

O'Donovan, Connell. "'Let This Be a Warning to All Niggers': The Life and Murder of Thomas Coleman in Theocratic Utah." Unpublished paper, 2008.

Oliphant, Mrs. [Margaret]. *Edward Irving, Minister of the National Scotch Church, London*. 2 vols. London: Hurst and Blackett, 1862.

Oliver, David H. *A Negro in Mormonism*. N.p.: n.p., 1963.

Oray, Georges. *An Analysis of Christian Origins*. Translated by C. Bradlaugh Bonner. London: The Secular Society, 1961.

Origen of Alexandria. *Commentary on the Gospel of John*. Washington, DC: Catholic University of America Press, 1989.

Owens, Lance S. "Joseph Smith and the Kabbalah: The Occult Connection." *Dialogue: A Journal of Mormon Thought* 27, no. 3 (Fall 1994): 117–94.

Parker, Richard A., trans. "The Book of Breathings (Fragment 1, the 'Sensen' Text, with Restorations from Louvre Papyrus 3284)." *Dialogue: A Journal of Mormon Thought* 3, no. 2 (Summer 1968): 98–99.

———. "The Joseph Smith Papyri: A Preliminary Report." *Dialogue: A Journal of Mormon Thought* 3, no. 2 (Summer 1968): 86–88.

Petersen, LaMar. *The Creation of the Book of Mormon: A Historical Inquiry*. Salt Lake City: Freethinkers Press, 2000.

———. "Memoirs of LaMar Petersen." Interviews by Kent Walgren. In Petersen, Papers, box 2.

———. Papers, 1829–2005. Ms0524, Marriott Library Special Collections, University of Utah.

———. *Problems in the Mormon Text*. Salt Lake City: n.p., 1957.

———. "Letter to the Editor." *Dialogue: A Journal of Mormon Thought* 1, no. 4 (Winter 1966): 9.

Petersen, Mark E. "Race Problems as They Affect the Church." Unpublished typescript of a talk given at a teachers convention, Aug. 27, 1954.

Peterson, H. Donl. *The Story of the Book of Abraham: Mummies, Manuscripts, and Mormonism*. Salt Lake City: Deseret Book, 1995.

Philagios, Nicholas. *Discourses of Nicholas Philagios*. Salt Lake City: by the author, 1961.

Prince, Gregory A. *Leonard Arrington and the Writing of Mormon History*. Salt Lake City: University of Utah Press, 2016.

Prince, Gregory A, and Wm. Robert Wright. *David O. McKay and the Rise of Modern Mormonism*. Salt Lake City: University of Utah Press, 2005.

Quinn, D. Michael. *Elder Statesman: A Biography of J. Reuben Clark*. Salt Lake City: Signature Books, 2002.

———. "LDS Church Authority and New Plural Marriages, 1890–1904." *Dialogue: A Journal of Mormon Thought* 18, no. 1 (Spring 1985): 9–105.

———. "The Mormon Hierarchy, 1832–1932: An American Elite." PhD. diss., Yale University, 1976.

———. *The Mormon Hierarchy: Extensions of Power.* Salt Lake City: Signature Books, 1997.

———. *The Mormon Hierarchy: Origins of Power.* Salt Lake City: Signature Books, 1994.

———. "Organizational Developments and Social Origins of the Mormon Hierarchy, 1832–1932: A Prosopographical Study." Master's thesis, University of Utah, 1973.

Reeve, W. Paul. *Religion of a Different Color: Race and the Mormon Struggle for Whiteness.* New York: Oxford University Press, 2015.

Report to the President by the Commission on CIA Activities Within the United States. Washington, DC: US Government Printing Office, 1975.

Richards, LeGrand. *Just to Illustrate.* Salt Lake City: Bookcraft, 1961.

Rigdon, Sidney. *Appeal to the American People: Being an Account of the Church of Latter Day Saint; and of the Barbarities Inflicted on Them by the Inhabitants of the State of Missouri.* Cincinnati: Glezen & Shepard, 1840.

Ritner, Robert K. "The 'Breathing Permit of Hôr' Thirty-Four Years Later." *Dialogue: A Journal of Mormon Thought* 33, no. 4 (Winter 2000): 97–119.

———. *The Joseph Smith Egyptian Papyri: A Complete Edition.* 2nd ed. Salt Lake City: Signature Books, 2013.

Roberts, B. H. *A Comprehensive History of the Church of Jesus Christ of Latter-day Saints.* 6 vols. Salt Lake City: Deseret Book, 1930.

———. *Defense of the Faith of the Saints.* 2 vols. Salt Lake City: Deseret News Press, 1907.

———, ed. *History of the Church of Jesus Christ of Latter-day Saints.* 7 vols. Salt Lake City: Deseret News, 1902–12.

———. *New Witnesses for God* II. Salt Lake City: Deseret News, 1909.

Robinson, Joseph Lee. Autobiography and Journals, 1883–1893. MS 1920, CHL.

Rogers, Brent M., Elizabeth A. Kuehn, Christian K. Heimburger, Max H. Parkin, Alexander L. Baugh, and Steven C. Harper. *The Joseph Smith Papers: Documents, Volume 5: October 1835–January 1838.* Salt Lake City: The Church Historian's Press, 2017.

Rogers, Horatio. *Mary Dyer of Rhode Island the Quaker Martyr that was Hanged on Boston Common, June 1, 1660.* Providence: Preston and Round, 1896.

Rubin, Jerry. *DO IT! Scenarios of the Revolution.* Intro. Eldridge Cleaver. New York: Simon and Shuster, 1970.

Sachse, Julius F. *The German Pietists in Provincial Pennsylvania.* Philadelphia: Printed for the Author, 1895.

Sackett, Chuck. *What's Going On In There?* Thousand Oaks, CA: Ex-Mormons for Jesus, 1982.

Salt Lake City Messenger. Newsletter published by Jerald and Sandra Tanner. Salt Lake City, Nov. 1964–present.

Sanford, Don A. *A Choosing People: The History of the Seventh Day Baptists.* 2nd ed., rev. & updated. Macon: Mercer University Press, 2013.

Schnoebelen, William J. "Joseph Smith and the Temple of Doom," *Saints Alive Journal* (Winter 1986).

———. "We Waited for Six Years." In *From Clergy to Convert,* compiled by Stephen W. Gibson, 67–73. Salt Lake City: Bookcraft, 1983.

Schnoebelen, William J., and James R. Spencer. *Mormonism's Temple of Doom.* Idaho Falls: Triple J. Publishers, 1987.

Scot, Reginald. *Discoverie of Witchcraft: Wherein the Lewde Dealing of Witches and Witchmongers is Notablie Detected … Whereunto Is Added a Treatise upon the Nature and Substance of Spirits and Devils.* London: Henry Denham for William Brome, 1584.

Scott, Ellen C. *Cinema Civil Rights: Regulation, Repression and Race in the Classical Hollywood Era.* New Brunswick: Rutgers University Press, 2015.

Scraps of Biography: Tenth Book of the Faith-Promoting Series. Salt Lake City: Juvenile Instructor Office, 1883.

Sears, L. Rex. "Punishing the Saints for Their 'Peculiar Institution': Congress and the Constitutional Dilemmas." *Utah Law Review* 2001, no. 3 (2001): 581–658.

Seixas, Joshua. *Manual Hebrew Grammar for the Use of Beginners.* 2nd ed. Andover: Gould and Newman, 1834.

Selden, Daniel L. *Hieroglyphic Egyptian: An Introduction to the Language and Literature of the Middle Kingdom.* Berkeley: University of California Press, 2013.

Select Committee on Presidential Campaign Activities. *Hearings before the Select Committee on Presidential Campaign Activities of the United States Senate, Ninety-Third Congress, First Session: Watergate and Related Activities, Phase I: Watergate Investigation.* Washington, DC: US Government Printing Office, 1973.

Sherman, Moroni. *Who Is Jesus?* Reese, MI: Moroni Sherman, [1956].

Shupe, Anson. *The Darker Side of Virtue: Corruption, Scandal, and the Mormon Empire.* Amherst: Prometheus, 1991.

Sillitoe, Linda, and Allen Roberts. *Salamander: The Story of the Mormon Forgery Murders.* Salt Lake City: Signature Books, 1988.

Skousen, Royal. *The Book of Mormon: The Earliest Text.* New Haven: Yale University Press, 2009.

———. *The King James Quotations in the Book of Mormon, The History of the Text of the Book of Mormon. Volume 3, Part Five* (Provo: Foundation for Ancient Studies and Mormon Studies, 2019.

Smith, Jason R. "Pauline Hancock and Her 'Basement Church.'" *The John Whitmer Historical Association Journal* 26 (2006): 185–93.

Smith, Joseph, Jr. Grammar and Alphabet of the Egyptian Language, ca. July–ca. November 1835. The Joseph Smith Papers. Online at www.josephsmithpapers.org.

——. *The Personal Writings of Joseph Smith*. Compiled and edited by Dean C. Jessee. Salt Lake City: Deseret Book, 1984.

Smith, Joseph Fielding. *Answers to Gospel Questions*. 5 vols. Salt Lake City: Deseret Book, 1957–66.

Smith, Joseph Fielding, ed. *Teachings of the Prophet Joseph Smith*. Salt Lake City: Deseret Book, 1938.

——. *The Way to Perfections: Short Discourses on Gospel Themes*. Salt Lake City: Genealogical Society of Utah, 1931.

Smith, Robert F. "Assessing the Broad Impact of Jack Welch's Discovery of Chiasmus in the Book of Mormon." *Journal of Book of Mormon Studies* 16, no. 2 (Fall 2007): 68–73, 98–99.

——. "If There Be Faults: They Be faults of a Man." *Interpreter: A Journal of Mormon Scripture* 8 (2014): 195–204.

——. *Oracles & Talismans Forgery & Pansophia: Joseph Smith Jr. as a Renaissance Magus*. Unpublished draft, Aug. 1987.

——. "Some 'Neologisms' from the Mormon Canon." In *1973 Conference on the Language of the Mormons*, 64–68. Provo: BYU Language Research Center, 1973.

Smith, Vida E. *Young People's History of the Church of Jesus Christ of Latter Day Saints*. 2 vols. Lamoni: Herald Publishing House, 1914–18.

Sorenson, John L., and Robert F. Smith. "Once More: The Horse." In *Reexploring the Book of Mormon*, edited by John W. Welch, 98–100. Provo: Foundation for Ancient Research and Mormon Studies, 1992.

Spaulding, Solomon. *Manuscript Found: The Complete Original "Spaulding Manuscript."* Edited by Kent P. Jackson. Provo: BYU Religious Studies Center, 1996.

Spencer, James R. *The Attack on Mormonism's Temple of Doom*. Boise: Thru the Maze, 1990.

Sperry, Sidney B. *Book of Mormon Compendium*. Salt Lake City: Bookcraft, 1968.

Stevenson, Russell. *Black Mormon: The Story of Elijah Ables*. N.p.: by the author, 2014.

——. *For the Cause of Righteousness: A Global History of Blacks and Mormonism, 1830–2013*. Salt Lake City: Greg Kofford Books, 2014.

Stewart, Isaac Dalton. *History of the Freewill Baptists for Half a Century, Vol I*. Dover, NH: Freewill Baptist Printing Establishment, 1862.

Stiles, Ezra. *Literary Diary of Ezra Stiles, D.D., LL.D. Vol. I January 1, 1769– March 13, 1776*. Edited by Franklin Bowditch Dexter; New York: Charles Scribner's Sons, 1901.

"The Story of Research on the Pearl of Great Price." In *Pearl of Great Price Conference December 10, 1960*. Provo: Brigham Young University, Dept. of Extension Publications, 1964.

Sussman, Barry. *The Great Cover-Up: Nixon and the Scandal of Watergate*. 4th ed. Potomac: Catapulter Books, 2010.

Talmage, James E. Collection, 1879–1933. MS 1232, CHL.

Tanner, Annie Clark. *A Mormon Mother: An Autobiography of Annie Clark Tanner*. Salt Lake City: Tanner Trust Fund and University of Utah Press, 1983.

Tanner, George Shepherd. *John Tanner and His Family: A History–Biography of John Tanner of Lake George, New York. Born August 15, 1778, Hopkinton, Rhode Island, Died April 13, 1850, at South Cottonwood, Utah*. Salt Lake City: John Tanner Family Association, 1974.

———. Papers, 1912–1992. Accn1361, Special Collections, Marriott Library, University of Utah.

Tanner, Jerald. *Confessions of a White Salamander: An Analysis of Mark Hofmann's Disclosures Concerning How He Forged Mormon Documents and Murdered Two People*. Salt Lake City: Utah Lighthouse Ministry, 1987.

———. *Does the Book of Mormon Teach Racial Prejudice?* N.p.: by the author, 1959.

———. *The Facts about the Book of Mormon*. [Salt Lake City]: by the author, [1962].

———. *Jerald Tanner's Testimony*. Salt Lake City: Utah Lighthouse Ministry, 1987.

———. *The Money-Digging Letters: A Preliminary Study*. Salt Lake City: Utah Lighthouse Ministry, Aug. 22, 1984.

———. *Mormonism: A Study of Mormon History and Doctrine*. Salt Lake City: by the author, 1963.

———. *Parallels to the Salamander Letter*. Salt Lake City: Utah Lighthouse Ministry, 1985.

———. *Pay Lay Ale: An Examination of the Charge that the Mormons Call upon Lucifer in their Temple Ceremony*. Salt Lake City: Modern Microfilm, 1982.

———. *Tracking the White Salamander*. 3rd ed. Salt Lake City: Utah Lighthouse Ministry, 1987.

———. *Suppression of the Records*. Salt Lake City: by the author, 1961/1962.

———. *Views on Creation, Evolution, and Fossil Man*. Salt Lake City: Modern Microfilm, 1975.

———. *What Hast Thou Dunn?* Salt Lake City: Utah Lighthouse Ministry, 1991.

———. *Will There Be a Revelation Regarding the Negro?* Salt Lake City: Modern Microfilm, 1963.

Tanner, Jerald and Sandra. "A Black Hole in the Book of Mormon: Computer Reveals Astounding Evidence on Origin of Mormon Book," *Salt Lake City Messenger* 72 (Jul. 1989): 1–15.

———. *Answering Dr. Clandestine: A Response to the Anonymous LDS Historian*. Enlarged ed. Salt Lake City: Modern Microfilm, 1978.

———. *Answers to Mormon Scholars I: A Response to Criticism of the Book Covering Up the Black Hole in the Book of Mormon*. Salt Lake City: Utah Lighthouse Ministry, 1994.

————. *Book of Mormon "Caractors" Found.* Salt Lake City: Modern Microfilm, 1980.

————. *Can the Browns Save Joseph Smith?* Salt Lake City: Modern Microfilm, 1981.

————. *The Case Against Mormonism.* 3 vols. Salt Lake City: Modern Microfilm, 1967–71.

————. *Changes in Joseph Smith's History.* Salt Lake City: Modern Microfilm, 1965.

————. *The Changing World of Mormonism: A Condensation and Revision of Mormonism: Shadow or Reality?* Chicago: Moody Press, 1980.

————. *Covering Up the Black Hole in the Book of Mormon.* Salt Lake City: Utah Lighthouse Ministry, 1990.

————. *A Critical Look: A Study of the Overstreet "Confession" and the Cowdery "Defence."* Salt Lake City: Modern Microfilm, 1967.

————. *Curse of Cain? Racism in the Mormon Church.* Salt Lake City: Utah Lighthouse Ministry, 2004.

————. *Did Spalding Write the Book of Mormon?* Salt Lake City: Modern Microfilm, 1977.

————. *Evolution of the Mormon Temple Ceremony: 1842–1990.* Salt Lake City: Utah Lighthouse Ministry, 1990.

————. *Excerpts from the Writings of Joseph Lee Robinson.* Salt Lake City: Modern Microfilm, 1960–1961.

————. *Falsification of Joseph Smith's History.* Salt Lake City: Modern Microfilm, 1971.

————. *The Father and the Son?* Salt Lake City: by the authors, 1960.

————. *Hofmann's Confession.* Photographic reprint of Mark Hofmann's interviews with Salt Lake County prosecutors. Salt Lake City: Utah Lighthouse Ministry, 1987.

————. *Howard Hughes and the "Mormon Will": Did Howard Hughes Really Leave $100,000,000 to the Mormon Church?* Salt Lake City: Modern Microfilm, 1976.

————. *Is the Book of Abraham True.* Salt Lake City: Modern Microfilm, 1968.

————. *Joseph Smith & Money Digging.* Salt Lake City: Modern Microfilm, 1970.

————. *Joseph Smith's Curse upon the Negro.* Salt Lake City: Modern Microfilm, 1965.

————. *Joseph Smith's Egyptian Alphabet & Grammar.* Salt Lake City: Modern Microfilm, 1966.

————. *Joseph Smith's Strange Account of the First Vision.* Salt Lake City: Modern Microfilm, 1965.

————. *Joseph Smith's Successor: An Important New Document Comes to Light.* Salt Lake City: Modern Microfilm, 1981.

————. *A Look at Christianity.* Salt Lake City: Modern Microfilm, 1971.

————. *The Lucifer–God Doctrine: A Critical Look at Some Recent Charges Relating to the Worship of Lucifer in the Mormon Temple*. Salt Lake City: Utah Lighthouse Ministry, 1987.

————. *Lucy Smith's 1829 Letter*. Salt Lake City: Modern Microfilm, Sep. 6, 1982.

————. *Mormons and Negroes*. Salt Lake City: Modern Microfilm, 1970.

————. *Mormon Church Fights Subpoena for Joseph Smith's Secretary's Diaries*. Salt Lake City: Utah Lighthouse Ministry, 1984.

————. *Mormon Spies, Hughes, and the CIA*. Salt Lake City: Modern Microfilm, 1976.

————. *Mormonism: Shadow or Reality?* Salt Lake City: Modern Microfilm, 1964. 5th edition published Utah Lighthouse Ministry, 1987.

————. *The Negro in Mormon Theology*. Salt Lake City: Modern Microfilm, 1967.

————. Papers, 1959–present. Utah Lighthouse Ministry, Salt Lake City.

————. *Problems in* The God Makers II. Salt Lake City: Utah Lighthouse Ministry, 1993.

————. *Revealing Statements by the Three Witnesses of the Book of Mormon*. Salt Lake City: by the authors, n.d.

————. *Serious Charges against the Tanners: Are the Tanners Demonized Agents of the Mormon Church?* Salt Lake City: Utah Lighthouse Ministry, 1991.

————. *Solving the Racial Problem in Utah*. Salt Lake City: by the authors, 1962.

————. *A Statement Concerning Some Charges of Immorality Made Against a Mormon Leader*. Salt Lake City: Utah Lighthouse Ministry, 1990.

————. *The Tanners on Trial*. Salt Lake City: Utah Lighthouse Ministry, 1984.

————. *Unmasking a Mormon Spy*. Salt Lake City: Utah Lighthouse Ministry, 1983.

————. *What Hast Thou Dunn?*

————. *Why Egyptologists Reject the Book of Abraham*. Reprint of *Joseph Smith, Jr., As a Translator* by F. S. Spalding and *Joseph Smith as an Interpreter and Translator of Egyptian* by Samuel A. B. Mercer. Salt Lake City: Utah Lighthouse Ministry, 1983.

Tanner, Mary Jane Mount. *A Fragment: The Autobiography of Mary Jane Mount Tanner*. Edited by Margery W. Ward with George S. Tanner. Salt Lake City: Tanner Trust Fund, University of Utah Library, 1980.

Tanner, Myron. *Biography of Myron Tanner*. Salt Lake City: Deseret News, 1907.

Tanner, Nathan, "Journal of Nathan Tanner." Catalogued (incorrectly?) as "Reminiscences, circa 1900." MS 15560, fds. 1 & 2.

Tanner, Obert C. *One Man's Journey: In Search of Freedom*. Salt Lake City: Humanities Center at the University of Utah, 1994.

Tanner, Sandra. "Dear Friend I." "Mimeographed letter. North Hollywood, 1959–60.

————. "Dear Friend II." Mimeographed letter. Salt Lake City, Jul./Aug. 1960.

————. "Evolution of the First Vision and Teaching on God in Early Mormonism." Online, www.utlm.org.

————. *Out of Darkness, into the 'Sonlight'*. Salt Lake City: by the author, 1960.

————. Recollections. Interviews and Personal Communications with Ronald V. Huggins, 2014–2020.

Thompson, Albert Edward, *Life of A. B. Simpson.* New York, NY: Christian Alliance, 1920.

Thurston, Elisha P., comp. *History of the Town of Greenwich, from the Earliest Settlement to the Centennial Anniversary of our National Independence.* Salem, NY: H. D. Morris, 1876.

Times and Seasons. Nauvoo, Il., 1839–46.

Tope, Wally. *"Poisoned" at Pizzaland: The Revealing Case of Ed Decker's "Arsenic Poisoning."* La Canada Flintridge, CA: Frontline Ministries, 1991.

Tullidge, Edward W. *The Women of Mormondom.* New York: By the authors, 1877.

Turley, Richard E., Jr. *Victims: The LDS Church and the Mark Hofmann Case.* Urbana: University of Illinois Press, 1992.

Turner, Wallace. *The Mormon Establishment.* New York: Houghton Mifflin, 1966.

Tuttle, Daniel S. "Mormons." In *Religious Encyclopedia or Dictionary of Biblical, Historical, Doctrinal, and Practical Theology,* 3 vols. edited by Philip Schaff, 2:1575–1581. New York: Funk & Wagnalls, 1882–83.

Tvedtnes, John A., ed. *The Book of Abraham Symposium: Papers Delivered at the [University of Utah] Institute of Religion Special Symposium April 3, 1970.* Salt Lake City: Institute of Religion, 1971.

————. "The Critics of the Book of Abraham." In Tvedtnes, *Book of Abraham Symposium.*

Van Wagoner, Richard S. *Natural Born Seer: Joseph Smith, American Prophet, 1805–1830.* Salt Lake City: Smith–Pettit Foundation, 2016.

Vogel, Dan. *Early Mormon Documents.* 5 vols. Salt Lake City: Signature Books, 1996–2003.

Wade, Stuart C. *Bottskill Baptist Church, Greenwich, Washington Co., N.Y.: Tombstone Inscriptions: A Copy of all Tombstone Inscriptions Existing in 1901.* Rpt. Alexandria, VA: Sleeper Company, 1995.

Wallace. Douglas A. *Under the Mormon Tree: The First 50 Years.* 2nd ed. n.p.: n.p, 2012.

Walters, Wesley P. "Joseph Smith's Bainbridge, N.Y., Court Trial." *Westminster Theological Journal* 36, no. 2 (Winter 1974): 123–55.

————. "New Light on Mormon Origins." *Bulletin of the Evangelical Theological Society* 10, no. 4 (1967): 227–44.

Ward, Margery W. *A Life Divided: The Biography of Joseph Marion Tanner, 1859–1927.* Salt Lake City: Obert C. and Grace A. Tanner Foundation and Publishers Press, 1980.

Wardle, James D. Papers, 1812–2001. Ms0578, Marriott Library Special Collections, University of Utah.

Warfield, Benjamin B. *Counterfeit Miracles: A History of Fake Miracles and Healings in the Christian and Catholic Traditions, with Arguments in Favor of Cessationism.* New York: Charles Scribner, 1918.

Waterman, Bryan, ed. *The Prophet Puzzle: Interpretive Essays on Joseph Smith.* Salt Lake City, Utah: Signature, 1999.

Wells, Emmeline B. "Biography of Mary Ann Angell Young." *Juvenile Instructor*, Jan. 1, 1891, 17.

Whitmer, David. *An Address to All Believers in Christ.* 1887. With an introduction by Jerald Tanner. Salt Lake City: Jerald Tanner, n.d.

Widtsoe, John A. *Joseph Smith: Seeker after Truth, Prophet of God.* Salt Lake City: Deseret News, 1951.

Williams, Roger. *Mr. Cottons Letter Lately Printed, Examined and Answered.* London, 1644.

Williams, T. W. *The Protest Movement: Its Meaning and Purpose.* Independence: The Church of Jesus Christ, 1926.

Wilson, John A. "The Joseph Smith Egyptian Papyri: Translations and Interpretations: A Summary Report." *Dialogue: A Journal of Mormon Thought* 3, no. 2 (Summer 1968): 67–85.

Wilson, William A. "The Paradox of Mormon Folklore." *BYU Studies* 17, no. 1 (1976): 40–58.

Winslow, Edward. *Hypocrisie Unmasked: A True Relation of the Proceedings of the Governor and Company of the Massachusetts Against Samuel Gorton of Rhode Island.* 1866. Rep., Providence: Club for Colonial Reprints, 1916.

Winthrop, John. *Winthrop's Journal: "History of New England," 1630–1649.* Edited by James Kendall Hosmer. New York: Scribner, 1908.

Wolfe, Tom. "The Me Decade and the Third Great Awakening." In *Mauve Golves & Madmen Clutter & Vine and Other Stories, Sketches, and Essays.* New York: Farrar, Straus, and Giroux, 1976, 126–157.

Wood, Samuel. *The Infinite God: Can Men Become Gods?* Independence: Lambert Moon Printing Company, 1934.

Wood, Wilford C. *Joseph Smith Begins His Work: Book of Mormon 1830 First Edition, Reproduced from Uncut Sheets.* Salt Lake City: by the author, 1958.

———. *Joseph Smith Begins His Work, Vol. II: The Book of Commandments, the Doctrine and Covenants, the Lectures on Faith, Fourteen Articles of Faith.* Salt Lake City: by the author, 1962.

Woodward, Bob. *The Secret Man: The Story of Watergate's Deep Throat.* New York: Simon & Schuster, 2005.

Wright, Stephen, comp. *History of the Shaftsbury Baptist Association, 1781–1853.* Troy, NY: A. G. Johnson, 1853.

Wunderli, Earl M. *An Imperfect Book: What the Book of Mormon Tells Us about Itself.* Salt Lake City: Signature Books, 2013.

Young, Ann Eliza. *Wife No. 19, or the Story of a Life in Bondage, Being ... Sufferings of Women in Polygamy.* Hartford: Dustin, Gilman, & Co., 1876.

Young, Brigham. Office Files, 1832–1878. CR 1234, CHL.

INDEX

About the Author

Ronald V. Huggins received his ThD from the University of Toronto/ Toronto School of Theology. He taught at Moody Bible Institute Northwest, Salt Lake Theological Seminary, and Midwestern Baptist Theological Seminary, where he also served as managing editor of the *Midwestern Journal of Theology*. He has published in the *Journal of Biblical Literature*, *Novum Testamentum*, *Ephemerides Theologicae Lovaniensis*, *Revue de Qumrân*, and the *Westminster Theological Journal*. His writings in the fields of world views, psychology, and comparative religion have appeared in *The Evangelical Dictionary of World Religions*, *The Journal of the Evangelical Theological Society*, *The Journal of Hindu–Christian Studies*, *Phanês: Journal of Jung History*, and *Dialogue: A Journal of Mormon Thought*. He and his wife, Marguerite, have four children and ten grandchildren.